Anti-Imperialist Marxism, Volume 2

Series Editors:
IMMANUEL NESS,
JENNIFER PONCE DE LEÓN,
& GABRIEL ROCKHILL

A Publication by:
CRITICAL THEORY WORKSHOP
& ISKRA BOOKS

Anti-Imperialist Marxism (AIM)

SERIES EDITORS
Immanuel Ness, Jennifer Ponce de León, and Gabriel Rockhill

INTERNATIONAL ADVISORY BOARD
Amiya Kumar Bagchi †, Radhika Desai, Cheng Enfu, John Bellamy Foster, Georges Gastaud, Ali Kadri, Annie Lacroix-Riz, Maxwell Lane, Torkil Lauesen, Linda Matar, Jacques Pauwels, Raúl Delgado Wise, and Helmut-Harry Loewen

EDITORIAL REVIEW BOARD
Daniel Benson, Jared Bly, Larry Busk, Daniel Cunningham, Salvatore Engel-Di Mauro, Bruno Guigue, Timothy Kerswell, Carlos Martinez, Aymeric Monville, Corinna Mullin, Nima Nakhaei, Eli Portella Perreras, Yin Xing, and Liu Zixu

CRITICAL THEORY WORKSHOP'S AIM series provides a platform for scholarly research and popular-form essays from around the world that challenge the widespread assumption, including within the Western left, that there is no real-world alternative to capitalism. Refusing to shy away from serious scholarly engagements with actually existing socialism, it opens up the spectrum of analysis to explore histories and contemporary developments that have either been ignored or misrepresented. In order to do so, it promotes innovative, non-Eurocentric research that overcomes the siloing effects of the disciplines and the ideological horizons of imperial knowledge production in favor of resolutely internationalist scholarship that deploys an anti-imperialist framework of analysis. The overall objective is thus to foster non-dogmatic theoretical work that has real use-value, precisely because of its relevance to concrete struggles for a more egalitarian and sustainable world.

FORTHCOMING AIM TITLES:

THE ACCUMULATION OF WASTE: A POLITICAL ECONOMY OF SYSTEMIC DESTRUCTION
Ali Kadri

THE COMMUNIST QUESTION: HISTORY AND FUTURE OF AN IDEA
Domenico Losurdo

How Paris Made the Revolution and the Revolution Made Paris

From France's Royal City to Bourgeois Babylon 1789-1889

Originally published, in part, in Dutch as *Het Parijs van de sansculotten. Een reis door de Franse Revolutie*, © Berchem [Antwerp]: EPO, 2007, extended and published as *Hoe Parijs de Revolutie maakte & de Revolutie Parijs*, © Berchem [Antwerp]: EPO, 2024.

Translated into English for this 2025 edition by the author.

First English Edition Published by *Iskra Books* © 2025.

10 9 8 7 6 5 4 3 2 1

All rights reserved.
The moral rights of the author have been asserted.

ISKRA BOOKS
WWW.ISKRABOOKS.ORG
US | ENGLAND | IRELAND

Iskra Books is an independent scholarly publisher—publishing original works of revolutionary theory, history, education, and art, as well as edited collections, new translations, and critical republications of older works.

ISBN-13: 979-8-3493-7538-5 (SOFTCOVER)
ISBN-13: 979-8-3493-7587-3 (HARDCOVER)

British Library Cataloguing in Publication Data
A catalogue record for this book is available from the British Library.

Library of Congress Cataloging-in-Publication Data
A catalog record for this book is available from the Library of Congress

ANTI-IMPERIALIST MARXISM SERIES
SERIES EDITORS: Jennifer Ponce de León, Gabriel Rockhill, and Immanuel Ness

Editing by DAVID PEAT
Typesetting by DAVID PEAT and BEN STAHNKE
Cover Art by BEN STAHNKE
Cover Art Inspiration from the Dust Jacket of *Urbino*, MIT Press, 1970

All images in the book are in the public domain and can be cited from *Wikimedia Commons* unless otherwise specified in the text.

How Paris Made the Revolution and the Revolution Made Paris
From France's Royal City to Bourgeois Babylon 1789 - 1889

Jacques R. Pauwels

ISKRA BOOKS
us | england | ireland

Table of Contents

PREFACE
Travel and History / **xi**

INTRODUCTION
Revolution and Democracy / **1**

PART I.
THE ANCIEN RÉGIME, FRANCE BEFORE 1789

1. *La France Profonde*: The Countryside / **13**

2. Paris: The "Royal City" on the Eve of the Revolution / **35**

PART II.
THE GREAT REVOLUTION, 1789-1799

3. The Road from Versailles to Paris / **87**

4. The Moderate Revolution: 1789-1792 / **111**

5. 1792: From Monarchy to Republic / **141**

6. 1793-1794: The Radical Revolution / **171**

7. 1794-1799: From Thermidor to Brumaire / **197**

8. Reflections on France's Great Revolution / **233**

PART III.
THE REVOLUTIONS OF 1830, 1848, AND 1871

9. 1830: Three Glorious Days in July / **265**

10. 1848: Red Flag on the Barricades / **273**

11. 1871: The Paris Commune / **289**

CONCLUSION.
PARIS, FROM FRANCE'S ROYAL CITY TO BOURGEOIS BABYLON / 303

BIBLIOGRAPHY / 317

"If we want to understand the genesis of modern democracy and the problems that it poses, we need to turn back to the era of the French Revolution."

—Domenico Losurdo

Preface
Travel and History

"WHOEVER UNDERTAKES A JOURNEY, is automatically immersed in history," writes the Austrian author of a theoretical as well as empirical study of the theme of travel and history.[1] Indeed, travel and history go hand in hand. On the one hand, even some elementary historical knowledge makes a voyage more interesting; the more one travels, the more one becomes interested in history. Conversely, studying history awakens the desire to travel. If you have become acquainted with Roman or Greek history, you will sooner or later want to take a plane and fly to Rome or Athens. The more one studies history, the more one experiences the desire to visit the sites where historical events took place.

While visiting some country, region, or city, it often happens that a specific important event, a certain epoch, or some famous personality comes to mind. Conversely, the study of some historical event or period may awaken the desire to travel to a certain destination. In Normandy, for example, it is impossible not to think of the Second World War, and for those who are interested in the history of that conflict, a pilgrimage to the beaches of that French province, where Allied troops came ashore in June 1944, is *de rigueur*. But Normandy also conjures up William the Conqueror, the Hundred Years' War, and Joan of Arc, who was burned at the stake in Normandy's capital, Rouen.

However, the case of Paris is historically even more complex and interesting than that of Normandy. The mere mention of the name of

---

1 Heppner, p. 2.

the French capital—the most beautiful and exciting city in the world, *n'est-ce pas?*—suffices to bring to mind countless historical episodes. Here are some examples: the sinister Cardinal Richelieu and the valiant Three Musketeers, Louis XIV, the pompous Sun-King, the meteoric career (and the love life) of the little Corsican, Napoleon Bonaparte, and the liberation of the city in August 1944, conjured up by the bullet holes that still pockmark the facade of the École Militaire, the training school for officers. And the French Revolution, of course, an extremely important and dramatic episode that, according to many if not most historians, constitutes the alpha of a "contemporary history" whose omega is far from ready to be written. It is that drama, France's "Great Revolution," that we will focus on here, that will lure us back to Paris for the umpteenth—or very first—time, and that will inspire and guide our sightseeing program in the City of Light.

Sites bringing back memories of the Revolution are still surprisingly plentiful in the French capital, but much of the Paris of 1789 has vanished forever, not only the Bastille, but also the Tuileries Palace and many other places that witnessed significant revolutionary events. However, even these vanished monuments are well worth a visit; in fact, what may be called "the invisible Paris of the Revolution" will be among the highlights of our visit there.

In any event, the topography of Paris is very closely connected to the history of the Revolution. Visiting the city, visiting this *space*, one cannot fail to come across the *time* of the Revolution. Conversely, the history of the French Revolution invites us to discover the relevant buildings, monuments, and sites—*lieux de mémoire* [sites of memory], to use an apt French expression—of the French capital. Indeed, the French Revolution was not exclusively, but certainly mostly, a Parisian affair, a drama played out on the stunning stage Paris happens to be. The French Revolution was in many ways a Parisian Revolution. The study of the French Revolution, a relatively brief but extremely dramatic and important moment in *time*, thus causes us to want to return to the *place* where the majority of the major revolutionary events took place.

Paris may be said to have made the Revolution, but the reverse is also true: France's Great Revolution, which started in 1789 but lasted until 1799, as well as the revolutions that broke out in the French capital in

1830, 1848, and 1871, have made, or rather, remade Paris. We will see that, in less than one century, those four revolutionary convulsions recreated the French capital: they transformed what had been France's "royal city," an urban reflection of monarchical France and its feudal order, featuring privileges for the nobility and the Church, into a "'bourgeois Babylon," a metropolis whose visage proclaimed not only to France but to the entire world that a new era had dawned: the era of the capitalist social-economic order and the attendant hegemony of the bourgeoisie.

To explore and get to know a place—a country, a region or, as in this case, a city—one needs a book as a travel guide; to learn about a period in time, one relies on a history book. This book is a combination of both, it is a travel guide for Paris in the time of France's Great Revolution—and, to a lesser extent, to the revolutions that rocked the country not much later, namely in the 19th century—but it is also a history of the revolutionary events that took place in the French capital. However, it is not easy to reconcile the history, the chronological account, with the topography, the description of the sites where the action took place. It is impossible to explore Paris in a way that perfectly reflects the chronology of the revolutionary events. The site of the disappeared Tuileries Palace, for example, will have to be visited more than once, because that edifice witnessed dramatic action not only in 1789 but also in 1792, 1793, and 1794; and Place de la Concorde—known as Place Louis XV before the Revolution and as Place de la Révolution during the Revolution, will likewise have to be visited more than once.

We have decided to give precedence to the chronology, the history, rather than the topography, with occasional flashbacks and flashforwards. But each phase of the Revolution will be described in the appropriate Parisian decor. The chronology of the early stages of the Revolution will thus take us from Versailles to the Palais-Royal in central Paris, hence to Place de la Bastille and then to the Hôtel de Ville. To witness the execution of King Louis XVI, we will head for Place de la Concorde, the vast open space in the middle of the city in the middle of the country, where the guillotine was deliberately installed—in the middle of the square, *naturellement*. We will visit ex-queen Marie-Antoinette, awaiting the relief of death in a medieval prison, the Conciergerie. And so forth. In this manner, a visitor to Paris is able to systematically explore the most important *lieux de mémoire* of the Revolution.

It is hoped that this approach will make this book interesting also for all those who do not intend to visit Paris. In fact, this book is intended as nothing more than an introduction to an extremely important historical drama; it was not written to impress experts in the field, but for the benefit of the general public. But it does take into account "classic" as well as recent studies of France's greater and lesser revolutionary convulsions. As examples of the former type of studies we should mention the work of Albert Soboul, and of the latter type, the opuses of Eric Hazan. And much inspiration was found in studies of books about recent history in general, above all those of the brilliant Italian philosopher-historian Domenico Losurdo.

As the aforementioned Austrian historian has written, travelling immerses us in history, travelling stimulates our interest in history. This book about the crucial role of Paris in France's Great Revolution of 1789-1799 and other revolutions, those of 1830, 1848, and 1871, and, conversely, the impact of those revolutions on the French capital, could not have been written if the author's interest in the city's history had not been stimulated by the countless occasions he has had to explore Paris since his very first visit there in 1968.

Introduction
Revolution and Democracy

THE FRENCH REVOLUTION is of interest not only to the people of France but to all of us. The reason for that is that it was not merely a French revolution, but an event of worldwide importance. The great Italian philosopher and historian Domenico Losurdo has written that it is necessary to "first carefully study the French Revolution in order to understand the origin and the problems of modern democracy." And understanding democracy, including its historical origins and development, is of crucial importance to all of us, wherever we live. Echoing Losurdo's words, it will be argued here that the French Revolution amounted to a first step, modest but very important, on the road towards genuine democracy, a destination that remains a bright but distant star even today. And we obviously mean the road towards democracy that has been taken in relatively recent history, an era usually referred to as "modern times" in the English-speaking world but as the "contemporary epoch" in France; however, in both cases it is usually defined as starting with the French Revolution, that is, in 1789. In any event, let us take a few moments to clarify what is meant with those terms.

The term democracy is of ancient Greek origin and contains the words *demos*, "people," and *kratos*, "power, rule." Democracy thus means "people's power." However, *demos* meant not the people in general but the common people, the large mass of "ordinary" or "little" people, also referred to at the time as *hoi polloi*, "the many," or the more recently coined expression, the "99 per cent." The Romans used to refer to these folks as the "plebeians," members of the *plebs*, a Latin equivalent of the Greek *demos*. For this kind of people to have power was an anomaly in the history of Ancient Greece; the celebrated Athenian democracy of the fifth century BC proved to be a short-lived, exceptional case. And it should be kept in mind that Athenian democracy differed in a number of important ways from modern democratic theory and practice; for example, it involved only a tiny minority of the city's inhabitants, since women, slaves, foreign residents, and the like were rigorously excluded from politics.[1]

The general rule of politics—the business of the typically Greek form of government, the *polis*, i.e. city-state—was a system in which power was monopolized by "the few" (Greek: *hoi oligoi*), by an elite, consisting of the rich upper-class folks who considered themselves to be "the best" (*hoi aristoi*), hence the terms oligarchy and aristocracy. The Latin equivalent of the Greek *oligoi* or *aristoi* was "patricians." Another common alternative to democracy was autocracy, the rule by a single person (*autos*), a *tyrannos*, "lord, master, sovereign, tyrant," hence the term tyranny; the analogous Latin expression was *dictator*. In any event, the idea of democracy was that ordinary people had political power, or at least a share of it, and—*nota bene!*—derived certain benefits from that.

Democracy meant not only power *by*, but also *for*, the ordinary people, the "99 percent," not the "1 percent." Moreover, the modern version of democracy must also be viewed as a two-sided coin. It features not only a *political* but also an equally important *social* side. In other words, in a democracy, the many of the demos, women as well as men, enjoy not only a measure of power, that is, provide input into the business of the state, they can also count on the state to provide them with some protection and certain benefits. For example, the right to engage in productive work and to receive an adequate wage in return; prohibition of child labor; legal limits on working hours; as well as access at little or no cost to public transportation, educational and medical services, the arts, sports, and other "public goods," "social services" or "entitlements."

Democracy is an abstract concept, an idea. It may be described as a utopia, meaning a "wonderful place" (from the Greek *eu*, "good," and *topos*, "place.") But the *eu* in utopia also conjures up an alpha privative,

---

1   Rockhill (2017), p. 65-66.

and an atopia is a "nonexistent place." Indeed, democracy does not (yet) exist, it is an ideal, a goal to which we, or at least most of us, aspire, to be achieved, hopefully, in the future. But here we are concerned with the past and the present, so we will continue to use the term democracy in the conventional sense, referring to systems that are "more-or-less" democratic, systems that provide a foretaste of the democratic utopia of the future.

In the past, democracies were rare, but societies with a remarkably high degree of democracy, admittedly an informal kind, did exist, for example many of North America's Indigenous Nations. Today, some countries are considered to be more democratic than others. Some lands are still authoritarian or even dictatorial, meaning there is no democracy at all. Others have achieved a decent, even considerable level of democracy.

Western countries are fully-fledged democracies, or so most of their own citizens think, if only because their leaders and their media tell them so. The relatively small collection of Western lands that are sometimes grandiloquently referred to as the "international community" has a hegemon, the United States. Its leaders and many of its citizens are convinced that their country is the *nec plus ultra* of democracy, the "exceptional" or "indispensable" nation, predestined to export its own brand of democracy all over the world, *manu militari* if necessary.

However, the Western world is not quite as democratic as its leaders, media, and most of its denizens believe. A thorough study by social scientists at leading US universities has recently arrived at the conclusion that the United States is not only not the world's finest democracy, but not even a democracy at all; that it is more aptly described as an oligarchy or, as former attorney general Ramsey Clark put it, "a plutocracy, a government controlled by an elite of ultra-wealthy citizens." Worse, a recent poll has revealed that the US is increasingly seen by people all over the world as a threat to democracy.[2]

One can also say that Western-style democracy is more style than substance, a kind of oligarchy disguised as democracy. In any event, the Western countries are far less democratic than we think. Conversely,

---

2   See the study by Page and Gilens; also Parenti, *Democracy for the Few*. Quotations from Clark taken from the article by Jensen, p. 7. Regarding the US as a threat to democracy, see the article by Patrick Wintour.

some countries that are generally perceived as undemocratic, at least from a Western point of view, are (or were) not entirely devoid of democratic merits of a social, if not political, nature. This may be said, for example, about the former "people's republics" behind the Iron Curtain, and also about Cuba, Venezuela, and the Libya of Colonel Gaddafi, Africa's only "welfare state," and also of China.

It is not easy to determine how democratic or undemocratic a country is; it all depends on the type of democracy one has in mind. Indeed, numerous types exist, as Canadian political scientist C. B. Macpherson, a specialist in the field, has emphasized.[3] In the Western world, the yardstick par excellence is *liberal* democracy, characterized by purported features such as freedom of speech, elections based on universal suffrage and the existence of multiple political parties. (One party is anathema, but for some mysterious reason just two parties is quite enough.)

Liberal democracy clearly focuses on the *political* side of democracy. As already mentioned, however, democracy also has a *social* side, it should provide protection and services—social services—for the ordinary or little people who constitute the demographic majority in every country and who need protection and social services much more than the rich and powerful minority. Different people have different democratic needs and expect different things from a democratic state. Access to quality medical services and education at low cost is essential to the demos, but not to the patricians whose wealth allows them to purchase the best education and health care in a "free market." Conversely, being able to choose between a Democratic or Republican nominee for the US presidency may loom important to middle-class burghers who appreciate the arcane difference between a "liberal" and a "conservative" would-be POTUS; but it is far less important to the masses, for example African Americans, for whom even a Black president achieved nothing worthwhile during eight years in the White House. It is therefore hardly surprising that a high percentage of Americans do not even bother to trek to a voting booth.

The Western countries are far less democratic than we have been conditioned to believe. Conversely, some countries that are considered undemocratic by the Western world are (or were) democratic on the social level. The former "people's republics" behind the Iron Curtain, for

---

3   See Macpherson's *The Real World of Democracy*.

example, and countries such as Cuba, Venezuela, China, and the Libya of Colonel Ghaddafi were more democratic, socially speaking, than many if not most Western "liberal democracies." Education and healthcare were affordable or even free of charge there.

A common, but mistaken, notion is that freedom is a hallmark of democracy. Freedom is an abstract concept, and it is of course impossible to be against it. But there are many types of freedom, *freedom to* do things, for example, a kind of freedom that can obviously not be absolute; but there is also the right to be *free from* evils such as poverty. This distinction was reflected in the famous "Four Freedoms" declaration by FDR and Churchill during the Second World War, which recognized the freedom of speech and of worship but also the freedoms from want and from fear. Freedom to do things is a hallmark of the ideology of capitalism, as demonstrated by its name, liberalism. But the freedom of liberalism is obviously a freedom to do things; more specifically, the freedom of the capitalist to operate in the (hypothetical) free market, competing freely with other capitalists and being free to accumulate riches. On the other hand, in its golden age, the nineteenth century, liberalism certainly did not want workers to be free to organize and to go on strike; unions and strikes were typically outlawed by liberal politicians. Liberalism also does not endorse the need of wage-earning and other ordinary people to be *free from* want, unemployment and so forth. We may conclude that the commitment of liberalism to freedom is far from unconditional; it is highly selective.

Democracy similarly promotes certain types of freedom while opposing others. Devoted to the emancipation of the demos, the *polloi*, historically all too often oppressed and exploited by the *oligoi*, democracy understandably favors and promotes freedom from poverty, violence and so on. It is no less understandable that it also seeks to destroy the freedom of those who have been guilty of oppression and exploitation. Democracy inevitably places restrictions on freedom, so it cannot, and should not, simplistically be equated with freedom.

How does a people, or rather, how does the demos, the lower class of a people, achieve democratic progress, in other words, its own emancipation? The answer is by flexing its muscle, by taking advantage of its greatest asset, its large numbers. When large numbers of people are involved in petitions, strikes, demonstrations, and other forms of collective action, they force the upper class to make concessions and introduce democratic reforms of a political and/or social nature, such as extensions of the right to vote and limitations on working hours. Ancient Rome thus occasionally witnessed a kind of general strike by its working class, the *secessio plebis*. In the course of modern history, "those below" gradually developed similar ways to make their collective action more effective, such as the organization of political parties and labor unions, and work stoppages. The increasing pressure exerted by "those below" thus forced "those above" to make more and more concessions and achieved considerable democratic progress. The direction of democratic progress is not "top-down" but "bottom-up."

Democracy's greatest leaps forward were achieved when, deliberately or not, the authorities representing the upper class ignored petitions and violently repressed massive demonstrations; sundry forms of collective action thus snowballed into major upheavals that brought about a partial or complete overthrow of the established political and social order and the introduction of radical changes for the benefit of the lower orders. When such an unprecedented scenario unfolded in France in 1789, a relatively new word, originally an astronomical term coined by Copernicus, was used to describe the phenomenon: revolution. More revolutions were to follow in the course of the nineteenth century, and not only in France. While some of them were repressed, many of them triggered additional democratic progress, especially in 1848, the revolutionary year par excellence, disparaged by counter-revolutionaries in Germany as *das tolle Jahr*, "the crazy year."

Revolutions, then, may be defined as movements that enjoy broad popular support, expressed in different forms of collective action, and seek to achieve radical political and/or socioeconomic change for the benefit of the lower-class and inevitably at the expense of the upper class. Revolutions are quintessentially democratic because their purpose is to emancipate the lower class, the *demos*, politically and/or socially. Paulo Freire thus views revolution as a liberation from oppression, defined as a situation in which "someone oppresses someone else," while in the "process of revolution" people "act in communion [to] liberate each other."[4]

---

4 Freire, p. 128.

The American historian Herbert Aptheker writes that the "revolutionary process ... far from being contrary to democracy, represents its quintessence. And the more fundamental the nature of the revolutionary process, the more democratic it will be"; and he even concludes that "the concept of democracy is born of revolution."[5]

Historically, some revolutions achieved a lot, producing major changes for the benefit of ordinary people, while other revolutions disappointed, producing only insignificant or cosmetic changes. Not all revolutions are alike: some revolutions are more radical, more far-reaching, more *revolutionary*, than others. And revolutions are not simple historical events but, as Freire noted, processes, complex historical phenomena that evolve and change over time. The French Revolution thus evolved between 1789 and 1799 from a moderate to a radical phase before being arrested and rolled back, not entirely, but to the nodal point where it had ceased being moderate and morphed into a radical phase. The result of this development was a dictatorship under Napoleon Bonaparte, an ambiguous historical personage who was simultaneously revolutionary and counter-revolutionary.

Revolutions are democratic by definition. In that respect, they differ greatly from rebellions or revolts, movements directed against any form of authority, movements that often benefit not the lower but the upper class and may in fact be counter-revolutionary and antidemocratic in nature. In Spain, for example, a 1936 revolt by army commanders against the democratically elected republican government purported to undo land reforms and other democratic, more-or-less revolutionary changes planned by that government.

Finally, some so-called revolutions are not revolutions at all, in the sense that they do not yield genuine democratic progress but merely some reforms, and not necessarily in the interest of the lower orders. England's 1688-1689 "Glorious Revolution," for example, was no revolution at all, yielding no benefits for the country's masses. As for the American Revolution, even though it received indispensable support from the lower-class colonists, it was not a real revolution but essentially a rebellion, a revolt against the authorities in London by the colonial elite, an "English" patriciate of owners of plantations and plenty of slaves as well as

---

5   Aptheker, pp. 104, 106.

wealthy merchants, including slave traders; and the liberty it sought, was essentially the liberty to expand westward at the expense of the Indigenous inhabitants.[6]

Much the same can be said about more recent "color revolutions," that is, fake revolutions. These manipulated movements sometimes enjoy considerable popular support, but they do not pursue genuinely democratic goals and are essentially counter-revolutionary in nature. However, their orchestrators shrewdly baptize these movements "revolutions" because that term conjures up a better future for the demos and is therefore useful for drumming up popular support, usually with the eager collaboration of the mainstream media, controlled by the elite. It would indeed be impossible to generate widespread enthusiasm for a movement that openly admitted pursuing "counter-revolutionary objectives."[7] And it was for the same reason that the collaborator regime of Marshal Pétain, while determined to liquidate the heritage of the French Revolution, presented its reactionary policy to the public as a "national revolution"![8] Similarly, in commercials new commodities are typically praised as being revolutionary, but are never described as counter-revolutionary!

Revolutions tend to involve violence, bloodshed and terror, and there are two reasons for this. First, extreme, intolerable violence always characterizes the pre-revolutionary status quo. In his influential book, *Pedagogy of the Oppressed*, Paulo Freire thus rightly stressed that

> [in] a relationship of oppression, violence has *already* begun. Never in history has violence been initiated by the oppressed. How could they be the initiators, if they themselves [i.e., the oppressed class] are the result of violence?[9]

We will see that the violence of the French Revolution was the direct response to the extreme poverty, oppression, widespread use of corporal punishment and torture, persecution of religious minorities, and other horrors that prevailed in France before 1789.

A second reason revolutions feature violence is that violence is used

---

6   "The American revolution," writes Amin, p. 44, "was merely a war of independence devoid of social importance ... Its objectives were above all a continued westward expansion and the preservation of slavery." See also Losurdo (2006), pp. 59-63.

7   Alleg, p. 77.

8   Ibid.

9   Freire, p. 41.

freely by counter-revolutionary forces seeking to suppress revolutions. As Arno Mayer has emphasized in his masterful study of the French and Russian Revolutions, *The Furies,* violence characterizes the counter-revolution because the elites of the old system always react violently even to peaceful attempts to dislodge them from their towers of power and privilege. The violence used by the revolutionaries is therefore "counter-violence, tactical violence purporting to abolish the strategic violence of the counter-revolution, against which nonviolence all too often proves to be useless."[10]

A counterexample is provided by Allende's embryonic revolution in Chile. He failed to consider the use of violence to prevent a counter-revolutionary coup by the military, led by Pinochet. But the result was a tsunami of violence orchestrated by the latter. Looking back, there would have been far less aggregate violence if Allende had taken drastic steps, including the use of violence if necessary, against the military counter-revolutionaries—and the revolution might have succeeded.

Of all forms of violence used by both sides in a revolutionary situation, war is unquestionably the most spectacular and deadliest and also the most complex. Wars may be fought to achieve revolutionary as well as counter-revolutionary purposes. The wars of liberation fought for the independence of colonies such as Vietnam were revolutionary wars; they constituted a form of revolutionary violence in response to, and purporting to overthrow, a system of foreign rule in which much greater violence was hardwired. Via such a *bellum justum,* colonized people sought to overthrow the oppressive colonial system and take power in their own hands, that is, to establish some form of democracy—and not necessarily one stamped with a *nihil obstat* by the former colonial masters. Conversely, all too many wars have been 24-carat counter-revolutionary; the Vietnam War is a prime example. That "American War," as the Vietnamese call it, exemplifies how wars can also be ambivalent, that is, can be fought for revolutionary goals by one side and against those goals by the other side. The Spanish Civil War of 1936-1939 likewise reflected this ambivalence, it was a revolutionary war for the republican side but very much a counter-revolutionary project for their "nationalist" enemies.

---

10   See Aptheker, pp. 89-100, 111-13, and Losurdo's in-depth study of nonviolence.

Armed conflicts abroad may also serve as an antidote to revolution at home and are therefore unleashed when the elite—that is, the ruling class—feels threatened and opts for a war against an *external* enemy to avoid revolution at home, that is, a conflict against an *internal* enemy, a class conflict. The ruling class can similarly decide to start a foreign war to arrest a domestic revolutionary process at a certain point, that is, to prevent it from radicalizing and threatening the wealth and privileges of the elite. We will see that this is how the French Revolution led to a series of foreign wars, fought far away from Paris, as far away as Moscow. In this book, however, we will focus not on foreign wars, but on the revolution, or rather, the revolutions, not only the so-called Great Revolution of 1789 but also the less famous revolutionary upheavals that rocked the French capital in 1830, 1848, and 1871.

This book constitutes an attempt to describe the French Revolution and to make it understandable via a visit to the great city where much of it happened, Paris. Answers will be offered to questions such as: how did people live in France before the Revolution, during the so-called Ancien Régime? How did things morph from an attempt to reform the existing order *from above* to a veritable revolution *from below*? Why did so much bloodshed have to occur? Who were the major actors of this drama—not so much individual personalities, but collectivities of people, that is, classes? Who were those (in)famous folks called sans-culottes? Why did the French Revolution spawn a long series of international wars? Why did the Revolution "devour its own children"? And why did the Revolution, an intrinsically democratic experience, yield a dictatorship by a military man, Napoleon Bonaparte, who happened to be—not coincidentally—the native son of the French province that was most distant from Paris? Why were new revolutions to rock France and especially Paris again later? With respect to the French capital, we will also explore the way in which the revolutionary upheavals of 1789, 1830, 1848, and 1871 transformed Paris from a "royal city," dominated by the nobility, of which the monarch was the *primus inter pares*, as well as the clergy, into the Babylon of the French and, indeed, international bourgeoisie, with as (phallic) symbol the Eiffel Tower.

If these issues are of interest to you, join us on this visit to Paris! *Allons-y*!

Part I.
The Ancien Régime: France Before 1789

IMAGE 1. Rural landscape in 18th-century France from the *Encyclopédie* by Diderot et d'Alembert.

1. *La France Profonde*
The Countryside

We are in the year 1785. With about 28 million inhabitants, France is, after Russia, the biggest country in Europe. It has been a kingdom, a Christian kingdom, ever since the pagan ruler of a barbarian tribe that had conquered the land hitherto known as Gaul, agreed to be baptized in Reims by that city's bishop, around 500AD, in the context of the collapse of the (Western) Roman Empire. Those barbarians were not Asiatic, like Attila's Huns, who had raided Gaul earlier, but a Germanic tribe known as the Franks. A region in the center of present-day Germany is still named after them, Franconia; but more important for our purposes is the fact that the kingdom that originated in Gaul under Clovis' auspices became known in Latin as *Francia*, and that eventually gave us the name France.

In 1785, France is still a monarchy tracing itself back to Clovis, even though different dynasties have occupied the throne during the many centuries that have elapsed since his lifetime, among them the Capetians and the Valois. But each new king, regardless of the identity of his dynasty, followed the footsteps of Clovis, trekking to Reims to be anointed by the bishop in the city's magnificent Cathedral; only after that ceremony was the king truly considered king of France. Now, the land is ruled by a member of the Bourbon Dynasty and, like many of his distant as well as immediate predecessors, he is called Louis: Louis XVI.

France is not only a monarchy, ever since Clovis it has been a Christian monarchy and it is reputed to be the primordial Christian kingdom, often referred to as the "eldest daughter of the Church." The symbol par excellence of the French monarchy is a stylized lily, the fleur-de-lis, whose three petals recall the Holy Trinity, thus affirming the Christian character of a state that is not separated from the Church. One of France's medieval rulers, crusader Louis IX, even achieved sainthood and became known worldwide as Saint Louis. And one of the icons of Christian and monarchical France is Joan of Arc, a fighter for France in the Hundred Years' War against England and simultaneously an icon of the Christian faith, though her canonization will have to wait until the 20th century; she is often represented holding a cross as well as a lily-covered flag.

France, then, is a Catholic kingdom. To its denizens, it seems that it has always been so, and most if not all of them expect that it will always be that way. Nobody has an inkling that, within a few years, a great revolutionary tsunami will roll over the land, traumatically transforming it into an entirely different world. Later, after 1789 and the many revolutionary years that followed that *annus horribilis*, people will look back at the old, pre-revolutionary France, the France of the Ancien Régime, either with disdain or with nostalgia. Even today, historians and politicians, inside and outside of France, find it virtually impossible not to display either their approbation or their loathing whenever the topic of the French Revolution arises.

In 1785, Paris has already been the French capital since time immemorial, and it is this great city that we are interested in. However, Paris is a kind of anomaly in a country that is still predominantly rural. It is therefore appropriate that we take a look at the rest of France, a rural universe sprinkled mostly with thousands of villages and hamlets but also with a fair number of provincial towns big and small, before we head for the capital.

Peasantry

It is not in the capital, but in the countryside, in *la France profonde,* "deepest France," as they say in Paris, where beats the heart of Ancien-Régime France. Pre-revolutionary France is indeed a *pre-industrial* society. This means that, like everywhere else in Europe—except in England, where the "Industrial Revolution" is already in full swing—and in the world, agriculture constitutes the most important sector of the country's economy, accounting for anywhere from 80 to 90 percent of the gross domestic product. Everything revolves around land, land is primordial. The majority of people live on the land, i.e., in the countryside, and make a living by working on the land. It is not a coincidence that the original meaning of the French word for work, *labor*, is "plowing," that is, the quintessential form of work on the land. It is the land that provides most people, at the price of hard work, with food and many other commodities they—as well as the minority who do not work the land—need to survive. In other words: most inhabitants of France—probably about 80 percent of the population—are peasants. Peasants work the land, and they live where they work, on the land, i.e. in the countryside, not in cities. Just before the Revolution, writes the American historian Arno Mayer,

> ... France was 85 percent rural. Twenty-two million out of 28 million French men and women lived in the countryside, the overwhelming majority engaged in agriculture and agriculture related work. At least one third of them were poor or destitute.[1]

For these peasants, their village (or hamlet) and its surroundings are their fatherland, their homeland, their country—which is what they like to call it, their "*pays*." (Many Italians similarly use the term *paesano* to refer, not to a fellow citizen of the Italian Republic, but to someone from their village or region of Italy.)

The peasants of the Ancien Régime do not inhabit individual farms surrounded by the land they own, as in the case of farmers in the US, Canada, and much of the rest of the Western World; they huddle together in villages and hamlets, where they live in small and humble houses, often primitive hovels. They labor on parcels of land dispersed around the territory of their village, one parcel nearby, in the valley, another one on the hillside, yet another one on the edge of the forest looming in the distance, etc.; this is the way in which the agricultural wealth—or "capital," if you prefer—of the rural locality is shared fairly by the inhabitants. It follows that one often has to cross a neighbor's land to reach one's own parcel, so there are no fences: the lots are not "enclosed" ; the system is based on "open fields." Moreover, the land is often worked collectively since each individual peasant does not own a plow or an ox needed to

---

1   Mayer, p. 413. According to Coquard, p. 45, "*les ruraux représentaient à peu près 75 % de la population*" of France. According to Hazan (2014), p. 16, approximately 23 million Frenchmen lived in the countryside.

pull it. Finally, each village features parcels of land that belong to, or rather, may be used by, the entire community, for example a space known as *le mail*, literally "the mall," but better translated as the "commons." On this parcel, all inhabitants' cattle are allowed to graze freely, and this privilege, or more correctly, this right, is called *la vaine pâture*, "free grazing." All this requires a high degree of collaboration and respect for the traditions of work on the land and social life in the village. Village life "remains subject to ancestral rhythms," as the historian Olivier Coquard has put, it is and must be strictly regulated; the peasants of the Ancien Régime are not individualists by any stretch of the imagination.[2]

Like most of their counterparts elsewhere in Europe, the peasants of Ancien-Régime France are preoccupied above all with the cultivation of one type of crop: cereals in general, and wheat in particular. They grow wheat so the people of France can eat bread, which is the main staple of their diet, providing them with the necessary carbohydrates. But wheat is a difficult crop to cultivate. It is very demanding: it will only grow on the best land and requires a lot of labor all year round—so that virtually every able-bodied person has to be involved in this type of work. Even so, the success of each year's harvest is never guaranteed. Poor harvests happen frequently, and this entails shortages, higher prices of wheat and therefore of bread, leading to undernourishment and even full-fledged famines. The existence of the French peasants is always precarious, and in the countryside many people have to resort for their survival, either temporarily or permanently, to activities such as begging, vagrancy, even crime, committed individually or in groups; banditry (*banditisme, brigandage*) is a major scourge.

The French peasants grow wheat because the French want to eat bread; and the French eat bread because French farmers grow mostly wheat. Mostly, but not exclusively. The French also want to drink wine. The vine is therefore another important crop, admittedly not primordial like wheat, but important, nonetheless. And some farmers, a minority but an important minority, focus on the production of wine, they are vintners. Fortunately, the vine does not compete with wheat. To the contrary, the vine is happy to grow on poor soils, for example on rocky soils where wheat could not possibly thrive, especially on hillsides where it

---

2   Kennedy, pp. 28 ff.; Coquard, p. 52.

would be impossible to labor with the plow. And tending the vine does not require as much labor as wheat. There are many vintners in rural France, but not nearly as many as ordinary peasants cultivating cereals.

On the menu of the French of the Ancien Régime, and of the great majority of Europeans in the pre-industrial era, bread and wine feature prominently, and they complement each other perfectly. It is not a coincidence that bread and wine are the symbols *par excellence* of the religion that dominates and virtually monopolizes Europe: Christianity.

But human beings also need proteins, and in pre-industrial France these are provided mainly by pork. Pigs do not compete with the indispensable cereals, neither with respect to land nor with manpower. One single swineherd is able to look after hundreds of pigs, and pigs are often allowed to roam freely throughout the village. These animals are happy to devour all sorts of leftovers, and in the fall—typically on Michaelmas, the feast of St. Michael, i.e. September 29—they are set free in the nearby forests to feast on acorns, mushrooms, etc. During five to six weeks, they thus grow fat. But the pigs are rounded up and killed on Martinmas, the Feast of St. Martin, which is November 11. "Every pig must some day face St. Martin" (*à chaque porc vient Saint Martin*) says an ancient French proverb! And the French have another proverb about pigs: *dans le cochon, tout est bon*!, "all of the pig is good [to eat]." The pig is indeed the only animal of which every little morsel can be consumed by humans, also the snout, the ears, the feet, the guts, used as casings for sausages, even the blood, destined to become blood sausage, known as *boudin*, a French word that slipped into English as "blood *pudding*." Moreover, mainly because of its high fat content, pork can easily be conserved through pickling, smoking, and salting. Such processes yield lard, bacon, hams, pâtés, potted meats known as *rillettes*, salamis, and other sausages, and all sorts of other types of porcine delicacies, known collectively as *cochonailles* or *charcuterie*. The pig thus provides enough meat to complement the ordinary people's diet of bread and wine for an entire year, at least in theory.

An additional source of protein is provided by cheese, which is typically made from the milk of goats or sheep. Like pigs, the latter are also domesticated animals that have minimum requirements in terms of land and labor: one single shepherd can take a flock of hundreds of animals to graze on non-arable land, if necessary even far away from the villages.

Especially in the south of France, the shepherds leave the villages in the spring and trek high into the mountain ranges of the interior, including the Alps, to allow their flocks to graze, and they return in the fall' this system is called the *transhumance*. In a village, the shepherd is therefore a rare bird, a social anomaly, a kind of nomad who does not fit perfectly in the village community, is not subject to its strict rules of conduct, and whose nonconformism is simultaneously admired and abominated by the other villagers; Jacques Brel has evoked this ambivalent relationship brilliantly in one of his songs, entitled *Les bergers* [*The Shepherds*].

Residents of, and visitors to, France, who munch baguette accompanied with charcuterie and goat cheese and washed down with some unpretentious regional wine, a *vin du terroir*, unwittingly mimic the eating habits of the denizens of France of the Ancien Régime. As for the less essential onions, shallots, garlic, and other herbs and vegetables that can make the meal more interesting, appetizing, and wholesome, and often serve to make hearty soups, especially in winter, they are grown in the *potagers*, the vegetable gardens that cling like barnacles to the hulls of the peasants' habitations.

For the conservation of pork, large amounts of salt are of course required. That salt is produced in the numerous salt flats that dot the endless Atlantic and Mediterranean coast of France, for example the *Pays Blanc* ("White Land") along the coast of Brittany's Guérande Peninsula. Salt is produced in abundance, and should therefore not be expensive, but it is, very much so, on account of the highly resented tax levied on salt, the so-called *gabelle*. This tax is typical for the Ancien Régime: it is a socially regressive *indirect* tax, which is most burdensome for the poorest people. This extremely regressive and widely detested form of revenue generation will be abolished during the Revolution but reinstated by Napoleon; its definitive abolition will have to wait until after the First World War!

Nobility

The peasants labor on the land but are very rarely owners of the land. Virtually everywhere, the land is owned by another class of people, namely the nobility or, if you prefer, the aristocracy. The general rule is *nulle terre sans seigneur* "there is no land that is not owned by a lord." (And this lord can also be a member of the clergy or ecclesiastical institution; the close ties between the nobility and the Church will be examined shortly.) It is estimated that, on the eve of the Revolution, approximately one third of the real estate of France belongs to the nobility.[3] Conversely, the owners of the land do not involve themselves in the hard work of laboring on the land, they leave that job to the peasants to whom they rent out the land in return for payment in cash or, more frequently, in kind, that is, a share of the harvest. The majority of the peasants of France are sharecroppers, *métayers*. Those who work on the land do not own it; those who own it, do not work on it.

The aristocrats—who are estimated to number somewhere between 300,000 and 400,000 persons, in other words, between 1 and 1.5 per cent of the population of Ancien-Régime France[4]—do reside on their land, preferably in the middle of their sometimes very vast landed estates. But they do not live in a farmhouse, they reside in a château, or at least a slightly less prestigious but still imposing habitation, a manor house (*manoir*). Members of the nobility also typically bear the name of their land. The marquess of Moulinsart, for example, resides in the château of Moulinsart and is the owner of all the land in and around the village of Moulinsart. But this does not exclude the possibility that he also owns land in other villages. As far as the nobility is concerned, the more land one owns, the better, and a nobleman is forever looking for opportunities to aggrandize his holdings, typically achieving this by means of marriage to an heiress.

The leading members of the nobility in the Ancien Régime thus control extremely vast holdings, and they still do today in countries such as Spain and Britain, that is, in countries where no revolution radically transformed the old established order. In a system dating back to the 14th century, for example, a foundation called "The Duchy of Cornwall" collects rent from 53,000 hectares of property in Cornwall to provide a huge income for Britain's Prince of Wales.[5]

The noble lords also benefit from all sorts of additional privileges,

---

3   Vovelle, p. 10; Coquard, p. 38. For a concise treatment of the role of the nobility on the eve of the Revolution, see the article by McManners.

4   Dupeux, p. 60; "Französische Revolution," p. 15.

5   Cooper.

collectively referred to as the "[feudal] seigneurial system." On the territory he controls, the local lord—or lady, but only on rare occasions, as this is a very patriarchal society—administers justice, for example, and he is the only one who has the right to hunt and to raise rabbits on enclosed lots known as *garennes*, "warrens." "His" peasants are forced to press their grapes in his wine press, to grind their grain in his windmill, and to bake their bread in his oven—all for payment, of course; and his exclusive ownership of bulls and boars mean that the locals also have to pay him for mating cattle and pigs. These obligations are known as the *banalités* or *droits de ban*, "banality-dues," and they apply not only to the lord's sharecroppers but to all those who inhabit his domain, his *seigneurie*, even those relatively few peasants who happen to own their own plot. And the peasants also have the duty to perform, and to perform free of charge, all sorts of occasional services for the lord, known as *corvées*.

The aristocrats are the high and mighty lords, and the peasants addresses his lord respectfully with *Monseigneur*, abbreviated as *Monsieur*, and with the formal pronoun *vous* (*vouvoyer*); conversely, the lord speaks informally with his peasant, using the familiar pronoun *tu* (*tutoyer*) and calling him *mon bonhomme*, "my [good] man." The aristocrats wear fine clothes, for example tight knickers known as *culottes*, silk stockings below the knees, and shoes featuring high heels and enormous buckles, and on the head, they sport a fancy wig and—when outdoors—a hat made of beaver fur imported from *Nouvelle France,* that is, Canada, and therefore very expensive, decorated with ostrich feathers.

The aristocrats also move around on horseback. The horse is the animal par excellence of the nobility, it is the *noble* animal. *Chevalier*, "knight," a term whose original meaning is "horseman," is technically a rank within the aristocracy but is virtually synonymous with aristocrat. The peasants do not have horses. Their plows are pulled by oxen, and they themselves normally trudge around in clogs sometimes stuffed with straw in lieu of socks. (The invention of the bicycle, in the 19th century, will make them much more mobile, and it is not surprising that in Germany the bicycle will originally be known as *Vice-Pferd*, "surrogate horse," a term whose shortened version, *Vice*, allegedly survives in the Dutch word for bicycle, *fiets*.) In any event, a peasant has to look up to see his lord, not only figuratively but even literally a member of the upper class, one of "those people high above," *ceux d'en haut*. And the peasant has to doff his cap, thus making himself even smaller vis-à-vis his *seigneur*, who in turn looks down from his "high horse," not only figuratively but even literally, on his *bonhomme*. The noblemen's felt hats are typically high, thus causing people who are usually already considerably taller than average because of their superior diet to tower even higher above the peasants; the latter look even shorter because they tend to wear a flat woollen cap (*casquette*) that truncates their profile. (But the famous cap known as a *béret*, originally from the Béarn-region and the adjoining Basque country near the Spanish border, is not yet the archetypical headgear of the French common man; it will only achieve that non-lofty status in the mid-nineteenth century, when Napoleon III and his wife, Empress Eugénie, will often vacation in Biarritz and thus cause things Basque to become trendy throughout France.)

The peasants slave away on the land and on their farmsteads, but the noble lords do not perform any manual labor, they are proud to constitute a "leisure class." They enjoy the good life in their chateaux. These aristocratic residences feature refined Rococo interior decoration, wall tapestries, busts and portraits of supposedly glorious ancestors, and high-quality furniture in a style said to be "characterized by lightness, comfort and harmony of lines." This furniture is named after the reigning King, Louis XIV, but in reality its style reflects the taste of his mistress, the famous Madame de Pompadour; the latter's pied-à-terre in Paris is the palace that will later become the official residence of the president of the French Republic, the Elysée Palace. The chateaux are also typically surrounded by pleasant gardens, mostly arranged *à la française*, "in the French manner," that is, "based on symmetry and the principle of imposing order on nature"; and they are often sprinkled with gazebos and with what are called *folies*, "little lunacies," about which more will be said later.

The aristocratic landowners consider manual labor to be the "the penance imposed by God on Adam for the original sin"; and they disdain having to work to survive as something ignoble, something dishonorable."[6] They also look down on "commerce and industry, the archetypical activities of the bourgeoisie in the cities," something that will be discussed soon.[7]

---

6 Coquard, p. 43.
7 Garrioch, p. 98.

The lifestyle of aristocrats is agreeable, pleasurable, more than a tad frivolous, often even decadent. This is reflected in paintings by contemporary artists such as Fragonard, Watteau, and Boucher, and conjured up in movies such as *Dangerous Liaisons* and *Valmont*, both based on adaptations of an 18th-century French novel by Pierre Choderlos de Laclos. The gentlemen flirt with the ladies, chamber music is performed, and of course one eats more and better than ordinary folks, and not only on the occasion of imposing big banquets or elegant little "intimate suppers," *soupers intimes*.[8] That is the reason why aristocrats are generally healthier and taller than the poorly fed, and often underfed little people. Like everyone else, the nobility eats bread. but the bread eaten in high society is fine *white* bread, not the coarse rye bread consumed by lower-class folks. And wines of high quality are served, for example, red wine from Beaune and elsewhere in Burgundy—but not from Bordeaux because, ever since the medieval times when the *bordelais* vineyard was part of the province of Aquitaine, a possession of the kings of England, its *clarets* have continued to be exported mostly to the other side of the English Channel. The most fashionable wine in polite society, however, is that still relatively new, elegant, sparkling white wine from the province of Champagne. That nectar is praised to the skies by Madame de Pompadour for "allowing the ladies to drink yet remain beautiful."[9]

The pleasurable existence in the chateaux in the countryside is interrupted from time to time by longer or shorter sojourns at the court in Versailles, or else in Paris or even some provincial capital such as Bordeaux or Dijon. In those cities, the aristocrats own imposing urban residences known as *hôtels*, to be discussed later. Life in the aristocratic residences in the country or in the city occasionally involves a "salon." A salon may be defined as a private gathering for the purpose of discussing arts, sciences, and above all literature, which is why it is also often referred to as "literary salon" (*salon littéraire*) or "conversation salon" (*salon de conversation*). The setting is usually an elegant boudoir, decorated in the Rococo style, and the happening tends to be hosted by the lady of the house, the *maîtresse de maison*. Only a small selection of members of high society attends, and they are mostly aristocrats, of course, but they may also involve a few handpicked members of the bourgeoisie, usually writ-

---

8   Wheaton, p. 194 ff.
9   Bonal, pp. 46-49.

ers, and intellectuals, especially philosophers such as Diderot, in other words, folks with celebrity status.[10]

In any event, as far as the nobility is concerned, in the time before the Revolution, life is good, very good. After the cataclysm of 1789, one of these aristocrats will write, alluding to his class: "Those who did not experience the Ancien Régime will never know how sweet life can be."[11]

Let us return for a moment to the important topic of bread. While the peasants and ordinary people in general settle for dark rye bread, the aristocrats and other well-to-do folks eat white bread made of real wheat, featuring additional ingredients such as sugar and eggs, in other words, various types of luxury bread collectively known as *viennoiserie* or "Viennese bread," such as the croissant. The latter, widely believed to be a quintessentially French delicacy, was in fact created in 1683 by the bakers of Vienna to commemorate their city's successful resistance against a siege by the Turks; hence the croissant's name and shape, that of the crescent moon, symbol of the Turks and their Islamic religion. Thanks to Marie-Antoinette, daughter of Habsburg Empress Maria Theresa, who came to France to marry the future king, Louis XVI, and brought croissant-bakers with her, this Viennese delicacy conquered the court of Versailles. The revolutionaries will put an end to the nobility's privileges with respect to the consumption of white bread and *viennoiserie* and make both available to the entire population, so that the consumption of dark rye bread will go out of fashion. During the Revolution, white bread will be known as "the bread of equality."[12]

The nobility is a "privileged" class. This means that its members enjoy the exclusive benefit of special, advantageous laws and political as well as social-economic arrangements. While the peasants and commoners in general have to pay taxes, for example, the rich—and sometimes extremely rich—aristocrats are not required to do so. And here is another example of this kind of inequality of people before the law, typical for the Ancien Régime: if found guilty of a serious crime, commoners are hanged or broken on the wheel, while noblemen are entitled to a less humiliating

---

10   See e.g. Noiriel, pp. 218-20.
11   Talleyrand (Charles Maurice de Talleyrand-Périgord, 1754-1838), quoted in M. Guizot's *Mémoires pour servir à l'histoire de mon temps*, published in 1858.
12   Soboul (1968), pp. 62, 224.

and less painful form of execution, decapitation. (Decapitation already constituted a privilege in the Roman Empire: Roman citizens, such as St. Paul, were beheaded, while foreigners such as St. Peter were crucified.)

The aristocrats also monopolize the higher levels of the hierarchy of the army and of the civil service, for which it is precisely in 18th-century France that the term "bureaucracy" starts being used. This privilege with respect to employment in the service of the state is not only advantageous but of cardinal importance. In noble families, the eldest son inherits not only the title of his father but the entire patrimony of the family; this system is called primogeniture or entail (*primogeniture, droit d'aînesse*). State employment functions as a kind of unemployment relief for the younger sons of noble families: they have easy access to prestigious and well-paid careers as officers in the army or high-ranking officials in the royal bureaucracy, for example as ambassadors in some foreign capital.[13]

The French nobility is characterized by hierarchy. The base of the pyramid features the lords of lower rank, the *chevaliers*; above the *chevaliers* loom the barons, above the barons the counts, dukes, and marquesses, and higher still one finds the princes of royal blood, known as *les fils de France,* the "sons of France"; and the king sits upon a throne at the very top of the pyramid. Like other aristocrats, the monarch is also a large landowner. Not surprisingly, he controls an enormous portfolio of real estate—arable land but also forests and other stretches of uncultivated land—spread all over the country. His possessions are known collectively as *domaine royal,* the king's "demesne." (This royal domain will become state property during the revolution, but the terminology will remain unchanged; even today, former royal forests are still identified as *forêt domaniale,* as readers who have motored through the French countryside may have noticed.)

The king is a member of the aristocracy, he identifies with that class and, conversely, the aristocrats consider him as one of theirs. Of all the noblemen of France, the king is the *primus inter pares,* the number one of his peers. It is expected that he will defend and promote the interests of the nobility. However, to be able to do that, he needs power, lots of power, including power over the noblemen themselves. That issue provides

---

13 In many countries the high ranks in the diplomatic service, e.g. the position of ambassador, were a virtual monopoly of the aristocracy.

the context of the historical development of royal *absolutism* in France (and elsewhere), a development that benefited the nobility in many ways, but simultaneously meant that they had to forego some the relative autonomy vis-à-vis the king which they had enjoyed in the Middle Ages.[14]

In the 18th century, the king is the absolute ruler of the country, of *his* kingdom. He enjoys total power; his will is the law of the land. Or, as Louis XIV laconically put it: *L'État, c'est moi,* "I am the state." Louis XVI will deliver himself of a similar statement in the early stages of the Revolution, at a moment when he has no idea that he is soon to be divested not only of absolute royal power, but of any kind of power: *C'est légal, parce que je le veux,* "it is the law because it is my wish."

Ordinary Frenchmen have no power whatsoever, they are the humble and powerless "subjects" of the king. The monarch has received his power from God, he rules "by God's grace," *de par la grâce de Dieu*. This idea, referred to by historians as the divine-right theory of kingship, implies that no earthly authority is higher than that of the king and that the king is not accountable to any human being. Even the nobility is politically impotent. To an aristocrat who does not wish to while away the time in his château in the countryside (and occasionally in his *hôtel* in the city), only one alternative option is available, namely that of a pleasant and supposedly prestigious but intrinsically useless sinecure at the court in Versailles, such as being put in charge of the royal chamber pot. Only a very restricted number of noble "favorites" may assist the king in ruling the country, in other words, serve as advisors or what are today called "ministers." Numerous noblemen are infected by "Anglomania," that is, they admire their English counterparts because—thanks to historical achievements such as Magna Carta and the so-called Glorious Revolution, which was not a revolution at all—they have managed to restrict the king's authority and therefore continue to enjoy much power themselves. "Anglomaniac" French aristocrats dream of the advent of a similar English system in their own country.[15]

Talking about Versailles, the king's vast and impressive château admittedly is only a stone's throw away from Paris but, like all the chateaux

---

14 This important historical development has been described brilliantly in a book by Perry Anderson, *Lineages of the Absolutist State*.

15 McManners, pp. 39-40; Furet and Richet, p. 32.

of the nobility, it is nonetheless located in the countryside. It is there that the king, assisted by an increasingly "bureaucratic" body of advisors and administrators, governs the country. Symbolically, the countryside thus rules the country—and supersedes the country's "kingless"[16] capital city, Paris.[17]

Versailles consists of a gigantic palace surrounded by a plethora of other buildings, including barracks for soldiers and stables for the horses, thus conjuring up a village; and it is adjoined by a vast park, just as countless French villages are situated near a forest. Versailles can thus hardly be considered to be a city, but it functions nonetheless—at the expense of Paris—as capital of the country. Approximately 10,000 people reside in the Palace of Versailles and its dependencies; the entire community features about 70,000 inhabitants.[18] In some ways, Versailles symbolizes, and externalizes, the aforementioned primordial characteristic of the Ancien Régime: the primacy of agriculture in the economy and, consequently, the preponderance of the countryside vis-à-vis the city; and also, last but not least, the social and political superiority of the large landowners not only vis-à-vis the rural as well as urban poor but even vis-à-vis the essentially urban class whose wealth, often considerable, is based on trade and other typically urban activities: *la bourgeoisie.* the middle class.

Versailles likewise symbolizes the king's alienation from the biggest of all French cities. As David Garrioch has observed, "Louis XIV had initiated the process of isolating the monarch from the kingdom's capital city by ordering the construction of the Château of Versailles and, once his court was ensconced there, had only rarely bothered to visit Paris"; later, "the Parisians resented Louis XV because they increasingly believed that he did not like their city and its inhabitants, and even distrusted them."[19]

Under Louis XVI, Queen Marie-Antoinette distanced herself even more from Paris, and even from the Château of Versailles itself, at least symbolically, by withdrawing from time to time into an idyllic but arti-

---

16 Expression used in Jones, p. 199.

17 The expression "kingless" was coined by Jones, p. 199.

18 Lévêque and Belot, p. 122. Mainly because of the return of the court to Paris, the total population of Versailles will decline to 25,000 during the Revolution.

19 Garrioch, p. 178.

ficial hamlet at the far end of the château's gardens, enveloped by vineyards, fields, orchards, and vegetable gardens, and overlooking a little village known as Saint Antoine—coincidentally the name of a saint who had withdrawn from a big city to live the life of a hermit in the wilderness. It is hardly surprising that, during the Revolution, the Parisian populace will force the royal family to move back to Paris; ironically, in their urban residence there, the Tuileries Palace, they will find themselves at only a stone's throw from another, far less peaceful, community named Saint-Antoine: the Parisian *faubourg* (suburb) of Saint-Antoine, which will reveal itself to be a kind of cradle of the Revolution. We will soon take a walk through that suburb.

In the Palace of Versailles too, the residents enjoy a most pleasurable and even frivolous lifestyle. The denizens of Versailles have no idea of the miserable existence of the majority of the common people in Paris, just as the nobleman in his château is not really aware of the misery of his peasants in their hovels. This ignorance, or indifference, is famously illustrated by a famous but probably apocryphal anecdote: Queen Marie-Antoinette, informed that trouble was brewing in Paris on account of the scarcity of bread, presumably quipped "let them eat cake!"—as if purchasing such high-quality and delicious but expensive type of pastry, an everyday feature in the diet of the denizens of Versailles, was an option for the poor Parisian working class. (The term allegedly used by Marie-Antoinette was actually *brioche*, which refers not to cake but to a type of bun concocted with expensive ingredients such as high-quality bread, eggs, and butter.)

Clergy

Other than the more or less numerous hovels of the peasants and one seignorial residence, a fancy château or more modest manor house, every French village also features a church, one single church, a Catholic church. The king is Catholic, so his subjects are also Catholic. The non-democratic principle that the religion of the ruler is the religion of the land, summarized in the saying *cujus regio, ejus religio* ("whose realm, his religion"), became the general rule in Europe in the 16th century, at the time of the Reformation: for reasons which had little to do with religious convictions but a lot more with considerations involving power and wealth, the continent's crowned heads had opted either to remain Catholic or to opt for a form of Protestantism. In the latter case, the monarch would typically close down the monasteries and confiscate their land and other possessions, thus replenishing his treasury.

The French kingdom actually constituted an exception to this rule. After decades of civil and religious wars, the country remained officially Catholic. But Protestantism—more specifically, Calvinism, imported from Switzerland and practised by the so-called Huguenots—was tolerated during the reign of King Henry IV: his Edict of Nantes, promulgated in 1598, had allowed Protestants to freely practice their faith. It was only during the reign of his grandson, Louis XIV, who officially revoked the Edict of Nantes in 1685, that Protestantism was no longer allowed. From then on, the king's religion was the religion of his subjects. Many Huguenots left the country, but Protestantism could not entirely be eradicated, and in the 18th century France, while remaining intolerant *de iure*, became tolerant *de facto*. However, the few remaining Protestants—and Jews—remained second-class citizens of the kingdom, with fewer rights than the Catholics.

And so the Catholic religion is the unchallenged state religion, the "established" religion, in the France of the Ancien Régime. The kingdom is a "clerical" society, in which Church and State are conjoined twins. The Catholic Church is rich, powerful, and omnipresent in the form of institutions—parish churches, monasteries, convents, priories, etc.—and persons—bishops, canons, priests, monks, nuns—who collectively constitute the "clergy." As in the case of the nobility, the power and wealth of the clergy repose on landed property. The Catholic Church is a large landowner, or rather, an extremely large, gigantic landowner. It controls at least five percent, but probably ten percent or even more, of the total surface of France.[20]

As for its share of the population, the personnel of the Church, the clergy, represents only 0.5 percent. The secular clergy has approximately 70,000 members, the regular—or monastic—clergy, approximately 60,000.[21] In Burgundy, for example, virtually all the vineyards belong to the famous great monasteries of that province, such as Cluny, Cîteaux,

---

20 Mayer, p. 414.
21 Dupeux, p. 57.

and Fontenay. Being a large landowner, the Church shares the economic interests of the nobility. In addition, the clergy, or at least the upper ranks of the clergy, is related to the nobility with respect to social origin. Because of the rule of celibacy, the bishops, cardinals, abbots, etc. do not establish great families or "dynasties"; they are not born into their position but are normally recruited within the nobility. The "princes" of the Church and the ecclesiastical "lords" in general are virtually exclusively gentlemen of noble origin, and they are respectfully addressed as *Monseigneur*. (Today, *Monsignor*, "my lord," is still an honorific form of address for high-ranking Church officials.) In this sense, the clergy may be considered to be a kind of colony of the nobility.[22]

Like the upper levels of the army hierarchy, those of the Church, featuring positions such as bishop and abbot, are likewise set aside for the younger sons—and, in the case of abbesses, the unmarried daughters—of aristocratic families. The incumbents of such careers—for which a genuine "vocation" is not de rigueur at all—enjoy great prestige, considerable power, and, above all, a hefty income. Indeed, the bishops and heads of monasteries and convents rake in, and administer, the rents and other revenues generated by the landed property of their diocese or monastic establishment. (A share of that income finds its way to the Papacy, of course.)

Moreover, the existence of a cardinal, bishop, or abbot is far from disagreeable. It is no secret that these ecclesiastical lords eat and drink very well, thus compensating for the sexual asceticism required by the rule of celibacy. What is less well known, is that the presumably strict rules of celibacy and chastity are systematically disregarded by numerous high-ranking members of the clergy. Many of them keep mistresses, and it is not a coincidence that Rome, as well as the papal enclave of Avignon, teem with prostitutes. The strict rules apply to the ordinary faithful, including the low-ranking clergy, whose members are not of noble origin but are recruited among the commoners, *la roture*; the majority of the countless parish priests, for example, has a petty-bourgeois or a peasant background. Financially, they can hardly make ends meet, as they receive only an infinitesimal part of the ecclesiastical revenue generated in their parish. A bishop's revenues typically exceed those of a parish priest by

---

22   Mager, p. 73.

about 200 percent.[23] Not surprisingly, then, this clerical underclass is far from well-disposed vis-à-vis its superiors and longs for far-reaching changes within the Church, changes that might improve their lot. A similar situation prevails within the regular clergy. The abbesses and abbots, virtually all aristocratic ladies and gentlemen, live extremely well, while ordinary nuns and monks do not. But it is not only on the material level that monastics are disenchanted. During the final decades of the Ancien Régime, the number of vocations has declined considerably, discipline has deteriorated noticeably, morale is low, and the general public looks down on the denizens of monasteries and convents, loathing them as a kind of parasites.[24]

Let us return to the essentials, the revenues of the "economic powerhouse" the Church happens to be."[25] Other than rents, the Church also collects an ecclesiastical tax, known as *la dîme*, the "tithe." It amounts to ten percent in principle, but a little less in reality, of the income of French Catholics, which means nearly the entire population of the country. The parish priest normally collects the tithe, he is the *décimateur*. But it is not uncommon for a large monastic institution to collect land rent from the local peasants and to relieve them of the tithe as well. The tithe is normally paid in kind, that is, in the form of a share of the harvest, which is deposited into *granges à dime* or *granges dîmières*, "tithe barns," imposing buildings of which a number still subsist in France today.

The economic base of the power and wealth of the Church is the same as that of the nobility, and the nobility controls the Church. The clergy does therefore not constitute a class in its own right, it really functions as a part of the nobility. Like the nobility, the Church is also organized along strict hierarchical lines: at the bottom of the pyramid, one finds the ordinary priests and monastics; above them loom the canons, the bishops, abbots and abbesses, archbishops, and cardinals; and the Pope is ensconced at the very top. In fact, the entire Ancien-Régime society of France (and other European countries) is perceived to feature a similar hierarchy, with the mass of the "common" or "little" people at the bottom, the lords of the nobility and the Church above them, the kings

---

23 Lagorio, p. 65.
24 Dupeux, pp. 55-59.
25 Coquard, p. 36.

even higher, and at the very top, at least in theory, the Pope, God's representative on earth.

However, the role of the church, of the clergy, differs from that of the nobility: it purports above all to legitimate the established order as a reflection of God's will. The Church teaches the people that every individual occupies her or his proper place in the God-given social hierarchy and has to accept the obligations associated with it; those who duly accomplish these obligations will receive their just reward—not in this life, but in the afterlife. The king is king "by the grace of God" and is accountable only to God for his political and other actions. The noble lord lives a pleasurable life in his château while the peasant labors "in the sweat of his brow" because that is what God has wanted. Everything is as it should be. The key word in the Christian prayer book, repeated again and again, is *amen*, translated into French as *ainsi soit-il*, "so be it."

That the doctrine of the Catholic Church functions in many ways as the ideology of the Ancien Régime, is also reflected in Christian language still very much in use today. God himself is described as "the Lord" (*le Seigneur*), but in prayers the French address him with the familiar *tu*, not the respectful *vous*. And Jesus, hardly a person of lofty social status, as he was the son of a carpenter, is "our Lord" (*notre Seigneur*); but he is often referred to as *notre Seigneur bien-aimé*, "our beloved Lord." If God in heaven is a lord, are lords here on earth not a little bit like God, or at least representatives of God? And do ordinary people not owe respect and unconditional obedience to them, even if most earthly lords, unlike Jesus, are from loveable and would not appreciate being addressed by members of the *polloi* with the familiar *tu*? There is much truth in an old saying that the priests kept the people ignorant while the lord kept them poor.

In the Ancien Régime, not only in France, but also elsewhere in Europe, there exists a dialectical relationship between poverty and wealth. The great wealth and the good life of the nobility and the clergy are unthinkable without the hard labor and the poverty of the peasantry, they are made possible by the poverty of the peasants; conversely, the poverty of the peasants is caused by the wealth of their aristocratic superiors. Wealth also goes hand in hand, in dialectical fashion, with social prestige and political power. It is because of their wealth that the *seigneurs* of the nobility and the clergy are powerful; and it is on account of their power and prestige that they are able to preserve their wealth—and to keep the peasants poor. Conversely, the peasants are powerless because of their poverty, and they remain poor because of their powerlessness. Will it always be like that?

CRISIS

In the 1780s, France is ravaged by a severe economic crisis. One of its causes is a strong and sustained population growth, sometimes described by historians as the "demographic explosion" of the 18th century. The determinants of this explosion cannot be elucidated here. However, let us focus on its effects on France. This demographic growth is less spectacular there than in England and quite a few other European countries. Even so, the kingdom's population increases from approximately 20 million inhabitants in 1700 to at least 26 and perhaps even 28 million on the eve of the Revolution.[26] But agriculture will continue for some time to remain primitive and therefore relatively unproductive, so that the production of essential foodstuffs cannot keep pace with population growth. This will lead to steep increases in the price of wheat and other cereals, and therefore of bread. The peasants, who work the land, do not benefit from this development, but the aristocratic and ecclesiastical landowners do, and so do the bourgeois merchants in the cities who distribute agricultural products via bakers to the population. Moreover, higher prices encourage landowners to increase production by means of mechanization and a rationalization of land cultivation. In France too, this results in the kind of "Agricultural Revolution" that has already been under way in England for quite some time. A peculiar aspect of this development is the appropriation by the large landowners of the commons that have been available to the peasants to graze their animals; the landowning lords similarly restrict access to the forests, where the villagers have traditionally collected firewood and fattened their pigs. (Hunting rights have always been severely restricted, commoners were sometimes hanged for poaching a hare!) In addition, the aristocrats demand that "their" underlings pay tributes and perform duties the *seigneurs* had traditionally been entitled to but had considered unimportant and therefore left un-

---

26 Vovelle, p. 16; Noiriel, p. 195. More on the "demographic revolution" of the 18th and 19th centuries in Habakkuk, p. 25.

enforced for a long time. To identify and enforce such ancient privileges, the landowners rely on professionals especially trained for this purpose; the young Gracchus Babeuf, later an ardent revolutionary, performs this function (called *commissaire à terrier*) in his native province, Picardy, in the early 1780s.[27]

In a context of rising prices, France's peasants also have to pay higher royal taxes and Church tithes as well as higher rents. In the 1780s, they thus find themselves increasingly under the gun. Things are made even worse by bad harvests and droughts, causing a peak in cattle mortality.[28] The vintners have a particularly hard time, because the price of the bread they must buy keeps climbing while the price of the wine they sell follows a downward trajectory.

The mid-1780s are good times for the land-owning nobility and high clergy. As far as they are concerned everything may—no: should—remain as it is. The Ancien Régime is *their* regime. The peasants, on the other hand, constitute a miserable and discontented rural under-class, a rural proletariat that urgently needs remedies for the evils that bedevil it and threaten to ruin it. The peasants long for an improvement of their lot. They expect such an improvement to be achieved within the parameters of the established social-economic order, they do not seek the overthrow of this order. Like their parents and ancestors, they fully accept what the Church has always taught them, namely, that all is as it should be, that the established order is a God-given order for which there is no alternative.

On the one hand, the peasants are attached in an arch-conservative manner to the established order, the Ancien Régime. On the other hand, a great number of them are growing disenchanted and hostile towards the noble and clerical lords who incarnate this order and subject the peasants to increasingly ruthless exploitation. During the Revolution, the peasants will display an ambivalent attitude: they will burn down chateaux and massacre priests and monks, but they will also take up arms to fight for the king and the Church and against the revolutionaries—at least in some French regions, most famously the Vendée.

---

27   Larue-Langlois, p. 13.
28   Soboul (1977), pp. 32-33.

IMAGE 2. To the left, the Pont Neuf, emblem of pre-revolutionary Paris, the "royal city", by Jacques Callot.

2. Paris:
The "Royal City" on the Eve of the Revolution

ON THE EVE OF THE REVOLUTION, Paris is a very big city, a metropolis that towers far above all other cities of France. Paris constitutes the great urban exception to the general rule specifying that Ancien-Régime France is rural. However, as suggested by the Chinese symbol of Yīn and Yang, the reality is never strictly black-and-white, and in the 1780s there still exist "mini-countrysides" within Paris. Arlette Farge has stressed that, in the 18th century, "the countryside is present in the city" (*la campagne est en ville*), featuring farms, vegetable gardens, orchards, non-cultivated open spaces, and so forth, for example the Grenelle Plain, the area where the Eiffel Tower will later arise.[1] These *rus in urbe* are the mirror image of *urbs in rure* constituted by the bigger or smaller urban centers that are sprinkled throughout the vast rural expanse of *la France profonde*.

In any event, compared with the countryside, Paris is an entirely different world, another planet. With somewhere between 600,000 and 700,000 inhabitants,[2] the French capital is almost the biggest metropolis of Northern Europe, surpassed only by London. In France and continental Europe, Paris is the city of cities, a *ville-monde* or "world-city," a modern Babylon. However, on the eve of the Revolution, Paris still features a

---

1   Farge, p. 69-71.
2   Between 650,000 and 700,000, according to Rudé, pp. 41-42; 600,000, according to Mayer, p. 413; 630,000, according to Varejka, p. 80. For a detailed study of Paris on the eve of the Revolution, see the study by David Garrioch, *La fabrique du Paris révolutionnaire*.

medieval look. Criss-crossed by a network of crooked streets and alleys, it is a very different city from today's City of Light. Only in the middle of the 19th century will Baron Haussmann, the Prefect of Paris, ruthlessly modernize the city by the creation of large avenues and squares. We will see later that his project served a counter-revolutionary objective: it was supposed to enable Haussmann's boss, Emperor Napoleon III, to employ cavalry and artillery in case of insurrections by his capital's pesky plebs. Since time immemorial, that Parisian plebs is to be found not exclusively, but primarily, in the eastern reaches of the city. It is there that we will begin our promenade through pre revolutionary Paris.

IMAGE 3. English tourist visiting Campania—painting by Carl Spitzweg (1808–1885).

Poor Folks...

We enter Paris via an eastern suburb, the previously mentioned Faubourg Saint-Antoine. This is a kind of big village that used to cling like a barnacle to the outside of the medieval walls of the city, erected during the reign of King Charles V, that is, in the middle of the 14th century. But these walls were torn down under Louis XIV to make room for a rosary of big boulevards. (Of the wall that used to separate Paris from suburbs like Saint-Antoine and above all from that other world formed by the countryside and the rest of France, a sliver is still visible in the Left Bank district, on Rue Clovis, near the Pantheon.)[3]

The Faubourg Saint-Antoine owes its name to a religious establishment located there since the 13th century, a Cistercian convent called Saint-Antoine-des-Champs, whose abbess, sometimes a princess of royal blood, is popularly known as *la Dame du Faubourg*, "the lady of the suburb."[4] Originally, however, this establishment belonged to the Antonines, a monastic order whose patron saint is not Anthony of Padua but the less well-known Anthony the Hermit, also known as Anthony the Great. This *Antoine* lived as an ascetic hermit in the Egyptian desert in the 4th century and is considered to be one of the founders of monasticism; he is therefore also known as Anthony Abbott. In painting and sculpture, he is always shown with a rather peculiar attribute, a pig, symbol of the carnal pleasures from which, as an ascetic hermit, he had abstained. He was the patron saint of butchers, and the Antonine monks raised pigs that were allowed to roam freely in the city streets, feeding on kitchen waste (and much else), thus serving as garbage collectors.[5] The convent may be located in a very poor part of the city, but it is one of the richest convents in France, with rents from Parisian houses one of its major sources of income.

The denizens of the Faubourg Saint-Antoine are mostly "little people," plebeian types, including many very poor people, In stark contrast to the affluent and elegant western districts of Paris, the city's eastern part is the Paris of ordinary Parisians, the habitat of the working class, *le peuple laborieux, les classes laborieuses*. Many people of that type are also to

---

3   Regarding the walls of Paris, see the study by Gagneux and Prouvost.
4   Le Faubourg Saint-Antoine, Paris.
5   Garrioch, p. 56.

be found in other eastern suburbs and in the center of the city, but the Faubourg Saint-Antoine is the heart of this popular Paris. However, very few factory workers live here. The factory, a center of mass-production by means of machines, is a phenomenon of the Industrial Revolution, and in the final quarter of the 18th century, this revolution has been under way in England for quite some time, but in France it has barely started. Paris is not yet an industrial city featuring big factories; in fact, it will never be one. The approximately 40,000 inhabitants of the Faubourg Saint Antoine—the "*Faubouriens*"—are mostly manual workers, artisans, that is, people who *manufacture* limited quantities of products, often quality products, typically in small productive centers known as *ateliers*, "workshops," or "manufactures"; they do not *fabricate* great quantities of products with the help of machines, as factory workers have started to do.

In the Faubourg Saint-Antoine, thousands of artisans—including numerous Germans, Flemings, and other foreigners—produce mostly furniture in "wretched, dusty workshops." (The raw material, consisting of logs of timber, originates in the Morvan Forest of Burgundy; it is driven from there via the Yonne and Seine Rivers to Paris, arriving at the Île Louviers, an island located just upstream from the Île Saint Louis at only a short distance from the Faubourg Saint Antoine; this islet is destined to disappear around 1850, when the narrow and shallow channel separating it from the Rive Gauche or Right Bank will be filled in, eventually becoming the Boulevard Morland.)[6] To this artisanal past, numerous furniture shops will continue to bear witness until the early 21st century. While cabinetmakers are prominent among the hard-working inhabitants of the neighborhood of Saint-Antoine, many other types of laborers are active here, including printers, barbers, tailors, watchmakers, shoemakers, cobblers, hatmakers, painters, butchers, grocers, etc.

The denizens of the Faubourg Saint Antoine are not well-to-do, far from it. Many of them are poor, sometimes very poor. But they typically work for rich customers, and for this chic clientele they produce tables and chairs, carpets and curtains, elegant clothes, boots and shoes, wigs, and all other sorts of products of quality and even luxury. They are therefore increasingly aware of the gap that separates them from the rich people of the noble and bourgeois elite. They are plebeians, they belong to

---

6   Hazan (2002), pp. 157-159; Garrioch, p. 28; "L'île Louviers, une île parisienne disparue."

the plebs, the common people, while the aristocrats and bourgeois may be described as patricians. On the other hand, the majority of these artisans and shopkeepers, while described as "workers," usually own some property, such as a house a workshop, a small *atelier*, a retail shop, and/or tools that are sometimes quite valuable and expensive; they are not wage-earners but dispose of an income of their own, no matter how modest. They may be described as "self-employed," as "auto-entrepreneurs." On account of this status and a corresponding mentality, it is permissible to define them as *petit-bourgeois*, "petty bourgeois"—lower-middle class, if you will.

The craftsmen's traditional sense of professional hierarchy—with the "masters" on top and the "apprentices" below—differentiates them from, and causes them to feel superior to, the many other common folks who dwell below them on the social scale. The latter include all those who will later be described as *ouvriers*, as "workers," that is, wage-earning factory workers, whose numbers are still extremely limited, because in France the Industrial Revolution is still in its infancy; the *journaliers* or "day laborers," willing to perform just about any type of work for a pittance; the unemployed, allegedly approximately 20,000 in number; the countless beggars; and the 10 to 15,000 *filles du monde*, the young and not-so-young women "for whom prostitution happened to be the only way of survival." These are the types of folks that will later be referred to by Karl Marx as "proletarians," meaning people who do not own property, or anything at all, except for their *proles*, the Latin term for "offspring." In any event, in the 1780s, Paris had a very large number of poor people: no less than 120,000, according to a police report. It had been like that for quite some time already. Leopold Mozart, who took his *wunderkind* Wolfgang Amadeus to the French capital in 1763, reported that the streets were teeming with beggars and that "it would not be easy to find a place with so many miserable and deformed people [*elenden und gestümmelten Personen*]." Moreover, during the years leading up to the Revolution, life in Paris has become increasingly expensive, and "the number of the poor, and people in a precarious situation, has been rising irresistibly." On the eve of the Revolution, writes David Garrioch, "the gap between the rich and the masses of poor people was widening, ... the poor were becoming more numerous—and poorer."[7]

---

7   Garrioch, pp. 51ff., 54, 61-62, 69. The number of unemployed in Coquard,

The Parisian *demos* has a lot in common with the peasants of the countryside and resemble them in many ways; like the peasants, the ordinary Parisians do not wear a hat, but a cap made of wool, similar to the beret still worn by many Frenchmen, and wooden shoes without socks but stuffed with straw. And also baggy, long-legged trousers or *pantalons*, which contrast starkly with the *culottes*, the knickers sported by aristocratic and bourgeois types in combination with silk stockings. During the Revolution, the aristocrats will be nicknamed *bas de soie*, "silk stockings"; the Parisian common people in general, and the artisans and shopkeepers in particular, will be known as sans-culottes, "those without knickers."[8]

The diet of the working masses of France's big city consists overwhelmingly of bread, ordinary grey bread, *le pain gris*, as it does for the peasants who inhabit *la France profonde*. On average, the French in general eat two to three pounds of this bread per day. The price of the "daily bread" is therefore extremely important. and it varies from year to year, depending on the outcome of the harvest. In addition, the bread price fluctuates greatly during the course of any given year. The price of bread peaks in July, high point of the so-called *soudure* ("soldered point"), the "lean" summertime, starting in June, when the supplies of flour from the previous year have almost run out and the new harvest is yet to come. A successful harvest causes the price of bread to drop back to low levels. The price of wine pursues a similar trajectory. The wine is lower in quality, but most expensive, just before the harvest in the fall. Each year, however, plenty of good new wine becomes available again, and at a low price, on Martinmas, the feast of Saint Martin, November 11; the vintners are not allowed to sell their wine before that date. This tradition lives on in the custom of releasing the new Beaujolais on the second Thursday of November.

A big difference between France's rural and urban, particularly Parisian, common people is that the majority of the latter have managed to benefit, much more than the former, from a basic education in parish schools run by the Church, whose attendance was made compulsory under Louis XIV, in 1698. The Parisian plebes are literate, have achieved a

---

p. 45. The police report is quoted in Varejka, p. 81. Leopold Mozart is quoted in Paumgartner, p. 118.

8   Hussey, p. 191, errs when he writes that the sans-culottes constituted "the lowest layer of the proletarian classes of Paris."

respectable cultural level, and are eager readers of the newspapers, magazines, and pamphlets that have been multiplying rapidly in the course of the 18th century, not coincidentally called the "age of enlightenment." They also can, and do, read the official public announcements posted on walls, by the royal, ecclesiastical, and municipal authorities. And many of them communicate with each other in writing.[9]

Numerous are the immigrants who have recently arrived from the countryside—and from other countries, such as Germany and the Austrian Netherlands, modern Belgium—in search of work as domestic servants or craftsmen. Approximately 40,000 domestic servants live in the capital, and there is a great variety of them, they range from snooty butlers and lackeys at the top to maids—*bonnes à tout faire*—at the bottom of the scale. Some seigneurs employ as many as 30, and even for a low-ranking nobleman four servants is *de rigueur*; bourgeois families have only one or two. One third of Parisian households feature at least one servant. But more than 90 percent of the domestic servants are not born in the city, "since Parisians themselves abominate the total loss of independence that is associated with this job." Shopkeepers and craftsmen "generally employ young women from the provinces, willing to work hard to save for a dowry."[10]

The ordinary folks we encounter here, in the suburb of Saint-Antoine, and also elsewhere in the city, have suffered a lot during an economic crisis that has raged during much of the 1780s. The agrarian crisis has caused prices to rise ceaselessly, undermined the purchasing power of Parisians, and thus reduced demand for the products manufactured by the artisans. That in turn has led to overproduction and unemployment in the manufactures and an increase in the number of jobseekers, so that wages have decreased, and demand dropped to even lower levels.[11] What is most crucial in this situation, is the evolution of the price of cereals and therefore of bread. Between 1785 and 1789, the price of wheat rises by no less than 66 percent. The revolutionary year 1789, and above all the month of July, witnesses a spectacular increase in the price of wheat and of rye, the main ingredient of the grey bread that is consumed daily

---

9   Noiriel, pp. 192-93, 216-18, 225.
10 Coquard, pp. 46, 60; Garrioch, p. 41; Noiriel, pp. 203-04.
11 Hartig, p. 71.

in great quantities by the ordinary people. On average, the purchase of bread requires half of the revenue of the Parisian working class; however, on the eve of the Revolution, this share rises to almost 90 percent of their budget.[12]

Unemployment, hunger, and poverty haunt the Faubourg Saint-Antoine. But neither the urban proletariat nor the artisans and shopkeepers threatened by pauperization understand the context of the economic crisis in general and of the increase in bread prices in particular. Rumours circulate about a conspiracy mounted by noblemen, merchants, bakers, and all sorts of other "usurers" seeking to profit from higher prices. The people are hungry and want the urban and royal authorities to find remedies; what is wanted above all, is the regulation of the price of bread. The fact that such a drastic measure is not introduced, causes considerable discontent. As a result of this, the inhabitants of the Faubourg Saint-Antoine and other popular districts will soon take action themselves and thus vent their frustration and anger. These people will constitute the shock troops of the Revolution, the revolutionary masses—or mob, as some prefer to call it—who will storm the Bastille. Albert Soboul, historian par excellence of the phenomenon of the *sans-culotterie*, will write about these hungry and disgruntled Parisian common people that "the Revolution was to a great extent their work, it was they who invested all their energy and hope in the Revolution, it was they who lived and suffered for the Revolution."[13]

Talking about the Bastille, suddenly we find ourselves in front of it. The real name of that edifice is Bastille Saint-Antoine. The word Bastille is a diminutive of *bastide*, a term of Provençal origin, meaning "fortification," "bastion." It is an impressive fortress dating back to the Middle Ages, rectangular and girded by high walls; these walls are reinforced by no less than eight round towers and are surrounded by a large and deep moat connected to the Seine and teeming with fish and frogs. The Bastille was constructed at the end of the 14th century in order to strengthen a weak point in the wall around Paris, namely where this wall reached the banks of the Seine. However, hundreds of years later, in the 1780s, the Bastille is situated within the city, because in the meantime Paris has

---

12 Soboul (1977), pp. 31-32; Rudé, pp. 21-22.
13 Soboul (1968), p. 9.

expanded well beyond its medieval city walls, "swallowing" the Faubourg Saint Martin and many other suburbs. Under Louis XIV, in the 1670s, the medieval city walls had been demolished to make room for a rosary of avenues, more than thirty meters wide and lined with trees; they were referred to with the term "boulevard," a French bastardization of the Dutch word *bolwerk,* meaning "dike, bastion, defensive wall," but the French term will later find its way into many other languages, including English, and even into Dutch itself.[14]

Since the time of Cardinal Richelieu, who was King Louis XIII's powerful Prime Minister in the first half of the 17th century, the fortress has served as a royal prison. The people incarcerated here are not ordinary criminals, but privileged personalities, jailed for unpaid debts and other relatively minor delinquencies. Voltaire was locked up there for some time for writings that were considered libellous, and the same fate befell the infamous Marquis de Sade. The Bastille has been aptly described as "a high, dark and threatening edifice, a sinister emblem of authority."[15] To the *Faubouriens,* the fortress, with its high walls and phallic towers, symbolizes the arbitrary power of the king; moreover, with cannon mounted on its high walls, it looms like a permanent threat to their suburb. That is why they will eagerly participate in the attack on the Bastille on July 14, 1789, and celebrate this event as their very own victory.

To leave the Faubourg Saint Antoine and enter the historical center of Paris, we have to pass to the right of the Bastille. There, at the beginning of the modern Rue de la Bastille, used to stand a monumental city gate, richly decorated, and resembling a kind of triumphal arch. But that city gate, the Porte Saint-Antoine, was demolished in 1778, since previously all persons and goods moving between the city center and the suburb had to squeeze through its three narrow apertures.[16]

...AND THE RICH

We now find ourselves in a part of Paris that had long remained uninhab-

---

14 Higonnet, p. 61, offers an "etymology of his own," he suggests that the term boulevard may come from *bouleversement,* "upheaval."

15 Hazan (2002), pp. 20-21.

16 Stammers; Gagneux and Prouvost, p. 124-127, 129.

ited because it was frequently inundated by the Seine; it was in fact the site of a former bed of that river. The district eventually developed into a center of market gardening, producing vegetables such as cabbages and leeks.[17] For these reasons it became known as Le Marais, "the marsh." It was only in the beginning of the 17th century, during the reign of Henry IV, that this "marsh" was reclaimed and protected from the Seine by means of solid dykes. A new district was planned around a central square, intended to be an urbanistic tip of the hat to the monarch and therefore baptized Place Royale; it featured a statue of the king's son and heir to the throne, to go down into history as Louis XIII, and surrounded by Italian-style arcades. The ambiance of this square, later to be called Place des Vosges, still conjures up the era of that particular Louis, the intrigues of the powerful Cardinal Richelieu, and the exploits of d'Artagnan and the Three Musketeers, described so vividly by Alexandre Dumas. We will later find out why the name of the square was to change to Places des Vosges.

In the 17th century, countless "*hôtels particuliers,*" some imposing and elegant, others less ostentatious, were erected in this district. These "seignorial residences" constitute a Parisian pied-à-terre which aristocrats, who normally reside in a château in the countryside, occupy occasionally or permanently for the purpose of business and especially pleasure. According to David Garrioch, the number of aristocratic inhabitants of Paris on the eve of the Revolution is unknown but is estimated to amount to about three percent of the population, which would amount to approximately 20,000 men, women, and children.[18]

The Parisian *hôtels* are imposing edifices, usually made of stone, and here in the Marais they are all constructed in the elegant style of the Renaissance. Via a monumental entrance gate decorated with sculptures and/or a coat of arms of the family, one arrives at an interior courtyard, where arriving noble ladies and gentlemen alight from their carriages. The building itself features many rooms for the comfort of the lord and his family and guests, and, on the highest floor, just under the roof, behind small round windows known as *œils-de-bœuf* ("ox-eye windows"), uncomfortable little rooms for the lackeys, kitchen staff, chamber maids, and other staff members; these attic rooms are called *mansardes*, after

---

17   Hazan (2002), p. 73.
18   Garrioch, p. 92.

their the architect François Mansart (1598-1666), wrongly considered to have been their inventor.

During the Revolution, countless *hôtels* will be confiscated, auctioned off, and bought up by well-to-do bourgeois who will transform them into establishments where travellers can rent a room for payment; this is how the term "hotel" will start to refer to a building for the accommodation of travellers, a type of establishment previously referred to as *auberge* or *logis,* "inn." But the term *hôtel,* referring to an imposing building in a city, subsists even today in France in terms such as *hôtel de ville,* "city hall," and *hôtel de la poste,* "post office." A number of these ancient aristocratic residences in the Marais are destined to serve as museums. The Hôtel Carnavalet, for example, one the home of Madame de Sévigny,[19] is the city's history museum, and the Hôtel Salé houses the Picasso Museum. Other fine seignorial residences of the Marais include the hôtels of Sully, Aumont, Rohan, and Beauvais. The latter, located at 68 Rue de Francois-Miron, accommodated the Mozart family during their visit to Paris in 1763-1764; at that time, his parents were touring Western European capitals to show off their prodigy, seeking employment for it in the service of royalty or high-ranking nobility or clergy.

The biggest and most elegant *hôtels* are owned by aristocrats. However, some grand residences in the Marais and in other classy districts of Paris belong to another type of rich folks, namely members of the higher ranks of the middle class or bourgeoisie. This class includes all those who dispose of a considerable income derived from commercial or professional activities, from service in the government bureaucracy, and even from landed property, but do not belong to the nobility or the clergy. These people are numerous in Paris and in the other cities big and small of France, but in the countryside, they are rare birds indeed. They are urbanites, not country folks. The American historian Charles Tilly has described this bourgeoisie as "not owners of big businesses, but rather merchants, lawyers, notaries, and others who make a living by managing capital."[20] He might have added that many bourgeois earned a considerable income from employment in the government bureaucracy, even though the most prestigious and best-paid positions were monopolized

---

19 Jones, pp. 165-68.
20 Tilly, p. 242.

by the nobility. Government jobs could in fact be purchased, and some positions brought the additional benefit of a noble title, so that the French bourgeoisie considered such a purchase an excellent source of prestige as well as revenue.

The term "bourgeoisie" is very broad. On the one hand, it refers to the *petite bourgeoisie* or "petty bourgeoisie," the lower-middle class, consisting of people such as small businessmen with limited incomes and more-or-less well-to-do artisans. On the other hand, this class also featured a higher but far less numerous level, namely the *grande* (or *haute*) *bourgeoisie*, an elite of rich merchants, bankers, high-ranking government bureaucrats employed in the service of the monarch or the city, lawyers, physicians, etc.—the type of people that will later also be referred to as *notables*, "persons of note," "persons of significance." These people are often as rich as many aristocrats and sometimes even (much) richer, so that they too can afford to live in seignorial residences. However, as already mentioned, their wealth does not normally spring from ownership of land, but is mostly the fruit of trade, industry, finance, and business in general—all of them activities looked down upon by the nobility, activities that may actually cause an aristocrat involved in them to lose his title, a penalty known as *dérogeance*. And to the extent that members of the bourgeoisie earn an income from employment in the government bureaucracy, sometimes earning a noble title in the process, they are resented by the nobility as intruders and *parvenus*, that is, upstarts.

Since at least one century, in France, as in England and elsewhere, much more money is to be made—or, put differently, much more capital is to be accumulated—in an activity other than land ownership, namely foreign trade, and especially trade in slaves, but also in wine. Because of that, many members of the bourgeoisie control much greater assets than most aristocrats, the more since France's landowning nobility has not bothered to make their land holdings more productive, as their English counterparts have done. The latter's methods to "improve" agriculture include specialization, (for example in the cultivation of cereals or rearing of sheep), mechanization, and the concentration and enclosure of their vast landed properties, which are no longer rented out to tenant farmers but worked by teams of hired laborers. Countless tenant farmers have suffered the consequences: they are ruthlessly driven from land their families had worked for centuries, becoming a rural proletariat doomed to leave their villages in search of land in the colonies or a job in the cities. Thus there has emerged an agrarian capitalism, to be followed by other manifestations of capitalism. The 17th and 18th centuries are the golden age of *commercial* capitalism, while the 19th century will witness the development of *industrial* and *financial* capitalism.[21] Colossal fortunes are being accumulated by means of international trade, especially in Great Britain and the Netherlands, but also in France, and above all thanks to the slave trade. However, in France it has not been in the capital, Paris, that capital has been accumulated in this fashion and that capitalist merchants have started to play a prominent social as well as economic role, but in the great Atlantic seaports, such as Nantes and Bordeaux, major centers of *la traite négrière,* the slave trade, and also of the wine trade.[22]

IMAGE 4. A French bourgeois family. Louis-Léopold Boilly, *Famille* (1797).

21   See Ellen Meiksins Wood, *The Origin of Capitalism: A Longer View.*

22   For the role of the slave trade in the development of the capitalist system, see the classic study by Eric Williams, *Capitalism and Slavery,* as well as the more recent treatment by Domenico Losurdo, *Liberalism: A Counter-History.*

The bourgeoisie is the social class that drives the development of this commercial capitalism, and profits from this development. In comparison with the fortunes earned from land ownership, the wealth thus amassed by the bourgeoisie is growing much more rapidly.[23] The upper-middle class, the *haute bourgeoisie*, has money, plenty of money, in other words: economic power, but politically it is powerless in comparison to the nobility; it has even less political power than it did in the time of Louis XIV, when members of the "vulgar bourgeoisie"—such as Colbert—could even become a minister, which is no longer the case. Moreover, even the richest bourgeois can only dream of achieving the kind of social prestige commanded by noble lords. Sometimes they try to imitate the manners and dress of the aristocrats, but this kind of mimesis tends to backfire, as if usually meets with ridicule, most famously so in Molière's 1670 comedy, *Le Bourgeois gentilhomme* (*The Middle-Class Aristocrat* or *The Would-Be Noble*).

The bourgeois "plutocrats" also try hard to infiltrate the aristocracy, sometimes successfully. The best way to achieve this goal is to have a daughter married to a nobleman. This stratagem requires payment of a sizable dowry. To the family of the aristocratic fiancé, such a marriage may provide relief from financial difficulties; it is sometimes referred to as *fumer son terroir*, "fertilizing one's land." And, as mentioned before, it is also possible to purchase—for a large sum of money—one of those positions in the royal bureaucracy that come with an admittedly minor noble title attached to it; however, the parvenus belonging to this "noblesse de robe" are looked down upon by the "old" nobility, supposedly the "real thing," the *noblesse de race*.

One of these upstarts is Pierre-Augustin Caron, a successful businessman whose fortune had been amassed at least in part by supplying weapons to the transatlantic British colonists who had rebelled against the government in London, thus achieving independence for a new nation that will become known as the United States of America. Via his excellent contacts at the court in Versailles, Caron managed to purchase the sinecure of "royal secretary," associated with ennoblement, but "he was never totally accepted by aristocratic society."[24] Beaumarchais refers

---

23 See e.g. Vovelle, p. 14; Guillemin, p. 16.
24 Garrioch, p. 114.

to a piece of land he has inherited from his deceased first wife, and this is the name he uses when he publishes *The Marriage of Figaro*, a satirical attack on the nobility. The performance of this play at the Parisian Odeon Theatre in 1784 will cost Beaumarchais three days of imprisonment, because the aristocratic ruling class finds his play far from amusing. The following lines from the *Marriage of Figaro* are particularly shocking to the nobility, and therefore enchanting to the bourgeoisie. It is a remark that Figaro dreams of addressing to his lord, Count Almaviva:

> Because you are a high lord, you think you are a great genius! ... Nobility, fortune, prestige, power. All those things make you so proud! But what have you actually accomplished to deserve all this? You went through the trouble of being born, that's all.[25]

Conversely, *Figaro* reveals itself to be extremely popular among the bourgeoisie, not only in France, but also abroad. (It is not a coincidence that a well-known, very bourgeois French newspaper was baptized *Le Figaro* when it was founded in 1826.) In Vienna, capital of the Habsburg Empire, Mozart will compose wonderful music for Beaumarchais' story, turned into the libretto for an opera, but this achievement will nip in the bud his potential career as a court musician. Contrary to Vienna, where the public defers to the taste of the emperor and the aristocracy, Mozart's opera will meet with resounding success in Vienna's great urban rival within the Habsburg Empire, Prague, a predominantly bourgeois and emperor-less city. (However, most denizens of Prague prefer to believe that Figaro's success in their city was due to their superior musical taste.)

The elegant hotel inhabited by Beaumarchais no longer exists. It was situated along the Boulevard Saint-Antoine, to which his own name would be conferred in 1831. His statue stands nearby on a small square along the Rue Saint-Antoine, and it faces the direction of the place where, in his lifetime, one entered the Bastille, the very spot where, on July 14, 1789, the sans-culottes forced their way into the fortress. Incidentally, today the Marais continues to be a very bourgeois district, and the trendy boutiques of its main street, the Rue des Francs-Bourgeois, are patronized by moneyed young customers who are sometimes described as "*bon chic, bon genre*" (BCBG) ['Good style, good class'].

The Faubourg Saint-Antoine and other eastern suburbs of the cap-

---

25   Beaumarchais, *Le mariage de Figaro*, quoted in Cohen and Major, p. 514.

ital are the virtually exclusive realm of the plebs. Countless "little people" also live and work in central Paris, which we entered through the Saint-Antoine gate, but the city center obviously belongs to the gentlemen of the aristocracy and the higher ranks of the bourgeoisie; as well as to the Church, as we will soon find out. The common folks we notice definitely do not "own" the city, they are merely tolerated here, because their labor and services are needed, for example as domestic servants, by the rich and powerful, the real owners and masters of the city. In fact, many of the lower-class folks here are domestic servants.

IMAGE 5. Statue of Beaumarchais.

The fact that central Paris is "owned" by an upper class of aristocratic, and, to a lesser extent, bourgeois, patricians, is externalized not only by the multiplicity of big and beautiful residences, but also by their abundant and arrogant use of horses and carriages. Ordinary folks trudge around on foot in the muddy streets, of which only very few have sidewalks, as noted by Louis-Sébastien Mercier in a lively passage of *Tableau de Paris*, a book published a few years before the outbreak of the Revolution. Mercier describes pedestrians being terrorized by horses "galloping as in the open country" and "the threatening wheels of the overbearing rich driving as rapidly as ever over stones stained with the blood of their unhappy victims." Such "traffic accidents" occur all too frequently and the victims are overwhelmingly the lower-class folks who constitute the majority of the pedestrians.[26] Making their way along the dirty streets, high on their horses or in the (relative) comfort of their carriages, the ladies and gentlemen of the upper class ogle the plebeian pedestrians, in their eyes worthless creatures "without faith or respect for the law" (*sans foi ni loi*), a kind of "beastly lot" (*peuple animal*) on which the patricians look down with disdain, indifference, fear, and fascination, as historian Arlette Farge has written.[27]

Riding horses or horse-drawn carriages, of which there are many different types, big and small, is a privilege reserved for the upper-class. Lewis Mumford, author of a book on "the city in history," made this comment about Paris in the 18th century:

> To keep a horse and carriage was an indispensable mark of commercial and social success; to keep a whole stable was a sign of affluence ..., the stables and mews crept into [the city], carrying there the faint healthy smell of straw and manure ... The restless stomp of a high-bred horse might be heard at night from rear windows: the man on horseback had taken possession of the city.[28]

We will find out later what was to happen to these "noble animals" when, as a result of the Revolution, the nobility on their "high horses" were forced out of their Parisian hotels and indeed, ceased to "own" the city. The horse stables would disappear, and *boucheries chevalines*, butcher shops specializing in horse meat, would spring up all over the capital.

---

26 Mercier, p. 111; 'La circulation parisienne au XVIIIe siècle.' See also Sournia, p. 13-15.
27 Farge, p. 35.
28 Mumford, pp. 369-71.

Churches and Monasteries in a "New Jerusalem"

Penetrating deeper into central Paris—while watching out for horse and carriage!—we saunter past yet another fine city residence, the Hôtel de Sens, then follow the banks of the Seine to the Pont Notre-Dame, which allows us to cross onto the Île de la Cité, historical nucleus of the city. There has been a bridge on this site since time immemorial: a wooden one arose here in 1413 and received the name it still bears today, but it was soon swept away by fires and a flood and replaced by a stone construction in 1507. The bridge is paved, which is unusual and has helped to earn the construction the reputation of being the "most elegant and pleasant" bridge in all of Europe. There used to be 68 houses on the bridge, most of them featuring shops, but they were torn down in 1786 for security reasons that will be discussed later. In 1671, a pump was added to the bridge to transfer water from the river to the city's many fountains for the benefit of the Parisians.[29]

We are now on the island where the city was born long before Julius Caesar and his legionnaires conquered Gaul around 50 BC. For a very long time, the city, then known as Lutecia (also Lucotecia), was limited to this island. The island was the city, hence its name Île de la Cité. It was only during the Middle Ages that Paris expanded to the Left and Right Banks of the Seine. The Celtic—more specifically: Gallic—people who inhabited this island were known as the *Parisii*, and this ethnonym produced the toponym, Paris. The first part of this name contains a very ancient root from the pre-Celtic (and even pre-Indo-European) "substrate languages"—of which Etruscan is a well-known example—namely *iber*, as in "Iberia," meaning "land near water," "land surrounded by water" or "peninsula," and occasionally also "island"; and the second part reflects the equally ancient term *issa* (or *ista)*, "city." This bestows on the toponym Paris the very plausible meaning of "island city," identical to that of the French term Île de la Cité.[30] Quite a few other cities share the *iber-issa* etymology, for example Byrsa, the original name of the Phoenician settlement that was to become Carthage; Bursa, in Turkey; Porec, on the coast of Croatia; and the village of Puurs in Belgium. The name of the

---

29   Hillairet (1969), pp. 74-79 ; "Le pont Notre-Dame."

30   The term *issa* also hides in the name of a legendary city, *la ville d'Ys*, somewhere on the Atlantic coast of France, swallowed up by the sea, and associated by an old Breton oral tradition with Paris.

Breton city of Brest has the same meaning, it reflects the combination of *iber* with *ista,* a term that is at the origin of the English word "city." About the name Lutecia, the French onomasticians Louis Deroy and Maryanne Mulon write that it is "a shorter version of an older term, Lucotecia, containing the Celtic word *luco,* 'marsh.'" The word *luco* is more likely of pre-Celtic, pre-Indo-European origin, namely, a variant of the term *lug,* referring to a combination of land and water, in other words, indeed, a marsh. This hypothesis is supported by Julius Caesar, who described Lutecia as a very marshy site.[31]

We pause in the middle of the Île de la Cité, on the square just in front of the triple portal of Notre-Dame Cathedral. This magnificent sanctuary was built in Gothic style in the 13th century on the same spot where a temple dedicated to Jupiter used to stand in the Roman era. In 528, during the reign of a Merovingian king, Childebert, a first Christian church was erected there. In many ways, Notre-Dame symbolizes the Middle Ages, feudalism, the former power of the Church as well as its links to the state in the Ancien Régime. In a gallery above the portals we notice 28 Gothic statues of men with crowns on their heads. They represent the kings of biblical Israel, but the Parisians think of them as medieval monarchs of France, that is, personalities such as Saint Louis, simultaneously kings of the land and protectors of the Church. During the Revolution, these statues will be destroyed. It is only much later that they will be replaced by the facsimiles visible today.[32]

The small square that faces the Cathedral, the Parvis ("forecourt") Notre-Dame, is considerably smaller than it will become in the middle of the 19th century and is surrounded by houses. A pillar once stood in its center, the *poteau de justice* or "stake of justice." This is where those who were condemned to death had to appear to publicly ask God for forgiveness for their crimes, a ceremony referred to as "public penitence and fine of honour" (*la pénitence publique et l'amende honorable*). The pillar was removed in 1769 and replaced by a marker—today a bronze star—indicating *point zéro,* "zero point," that is, the spot from which distances are calculated between Paris and all other places in France. After the ceremony, the convicted person was taken to Place de Grève, a square

---

31   Hillairet (1969), pp. 10-11; Deroy and Mulon, p. 368; Pauwels (2009), pp. 113-114.

32   Kennedy, pp. 204-06.

overlooking the banks of the Seine near the City Hall, the Hôtel de Ville; this is where the executions took place. The square used to be bordered by a kind of beach, hence the name *grève*, meaning "beach" or "riverbank." The day laborers of the district used to gather here in the morning, looking for work, which gave rise to the expression "*faire la grève*," which originally meant "waiting for work" but eventually "refusing to work," "going on strike."

On March 28, 1757, having absolved his *pénitence et amende honorable*, a man named Robert François Damiens, who had attempted to assassinate "the sacred person of the king," Louis XV, but had only managed to wound him lightly with a knife, was brought here to be atrociously tortured, quartered, and burned. In the supposedly already "enlightened" 1780s, people continued to be drawn and quartered and burned alive in Paris. From God, one might receive a pardon, but not from the king. Quartering, like burning at the stake, was also believed to prevent a person from being resurrected on the day of the last judgment, as resurrection presupposed an intact body.[33]

One should definitely not idealize France's Ancien Régime in general and its monarchy in particular. Equally, things were not better in other European countries in those supposedly "good old days." Whenever kings or other lords were, or believed themselves to be, threatened, they responded in a particularly cruel manner, and persons found guilty of lese-majesty and other rebels were frequently tortured in bestial ways before being put to death. Yemelyan Pugachev, for example, the leader of a rebellion by Cossacks and peasants in the Russia of Catherine II, was tortured and broken on the wheel in Moscow on January 10, 1775.

We continue to the Petit-Pont or "little bridge," likewise featuring houses but also watermills. Because of the dangers involved, especially of fires, it had been just 'recently' decided, namely in 1785, to demolish the houses and mills; work on that undertaking has already started, but it will take some time—until the early 1800s—before this will be a fait accompli.[34] Having crossed the bridge, we find ourselves on the Rive Gauche, the Left Bank, that is, the part of Paris to the left of those who are heading downstream on the Seine River. This terminology dates back

---

33   Obeyesekere, pp. 235-36; Arasse, p. 21.
34   "Les maisons sur les ponts."

to the days when Lutecia was a community of boatmen and fishermen, which happens to explain the boat displayed on the city's coat of arms. Since the middle of the 13th century, the Left Bank has been the home of the university of Paris. This venerable institution was founded by Robert de Sorbon, the father confessor of King Louis IX, or Saint Louis, and is therefore known as the Sorbonne. For many centuries, the language used by the professors and students was Latin, which is why the Parisians baptised this district the Latin Quarter, *le Quartier Latin*.

The main street of the Latin Quarter is the Rue Saint-Jacques. In Roman times this was the *cardo maximus,* the major, 9 meter wide artery of Lutecia, connecting the northern and southern banks of the Seine via the island and predecessors of the bridges we just used, the Pont Notre-Dame and the Petit-Pont. This cardo was actually part of a road leading to distant Spain, but a few hundred meters to the south of the Seine, another road, eventually known locally as the Rue Galande, veered off to the southeast, in the direction of Italy. That was the road that exited the city via the Rue Mouffetard and led via Lyons to Rome. It is likely via this thoroughfare that Caesar and his legionnaires arrived in Lutecia, and it is in this part of the city that a Roman Paris arose, complete with baths and an amphitheatre, now known as the *arènes de Lutèce*. However, after the fall of the Roman Empire, this Roman connection gradually dwindled in importance. As a result, the Rue Galande became an unimportant and narrow alley.[35]

More important was henceforth the wide and straight road heading straight south, or rather slightly southwest, to Spain, via Tours and therefore known as the *via turonensis*. It was via this thoroughfare that pilgrims set off for Compostela, in Spain's northwestern province of Galicia, to pray at what was believed to be the tomb of one of the two apostles called James, Jacques in French, namely the elder one, James Major. In the Galician language, James is Yago, and Saint James is Santiago, hence the expression Santiago de Compostela, "Saint James of Compostela." The road to Compostela crossed the land of the Basques, today divided by the French-Spanish border. It is very likely from the Basque language, in which James is called Jakue, that Yago/James became famous in France under the name of Jacques.

---

35 More about the Rue Galande and the Rue Saint-Jacques in Tisserand, p. 207-208, 249-250.

Before leaving Paris to undertake their long journey, these pilgrims used to pray in the chapel of a monastery established there in 1217 by the "order of preachers" (*ordo predicatorum*, OP), better known as the Dominicans. This order of mendicant monks, similar to, and in many ways competitors of, the Franciscans, had been founded in Toulouse only two years earlier by a Castilian Spaniard called Dominic de Guzmán, destined to be canonized and henceforth known as Saint Dominic. The chapel happened to be dedicated to Saint James, the patron saint of Spain, for whom the Dominicans had the same special kind of devotion as the pilgrims. Because of their fondness for James/Jacques, the monks acquired the nickname Jacobins, meaning worshippers of Jacob(us), which is the Latin version of the name James. The pilgrims heading for Santiago, on the other hand, were commonly known in France as *Jacquets,* worshipers of Jacques. It is extremely likely that Saint Dominic had brought the cult of James, patron saint of Spain's Christian fighters against Islam, with him when he moved to southern France to combat another "heresy," Catharism.

And so, the Dominican monastery in Paris proved to be a most appropriate place for a symbolic meeting of Frenchmen heading for Spain to simultaneously worship James and Dominic, the Spaniard who had imported the cult of James into France. The Dominican establishment also happened to be conveniently located near the southern section of the city walls and the city gate they had to use to exit the city, unsurprisingly also named after James, the Porte Saint-Jacques. That gate was demolished in 1684, under Louis XIV, when it was felt that Paris no longer needed a defensive wall, and certainly not one of the outdated medieval types. The stretch of city wall, punctured by the gate where it crossed the cardo, together with the adjoining moat, corresponds to the former *decumanus*, the major east-west thoroughfare of Roman Paris; and the gate found itself on the site of the forum.

The Dominican monastery and its chapel were located along the former Roman cardo, and so the ancient thoroughfare became known as "*Grand Rue Saint-Jacques des Prêcheurs*," "the Great Street of Saint Jacques of the Preachers," and eventually as simply Rue Saint-Jacques. The site is presently occupied by number 158 Rue Saint-Jacques as well as 14 Rue Soufflot. In the 17th century, however, the Dominicans moved into a new monastery, located near the Rue Saint-Honoré, built on land donated by Louis XIII.[36] It is in that monastery that, during the Revolution, the most ardent revolutionaries will get together and thus also become known as 'Jacobins.' Those radicals will reveal themselves to be worthy heirs to the apostle James who, according to an ancient legend, had been as a "fanatic" follower of Christ and who, as patron saint of Christian Spain, had been a hot-headed fighter for Christianity against the Muslim "infidels," and also of the Dominicans who, in contrast to their supposedly softhearted Franciscan competitors, were considered to be an extremely militant lot.

There exist Jacquets and Jacobins, but also Jacobites. The latter term designates all those citizens of Great Britain who support the Stuart Dynasty, removed from the throne during that country's so-called "Glorious Revolution" of 1688, and above all King James II. Exiled in France, James II resided in Saint-Germain en Laye, a town to the west of Paris and close to the royal palace of Versailles, where he died in 1701. He was buried in a chapel in the Monastery of the English Benedictines, situated in the ... Rue Saint-Jacques, at numbers 269-269 *bis*. The building is now home to the Schola Cantorum, a school of music and dance.

Continuing our exploration of the Left Bank, we suddenly find ourselves in front of a magnificent Gothic building. It is yet another hôtel, obviously dating back to the Middle Ages, but this one belonged to a different category of lords, namely the abbots of the famous Benedictine Monastery of Cluny, situated in the southern reaches of the province of Burgundy. This is their Parisian pied-à-terre, and it is known as the Hôtel de Cluny. The Cluniac abbots happen to be powerful men, veritable "princes" of the Church, and a number of them even became Pope. It goes without saying that they have always been *fils cadets,* younger sons, of major noble families, because theirs was an ecclesiastical position commanding not only great prestige but also huge revenues. As abbot of Cluny, one disposes of more than sufficient manpower to handle all the work that needs to be done in the monastery in distant Burgundy—and above all in the vast vineyards that form a substantial part of the Cluniac real estate portfolio. (In the monasteries, even the ordinary monks tend to be of superior social origin, and they occupy themselves mostly with copying, illustrating, and/or commenting on, manuscripts, and with oth-

---

36   Péricard-Méa, pp. 129-30; Hillairet (1969), vol. 2, p. 125.

er intellectual pursuits; the hard work on the fields is usually entrusted to friars of humbler social background.) However, the abbots do visit their monastery in Burgundy quite often, if only to collect their share of the rents and tithes. And this involves major amounts of money because Cluny controls countless properties inside and even outside of France. According to a popular saying, the Monastery of Cluny collected rent "wherever the wind blows": *Partout où le vent vente, l'abbaye de Cluny a rente.* However, the abbots find life more interesting in the big city on the banks of the Seine than in the Burgundian countryside, no matter how bucolic. Therefore, they are more often to be found in their seigniorial residence in Paris. Some of these abbots have a soft spot for James the Apostle, which is why the facade of their hôtel is abundantly decorated with sea scallop shells or *coquilles Saint-Jacques*, the preeminent attribute of this saint.

During the Revolution, the Monastery of Cluny will be closed and its vast archipelago of buildings, including the grandiose church, once the biggest in Christendom, will be mostly demolished; even so, the remains are impressive and make it worthwhile to visit that Burgundian village. The Parisian Hôtel de Cluny, on the other hand, managed to survive the Revolution without much damage, and that beautiful Gothic building is today the home of a museum devoted to medieval art. The famous tapestry of the "Lady of the Unicorn" is among the many treasures on display there, and so are a few original heads of the statues of biblical kings that used to adorn the façade of Notre-Dame.[37] And in the basement one can admire the impressive ruins of the baths of Roman Paris. The Hôtel de Cluny is a jewel, a must for tourists visiting the French capital.

Just down the street stands the church of the Sorbonne. Before the Revolution, the famous Parisian university was an ecclesiastical institution, so it was only normal that a sanctuary was attached to it. This domed church was erected in the 1640s by famous Cardinal Richelieu, the "prime minister" of King Louis XIII, and it contains his tomb. It is in many ways thanks to him that the monarchy has been able to acquire so much power, in other words, has been able to become an *absolute monarchy*, whose fate is intimately linked to that of the Catholic Church, which was not yet the case at the time of Louis XIII's predecessor, Henry IV. For

---

[37] See http://www.musee-moyenage.fr/collection/oeuvre/tetes-rois-juda-notre-dame.html.

one thing, Richelieu managed to reduce the power of the great noblemen to the advantage of their *primus inter pares*, the king. Second, while he proved unable to eradicate Protestantism entirely in his country, he did manage to strictly limit the influence of the French Protestants, the Huguenots. Richelieu functioned as a kind of godfather of the monarchical and clerical France that will be consumed by the flames of the Revolution. The church of the Sorbonne is one of the many imposing sanctuaries that arose in Paris after the religious wars of the 16th century, in the context of the Counter-Reformation, purporting to turn Paris into a Catholic "New Jerusalem" in which the Huguenots would feel very much out of place.[38]

We exit the city at the site of the former gate named after the Archangel Michael, the Porte Saint-Michel. The name was transferred to a big boulevard that was to be constructed in the 19th century, the Boulevard Saint-Michel, which will replace the Rue Saint-Jacques as main artery of the Latin Quarter. We now find ourselves on the southern periphery of Old Paris, just outside of the former city walls. To our left, we perceive in the distance the mighty silhouette of the new abbey-church of Sainte Geneviève, which was finished in 1773. To reach it, we would have to follow the line of the demolished city walls past the site of the former Porte Saint-Jacques. This stretch, once the *decumanus* of Roman Paris, will eventually become a wide street named after the architect of the new sanctuary, Jacques-Germain Soufflot (1713-1780). During the Revolution, his gargantuan domed construction in the neo-classical style will be transformed into the resting place of heroes of the French nation and henceforth be known as the Pantheon.[39]

On the right-hand side, an equally imposing secular edifice comes into view: the Luxembourg Palace. Around 1620, this was the residence of the widow of Henry IV, Queen Maria de Medici. The original owners of the edifice were the dukes of Luxembourg, but she had acquired it and transformed it into a vast complex in the style of the Pitti Palace, the sumptuous residence of her illustrious family in Florence; and the gardens of the palace were inspired by the famous Florentine Boboli Gardens. Since 1778, the Luxembourg Palace has been the home of a younger brother Louis XVI, Louis-Stanislas-Xavier, who bears the title of Count

---

38 Jones, pp. 168-73.
39 Jones, pp. 208-09; Sournia, p. 61-63.

of Provence; during the Revolution he will flee the country, but return after the fall of Napoleon to reign, from 1814 to 1824, under the name of Louis XVIII. (We will learn later what happened to Louis XVII.) During the Revolution, the cellars of this royal residence will serve as a prison. To the famous revolutionary tribune, Georges Danton, it will be the antechamber of death. Today, the palace is the home of the French Senate, the upper house of the country's Parliament, established in 1799.

We walk by a huge monastery, inhabited by monks of the Franciscan Order, also known as the Friars Minor; on account of the knotted rope (*corde*) used to hold up their habit, allegedly an allusion to the ropes that bound Jesus, the Parisians like to refer to them as the *Cordeliers*, "the men of the rope." This religious establishment was founded shortly after the death of Saint Francis of Assisi by none other than French King Louis IX, who was himself canonized after his death, henceforth to be known as "Saint Louis." This was in the 13th century, at a time when the Franciscans were ensconcing themselves in virtually every major city in Europe, aiming to keep the swelling masses of urban poor out of the clutches of heresy by convincing them of the benefits of poverty, presumably a condition facilitating salvation in the afterlife. During the Revolution, this Franciscan monastery will become the meeting place of a political club whose particularly radical members will be nicknamed "Cordeliers."[40]

On the eve of the Revolution, Paris is teeming with churches and monasteries. The French capital counts approximately fifty parish churches, almost forty monasteries for men and no less than eighty convents for women. Every religious order is represented in this city.[41] With approximately one thousand priests, curates, and other staff of about fifty parishes, the secular clergy cannot compete in numbers with the regular clergy, which boasts close to one thousand monks and no less than five thousand five hundred nuns! Approximately one quarter of the city's total surface belongs to the Church. The Abbey of Saint-Germain-des-Prés alone owns no less than two thousand hectares—about five thousand acres—in the southern part of the city.[42] And in Paris, as in the rest of France, it is

---

40 In French, Cordeliers is capitalized when the term refers to the monks, but not when designating the members of the revolutionary club.

41 "Les fondations religieuses au XVIIe siècle."

42 Tulard, p. 43; *Tableau de Paris*, p. 222; Rudé, p. 12; Mayer, p. 414.

not only the *space* that is dominated by the Church, but also the *time,* as the historians François Furet and Denis Richet have emphasized:

> Time, too, is Catholic: the calendar, the working hours, the numerous holidays, the great moments in the life of an individual are unthinkable without divine blessing.[43]

In this respect, the Revolution will likewise trigger profound changes.

Coffee-Drinking Intellectuals

The Latin Quarter, the district around the Sorbonne, is a haven for intellectuals. They like to get together in a relatively new type of establishment, the coffee house or café. Until the end of the 17th century, coffee had hardly been drunk in Europe. It is a beverage that belongs to the world of Islam, where wine and other alcoholic drinks are forbidden. And the coffee bean is a seed of a plant that is at home in the Horn of Africa and the southern reaches of the Arabian Peninsula, where one of its export harbours, located on the shores of the Red Sea, bears a name that conjures up fine coffee: Mocha.[44] In Europe, coffee was introduced by the Arabs, namely in territories they were to occupy for a shorter or longer period of time, such as Spain and Sicily. Later, coffee made its appearance in the Balkan Peninsula, where it was brought by the conquering Turks. And it was after the great siege of Vienna by the Turks, in 1683, that the first coffee houses sprang up in the Austrian capital, soon to become a kind of "coffee capital." It was also in the 1680s, in 1684, to be precise, that an immigrant from Palermo, Francesco Procopio dei Coltelli, opened what was reputedly the French capital's first—but more likely second[45]—coffee house in the Latin Quarter. That café received the name of its owner, and it will continue to occupy its original premises at number 13 of the Rue de l'Ancienne-Comédie until well into the 21st century. But it will become a restaurant and in 1989, at the time of the Bicentennial of the French Revolution, it will be renovated in the style of the late 18th century.

---

43 Furet and Richet, pp. 29-30.

44 **Ed. Note:** Also written as Mokha, a port city on the Red Sea coast of Yemen.

45 According to some authors, it was an Armenian, Harouthian, who, in 1672 had already opened the very first café on the Quai du Louvre; see Garrier, p. 131.

In the 18th century, the café conquers Paris and indeed all cities of France. In 1721, there are already three hundred such establishments in the capital, by the time of the Revolution there will be two thousand of them. But not all Parisians and all Frenchmen flock to the cafés. As in other countries, it is the bourgeoisie that enjoys coffee and likes to meet in coffee houses, whose typically elegant interior decoration "contrasts strikingly with the simple, vulgar, often shabby interiors of the cabarets,"[46] the establishments where the capital's common folks gather to drink and socialize. And where coffee is served, a stimulating drink that generates and accompanies lively discussions about business, politics, literature, philosophy, art, etc. The café has become the quintessential social center for the bourgeoisie, it is that class's favored alternative not only to the plebeian cabaret but also to the aristocrats' salons, where the guests prefer to sip hot and very sweet chocolate; the latter is a relaxing rather than stimulating refreshment, perfect while languidly contemplating life and the world, sometimes flirting with the new ideas concocted by bourgeois philosophers and other intellectuals, but typically reaching the conclusion that, as Voltaire sarcastically put it, *tout va pour le mieux dans le meilleur des mondes possibles*—"all is for the best in the best of all possible worlds."

Things are quite different in the coffee houses. There, the bourgeois gentlemen likewise share contemplations about life, and inspiration comes mostly from the trendy philosophy of the Enlightenment, *Les Lumières*. Typical for this philosophy is an optimistic faith in the intrinsic goodness of man as well as a firm belief in the unlimited potential of human reason, *la raison*. Thanks to human reason, to rational thinking, everything can and will change for the better. Does a better society, a better state, a better human being also belong to the realm of the possibilities? This is what is being discussed endlessly over cups of coffee, and occasionally also while enjoying a Sicilian ice cream. Numerous bourgeois intellectuals agree with Voltaire, a merciless critic of the Ancien Régime. As he and other enlightened philosophers saw it, things were not going well in France, and much had to be changed.

Most of Procope's patrons belong to this middle class, and they agree with the critical views expressed by Voltaire. Another regular at Procope

---

46   Brennan, p. 128.

who agrees, is Napoleon Bonaparte, as yet an unknown young officer, who is often seen there, sipping espresso. (Procope still proudly displays a hat Napoleon allegedly forgot there after one of his many visits.) But later, as emperor, he will blame the philosophers for the Revolution and the excesses associated with it—which is what most conservative Frenchmen have done to this very day. During a visit to the tomb of Jean-Jacques Rousseau in Ermenonville, a village to the north of Paris, he will opine that it would have been better if that philosopher had never lived; one of his companions courageously quips that the same thing could be said about Napoleon himself! It is to the Corsican's credit that he agreed with this remark. In any event, on the eve of the Revolution, in the context of the slow diffusion of the ideals of the Enlightenment philosophy, "a spirit of scepticism is on the rise, not only among intellectuals, but also increasingly among the Parisian middle class."[47] However, Rousseau, Voltaire, and the other Enlightenment philosophers can hardly be considered as intellectual godfathers of the French Revolution. The reason for this is that they do not dream of radical political, let alone social, changes, and certainly not of "bottom-up" changes, but only of reforms introduced by the existing authorities, of "top-down" changes, such as those that are already being introduced by "enlightened despots" like Frederick the Great—a personal friend of Voltaire—in Prussia and by Emperor Joseph II in the lands controlled by the Habsburgs, including not only Austria but also Belgium.[48]

The premise that constructing a better society belongs to the realm of possibilities appears to have been confirmed by the recent birth of a new state, not a monarchy but a republic, on the other side of the Atlantic Ocean, following a revolution that would never have succeeded without considerable military support provided by the French monarchy.[49] The ambassador of this new country, Benjamin Franklin, and another one of the fathers of American independence and future president, Thomas Jefferson, eagerly patronize the Procope. In their company, one regularly notices the Marquis de Lafayette, who commanded the French troops

---

47   Garrioch, p. 204.

48   See Jourdan, p. 376 ff.; Furet and Richet, pp. 21-22; Guillemin, pp. 20-21.

49   The United States proclaimed its independence on July 4, 1776; now celebrated as a National Holiday, in the country that became officially independent from Britain after a long war, with a treaty signed at Versailles in 1783.

sent to the other side of the Atlantic by Louis XVI to assist George Washington in his struggle against the British. They all speak with great enthusiasm about liberty and equality but mostly in abstract terms and without worrying about the fact that Jefferson, Washington, and other "fathers of independence" saw nothing wrong with owning slaves. Slavery—constitutionally enshrined unfreedom for Black people—will continue for a long time to exist in the self-styled land of liberty on the other side of the Atlantic. In many important ways, the American Revolution was not a genuine revolution at all, but rather a "restoration," a movement "driven by traditions, as the American historian Arno Mayer has put it: the American "rebels never intended to bring about major changes in the colonies' moral, social, or economic values or institutions," but aimed at achieving "political and civil freedoms [that] were not [to be] extended to Blacks and Native Americans," even though those two groups represented at least twenty percent of the population.[50] However, one of the basic ideas associated with the American Revolution—the right of a people to rid itself of a monarchical "tyranny"—unquestionably reverberated far and wide and influenced the French Revolution.

Exiting the Procope, a short walk along Rue Dauphine takes us to the banks of the Seine. We reach the river near a restaurant that was established recently by a man named Lefèvre, *'limonadier*, that is, "[licenced] purveyor of drink," of King Louis XV. That eatery will become famous after acquiring the name of a new owner, Lapérouse, in the middle of the 19th century. On the eve of the Revolution, however, this is one of the very first restaurants of the French capital. The term 'restaurant' has only just entered the French language, it was first used only a few years earlier. Restaurants are a new phenomenon, and they are inspired by eateries that have existed for some time in England and are known there as taverns. This explains why one of the first restaurants in Paris, opened in 1782, it is called *La Grande Taverne de Londres*, "The Great Tavern of London." The restaurants offer their customers refined food in a setting characterized by the "peace and quiet" that prevailed inside, by "the cleanliness and even luxury of the interior decoration ... and, above all, by the fact that they introduce the public to fine cuisine [*la grande cuisine*]." Previously, one could have meals served in establishments that were too basic and/or plebeian—and too noisy—to suit the taste of the bourgeoisie and, *a for-*

---

50   Mayer, p. 26.

tiori, the nobility, such as the inns (*auberges*) and above all the so-called *bouillons*. Those were eateries where it was possible, after some hard work, to "to restore [one's forces]," *se restaurer*, by the consumption of nutritious dishes such as soups made of meat and vegetables, vegetables and meat broth (*bouillons*); thus originated two words for eateries, namely 'restaurant,' which was adopted by countless other languages, and 'bouillon,' to be used relatively rarely even in French. Even today, however, Paris continues to boast a handful of ancient eateries that call themselves "bouillon," for example Chartier, an establishment dating back to 1896, located at number 7 of the Rue du Faubourg-Montmartre.[51] Lapérouse, on the other hand, became a deluxe restaurant and has remained so. It charges high prices, but its patrons may partake of refined food served in a decor that has hardly changed since the 18th century, including comfortable small private rooms (*cabinets particuliers*) in which one could imagine being at home; the dining pleasure is further enhanced by the knowledge that one was preceded there by celebrities such as Alexandre Dumas, George Sand, Alfred de Musset, Victor Hugo, Émile Zola, Guy de Maupassant, Gustave Flaubert, Marcel Proust, the Duke of Windsor and Wallis Simpson, Jean-Paul Sartre, Simone de Beauvoir, Albert Camus, Albert Einstein, Emperor Hirohito, Charles de Gaulle, and virtually all his successors as president. Auguste Escoffier (1846-1935), the world-famous "king of chefs and chef of kings," spent many years ruling over the kitchen of Restaurant Lapérouse.

Royal Squares and Monuments

We follow the Seine downstream past another big monastery that is doomed to be closed and demolished during the Revolution; it belongs to the Augustinians. To our right, the oldest bridge of Paris comes into view, stretching to the Right Bank via the western tip of the Île de la Cité; paradoxically, however, it is called Pont Neuf, the "new bridge." When its construction, which had started in 1578, was finally completed in 1606, it was not just new, but new in spectacular fashion, for a number of reasons. First, while Paris boasted plenty of wooden bridges, this happened to be the very first bridge made of stone. Second, with a length of 278 metres and a width of 28 metres, it was colossal in comparison to

---

51 Revel, p. 222-227; Mennell, p. 197 ff.

all other bridges. Third, it was not built up with houses, as was the case with existing bridges.⁵² Furthermore, the pedestrians could benefit from an innovation: sidewalks. Crossing the bridge thus revealed itself to be a kind of promenade making it possible for Parisians to meet, socialize, be entertained by street singers and other buskers, and shop, as all sort of goods were offered for sale by ambulant vendors, including the first *bouquinistes* or "booksellers" who were eventually to set up shop along the nearby quays of the Seine. This was also the first bridge that offered unobstructed views of the Seine as well as cityscape, a minor inconvenience being the fact that pedestrians were exposed to "unpredictable puffs" of wind that tended to carry away hats and wigs. The Pont Neuf became a major attraction and even the emblem of the city, an achievement to be emulated a century later by the Eiffel Tower. On the eve of the Revolution, a Parisian compared the bridge to a human heart, that is, as "the center of all movement and circulation."⁵³

IMAGE 6. The Pont Neuf in 1763.

The Pont Neuf was a present by the king to the city and became a symbol of the monarchy, it was very much a royal bridge. There exist-

---

52   "Les maisons sur les ponts."
53   Mercier, p. 71.

ed solid reasons why a monarch wanted to associate himself with such a construction. Bridges symbolized a connection between heaven and earth, and the builder of a bridge—*pontifex* in Latin—is an intermediary between humans and God. The pope is traditionally called *pontifex maximus*, as the one who is supposed to be the foremost amongst all builders of bridges or, as one can also see it, the bridge par excellence between heaven and earth.[54] A royal bridge like the Pont Neuf similarly promoted the idea that the king was God's representative on earth, accountable only to God.

When this new bridge—eventually to become the city's oldest, while keeping its name!—was inaugurated in December 1607, France was ruled by Henry IV, and he was the first to cross it, on horseback and followed by a large retinue. A bronze statue of that king, the first monarch of the Bourbon Dynasty, was erected in the middle of the bridge soon after his death by order of his widow, Maria de Medici. It was to be followed, at least for some time, by statues of other kings occupying the semi-circular bastions on top of the bridge's pillars. The Pont Neuf was the capital's first decorated bridge: it featured no less than 381 mascarons, sculpted faces of grotesque, satyr-like mythological figures; like the similar but more famous gargoyles of Notre-Dame Cathedral, they served to ward off evil spirits.[55] But they were to prove powerless against the evil spirits of the Revolution.

Henry IV was one of the few kings to be genuinely popular, and he was often referred to as "good King Henry." There were two reasons for this: First, as mentioned before, he was tolerant with respect to religion, allowing the Huguenots to freely practice their faith in an officially Catholic kingdom. Henry was originally a Protestant himself, but he had converted to Catholicism to be acceptable as king to the Catholic majority of the country's nobility. As every French schoolchild knows, at his conversion he supposedly mumbled *Paris vaut bien une messe*, "Paris is well worth going to Mass for." In the depth of his heart, he always remained a Protestant, which was a public secret, and for this reason he was assassinated by a *dévot*, a fanatic Catholic, in 1610. A second reason for the popularity of Henry IV was that he was sincerely concerned about

---

54   Chevalier and Gheerbrant, p. 777.
55   Jones, pp. 156-59; Hillairet (1969), pp. 87-88 ; "Les secrets du Pont-Neuf."

the well-being of his subjects. The economic program of his government aimed at making it possible for the French people to eat well. He is said to have solemnly declared that he "would do everything in his power to ensure that there would not be a single laborer in his kingdom who could not afford to enjoy a chicken dinner on Sundays."

In the early stages of the French Revolution, when a constitutional monarchy will still be an option, the Parisian populace will loudly invoke the name of Henry IV, for example during a demonstration in front of the Palace of Versailles; thus they let it be known that they wished for a kind king like him. But Louis XVI cannot and will not morph into another "good king Henry." Consequently, the monarchy will be forced to make way for a new form of government, the republic. During the Revolution, the statue of "good king Henry" on the Pont Neuf will be taken down, but in 1818 a copy will be placed on the very same spot.

Our visit to the Pont Neuf would not be complete without an examination of the large edifice that is attached to it close to the Right Bank. It was built between 1605 and 1608 to accommodate a waterwheel and pump, used to provide water from the Seine to the nearby royal residences, the Louvre and Tuileries Palaces, as well as their gardens. The edifice was designed by a hydraulic engineer of Flemish origin, Jean Lintlaër, and received the name La Samaritaine, a tip of the hat to a biblical figure, the Samaritan "woman at the well" who gave Jesus water to drink; a bronze statue of her is decorating the building's façade. The pumping station will be demolished in 1813, but its name will be inherited by a department store that will arise in 1870 on the Right Bank, right in front of the Pont Neuf; this famous *grand magasin* was closed for many years but reopened recently, in 2021.[56]

We resume our walk and pass by the Hôtel des Monnaies, another impressive building, neoclassical in style. Its construction was finished only recently, in 1777, and it is not the residence of a noble family, but the royal mint. At the end of its long façade, which runs parallel to the quay of the Seine, we reach the site where the famous Tour de Nesle (Nesle's Tower) used to stand, a high-rise fortification constructed in the early 13th century on the strategic—and militarily vulnerable—spot where the city walls used to abut the Seine embankment. In 1665, this

---

56 "La pompe de la Samaritaine."

building was demolished to make room for the Collège des Quatre-Nations ("College of the Four Nations"), funded by Cardinal Mazarin and therefore also known as the Collège Mazarin. Jules Mazarin, an Italian whose real name was Giulio Raimondo Mazzarino, and whose tomb is located in the college chapel, used to serve as chief minister when King Louis XIV was still too young to take the reins of power into his own hands, as he would do soon enough. Mazarin was an energetic champion of the power of the monarchy at a time when it was seriously challenged: as in 1650, by the ambitions of the aristocrats, and he repressed their revolt, known as the Fronde; he continued the project originally undertaken by Richelieu, namely the construction of royal "absolutism," that is, a system in which the king dominates unconditionally while the nobility does not have much, if anything, to say in the realm of national politics. Instead, the noblemen were in many ways forced to participate in life at the royal court in Versailles, but merely as extras in a ritual in which the "great monarch" plays the key role. It was thanks to Mazarin that, as adult, King Louis XIV would be able to declare with supreme arrogance: "I am the state," *L'État, c'est moi!* Indeed, throughout his long reign, political life would revolve around the person of the king, much like the planets revolve around the sun—something that had become known only shortly before thanks to scientists such as Galileo and other heroes of the "Scientific Revolution." It was not a coincidence that the sun became the emblem of Louis XIV, and that this monarch was to go down in history as *le Roi-Soleil*, the "Sun-King." The plan of the city of Versailles, featuring wide avenues converging to the royal palace, likewise conjures up a kind of urbanistic solar system. Here is another anecdote about Mazarin: he refused to give in to young Louis' desire to marry an Italian beauty with whom he had fallen madly in love, namely Mazarin's own niece, Maria Mancini. Instead, the Cardinal forced the young king to marry a daughter of the King of Spain, Maria-Theresa, a union that served the interests of the French state.

The College of the Four Nations is an impressive domed building, designed by Louis Le Vau, one of the favorite architects of Louis XIV, who also did work on the Palace of Versailles and on the Louvre. Its name refers to the "nations" of students at the original Parisian university—French, English, Normans, and Picards—but the establishment was set up for the benefit of students from territories recently acquired by France, such as Rousillon and Artois, regions in southern and northern France, respectively. The college is a monumental building, and the giant triangle it constitutes together with the Louvre, located just across the river, and the nearby Pont Neuf, amounts to an impressive urbanistic "statement of dynastic power," as Colin Jones has put it. During the French Revolution, the university colleges will be dissolved, and the edifice associated with Mazarin will eventually (in 1805) become the home of the Institut de France, and therefore of one of its academies, the prestigious Académie Française, established by Richelieu in 1635.[57]

We turn left and after a short walk we find ourselves in front of yet another abbey. This one belongs to the Benedictine Order and is called Saint-Germain-des-Prés. The name reflects the fact that the site of this venerable institution used to be just outside the medieval city walls, in other words, in the countryside—or "in the fields," *les prés*. It is a very ancient monastery, founded at the time of the Merovingian Dynasty, which ruled the land in the 7th-8th centuries; its kings are often referred to in French history books as *rois fainéants* or "do-nothing kings," but this is something that might be said of quite a few kings of France—and of other countries! It is in this building that these kings arranged to be buried, while later monarchs would prefer another monastery as their burial place, namely the Abbey of Saint-Denis, located to the north of Paris. Germain was an obscure bishop of the Merovingian era who, after a long and presumably very pious existence, was rewarded with a canonization. During the Revolution, Saint-Germain Abbey will be closed down and its buildings—except for the church—will be demolished and auctioned off together with the institution's vast portfolio of real estate. A wide new avenue will soon slice through the site of the monastery and its lands, eventually becoming the major east-west artery of left-bank Paris: the Boulevard Saint-Germain.

We head west, even further away from the historical city center and into a suburb that contrasts starkly with the eastern Faubourg Saint-Antoine We are in the Faubourg Saint-Germain where, in the late 17th and early 18th centuries, large and sumptuous seigneurial dwellings were erected, often with vast gardens to the rear. The *crème de la crème* of the nobility had started to abandon the Marais when that district was becoming

---

[57] Jones, pp. 184-85.

more crowded and unfashionable as it was being penetrated by bourgeois types. As Eric Hazan has written, the aristocracy "having crossed the river, ensconced itself more comfortably in the Faubourg Saint-Germain." In contrast to the Marais, a neighborhood squeezed between de Faubourg Saint-Antoine and the equally plebeian old neighborhoods of central Paris, Saint-Germain was far from popular eastern Paris and totally uncontaminated by the presence of "little people." This exclusively noble western faubourg offered aristocrats the additional advantage of being closer to the court in the Palace of Versailles, which they often had reason to visit. In any event, by the end of the reign of Louis XIV, that district had become "the ultimate in fashionable living."[58]

The Palais Bourbon is a fine example of the residences in the Saint-Germain neighborhood, of which many are indeed more aptly described as palaces rather than just hôtels. It was constructed in the 1720s for Louise-Françoise de Bourbon, daughter of Louis XIV and his mistress, Madame de Montespan. On the eve of the Revolution, this architectural marvel belongs to the Prince of Condé, one of the richest and most powerful noblemen in the land; but when, in 1789, Condé will emigrate from revolutionary France, the Palais Bourbon will be confiscated by the state. Eventually it will become the home of the lower house of the French Parliament, the *Assemblée nationale* or National Assembly. The term Palais-Bourbon is hyphenated when it refers to the institution, but when it refers to the building it is not hyphenated. It is rather ironic that a central institution of the French Republic bears the name of the former royal family.[59]

On its western outskirts, the Saint-Germain district also features a huge hôtel that was not constructed for some aristocratic family, but for war veterans: the Hôtel des Invalides. Louis XIV had ordered the construction of this gigantic complex, whose impressive dome recalls the cupola that crowns St. Peter's Basilica in Rome. Not far from there we can admire the École militaire or Military Academy, founded in 1751, an institution for the training of future officers in the royal army. A young man from Corsica, an island sold to France in 1769 by the city state of Genoa, thus becoming a French possession without the consent of its inhabi-

---

58   Hazan (2002), pp. 86, 134-35; Jones, p. 162.
59   Hillairet (1956), volume 2, p. 254.

tants, studies here in 1784-1785: Napoleon Bonaparte. He is the scion of a low-ranking noble family—or is it a bourgeois family with aristocratic pretensions?—residing in the city of Ajaccio. Napoleon studies to be an officer in the artillery. Because it involves difficult studies in chemistry, mathematics, and so forth, this field is not favored, and therefore monopolized, by sons of the upper levels of the nobility; they prefer traditional branches, and above all the prestigious cavalry. Cavalry may have a great past, but, unlike artillery, it does not have a great future. With respect to artillery, France happens to be Europe's leading power, and it thanks to his intelligent use of cannon, learned at the École militaire, that Napoleon will prove to be extraordinarily successful for so long during battles against the enemies of his country.[60]

Napoleon will die in exile on the Island of St. Helena, but in 1840 his remains will be returned to France, to be buried in a monumental sarcophagus below the dome of Les Invalides. Napoleon's spectacular social climb, from petty-aristocratic origins in a distant, barely French province, to emperor of France, could not be symbolized more effectively than by his being buried in one of the most magnificent buildings in the most aristocratic of all neighborhoods in the nation's capital. Today, this neighborhood is extremely bourgeois and, as we will see later, Napoleon played a crucial role in this *embourgeoisement* of an originally uber-aristocratic part of Paris.

Without exception, the Palais Bourbon, the Hôtel des Invalides, the École Militaire, and the many other edifices of the prestigious Saint-Germain district are monuments that will continue even into the 21st century to radiate the glory of the Ancien Régime. But we should also mention the Champ-de-Mars, the "Field of Mars," which stretches from the École militaire to the site where the Eiffel Tower will be erected, to be inaugurated in 1889 on the occasion of the centenary of the Revolution. The Champ-de-Mars was originally a low-lying and marshy area along the Seine, situated at a stone's throw from the city walls. It used to be known as the Plain of Grenelle. This toponym reflects the distinctly non-urban character of the district. "Grenelle" comes from the Latin word *garanella*, diminutive of *garenna, garenne* in French, a walled piece of land where one raised—and hunted—rabbits. The area was a *rus in urbe,* a minia-

---

60   Rothenberg, pp. 24-28.

ture countryside within the city. Not so long ago, peasants and shepherds could still be seen at work there and rabbits will continue to be raised there for a long time.[61] However, after the construction of the École militaire in the 1760s, this lowland was drained and started being used for training soldiers. During the Revolution, some festive events will take place there, for example the *Fête de la Fédération* or "Celebration of the Federation" of July 14, 1790, a commemoration of the storming of the Bastille exactly one year earlier. And in 1796, a military barracks erected in the Grenelle plain will witness one of the many dramatic events of the Revolution, as we will see later.

In the vicinity of the Palais Bourbon, we take a "flying bridge" (*pont volant*), that is, a ferry, to cross over to the Right Bank. In this western part of Paris, bridges do not yet span the Seine. The beauty named after a Russian czar, for example, the Pont Alexander III, richly decorated with columns, statues, and pretty gas lanterns, will appear in 1900, during the so-called Belle Époque. In front of the Palais Bourbon itself, work is already in progress on a new bridge that is supposed to receive the name of Louis XVI. It will link the Palais Bourbon and the rest of the Rive Gauche with a vast octagonal square on the other side. The planned bridge aims to connect the Palais Bourbon and the rest of the Left Bank with a vast square on the other side of the Seine. This will be yet another one of one of those *places royales*, "royal squares," that have made their appearance in many French cities, purport to glorify the absolutist monarchy, and always feature an imposing statue of some king in the middle. The idea is to create a space to celebrate occasions such as military triumphs, the conclusion of peace treaties, royal weddings, and other dynastic events.

We have already visited the prototype of these squares, the one located in the Marais and named after Louis XIII, destined to become the Place des Vosges. But this square here in western Paris bears the name of King Louis XV, and his equestrian statue is visible in the center, on the very spot where an Egyptian obelisk will be erected in 1836. It is this Louis who ruled France when this place, a grandiose urbanistic project by the architect Ange-Jacques Gabriel, was constructed.[62] The site of Place Louis XV marks the western limits of the city, and the square is supposed

---

61 Hillairet, deel 3, p. 45.
62 Garrioch, pp. 222-23; quotation from Jones, p. 207.

to constitute a harmonious transition from the gardens of the Tuileries to the new, wide avenue, the Champs-Élysées. That thoroughfare leads west through a still rural area, featuring gardens, farms, woods, etc., to a hillock, called Montagne du Roule, that will later be crowned with the Arc de Triomphe, a monument in honour of Napoleon's army. The name of the avenue, "Elysian Fields," alludes to the bucolic character of the area but simultaneously conjures up the afterlife. In Greek mythology, those fields, known as the Elysion, were the resting place of the Greek heroes in the afterlife, and they were believed to be situated in the west, the area of the setting sun, the direction to which the avenue pointed the way.

The Champs-Elysées run parallel to the Rue du Faubourg-Saint-Honoré, the continuation of the Rue Saint-Honoré, the main east-west artery of old Paris. It is in the Rue du Faubourg-Saint-Honoré that we discover the main entrance of an impressive residence inhabited by Madame de Pompadour, the official mistress (*maîtresse en titre*) of Louis XV. Erected around 1720, it was originally the home of an aristocrat from Normandy, the Count of Évreux, and known as the Hôtel d'Evreux. Much later, long after the death of the original proprietor and a number of changes in ownership, the building was to be baptized Palais de l'Elysée because its gardens abut the Champs-Élysées. Louis XV bought the property for his mistress 1753. In February 1764, a very young Wolfgang Amadeus Mozart was brought there by his father to show off his musical talent, but the visit was marred by a false note: after his successful performance, Lady Pompadour spurned the Wunderkind's attempt to embrace her, as he had managed to do with Empress Maria-Theresa after a concert in her palace in Vienna. Pompadour, a woman of bourgeois origin, who had been named marquessa by her royal lover, obviously disliked physical contact, even in the shape of an innocent little kiss, with commoners, no matter how small, cute, and talented. But perhaps she worried about being infected with some Covid-like contagious disease, and she may already have been in poor health. Although only forty-two years of age at the time, Pompadour was to die two months later, on April 15, 1764, of pneumonia. Her position as mistress to Louis XV was taken over by Madame du Barry who, on December 8, 1793, will be guillotined kicking, fighting, and screaming.[63] Later, Napoleon will live for quite some time in the Élysée, and it is through its back door that he will sneak out to the

---

63   "Französische Revolution." p. 24.

Champs Élysées and head west, to the Atlantic coast and to exile in Saint Helena. After his downfall, the premises will be occupied temporarily by some of his victorious enemies, namely Russia's czar Alexander and the Duke of Wellington. At the time of the 1848 Revolution, when a republic will be proclaimed for the second time, this palace will become the official residence of the president of the French Republic.

Returning towards the center of the city, we pause again in front of the equestrian statue of Louis XV. The proud monarch is dressed like a Roman emperor and crowned with laurels. A contemporary (1787) tourist guide to Paris has praised this statue as "a superb monument, noble, simple, in an authentic ancient style."[64] This Louis fancied himself to be very popular and liked being nicknamed *Louis le Bien-Aimé*, "Louis the Beloved," at least by sycophants. When a careful attempt was made to make him understand that all was not well in the land and that this might some day generate serious difficulties, he made it clear that he was not worried at all and uttered one of his infamous remarks: *Après moi, le déluge!*, "If the flood comes, it will be after me!" And that royal prophesy proved to be correct: the "flood" of the Revolution was to inundate France only after his death.

Folies and Guinguettes

Walking to the end of the attractive Rue Royale or "Royal Street," laid out in 1758 as part of the royal square named after Louis XV, we arrive at a major construction site. For about twenty years, they have been working here on the construction of a church that is supposed to provide the Rue Royale with an imposing yet elegant architectural termination; its portal therefore faces the south, and not west, as the church-building tradition demands.[65] It is supposed to be an edifice in the trendy neo-classical style. Greco-Roman Antiquity has been extremely fashionable for some time, which explains why many of the new buildings in Paris reflect neo-classical architecture. That style conjures up ancient Athens and Rome and associates the French monarchy with their glory and power, it is a style

---

64   Thiéry, p. 101.

65   Entering a church, one proceeds normally from the west, the direction of the setting sun and symbol of darkness and ignorance, to the east, the direction of the rising sun, of Christ and of the "light" of Christianity.

that "expresses dynastic grandeur."[66] The new church at the end of the Rue Royale will look like a Greco-Roman temple; and its facade with pillars crowned by Corinthian capital will mirror the colonnade of the Palais Bourbon on the opposite side of Place Louis XV. However, the construction will be interrupted by the Revolution. Later, Napoleon will toy for some time with the idea of transforming the building into a temple in honour of his armies, but nothing will come of that project. In the end, a church will arise here after all, and it will be dedicated to Mary Magdalen. The Église de la Madeleine will be inaugurated only in 1845.

We continue along Rue Basse-du-Rempart, which corresponds more or less to what will later be called the Boulevard de la Madeleine. This is another "boulevardized" stretch of the former city walls. We turn left at the site where the Opera will arise later, in the 1850s. Via a street that is already called Rue de la Chaussée-d'Antin but is colloquially referred to as the Chemin de la Grande-Pinte, we enter a district known as the Faubourg Montmartre. The term *chaussée* reflects the street's origin as an elevated thoroughfare, a kind of causeway, because this used to be another low-lying, marshy area, bisected by the city's two-meter wide "Great Sewer," *le Grand Égout de Paris*. This sewer—once a small stream descending from the hills of Ménilmontant, Belleville, and Montmartre—was covered in 1771, which gave birth to a new street called Rue de Provence in honour of a younger brother of Louis XVI, the Count of Provence. This count will flee France during the Revolution but return in 1814 to become king as Louis XVIII.

Not so long ago, this district featured vegetable gardens, orchards, farms, and popular taverns, but recently they have had to give way to hôtels owned by noblemen or rich members of the bourgeoisie. A famous revolutionary, Mirabeau, will move into this very trendy part of the capital and will breathe his last here in 1791. And Napoleon will live for some time in a comfortable home just around the corner, in the Rue Chantereine (sometimes called Rue Chanterelle), formerly known as the Ruelette aux Marais des Porcherons; it was the (rented) residence of Josephine de Beauharnais, and the couple lived there after they were married on March 9, 1796. Towards the end of 1797, this street will be rebaptized Rue de la Victoire, "Street of Victory," in honor of the triumphs achieved

---

66   Jones, p. 208.

by Bonaparte in Italy, confirmed in the Treaty of Campo-Formio of October 18 of that same year. The house no longer exists; it used to stand on the site now occupied by numbers 47 to 51 of Rue de la Victoire.[67] It was after his return from Egypt that the couple would move to the Château of Malmaison, located in the village of Rueil, to the west of the city.

Prominent among the inhabitants of the district of the Chaussée d'Antin are the financiers who collect taxes on behalf of the government and make a lot of money by doing so; they are known as the "farmers general" (*fermiers généraux*). As for the fine residences of all these mostly *nouveau-riche* denizens, they often include vast gardens featuring gazebos (*gloriettes*), fake ruins, and similar *folies*, "frivolities." These architectural or horticultural accessories allow the owners to enjoy the beauty and pleasures of nature within the city limits; but on ordinary Parisians they have the same effect as a red rag on a bull. During the Revolution, quite a few of them will be transformed into municipal parks or "tivolis," that is, public amusement parks. Perhaps the most famous of these was located on the site later occupied by the Saint-Lazare railway station; it was the former *folie* of Simon-Gabriel Boutin, the son of a farmer-general, who had called it "Tivoli," after the town near Rome, home of the Villa d'Este with its magnificent gardens.[68]

Nearly at the end of the Rue de la Chaussée d'Antin, a.k.a. Chemin de la Grande Pinte, we enter a neighborhood known as Les Porcherons. Porcheron was the name of a wealthy bourgeois family that owned much real estate here in the Middle Ages and especially along the perpendicular Rue Saint-Lazare that is coming into view and happens to be part of a wall around Paris that should not be confused with the aforementioned medieval city walls. It is the "fiscal perimeter" (*périmètre fiscal*) or "customs barrier" (*barrière douanière*) that separates Paris from the suburbs and the rest of France; the capital is subject to a different taxation system, duties have to be paid on goods imported into the city, and this is task is absolved in a tollgate (*barrière d'octroi*).

The customs barrier generates revenue for the royal coffers, but it also causes prices in Paris to be considerably higher than elsewhere. Wine, subject to extra high duties, is three times more expensive than

---

67 Sand et al., p. XXXIX; Masson, p. 48-49, 55; Beaumont.
68 "Les folies au XVIIIe siècle."

outside of Paris. But Parisians crave the fruit of the vine, they consume huge amounts of it; each year, male adults drink an average of 250 or even 300 litres of wine, compared to 20 litres of beer and six litres of cider.[69] This explains the existence, just outside the fiscal perimeter, of numerous big taverns, known as *guinguettes*, which offer wine at considerably lower prices than in the city, as well as music, dance, gambling, and other forms of entertainment. The best known and most popular of these institutions is called La Grande Pinte, and the street leading to it is therefore informally called Chemin de la Grande Pinte. The tavern rises in front of us, on the other side of the Rue Saint-Lazare, which marks the fiscal perimeter, and just beyond the toll gate known as Barrière des Petits-Porcherons; it occupies the site where a church will be built in the 19ᵉ century, the Église de la Trinité.[70] Of all the guinguettes on the outskirts of Paris, La Grande Pinte is closest to the city center and therefore easily accessible to Parisians, who trek to it in great numbers. The guinguettes attract mainly "little people" such as gardeners, masons, and other laborers, artisans, soldiers, and street walkers, but also rich ladies of aristocratic or bourgeois background who come here, disguised as maidservants or milkmaids, to frolic with sturdy workers or mustachioed military fellows.[71]

However, when we undertake our promenade in Paris, in the year 1785, only shortly before the outbreak of the Revolution, the situation with respect to the fiscal boundary and the guinguettes has been changing dramatically. A new enclosure with a much larger perimeter was recently erected and is called the "Wall of the Tax Farmers" (*enceinte/mur des fermiers généraux*), that is, wall of the collectors of taxes and excises. It is a formidable stone construction with a height of 3.5 meters and a total length of 23 kilometers, "bordered by a circular path on the inside and a wide boulevard on the outside." And it is punctured by no less than fifty-five *barrières*, that is, tollgates, mostly creations of Claude Ledoux, one of the masters of French neo-classical architecture. One of them, finished in the revolutionary year 1789, is destined to survive into the 21ˢᵗ century; it will be visible on the square named after the Battle of Stalingrad:

---

69 Brennan, pp. 189-91; Plack.
70 Brennan, p. 81-84, 138-139, 158-186.
71 Garrier, p. 132-133; Brennan, p. 81-84, 138-139, 158-186. More about the guinguettes, La Grande Pinte, and its owner, Ramponeau, in Dion, p. 505-511; Lachiver, p. 351-353; Béric Le Goff.

the Barrière Saint-Martin, better known as the Rotonde de la Villette.

These tollhouses are usually impressive monuments, a kind of palace, surrounded by powerful pillars in Greco-Roman style and clearly inspired by models dating back to Antiquity or the Renaissance, such as the Roman Pantheon and Palladio's Villa Rotonda.[72] The Parisians are offended by the in-your-face architecture of the new *barrières*, perceived as oozing ostentation as well as arrogance.[73]

Particularly traumatic is the fact that the new arrangement spells the end of the cheap wine and good times in La Grande Pinte and the other *guinguettes* of the Porcherons District. This neighborhood now finds itself inside the city limits and has to charge higher prices. Most guinguettes move to more distant locations beyond the new customs wall, mostly in the districts of Belleville and Montmartre. La Grande Pinte does not move, will remain in business for some time despite higher prices, but will have to close its doors in 1790. In any event, in the *guinguettes* the happy mood gives way to resentment, as reflected in the sarcastic lyrics of this contemporary little poem:

Le peuple Parisien persiflait:	The Parisians scoffed:
Pour augmenter son numéraire	To increase its revenues
Et raccourcir notre horizon	And shorten our horizon
La Ferme a jugé nécessaire	The taxman deemed it necessary
De mettre Paris en prison.	To put Paris in prison.

A conspiracy theory emerges: all that misery is the fault of unconscionable usurers who team up with aristocratic landowners and their friends at the court in Versailles. And the new wall is said "to make Paris grumble" (*le mur murant Paris rend Paris murmurant*). Among the capital's demos, it increases a general discontent that will not cause the Revolution, but certainly help to make it possible.[74] It is hardly surprising that, during the Revolution, these taverns will reveal themselves to be "places where people gossip, news is exchanged, and rumors are spread," as hotbeds of revolutionary propaganda and indoctrination, and as centers for the recruitment of participants in the great revolutionary events, such as the storming of the Bastille as well as attacks on many of the toll barriers

---

72   Hazan (2002), p. 144.

73   Hazan (2002), p. 144. For a comment by a contemporary, see Mercier, p. 50-51.

74   Garrier, pp. 126-27; Cetekk, p. 22.

of Ledoux.[75]

After a northerly walk of a little less than one kilometer, we reach a wide perpendicular street, later to be known as Boulevard de Clichy; it runs from west to east at the foot of the *butte* or hill of Montmartre and constitutes the perimeter of the new toll barrier. At the intersection we have just reached, a tollgate is being erected that will replace the Barrière des Petits-Porcherons that we have left behind. An imposing stone cross used to rise here, white because of the dust from carts constantly passing by on their way to construction sites throughout Paris, loaded with the famous "plaster of Paris." That important construction material, also known as "gypsum plaster," has been quarried on the hill of Montmartre. The cross inspired the name of an inn, La Croix Blanche, and the new tollhouse inherited this name, eventually to become just Barrière Blanche. The intersection becomes a square with the same name, Place Blanche. In the late 19th century, the famous Moulin Rouge nightclub will arise here, to survive into the 21st century, but the tollhouse disappeared shortly after the definitive abolition of the customs barrier in 1860.

In front of us we now perceive the 130-meter high hill of Montmartre, whose slopes are covered with vineyards and sprinkled with windmills, of which names such as Moulin Rouge and Moulin de la Galette will remind visitors much later, when the rural character of the area will have been obliterated by urban sprawl. On this hill there are countless quarries yielding the Paris plaster that was just mentioned, a favorite construction material since Roman times, not only because it is cheap in comparison to wood but also because it is virtually fireproof. The great fire of London in 1666 triggered a decree by Louis XIV, promulgated in the following year, making the use of plaster compulsory for the interior as well as the exterior of new buildings. Demand for plaster thus skyrocketed, the more so since in the 18th century the capital witnessed rapid demographic growth. Consequently, a large-scale production of plaster developed in Montmartre and elsewhere in the capital.[76]

The village of Montmartre, until 1860 an autonomous village just outside the northern boundary of Paris, destined to retain a village atmosphere even after its absorption by the city, occupies the top of the

---

75 Rudé, pp. 217-18.
76 Farge, p. 25.

hill. Its hub is a little square called Place du Tertre, but nobody seems to know anything about the origin or meaning of this name. A gallows rises in the middle of the square, and the last time someone was hanged here was not that long ago, in 1775. Just beyond the village square we discover a small Romanesque church that is dedicated to Saint Peter. According to an ancient tradition, it was erected on the spot where, a very long time ago, a holy man named Dionysios, Saint Denis in French, was martyred, namely by decapitation. A modest chapel, a so-called martyrium, was built there and developed into a monastery. Thus originated the toponym Montmartre: *mons martyri*, "martyr's mountain." But it is also permitted to believe that, in the Roman era, a temple stood here, dedicated to the god Mars, and that the toponym reflects the Latin term *mons Martis*, "hill of Mars."

The abbey of Montmartre is actually a Benedictine nunnery, whose history has known ups and downs and whose abbess has always been a lady of high noble origin. Most of its buildings are not to be found on top of the hill, but somewhat lower, on a site that will later be named after those ladies, Place des abbesses.[77] The monastery, proprietor of much land, is predestined to be closed during the Revolution, and its landed property will be parceled out and auctioned off. The former martyrium, that is, the little church of Saint Peter, will escape that fate. About one hundred years later, the Sacré-Coeur, the huge Basilica of the Sacred Heart, will arise just next to it and cast its cold shadow over the tiny Romanesque edifice. It is then that Montmartre will experience its golden age, with the arrival of painters such as Toulouse-Lautrec, writers, and all sorts of other nonconformists known as *bohémiens*. By that time, the metropolis will have swallowed the once bucolic hilltop village, and precious little will remain of its vineyards and windmills. But in the 1780s things have not gone that far yet.

Gazing northward from the top of the hill of Montmartre, one can perceive the abbey church of Saint-Denis, allegedly constructed on the site where the martyr was buried. Ever since the Middle Ages, that monastery has functioned as a mausoleum for the kings of France. Countless monarchs named Louis, Henry, Charles, etc., rest there in imposing tombs, but not for eternity. During the Revolution, republican fanatics

---

77 For more details on the history of the abbey, see Hillairet (1956), part 3, p. 133-138.

will vandalize the royal tombs and discard the remains of kings, queens, and other royals.[78] In any event, the architecture and art of the mausoleum in Saint-Denis constitute yet another proof of the narrow ties between the monarchical state and the Catholic Church in France's Ancien Régime. The fact that the tombs of the French kings are to be found outside of the capital also reflects the reality that, ever since the time of Louis XIV, the monarchy has not been fond of Paris, even though it was very much a "royal city," and have spent as little of their time there as possible during their lifetime, and, after their death, wanted to stay away from the city for eternity.

IMAGE 7. Montmartre and its monastery, with Paris in the distance on the left, in the 16th century.

---

78   Kennedy, pp. 206-210.

Part II.
The Great Revolution, 1789-1799

IMAGE 8. The March of Women to Versailles on the 5th and 6th of October 1789.

3. The Road from Versailles to Paris

Rendez-vous in Versailles

THE ROYAL FINANCES are virtually depleted, and the king is in urgent need of money. His predecessors have borrowed large sums of money to construct the Palace of Versailles and these loans have not yet been paid off. Moreover, living in luxury in Versailles is expensive, very expensive; it absorbs no less than six percent of the state's income. Very costly, also, are the wars that were waged recently, presumably for the glory of the monarch and/or in the interest of the kingdom, especially the recent War of American Independence. That war actually came down to a conflict between English colonists in Britain's transatlantic possessions and the government in London and was really of no concern to France, but Versailles eagerly supported the rebels for no other reason than that Britain happens to be the traditional enemy of France—and to obtain some sort of revenge for defeat in the previous conflict, the Seven Years' War (1756-1763), when New France was lost to Britain. To finance the French effort on behalf of the "American" rebels, enormous loans were contracted, and the interest that needs to be paid accounted for almost half of all state expenditures.

It is explained to Louis that there are essentially two ways to resolve the fiscal crisis. First, by reducing the state expenditures. However, that amounts to curtailing the king's lavish spending habits, and that he finds out of the question. Second, the state's revenues can be increased, and that implies levying new or higher taxes. To that option, the monarch has no major objections, but there is a practical problem. Direct as well as indirect taxes are already very high. And the majority of Frenchmen are poor and dispose of very low incomes. Is it feasible to impose more taxes on them? As for the kingdom's rich denizens, above all the nobility and the high ranks of the clergy, these classes enjoy the king's favor and are legally privileged, which means that they are exempted from paying taxes. In other words, the numerous poor Frenchmen—the 99 percent, as we might say today—cannot pay, and the minority—the one percent—of rich Frenchmen do not have to pay.

The monarchy's absolutist system calls for the king, first, to obtain the advice of his councillors, and then to unilaterally issue a decree outlining the measures that he has decided on. However, Louis XVI finds this procedure too risky. He does not want to assume sole responsibility for the measures that are to be announced, because they are certain to be unpopular. That is why he decides, in the summer of 1788, to schedule a meeting of the country's Estates General in Versailles, in the following spring. This institution is some kind of parliament in which the people in general are not represented, but instead the three "estates," that is, the nobility, the clergy, and the so-called Third Estate, representing the rest of the population, including the upper and lower ranks of the bourgeoisie, the peasants, the working masses, etc. Under Louis XIV and Louis XV, the Estates General had never been asked to convene,[1] but this time its intervention is deemed necessary to help find a solution for the fiscal crisis and to give legitimacy to the reforms that are to be introduced. It is hoped that the nobility and the clergy will agree to pay at least some tax on the income from their landed property and that the Third Estate will likewise make concessions. However, this hope will be sadly disappointed.

The aristocrats are not prepared to make concessions, to the contrary. They view the king's difficulties, and his order for the Estates General to convene, as an opportunity to recover at least a part of the power the nobility had lost at the time of Richelieu and Mazarin, the architects of royal absolutism. In fact, the suggestion to convene the estates emanates from the nobility. In that institution, voting traditionally takes place per class, per estate. This means that the aristocrats, knowing the clergy to be

---

1   This parliamentary institution first met during the reign of Philippe the Handsome, around 1300; its last previous meeting had taken place in 1614.

on their side, can look forward to having the majority and thus be able to introduce all kinds of reforms to their advantage and to the disadvantage of royal absolutism. (This had even caused some historians to write that the French Revolution started with an "aristocratic revolution."[2]) What the aristocrats do not realize, as the British historian Perry Anderson has noted in his book, *Lineages of the Absolutist State*, is that royal absolutism actually serves to protect the privileges of the nobility in the face of the growing power of the bourgeoisie. The nobility thus plays a risky game, it will end up losing, and it will pay a high price. "The nobles failed to see," writes Soboul, "that by whittling away the power of the monarchy, they were destroying the natural protector of their privileges."[3] In any event, from the fall of 1788 to the spring of 1789, the aristocrats of France are ambitious, optimistic, and full of confidence.

The king, then, cannot look forward to concessions from the part of the nobility. To make things worse, the little people also reveal themselves to be in a nasty mood, at least in Paris. The winter has been very cold and miserable. Unemployment has increased, and the price of bread has risen steeply. But the royal government and the church continue to collect taxes and tithes. Among the Parisian poor, the news of the upcoming meeting of the Estates General raises high expectations, and particularly the hope that improvements will be forthcoming, above all a freeze on the price of bread; but the news also triggers fears, especially the fear of what is called an "aristocratic conspiracy." It is suspected that noblemen entertain ambitions and forge plans that will be disastrous for ordinary people. Rumors are circulating that the increases in the price of flour and bread are the product of a plot of the noble and clerical landowners, a plot also involving merchants, baker, and even members of the royal court, including the king himself. Towards the end of April 1789, riots break out in the suburb of Saint-Antoine, following a wage reduction for the approximately 400 workers in the Réveillon wallpaper factory; about thirty people are killed. A royalist pamphlet provides this commentary: "Majesty, our recent misfortunes are due to nothing other than the high price of bread."[4]

---

2   Rudé, p. 27, quotes Chateaubriand, who wrote that "the patricians started the revolution, the plebeians finished it."

3   Soboul (1977), p. 15.

4   Rudé, p. 43.

The Réveillon factory is located at the present number 31 of Rue de Montreuil, and the riots took place on the corner of that street and the Rue du Faubourg-Saint-Antoine, around a fountain that had been erected there in 1719 and still subsists today. Incidentally, it was only a decade before the Revolution, in 1779, that house numbers were introduced in Paris.[5] Before that, houses were identified by means of a sign (*enseigne*), but these were disliked by many Parisians because, dangling above the heads of the pedestrians in the crowded streets, they often fell down and wounded or even killed passersby.[6] This little verse provides a critical comment on these house signs:

Je voudrois ...	I wish ...
Que l'on n' mit plus l'effigie	They would stop putting up signs
Ni du bon Dieu ni de ses saints,	Not even of God and his good saints
Dont les irrévérends humains	Used by disrespectful humans
Signalent les lieux plus profanes.	To mark even the profanest places.
Il est des Vénus, des Dianes,	There are plenty of Venuses, Dianas,
Des Cupidons, des Adonis	Cupids, Adonises
Et d'autres objets infinis,	And a multitude of other objects
Pour indiquer tous domiciles	To identify the houses
De cette plus grande des villes[7]	Of this greatest of all cities.

As already mentioned, the triad of the Estates General consist of the nobility, the clergy, and the Third Estate, and represents no less than approximately 90 percent of the population of France. This demographic mass may be described as a kind of pyramid with, at the top, the rich members of the haute bourgeoisie, the upper-middle class, and at the bottom the rural and urban proletariat, with all sorts of petit-bourgeois types in between; in other words, members of the lower-middle class such as artisans, more or less well-to-do peasants, and so forth. The delegates who populate the Estates General have been elected on the basis of a quasi-universal suffrage, but via an indirect and very complex electoral system that excludes a huge number of Frenchmen, if not as voters, then as candidates.[8] As a result, the delegates (*députés*) of the extremely heterogeneous Third Estate are virtually without exception members of

---

5   Varejka, p. 86.

6   Varejka, p. 86; about the house signs, see the book by Fournier and Cousin; also Farge, pp. 110-13.

7   Fournier and Cousin, p. 15.

8   Furet and Richet, p. 73; Canfora, p. 98.

the bourgeoisie, and mostly the upper levels of that class: bankers, businessmen, merchants, artists, intellectuals, high-ranking officials, and prosperous artisans plus, of course, numerous lawyers, brought up, as a French historian writes, "with the dreams of Montesquieu, the sarcasm of Voltaire, and the sentimentality of Rousseau."[9] Alongside the electoral system, there is another reason why few petit bourgeois and hardly any workers or peasants are to be found in the Estates General, namely the fact that this type of people does not dispose of the time and the money that is required to head for Versailles and remain there for an indeterminate period of time at their own expense. In addition, they lack the intellectual and oratory qualities that are indispensable weapons in the arena of the Estates General.

The delegates of the Third Estate, then, are members of the middle class, not of the lower class. What distinguishes them from the nobility, is not so much money and property, of which they often have as much (and frequently more) than the average aristocrat, and not even social status and prestige, but rather written and unwritten *privileges* of the nobility and its ally, the clergy. As for the political level, the bourgeoisie does not really crave political power, because in the country's absolutist system the nobility also lacks political power; what the bourgeoisie wants is a different role for the state. Its members dream of a state that will be at their service instead of defending and promoting the interests of the nobility (and the clergy), which is what the monarchy has been doing. Such a state, whether a monarchy or not, is to feature equality before the law between nobility and bourgeoisie, and it will do away with whatever goes against the economic interests of the bourgeoisie.

Here are two examples of measures or institutions that the bourgeoisie detests and wants to eliminate: an economic policy that favors land ownership, the basis of the wealth of the nobility (and the church); and the numerous regulations that inhibit "trade and industry," the basis of the wealth of a large part of the bourgeoisie, such as royal monopolies, interior customs barriers, and the bewildering multiplicity of weights and measures. Forced government loans provide yet another reason for bourgeois discontent with respect to the function of the monarchical state. A state controlled by the bourgeoisie, or at least functioning to its advan-

---

9   Morazé, p. 159.

tage, will enshrine the "freedoms" cherished by that class: the freedom to own property, freedom of enterprise, free markets, and free competition; and, last but not least, free labor, that is, a labor force whose price, in other words whose wages, will be determined, like the price of commodities, by the supposedly natural interplay of supply and demand in a free market. It is in 1776, in Great Britain, that these *liberal* ideas, promoting "laissez-faire," were codified by Adam Smith, the theoretician of "liberalism," in a famous opus, *An Inquiry into the Nature and Causes of the Wealth of Nations*. In France, similar liberal ideas, contrasting starkly with the mercantilism that has hitherto dominated the emerging science of economics, are simultaneously being formulated by economists such as François Quesnay, who will become known as "physiocrats."[10]

What differentiates the bourgeois delegates in the Third Estate from those below them on the social ladder, and above all the workers and other "proletarians," are money and property, of course, but also education, the ability to speak refined instead of crude French, fine clothes, good manners, and of course also a bourgeois world view, which comes down to liberal ideas with respect to issues political and social-economic. For the members of the bourgeoisie, being segregated from the *menu peuple* does not present a problem. This barrier may continue to exist, in fact, it must continue to exist. The bourgeoisie wants equality in the sense that it wants to end inequality between itself and the nobility; what the bourgeoisie does not want, is the end of inequality between itself and the lower orders, the "little people."

In the arena of the Estates General, the bourgeoisie seeks to challenge the nobility and the latter's ally, the clergy. Its great ambition is to transform the feudal regime, which the Ancien Régime happens to be, into a new, bourgeois regime; and it aspires to achieve this objective by legal means, the idea of a revolution does not come to mind. But this transformation can only be achieved with the support of the people, particularly of the "little people" of Paris, the "sans-culottes." These plebeians are not present during the debates of the Estates General in Versailles, but they are very much present, even dramatically so, in the streets and squares of the capital. The bourgeois delegates in the Estates General will learn to manipulate "the street," to assume leadership over the Parisian

---

10   Furet and Richet, p. 65; Noiriel, pp. 230-32.

populace. They do this not only to put pressure on their aristocratic and clerical adversaries within the Estates General, but also to extort from the king, the champion of the cause of the nobility and the clergy, concessions of which they could otherwise only dream.

The first meeting of the 1,165 members of the Estates General took place on May 5, 1789, in a building in Versailles known as the Hôtel des Menus-Plaisirs. This big edifice, situated on the avenue leading towards Paris, had hitherto served for the storage of all sorts of paraphernalia used for feasts organized for *les plaisirs*, "the pleasures," of the king.[11] But Louis XVI will derive little or no pleasure from the series of events that is about to get under way in this building.

The representatives of the bourgeoisie immediately move to the offensive. A few months earlier, on December 27, 1788, they had already obtained the king's authorization to have as many delegates—about six hundred—as the combination of nobility and clergy, since they represent the overwhelming majority of the country's population. This time, they demand that voting will no longer be done by class or "estate," as tradition required, but by head. That should normally ensure a majority for the bourgeoisie because numerous representatives of the clergy's lower ranks have been influenced by the Enlightenment and may therefore be expected to side with the Third Estate. Moreover, such "enlightened spirits" are also to be found within the ranks of the nobility, for example, the Marquis de Lafayette and other "Americans," that is, noblemen who returned from the American War of Independence in the "new world" with a new, "progressive" view of the world. The representatives of the Third Estate claim to speak in the name of the French people in its entirety[12] and to pursue objectives that are in the interest of the people, the community of all Frenchmen or, as they call it, "*la nation*." They therefore invite the aristocratic and clerical delegates to join them so that they can work together in the search for a solution to the country's problems. One June 17, the Third Estate takes one more step in that direction and proclaims itself to be the "National Assembly."

King Louis XVI navigates between Scylla and Charybdis. Some of

---

11   Popkin, pp. 190-91.

12   That was the central thesis of a famous pamphlet, "What is the Third Estate?," written by a clergyman, Abbé Emmanuel Joseph Sieyès.

his advisors recommend making concessions. Others, for example his younger brothers and Queen Marie-Antoinette, argue in favor of obduracy. By making concessions with respect to the issue of representation in the Third Estate, he has stimulated expectations on the side of the Third Estate but exasperated the nobility and the high clergy. But when the Third Estate declares itself to be the National Assembly, he decides that is too much and he sides with "his" nobility. He suspends the meetings and orders the doors of the Hôtel des Menus-Plaisirs to be locked until further notice. On June 20, the delegates of the Third Estate respond by convening in a hall used to play a kind of tennis known as *jeu de paume*, located in a side street in the vicinity of the palace. There they swear to remain together until they have worked out a constitution for France. This "oath of the *Jeu de paume*" will be immortalized by Jacques-Louis David—soon to be known as the "artistic dictator of the Revolution"[13]— on a painting preserved in the Palace of Versailles. A few days later, the king condemns this act of insubordination, but, to his great consternation, more and more delegates of the clergy and even a few "enlightened" noblemen move to the National Assembly. He finally gives in and, on June 27, orders the nobility and the clergy to join the National Assembly. On July 9, this body solemnly rebaptizes itself "Constituent Assembly." We are on our way to a new France.

The events in Versailles make a great impression on the people in Paris. Among those who find themselves in dire straits, they raise the hope that their lot will improve, above all by the introduction of a lower price for bread. However, they simultaneously cause fears that things may get worse, that the aristocrats may conspire to create a famine in order to raise bread prices even more. In addition, it is learned that troops are being concentrated in and near Paris and the Parisians therefore fear that the king may use violence to put an end to the initiatives undertaken in Versailles by the delegates of the Third Estate for the benefit of the common people. In the meantime, prices continue to increase. The reason for this is that we are in the month of July and therefore on the eve of the harvest, which means that the supplies of wheat from the previous year are at their lowest. This situation has traditionally caused prices to rise, but this year the consequences will be dramatic.

---

13   On the role and importance of David during the French revolution and under Napoleon, and on the relation of revolution and art in general, see Hauser, pp. 662-70.

From the Palais-Royal to the Bastille

In Paris, those who want to find out what is going on in Versailles, head for the Palais-Royal. This is a big and beautiful hôtel, or rather, "a complex of houses, hôtels, and open spaces,"[14] worthy of being called a palace. It was originally constructed for Cardinal Richelieu and is located in front of the Louvre, which was still the main royal residence at the time. Later, the place became the property of a younger brother of Louis XIV, Philippe. His descendants are likewise always called Philippe, or sometimes Louis-Philippe, and bear the title of Duke of Orleans. They are ambitious fellows, and it is widely believed that they dream of seeing a Philippe of Orleans, rather than a Bourbon Louis, occupying the royal throne.

To finance their lavish lifestyle, the dukes of Orleans need lots of money. That is why they had the garden of their hôtel surrounded by a gallery of boutiques, with apartments on the higher floors, yielding a handsome rental income. The ground floors feature fine shops and restaurants such as the Trois Frères Provençaux, which "offers Parisians culinary specialties from southern France such as bouillabaisse and *brandade* of salt cod,"[15] and will only close its doors in 1867, and chic cafés like Le Café de Chartres, founded in 1784; many years later, this establishment will become a restaurant, the famous Grand Véfour, which will preserve its magnificent 18th-century interior decoration. The Palais-Royal—"a luxurious little city, hidden inside a big city"[16]—quickly morphed into the trendiest spot in the entire capital. In this establishment, one can carry on endless conversations with friends and strangers while sipping coffee, or flirt with women patrons, of whom a large number practised the "world's oldest profession." (One of these professionals relieved a young Corsican of his virginity here in November 1787; his name was Napoleon Bonaparte.)

On the upper floor are a number of "salons," meeting places of enlightened spirits, but of the bourgeois rather than aristocratic variety. The Salon de Montpensier, for example, just above what is now the Grand Véfour, attracts men who will play important roles in the drama of the

---

14 Hazan (2002), p. 29.
15 Castelot, p. 267.
16 Hazan (2002), p. 30.

Revolution, men such as Danton, Marat, and Robespierre. One floor higher is where Paul Barras lives. He will be one of the leading actors in the later stages of the Revolution, known as the Directoire. He will offer one of his mistresses, Joséphine de Beauharnais, to a general with political ambitions, Napoleon Bonaparte, and also assist in hoisting the Corsican into the saddle of power. But that is a story that will be told in a later chapter of this book.

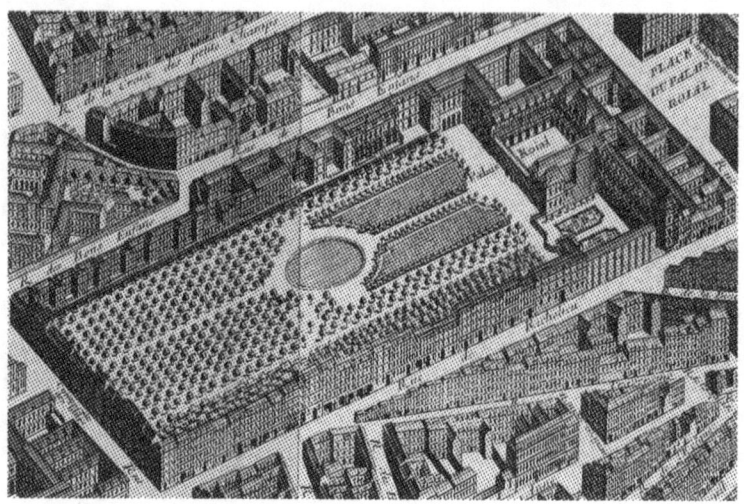

IMAGE 9. The Palais-Royal and its Garden, from the city map of Turgot (1739).

Here, in the Palais-Royal, messengers keep on arriving from Versailles. They bring the latest news about the events that are occurring over there. Thus we recently learned something very surprising: in the Estates General, Louis-Philippe-Joseph, the duke of Orléans, has quit the nobility and joined the Third Estate. It is suspected that, by doing so, he seeks to demonstrate that he is ready to take on the role of constitutional monarch in case Louis would not be willing to abandon absolutism. In any event, the Palais-Royal increasingly attracts large crowds of Parisians, especially members of the city's bourgeoisie, who make no secret of their enthusiasm for the cause of the Third Estate. Here they discuss the latest news, criticize the king, the queen, the court, the nobility, and the clergy, and it is from here that rumours spread throughout the capital like wildfire.

When, in the fall of 1792, the monarchy will have to give way to a republic, Philippe of Orléans, still the owner of the Palais-Royal, will change course entirely. He will adopt a new name, Philippe Égalité, and rename his hôtel Palace Égalité, while the garden will be called Garden of the Revolution. The "former [*ci-devant*] duke of Orléans" will be elected as a member of a new legislative body, the Convention, participate in the trial of Louis XVI, and even vote to have him executed. But afterwards he will fall into disgrace and will also be guillotined, namely on November 6, 1793. His palace will be confiscated, but after the fall of Napoleon, his son, named Louis-Philippe, will recover the property. Louis-Phillipe will realize the big Orleanist dream by ascending the throne as (constitutional) king in 1830. However, in 1848, he will lose his crown as well as the Palais-Royal, which will again become property of the state. Under Emperor Napoleon III, the palace will serve for some time as residence of the Bonaparte family. State property again since 1870, it will eventually become the home of the Conseil d'État, an institution established to advise the government in administrative and legal matters.[17]

On July 12, around noon, the news arrives at the Palais-Royal that the king sacked Jacques Necker, the minister who personified the hope for reforms. (It was he who had persuaded Louis to give in to the demand to double the representation of the Third Estate in the Estates General.) It is not a good time for such tidings, because in Paris the price of bread has just shot up again. But who pays attention to such trivialities in the Château of Versailles? In any event, the "great hope" (*grande espérance*) collapses like a failed soufflé and the Parisian populace are furious. In the suburb of Saint-Antoine and others popular districts, the bells sound the alarm and crowds gather. The crowds shout "patriotic" slogans, that is, slogans expressing hostility to the monarchy, the aristocracy, and the clergy. And it gets worse: a number of toll gates of the detested tax wall around the capital are attacked, looted, and set on fire, and the staff members are lucky when they get away with only a beating. Royal troops are

---

17   Hillairet (1956), Tome 1, p. 185 ff.; de la Batut, tome 1, pp. 24-29.

called in to restore order, for example on Louis XV Square, now Place de la Concorde, site of noisy demonstrations. The cavalry, commanded by the Prince of Lambesc, intervenes with great brutality, which shocks the eyewitnesses.[18]

But restoring order proves to be a sort of mission impossible, because many soldiers sympathize with the demonstrators and join their ranks. Frustrated, the commanders see no other solution than sending the rest of their men back to the barracks. This leaves the demonstrators, the populace, in control of Paris. But what if the next day other, more disciplined troops might show up? It is for that reason that, during the night of July 12 to 13, small groups of Parisians undertake a search for knives, swords, and other weapons—but also flour!—at the workshops of arms dealers, locksmiths, and in monasteries such as that of Saint-Lazare, situated on what is now the Rue du Faubourg-Saint-Denis.

The next day, July 13, the Palais-Royal witnesses heated debates. A journalist suspected of Orleanist sympathies, Camille Desmoulins, climbs onto a chair in front of the Café de Foy (numbers 57-60 of the Galerie Monpensier) and—pistol in hand!—launches into a diatribe in which he exhorts his audience to take up arms. The crowd responds by trekking to the armouries of the Hôtel des Invalides and loudly demanding that its governor provide them with weapons. As his soldiers refuse to intervene, the poor man has no choice but to give in, and the demonstrators, consisting mainly of sans-culottes, depart with no less than 30,000 muskets. Suddenly a cry is heard, "to the Bastille!," and the mob sets in motion in the direction of that fortress. Nobody knows what the original intention may have been. Probably the idea was to obtain powder that was known to be kept there, but the fear that the king may order the nearby Saint-Antoine suburb to be shelled by the Bastille's artillery, may also have played a role. Finally, the Bastille also symbolized the royal "despotism" that was thoroughly despised by the Parisian "patriots." In any event, during the night of July 13 to 14, inhabitants of the main streets leading to the Bastille notice men "armed with rifles, pitchforks, and pikes" trekking eastward in the direction of the Bastille, occasionally "forcing their way into houses to demand food or drink, money, weap-

---

18   The events leading to the storming of the Bastille are described in Quétel, pp. 354-59.

ons."[19]

In the morning of July 14, the vanguard of a mass of tens of thousands of demonstrators invade the Bastille via a courtyard situated on the site of what is now number 5 of the Rue Saint-Antoine. At first, everything goes smoothly. Spokesmen for the demonstrators negotiate with the commander of the fortress, the Marquis de Launay, and for some time it looks as if here too, as earlier in the Invalides, bloodshed will be avoided. But the crowd in the back has no idea what is going on and becomes impatient. Some people start swearing, shouting, pushing... The defenders panic and suddenly open fire, killing about one hundred sans-culottes. The ensuing "battle of the Bastille" does not last very long. Some cannon are brought in by soldiers who have changed sides, and that causes de Launay to surrender. The seven prisoners found in the dungeons, who have not the faintest idea of what is going on, are set free. A relatively small number of defenders, on the other hand, fall victims to the wrath of the mob. De Launay is one of them. He is lynched and, with his head as trophy on a pike, the crowd heads for city hall. The pike (*pique*), a cheap weapon that many artisans are capable of fashioning themselves, if necessary, will become the weapon of choice for the Parisian sans-culottes; with a mixture of affection and respect, they will call it "Saint Pike," and the sans-culottes themselves will eventually be nicknamed "the pikes." However, they also arm themselves with rifles and will even manage to acquire artillery![20]

At the end of this fateful 14th of July, the capital's first great "revolutionary day" (*journée*), and a date later to be known as "Bastille Day," Louis XVI writes in his diary: "Nothing." In reality, it has been a particularly interesting and important day, but perhaps his entourage did not have the courage to tell him what had happened. In any event, the dramatic demonstration of the power of the Parisian populace changes the power relations in Versailles. The representatives of the Third Estate, taking on the role of spokesmen of the Parisians and the entire French people—or the "nation"—will manage during the following days to intimidate not only their adversaries in the Constituent Assembly, the nobility and the clergy, but also the king and the court, and to force them

---

19 Quétel, p. 357.
20 Soboul (1968), pp. 107, 212-13. For a detailed description, see Quétel, pp. 359-66.

to make important concessions, such as the reinstatement of Necker and the withdrawal of all troops from Paris. Moreover, the champions of the hard line against the Third Estate, for example the Count of Artois and the Prince of Condé, can no longer tolerate the situation and flee abroad. It is thanks to its de facto alliance with the Parisian sans-culottes that the bourgeoisie will be able to introduce its program of political reforms.

IMAGE 10. Demolition of the Bastille in July 1789.

However, the Parisian demos has a program of its own, which happens to be economic, rather than political, in nature. The little people want lower prices. Whether the bourgeois delegates in the Constituent Assembly who claim to represent the Parisians and to take their interests to heart, can or want to introduce lower prices, that is another question. The events of July 14—and the riots that flare up again on the 23rd—indicate that the sans-culottes are prepared to use violence to achieve their goals, and this terrifies even their bourgeois allies. Like the king, the nobility, and the clergy, the latter fear the fury of the populace, they worry about their property and even their lives, they are appalled by the threat of "anarchy." Arno Mayer offers the following comment:

> While some notables applauded, albeit reluctantly, the lower orders for their heroic contribution to the struggle for freedom, others almost instantly fretted about the risk of unbinding them. The ghastly murder and dismemberment of several notables following the fall of the Bastille merely confirmed the upper ten thousand in their profound disquiet about the coarseness, savagery, and irrationality of the rabble, for which they disclaimed all responsibility. Indeed, ... the reformists' flirtation with the ordinary people, including their crowds, was short lived.[21]

To prevent the sans-culottes from providing any input at all into political matters, it is decided that the members of what is called the Commune, that is, the municipal authorities who meet in City Hall, may only be elected by "active" citizens, meaning people who pay a relatively high amount of taxes. It is in this context that Lafayette allegedly coined the term "honest people" (*honnêtes gens*) to refer to propertied people, the "property-owning class" (*gens de bien*).[22] Those who do not own the required minimum of property as measured by the amount of taxes they pay, in other words the propertyless people (*les non-possédants*) or "have-nots" (*gens de rien*), are classified, or rather, downgraded, as "passive" citizens. The same tax-based voting system (*suffrage censitaire*) will shortly also be introduced for elections to the National Assembly.

In this ambiance, it is hardly surprising that the bourgeois authorities start judicial proceedings against all those who, during the troubles—for example, during the attacks against the toll gates—committed theft, engaged in looting, vandalism, and similar crimes against property. To maintain the desired respect for property and order, a bourgeois militia (*milice bourgeoise*) is also set up during the days following the storming of the Bastille. Only "active" citizens may join. Later, this militia will receive a more neutral name, "National Guard" (*garde nationale*). Its members will be easily recognizable on account of their blue uniforms, which contrast starkly with the white uniforms of the royal troops, who have in any event been withdrawn from Paris. The National Guard has the task to maintain order, enforce respect for property, and ensure that the sans-culottes do not undertake anything that may not suit the objectives of the

---

21 Mayer, p. 117.
22 Guillemin, pp. 9, 38.

bourgeoisie.

On October 21, 1789, a martial law will be introduced, giving the authorities the right to send in the National Guard to quell any new riots. Such states of emergency are to be announced by hoisting a red flag on the façade of the Hôtel de Ville, and it is by means of a red flag that the National Guard will warn the "populace" that, in case of unrest, force may be used to restore order. A red flag will thus serve to warn the people, but we will see that the people will adopt this symbol to declare its own power and make demands.[23] Already on July 15, the sans-culottes are urged to surrender the rifles they had obtained at the Invalides and used to storm the Bastille. Most of them comply, because they receive a rather generous premium of 40 sols (*cents*), the equivalent of two days' wages.[24]

Within days after the storming of the Bastille, 800 workers began demolishing the edifice, because it was despised as a symbol of royal absolutism. But that was not the only reason why, as far as the sans-culottes were concerned, the fortress had to go. As already mentioned, the neighboring Porte Sainte-Antoine had already been demolished some years earlier, in 1778. And so there emerged, between central Paris and the Faubourg Saint-Antoine, a vast open space where there used to be only a narrow passage in the shadow of a huge and forbidding fortress. Even large numbers of people and goods—including weapons—could henceforth move easily from the faubourg into the city center. An obstacle, minor physically but major symbolically, that had made it difficult for the *faubouriens* to enter the center of the "royal city," thus disappeared. Henceforth, the capital lies defenseless, so to speak, against attack by the restless denizens of the eastern suburb that had proved to be the cradle of revolution in 1789. Later, in 1830 and 1848, descendants of the sans-culottes of the Great Revolution will once again invade central Paris with revolutionary intentions, intentions even more radical than before, as their red flags will testify. We will deal with these new revolutionary incursions towards the end of this book.

In the 21st century, precious little will remain of the Bastille. A few stones from the base of one of its eight towers are displayed in a small park on Square Galli situated alongside Boulevard Henri IV, close to the

---

23 Dommanget, pp. 20-21.
24 *Ibid.*, pp. 30-31; 36-37.

Seine. The stones were discovered in 1899 during the construction of the subway. However, most of the large building stones of the prison were recycled as construction material. Some were used in 1791 to build a theatre, the Théatre du Marais, not far from the site of the Bastille and of the residence of Beaumarchais, whose plays were performed there; its façade may still be seen at number 11 Rue de Sévigny. The home of Beaumarchais was to be found nearby, along the boulevard, which will be named after him, leading towards Place de la République.[25] Other stones ended up being used to finish the bridge connecting Place de la Concorde with the Palais Bourbon; plans for such a bridge had already been made in 1772, but its construction was subject to many delays, financial problems being the main issue. But it became possible to finish the job when inexpensive building material suddenly became available thanks to the demolition of the huge Bastille Fortress. When finished in 1791, that bridge will not be named after Louis XVI, as originally planned, but be called Pont de la Révolution; the idea is that Parisians will be able to demonstrate their disdain for royal absolutism, of which the Bastille had been the symbol, by stepping on its stones.[26]

A relatively small number of stone blocks, 83 in total, were carved into models of the Bastille. They were sold or sent to other cities in France to be displayed in their city hall or some other prominent spot to commemorate the original revolutionary act of the French people. These models can still be seen in the Paris History Museum, the Hotel Carnavalet, located in the Marais district, not far from the square where the Bastille once proudly stood. This same museum also holds a number of keys from the ancient fortress, but Lafayette offered one to his American friend George Washington, who decided—or maybe it was his wife, Martha?—to hang it in the kitchen at his Mount Vernon plantation, not far from the American capital, where it remains to this day.[27]

In the spot where the Bastille once stood, there is now a large square. The outline of the foundation is clearly marked out on the ground by colored stones. At the Bastille metro station, at the other side of the square, close to the "new" opera, one can still see part of the foundations

---

25   Poisson, p. 32.

26   Quétel, pp. 409-14; Poisson, p. 32.

27   Quétel, pp. 401, 411.

of the exterior wall, the counterscarp of the fortress. The numbers 1 to 3 of Place de la Bastille are occupied by a brasserie-bar called "Le Café Français," whose façade displays a plan of the old fortress.[28] In the summer of 1830, during what was known as the July Revolution, which lasted three days, fighting once again took place in Bastille Square. It is these "Trois Glorieuses" (Three Glorious Days), and not the 14th of July 1989, that are memorialized by a column, 47 metres tall, that stands in the center of the square, the July Column; more about it later.

Every year, on July 14, which became the national holiday in 1880, the square serves as the location of a great, popular ball called the "Quatorze Juillet." Leftist groups come here to celebrate May Day on the first of that month, and their demonstrations and marches through Paris often end here with a symbolic re-enactment of the storming of the Bastille. Groups on the right of the spectrum tend to hold demonstrations in the west of the city, posher and more bourgeois, at the Place des Pyramides, near the statue of Joan of Arc, symbol of the monarchist and Catholic France of old. The popular district surrounding the Place de la Bastille was renovated in 1980, as François Mitterrand, a socialist, became President of the French Republic. He also invested huge amounts in other districts to the east, such as Bercy and La Villette, which remain the Paris of the working class, immigrants, the less affluent, and the "little people." As such, the Place de la Bastille and surrounding area make up a vibrant and pleasant neighborhood that attracts many young people, tourists, and even affluent bourgeois from the west of the city.

City Hall and Commune

The conquerors of the Bastille move on in triumph to the Hôtel de Ville, the capital's city hall, a stately Renaissance building surrounded by houses and a square overlooking the Seine, the already mentioned Place de Grève, where executions used to be carried out. After the fall of the Bastille, the Hôtel de Ville becomes the meeting place of the Commune. This is the government of the city, but during the Revolution it begins to function as a de facto government of the entire country. In any event, the Commune does not represent the nation in its entirety. It is the executive body of some fifty electoral districts or "sections" of Paris. Each section represents

---

28   *Les lieux de l'histoire de France*, pp. 412.289-291.

a well-defined district of the capital, whose members are elected by the local "active citizens" and are therefore virtually exclusively members of the well-to-do bourgeoisie. They are nevertheless under constant pressure from the "passive citizens." With the taking of the Bastille, the latter have demonstrated their power, they have become aware of it, and they expect to use it to obtain satisfaction of their needs and wants. If this does not happen, big trouble may occur, as will be shown frequently during the days following July 14: from time to time, severed heads appear on pikes, and a number of real or presumed enemies of the people end up "on the lantern" (*à la lanterne*), that is, hanged without due process from a lamppost in the vicinity of the Place de Grève.

After July 14, the Parisian revolutionary crowd, mainly denizens of the Saint-Antoine area and other popular districts, and hence known as the "sans-culottes," gather again and again in the square in front of the Hôtel de Ville. Thus they exert strong pressure on the members of the Commune. These in turn harass the deputies of all of France, gathered in the Constituent Assembly who are likewise mostly members of the haute bourgeoisie. And this assembly works hard to influence the king and his entourage. The Hôtel de Ville of Paris henceforth symbolizes the power of the people as it confronts the nation's representatives and the king, the influence of the people—of "the street"?—on the legislative and executive branches of the government. Since these two pillars of power stand in Versailles, the Hôtel de Ville symbolizes the power Paris henceforth enjoys vis-à-vis Versailles and over the rest of the country and, more in general, the power of the city vis-à-vis the countryside.

In the weeks that follow July 14, this power is also displayed, admittedly still symbolically, but nonetheless effectively, in two ways. First, by means of a national flag. Prior to the Revolution, France had no genuine national flag, but white as well as blue were the typical colors of the monarchy, used by royal institutions such as the army and the navy. The white cross of Saint Michael on a blue background had been used by French armies during the Hundred Years' War, when it contrasted starkly with the English flag featuring the red cross of Saint George on a white background. And the same blue-and-white flag with a cross was also used by French ships such as that of Samuel de Champlain, founder of Nouvelle France, and thus ended up on the flag of Québec together with fleurs de lys, symbol *par excellence* of the French monarchy. After the storming of the Bastille, the blue and white of the flag of the monarchy are combined with the colors of Paris, blue and red (Lafayette supposedly came up with this idea). Thus is born—first as a cockade, subsequently as a flag—the French *tricolore*: blue, white, and red. The combination of these three colors had been associated elsewhere with liberty and democracy, they first made their appearance on the flags of the Republic of the Netherlands as well as of the young American republic. After the abolition of the monarchy, in 1792, this intrinsically Parisian *tricolore* will become the symbol of the French Republic.

IMAGE 11. Louis XVI greets the Parisians from a window of the Hôtel de ville on July 17, 1789.

Second, on July 17, 1789, only three days after the storming of the Bastille, King Louis XVI considers it necessary to abandon the familiar environment of Versailles, if only temporarily, and make an official visit to the Hôtel de Ville in Paris. He goes there to pay homage to the rebellious people of Paris who no longer wish to be his meek subjects but do not (yet) want to get rid of him. But it is quite a humbling experience for the descendant of absolute monarch Louis XIV, he of the famous phrase *L'État, c'est moi,* "I am the state." In the city hall, the monarch has a red, white, and blue cockade pinned to his hat, the first confirmed instance where these three colors were used. To curry favor with the crowd, he has wine served, so that the people can drink a toast to his health. It is an important symbolic gesture, since the rising price of wine in Paris, along with the rising cost of bread, has also fanned the flames of discontent.

In many ways, Paris, or at least its *menu peuple* or ordinary people, constitutes the dynamo of the Revolution. But this is not to say that the rest of France has no role to play in the events of 1789 and the following years. Without the consent and collaboration of the rest of the country, the Revolution would have been impossible. After the fall of the Bastille, the flames of Revolution spread like wildfire from the city to the countryside. At the end of July and during the entire month of August, the French provinces experience what will be called *la Grande Peur*, "the Great Fear."[29] The peasants take up arms to defend themselves against the real or imaginary intrigues of their aristocratic lords. The latter are suspected of inciting the countryside's unemployed, vagabonds, and assorted criminal elements (*brigands*) to murder peasants who are henceforth reluctant to honour their feudal obligations to the lords. Calls to that effect have been emanating from representatives of the Third Estate. Armed bands are being formed and move onto the offensive, mistreat aristocrats and even, albeit in rare cases, put them to death. They attack the chateaux and often burn down buildings, furniture, and especially the archives, making sure that the lists of names of peasants who owe feudal services go up in smoke.[30]

---

29   The classical study of this episode is *La Grande Peur de 1789*, by Georges Lefebvre; See also the short article by Hartig, pp. 88-135.

30   Hartig, pp. 130-31.

IMAGE 12. The "Great Fear" of 1789 in the countryside.[31]

Besides the revolution in Paris, there is thus also a revolution in the countryside. This "peasant revolution" (*révolution paysanne*) is in many ways a response to the initiatives undertaken by the nobility on the eve of the Revolution, aimed at forcing the peasantry to submit to the enforcement of feudal privileges that had long been neglected. The violence used by the peasants also recalls the famous peasant uprisings in France during the Middle Ages, the so-called *jacqueries*.[32] This violent peasant rebellion, a kind of echo from a past era, combined with the "modern" revolutionary events in the capital, trigger a mass exodus of the French

---

31   Source: https://www.worldhistory.org/image/15880/the-great-fear.

32   Jacques, James in English, was a nickname designating a peasant.

aristocracy to countries such as Germany (where Koblenz will become a famous haven for counter-revolutionary émigrés), England, and the Austrian-controlled Low Countries, now Belgium.

This is the context in which a dramatic step is taken by the National Assembly in Versailles on August 4, 1789, namely the abolition of all the privileges hitherto enjoyed by the nobility and the clergy, including the widely hated tithe; noble titles will be abolished later, on June 19, 1790. This means the demise of the ancient feudal system, at least in theory. The reality is a bit less spectacular: the bourgeois deputies recognize the traditional privileges of the noble lords as a form of legal *property*, the abolition of which needs to be compensated for with payment; otherwise, a precedent would be set that might also jeopardize other forms of property. As for the question how the poor peasants of France can possibly come up with the money needed to buy back the seignorial privileges, that is not a cause for much concern for the delegates of the Third Estate, even though they supposedly represent not only the bourgeoisie but also the peasantry and the rest of the nation.[33]

The hot summer of 1789 ends symbolically on August 26 with the Constituent Assembly's formulation of a set of high-minded principles, the Declaration of the Rights of Man and the Citizen. These are the basic principles, inspired by the ideas of the Enlightenment, of a constitution that the Constituent Assembly plans to work out for the benefit of the country. These principles, now universally accepted, at least in theory, include the sovereignty of the people (or "the nation") instead of the monarch; the equality before the law of all citizens (*citoyens*); the separation of powers (legislative, executive, and juridical); freedom of expression; and the right to hold property, declared to be '*inviolable*' and even sacrosanct (*sacrée*). This clearly reflects the bourgeois character of the Assembly, and, in the end, of the Revolution itself. Karl Marx was to criticize the Declaration of the Rights of Man and the Citizen for not defending "man," i.e. the human being, not as human being per se but "as an individual, as owner, as egotist" and not the ordinary person.[34]

---

33 Hazan (2014), pp. 76-79.

34 Morange, especially on p. 23, writes that the right to hold property "will be one of the most hotly contested items of the Declaration. It is the item that most clearly reflects its liberal character with respect to economic issues." See also the remark by Guillemin, p. 33.

For the common Parisians, holders of precious little property, if any, the Declaration amounts to nothing more than empty phrases. Their own ambitions do not focus on noble principles but on practical solutions to everyday problems, especially the problem of putting the "daily bread" on the family table. As Bertolt Brecht put it: "*Erst kommt das Fressen, dann kommt die Moral.*" In plain English: it is hard to be philosophical when you have an empty stomach. Consequently, the Declaration of the Rights of Man and the Citizen does not still the revolutionary appetite of the Parisian demos.

4. The Moderate Revolution: 1789-1792

A BAKER IN THE TUILERIES PALACE

WITH A NEW AND BOUNTIFUL HARVEST, the price of bread goes down over the summer of 1789. But at the end of August, around the time when the deputies adopt the Declaration of the Rights of Man and the Citizen, a great drought suddenly causes it to shoot up again. What makes this even more painful is the increasing unemployment among the servants, wigmakers, and producers of other luxury goods who, with the flight of the aristocrats, have been losing their clientele. Soon, one can again hear the growling of the humble Parisians as they curse the hoarders and spread rumours about a "famine plot." The women are particularly active in the popular reaction against the bread's shortage and rising cost. They are involved in riots at the bakeries, and they loudly voice their discontent in front of the entrance to the Hôtel de Ville.

In Versailles, the political power struggle between the bourgeois deputies and the king, who continues to defend his own cause, as well as that of "his" nobility and "his" clergy, remains far from resolved. The king has lost ground, but he has not yet been defeated and is still in a position to bounce back after the losses he suffered in July. After all, in Versailles he plays on his home ground, so to speak. In any event, he feels strong enough to refuse to put his signature to the Declaration of the Rights of Man and the Citizen, whose principles contravene those of royal absolutism and of the Church. The more radical bourgeois elements of the Constituent Assembly in Versailles, like their counterparts and sympathizers in Paris, realize that they can take advantage of the discontent of the Parisian plebs and that it would be easier to do so in the capital itself.

In the Palais-Royal, agitators like Desmoulins, Danton, and Marat start promoting the idea that the king should return to Paris, presumably to be closer to his needy people. This idea appeals to the sans-culottes, many of whom still believe, like their medieval ancestors, that the king is a kind of father of his people, a well-intentioned protector who, as in the time of good king Henry IV, will certainly do something to lower the price of bread if only he realizes how much his loyal subjects are suffering, as he is sure to learn if he would spend more time in the capital.[1]

On October 2, in Versailles, during a military banquet attended by the royal family, the recent reforms are severely criticized. The emblem of the Revolution, the tricolor cockade, is even trampled on. This provokes great indignation at the Constituent Assembly, among the "patriots," as the bourgeois deputies have started referring to themselves. And at the Palais-Royal, the demagogues cry out for vengeance. Unrest spreads to the Saint-Antoine suburb where, on October 5, a crowd of women hold a demonstration and arrange for the alarm bells to ring. A crowd gathers at the Hôtel de Ville and forces the leaders of the Commune, as well as Lafayette, commander of the National Guard, to accompany them to Versailles. The idea is not only to demonstrate there against the counter-revolutionary attitude of the court, but also to demand action against hunger: Paris needs bread, and the king has to provide it!

Some 15,000 people take the road to Versailles. Among the many women, one notices not only popular types such as fishwives (*poissardes*), but also ladies of bourgeois origin, easily recognizable because they are well dressed and even wear fancy hats. As was the case with the assault on the Bastille, the protagonists are not the dregs of Paris, malcontents with wanton destruction in mind and obsessed with looting, as some past historians have depicted them. The revolutionary crowd is not a savage "populace," an undisciplined mob; to the contrary, they are remarkably disciplined and display respect for life and property. When things escalate to violence, it is usually in response to provocation.[2]

Arriving at Versailles at the end of the afternoon, the crowd demon-

---

1   Rudé, p. 227.
2   This was convincingly demonstrated in the study by Rudé.

strates noisily in front of the king's balcony. The night passes by in relative calm but in the early morning there occurs an incident. When some demonstrators force their way into the palace, one of the king's personal guards loses his nerve and fires, killing one. This triggers a brawl that leaves a number of dead on both sides. Lafayette's National Guard manages to restore order, and cries of "long live the king!," "our good king!" and "long live Henry IV!" can be heard. Despite the circumstances, the king refuses to resort to violence despite the advice of some members of his entourage. Instead, he agrees to receive spokespeople for the crowd, and when they appear they turn out to be women. In their presence, he solemnly signs the Declaration of the Rights of Man and the Citizen, hoping to defuse the situation. But when the news reaches the crowd, there are cries of "What good is that? It's bread we need!"[3] soon followed by the demand "To Paris with the king!"

Exasperated, Louis XVI agrees, and his carriage departs on October 6, around 1 p. m., followed by the crowd. The trip will turn into an odyssey of no less than six hours in the rain and cold. The crowd triumphantly sing that they are bringing back "the baker, his wife, and the little baker's boy" (*le boulanger, la boulangère et le petit mitron*) For the sans-culottes everything revolves around bread, its scarcity and its high cost, and they are happy and proud to bring back the baker-king who will make cheap bread available. He will, won't he?

The centrality of bread and the fact that Parisians expect the king to do something about it, like a good father providing for his children, is reflected in a few couplets of a revolutionary song of the era called *Courage patriotique des dames de la halle*, 'Patriotic courage of the market women':

J'voyons ben qu'on nous veut du mal,	We can see they mean us harm,
J'irons jusqu'au trône royal	Let's go right to the royal throne
Trouver not' bon Roi, not' bon père,	Find our good king, our good father,
L'y dir' que j'somm' dans la misère.	And tell him our woes.
J'l'y dirons qu'avec not' argent,	We'll explain that we have no money,
Que l'pain nous manque à tout moment,	That we're always without bread,
J'savons ben qu'i n'a pas d'malice,	We know he means us well.
Et qu'i nous rendra bonn' justice.[4]	And will give us justice

---

3   Lévêque and Belot, p. 126.
4   *Chansonnier révolutionnaire*, p. 48.

Abandoned by the king and his court, the palace of Versailles looms like a huge white elephant. The enormous building will be emptied, with all of its paintings, statues, tapestries, jewellery, and objets d'art transferred to the Louvre Palace. From the 16th to the 17th centuries, before the construction of Versailles, the Louvre had served as the royal residence. During the revolution, the building will be transformed into a national museum with the objective of "the education of the people." Its doors will open in summer 1794. The embryo of the Louvre's magnificent collection is constituted by the numerous masterpieces collected over the centuries by the kings of France from within the country but also abroad. Following the Revolution and under the reign of Napoleon, the collection will be increased by canvases and art pieces from conquered lands such as Belgium and Italy. However, many of the furnishings of the palace of Versailles are not transferred to the Louvre. They are auctioned off publicly at discount prices. The idea is to demolish Versailles, but Napoleon will decide to keep the palace as one of his imperial residences, But he prefers Fontainebleau and never spends a single night in Versailles.

In 1830, the palace of Versailles will likewise be turned into a museum and all sorts of furniture and works of art are brought together there in an attempt to bring back the ambiance of the palace's monarchical *age d'or*. That will prove to be useful during the Franco-Prussian war of 1870-1871, particularly during the long siege of Paris, when the King of Prussia and his entourage move in. In the Hall of Mirrors, on January 18, 1871, he is proclaimed Emperor of all Germany. This he owes mainly to his chancellor, Otto von Bismarck, the most capable European statesman of the era. It is a great humiliation to the French, who will exact revenge at the end of the First World War. In the same Hall of Mirrors, on June 28, 1919, the German delegates will have to sign the humiliating Treaty of Versailles. It will only be thereafter that the palace will slowly morph into a major tourist attraction.

After arriving in Paris, the king settles into the Tuileries Palace, located between the gardens of the same name at the complex of the Louvre. (The western extremities of the two wings of the V-shaped Louvre, known as the Marsan pavilion to the north and the Flore pavilion to the south, next to the Seine, form part of the Tuileries palace at this time.) The Tuileries owes its name to the tile (*tuile*) factory that occupied this site many centuries ago. Constructed towards the end of the 16th century, the edifice was restored and enlarged from time to time, becoming a longer building with a façade of more than 200 metres. Henry IV and the young Louis XIV had resided there at one time.

Louis XVI and Marie-Antoinette thus move into a truly royal residence, albeit considerably more modest than Versailles. In this palace, the royal family will remain virtually uninterruptedly until August 10, 1792, when the sans-culottes will forcibly evict them. After the abolition of the monarchy and the proclamation of the republic, the final sessions of the king's trial will be held here and, on January 17, 1793, Louis will be condemned to death in the palace that had been his home for a few years. A few months later, the Assembly, then known as the Convention, will meet in this building. Later still, Napoleon will move in, to be followed quite a few decades later by his nephew, who will rule France from 1859 to 1870 as Emperor Napoleon III. He will lose his throne after the Battle of Sedan during the disastrous Franco-Prussian War of 1870-1871. And during the subsequent uprising known as the Paris Commune, in May 1871, the Tuileries will be burned to the ground and thereafter the remains will be removed. Today there is talk of a possible reconstruction of this historically important palace, the locale of such dramatic and bloody events.

As for the Tuileries gardens, located between the former palace and the modern Place de la Concorde, they have barely changed since the time of the French Revolution. Louis XVI and Marie-Antoinette often strolled through them with their young son, the dauphin, for whom a small children's playground was built at the end, bordering the Place de la Concorde.[5] Later, in these gardens, great republican feasts will be orchestrated, for example the great *Fête de l'Être suprême* (Celebration of the Supreme Being) of June 8, 1794, an initiative of Robespierre but staged with great pomp by the painter David. During the Revolution, in times of shortage and famine, the Tuileries Gardens are also used to grow vegetables, especially potatoes. At the time, this humble tuber from the Andes is becoming a cheap and nutritious addition to the French diet, although to this day, the French prefer bread.

When the royal family departs from Versailles, it is followed by the Constituante which, on November 9, 1789, moves into an edifice known

---

5   Jacquin et al., pp. 145, 148, 152.

as the Manège, the "horse riding arena," since it serves for indoor equestrian purposes. It is part of the Tuileries palace complex, as it is conveniently located just outside of the palace's gardens. Similar buildings in the immediate vicinity are the Orangerie, a greenhouse that produces oranges for the royal table, and the Jeu de Paume, a hall for tennis playing. The latter two buildings will survive into the 21st century. But after the Revolution, at the beginning of the 19th century, the Manège was to be demolished to make way for a new street, the Rue Rivoli; the riding arena stood on a site located between the Tuileries gardens and the place where the Hotel Meurice will be constructed. A commemorative plaque can be seen near the entrance of the Tuileries, across from number 230 of the Rue de Rivoli.

The Manège is a long building not very well suited for the gathering of hundreds of deputies. They have to be seated in two long rows of benches facing each other. From the perspective of the president, whose rostrum stands at one end, half the deputies are to his left, the other half to his right. Those whose political view align with each other tend to sit together. And the president soon notices that those who want change, even a lot of change, in other words, the progressives or radicals, gather on the left; the deputies who want little to no change, on the other hand, the conservative elements, huddle on the right. Thus originates the political designations of "the left" and "the right." Eventually it will turn out that, on the left, the radical elements like to take place on the benches at the top, and so they will become collectively known as *la Montagne*, "the mountain." The more moderate left-wingers—"revolutionaries, *ma non troppo*," as an Italian author has described them[6]—occupy the lower seats and become known as *la Plaine*, "the plain," or, more pejoratively, *le Marais*, "the marsh." The sessions of the Constituent Assembly are open to the public. From balconies constructed for that purpose, spectators can listen to the often pompous declarations and passionate debates and freely (and loudly) express their opinions by cheering or jeering at the speakers. The meetings thus become a kind of show, a theatrical performance, sometimes even a circus.

The deputies have different ideas about issues ranging from general principles and specific policy objectives to tactics and strategies to be fol-

---

6 Del Tufo, p. 7.

lowed to achieve more or less radical objectives. Delegates with similar opinions form associations called "clubs," which are in fact embryonic political parties. One group that starts with rather moderate ideas but becomes increasingly radical as it grows in numbers, starts to meet in November 1789 in the new monastery of the aforementioned Dominicans, located at the modern-day site of the Saint-Honoré market; its entrance is on the street of the same name, only a stone's throw from the Manège. These meetings initially take place in the monastery's library, on the floor above the chapel, actually the attic. The annual rent paid to the monks is 200 Francs. Later, after the monastery is closed in the autumn of 1790, the deputies gather in the chapel itself.

IMAGE 13. To the left, the Manège, to the right, the Tuileries Gardens and Palace. (Source: Anthony Pascal, les-dentus.blogspot.com/2015/10/des-meteorites-devraient-froler-la.html.)

As previously mentioned, the Dominicans are nicknamed the Jacobins, due to their devotion to Saint James. The members of this club, whose official name is the *Société des amis de la Constitution* (Association of Friends of the Constitution), acquire the nickname of the monks; they become known as the Jacobins. James was said or at least believed to have been a fanatic and belligerent saint and that reputation is transferred to the new, revolutionary kind of Jacobins. They will be considered by contemporaries and, later, by historians, as the most fanatic of revolutionaries—especially those, of course, who join the Montagne in the Manège.

Although the Jacobins started off as moderates, they gradually become more radical. They will be the first to call for the abolition of the monarchy and the declaration of a republic. Their club becomes very popular, not only in Paris, where it will boast 1,200 members by June 1791, but also in many other cities, where hundreds of Jacobin sections spring up. [7]

The more moderate elements, such as Lafayette, Sieyès, and Barnave, soon turn their backs on the Jacobins and start their own club, with a platform featuring support for a constitutional monarchy. They are called the Feuillants because they hold their meetings in another monastery, also located close to the Manège, whose monks are known by that nickname. These are Cistercians, that is, members of the order of Saint Bernard, and therefore also known in France as *Bernardins*. But their nickname is Feuillants, a reference to their very first monastery in France, originally a Cistercian establishment, was that of Notre-Dame de Feuillant, situated close to Toulouse. Like the abbey of the Jacobins/Dominicans, the establishment of the Feuillants/Bernardins is doomed to disappear from the cityscape. It stood in the area that will be occupied much later by the luxury hotels Westin Paris-Vendôme (formerly the Inter Continental) and Meurice, at the corner of the Rue de Castiglione and the Rue de Rivoli. The monastery of the Feuillants and the club bearing its name are commemorated nowadays by a luxury restaurant on that spot, Le Carré des Feuillants. [8]

---

7   Miquel, p. 315.
8   "Église des Feuillants."

Visiting the Cordeliers

The Jacobins have not only conservative but also radical competitors. To find them, we must trek to the Left Bank of the Seine, to the little square Henri Mondor along the Boulevard Saint-Germain. In the middle of that square, the statue of Georges Danton, one of the most prominent of revolutionary demagogues, greets the folks who enter or exit the busy Odéon subway station. His house used to stand here, but it was demolished a long time ago, namely, in the 19th century when the Boulevard Saint-Germain was laid out.

This neighborhood used to be known as the Cordeliers district because its paramount edifice was the monastery of the Franciscans. The Parisians colloquially referred to them as the Cordeliers, that is, "the men of the rope," because they used a rope to fasten their robe around their belly. Starting in April 1790, the chapel of the monastery is used for meetings of a club of revolutionaries officially called the "Society of Friends of Human Rights and of the Citizen," but the association with the Franciscans causes its members to receive the nickname Cordeliers. The Cordeliers, i.e. Franciscans, traditionally focus on working with the "little people" in the cities and compete for the favors of the plebs with the Dominicans, also known as Jacobins. Many members of the club, and most of its leaders, belong to the bourgeoisie; Danton is one of them. But the rank-and-file includes a much higher percentage of folks of plebeian background than the Jacobin Club. That helps to explain why the Cordeliers are even more radical revolutionaries than the Jacobins. With the latter, the Cordeliers are in keen competition to curry favor of the sans-culottes and ordinary Parisians in general. In some respects, the Cordeliers resemble the Franciscans, a monastic order that traditionally catered to, and identified with, the urban poor, and competed for this constituency with ... the Dominicans, a.k.a. Jacobins. During the Middle Ages, these two orders usually established themselves on opposite ends of cities. In Florence, for example, the Dominican church of Santa Maria Novella was to be found in a northwestern district, while the Franciscans of Santa Croce occupied a site in the southwest of the city. In revolutionary Paris, the Jacobins and Cordeliers similarly kept their distance, the former entrenched on the Right Bank, the latter, on the Left Bank.

In 1793, the Cordeliers Club will split into a more moderate wing, known as the "indulgents" and a very radical one, the *"exagérés"* (exaggerators); they are also referred to as "Dantonists" and "Hébertists" since their respective leaders are Georges Danton and Jacques René Hébert. The figurehead of the Cordeliers is Georges Danton. As already mentioned, he lives in a house that stands on the site where later, in 1891, his statue will arise. Other famous members of the club are Jean-Paul Marat and Camille Desmoulins. The latter is the founder of the club. He and his wife Lucille used to live on the third floor of number 2, Place de l'Odéon, where a restaurant called La Mediterannée will later be established. Marat is the publisher of a newspaper that has been very popular among the sans-culottes, *L'Ami du Peuple,* and he himself has thus become known as "the friend of the people." His printing press is located in the house at number 6 of the Cour du Commerce, later to be referred to as Cour du Commerce-Saint-André. In the 21st century, this narrow, picturesque alley with its cobblestones and old houses will still look much as it did at the time of the Revolution.

It is in his home on the nearby Rue des Cordeliers, now located at number 20 of the rue de l'École-de-Médecine, that, on July 13, 1793, Marat is visited by a charming young woman from Normandy, Marie-Anne Charlotte de Corday d'Armans, better known as Charlotte Corday. He receives her as he takes a bath, and suddenly she plants a sharp knife in his chest, which she had bought for two francs in a store at number 177 of the Galerie de Valois, in the Palais-Royal. The famous painter Jacques-Louis David has immortalized Marat, pictured dead in his clog-shaped bathtub, on a canvas that can be seen today at the Royal Museum of Fine Arts in Brussels. This painting is praised by connoisseurs as David's masterpiece, and as "perhaps the greatest political painting of all time."[9] The bathtub, in the shape of a wooden shoe, subsists and can be seen at the Grévin Wax Museum, located in Paris on the Boulevard Montmartre, at number 10.

Right in front of Marat's printing house is number 9 of the Cour du Commerce. They are experimenting here with a technological innovation for the purpose of human executions, the guillotine. The intention is that all who are sentenced to death will be dispatched in the same fashion. In the Ancien Régime, decapitation was a "privilege" reserved for

---

9   Mayer, p. 195. See also Hadjinicolaou, pp. 125-28, and Hauser, p. 670.

the aristocrats, but from now on, everybody will be able to "enjoy" it. Moreover, the introduction of a new mechanical form of decapitation will make executions precise, quick, and therefore more humane than before, since in the past the executioners often bungled their task. (Indeed, "decapitation was the most difficult execution method, since it required great experience, which not all executioners had.")[10]

A more perfect, quasi-industrial version of the guillotine has actually been in use for centuries, for example in Germany. A humane and efficient instrument for executions is wanted and is being developed here, in the Cour du Commerce. The machine will be named after Joseph Ignace Guillotin, who, before the Revolution, was the attending physician of the Count of Provence; he was also a deputy of Paris in the Estates General and one of the initiators of the oath of the *Jeu de paume*. After the Assembly decides, in the spring of 1791, not to abolish the death penalty, this champion of the revolutionary principle of equality will propose to carry out all executions in the same way, regardless of the social rank of the person condemned to death. The deputies agree with him and on October 6 of that same year, a new law stipulates that "*tout condamné [à mort] aura la tête tranchée,*" that is, that "everyone condemned to death is to have their head cut off." The new law also prohibits torture and abolishes "imaginary crimes" such as witchcraft and heresy.[11]

The new version of the chopper to be used for this purpose will be given the name "guillotine," but its designer is another medical doctor, Antoine Louis, secretary of the National Academy of Surgery. And it is a German maker of musical instruments living in Paris, Tobias Schmidt, who wins the contract to manufacture the revolutionary death-machine in April 1792. He goes to work immediately. Schmidt's workshop is on number 9 of the Cour du Commerce. It is here that he mounts the prototype of the new machine and experiments with it in the presence of Guillotin, Louis, and the official executioner, Charles-Henri Sanson. It turns out that Louis' invention, which for a time will be called the "Louisette" or "Louison," works very well, at least on the sheep that serve as guinea pigs for testing purposes. (Later, at the Bicêtre prison hospital, other trials are carried out on three human corpses.) The effectiveness

---

10   See Thibault's article, featuring examples of failed beheadings.
11   Coquard, p. 115.

of the instrument will be further increased by an oblique cutting edge, which was initially shaped like a crescent moon.

In the Assembly, Guillotin proudly reports that henceforth, the condemned would find themselves in the afterlife in the blink of an eye. "The patient [sic] will only feel a slight breeze on the neck," he explains triumphantly!12 But skeptics question whether death by the guillotine will be truly painless. Careful observation of the freshly sliced heads will lead to the conclusion that consciousness continues for a short time, at least as long as blood is still circulating in the brain. Or perhaps not? Even today, we cannot say for sure.13 In any event, the guillotine is approved for its deadly revolutionary purpose, and it is used officially for the very first time on April 25, 1792, for the execution, at place de Grève, of an ordinary criminal, Nicolas Jacques Pelletier.

Before the Revolution, the executioner Sanson first tortured the condemned, which produced a spectacle of considerable duration. He then proceeded to the decapitation itself, using either the sword or the ax, which required a fair bit of dexterity, so that he had the spectators' full attention; in other words, the executioner was the star of the show. But the guillotine downgrades his role to the menial task of pulling on a rope, after which the body without head and the head without body are quickly made to disappear. (Furthermore, Sanson does not even pull the rope himself; he simply gives a sign to an assistant, who carries out the fatal deed.) At the very first execution by guillotine, the crowd is clearly disappointed by the lack of show or drama normally provided by an execution, as well as by the brevity of the whole affair. Sanson is likely also disappointed. It is possible that Pelletier is happy with the guillotine's efficacy but, if so, his satisfaction is very short-lived.

Before it became an Italian trattoria, a traditional restaurant occupied the house where Tobias Schmidt set up the very first guillotine. The lamb chops featured on its menu remind us of the sheep that served as the very first victims of the revolutionary cleaver; and the house cocktail was called the "Guillotine," those who over-indulged ran the risk of losing their head. Next to Schmidt's house, in the Cour du Commerce, is the rear entrance to the aforementioned Café Procope. The Cordeliers and

---

12   Poisson, p. 101.
13   Poisson, p. 101; "Les morts violentes de l'histoire: Robespierre."

other radicals are regular customers of this establishment, for example Marat, Danton, Desmoulins, and Fabre d' Églantine. And it is a Procope customer who, in 1789, first appears with a Phrygian cap on his head, later to become the favorite headgear of all the revolutionary believers, including the sans-culottes and, of course, the Cordeliers.[14]

Down with the skullcap!

The relocation of the king and of the Constituent Assembly constitutes a victory for the revolutionary bourgeoisie over the conservative supporters of the Ancien Régime. But there is not yet talk about a possible abolition of the monarchy. The revolution seems to be moving towards a constitutional (and parliamentary) monarchy, a system in which the king represents the executive branch, in other words, where he functions as head of state with limited power. In Paris, the king no longer plays on his home turf, and the chances are therefore much greater that he will have to resign himself to a drastic curtailing of the absolute power he previously held. On the other hand, from now on events will play out in the very heart of revolutionary Paris, in proximity to the Hôtel de Ville, with its Commune, and close to the Faubourg Saint-Antoine, bulwark of the Parisian sans-culottes.

Although now enjoying a much stronger position vis-à-vis the king, the Constituent Assembly, with an almost exclusively bourgeois membership, also finds itself facing the ascending power of the common people of the capital, the Parisian demos. To appease this useful but dangerous ally, the Assembly in Paris will immediately set to work to ensure that Parisian bakers receive more flour, so that cheaper bread becomes available. It is not the king but the Constituent Assembly that reveals itself to be "baker." The price of bread remains high, but at least the sans-culottes have it back on their tables.

Peace and quiet thus return to the capital, at least for the time being. The deputies of the Constituent Assembly are therefore free to focus on the great task they have set for themselves, the drafting of a constitution for the country and for the people, in short, for the *nation*. But it is hardly surprising that, in this context, attention will have to be paid not only to

---

14   *Ibid.,* pp. 100-101; Wilde.

the fine principles of the Declaration of the Rights of Man and of the Citizen, but also to more practical considerations. One of the great issues is the fiscal crisis that has led to the convening of the Estates General and still awaits a solution.

The deputies have no desire to solve the problem of the national debt the way Lenin and the Bolsheviks will later do in Russia, when those revolutionaries will liquidate a similar debt, accumulated by the overthrown tsarist regime, by simply repudiating it at the expense of the creditors. The reason for that reluctance is rather simple. The majority of deputies are wealthy citizens who, through the purchase (sometimes compulsory) of government bonds from successive kings, are the very same ones who lent the money used to build palaces and fund wars. The majority of the state bondholders are the same kinds of people who now find themselves in power. Unsurprisingly, they find it imperative that the debt be paid back. But how? The answer to that question is quickly found: at the expense of the Church, which, in France, has enormous wealth, mainly in the form of real estate.

It is a particularly opportune time for the financial plunder of the enormous ecclesiastical wealth because in France, and especially in Paris, the Church has never been so unpopular. Like the nobility and the monarchy, the Church was a bastion of the Ancien Régime and is therefore hated by all those who want an overthrow of the system, or at least to reform it considerably. In a revolution directed against a system in which the State and the Church are intimately linked, it is impossible to attack only the State while sparing the Church. The clergy is the conjoined twin of the nobility, its ally and supporter, and opponent of the Third Estate, first in the Estates General and then in the Assembly; like the nobility, it now has to face the music. The holdings of the nobles who fled France have been confiscated, so it is only logical that the revolutionary government, finding itself deep in the red, set its sights on the vast possessions of the Church.

Many bourgeois members of the Constituent Assembly are openly anticlerical and hostile to the clergy, but not necessarily towards religion. They have been influenced by the Enlightenment and have read the works of Voltaire, in which he attacked the Church with a particular virulence. But the Parisian sans-culottes, who have likewise taken a page from Voltaire, also reveal their anticlerical bent during the summer of 1789. The slogan "*À bas la calotte!*" ("Down with the skullcap!") is increasingly heard during their rallies. What is particularly surprising is the anti-clericalism displayed by women.[15] With regard to the political conflict within the Constituent Assembly, the sans-culottes identify with the Third Estate, whose enemies are also their own enemies, and their hostility towards the Church is the inevitable corollary of their hostility towards the nobility. "This nobility and this clergy are but one, they pull together," went a revolutionary song that was very popular among the sans-culottes.[16]

In this increasingly anticlerical revolutionary climate, the confiscation of the enormous wealth of the Church looms like the ideal solution to the fiscal crisis. With one bold financial uppercut, the ecclesiastical ally of the nobility is put out of action, the finances of the State are (hopefully) sanitized, and the well-to-do burghers ensconced in the Constituent Assembly can recuperate the money they had invested in royal bonds. Consequently, on November 2, 1789, the property of the Catholic Church is "made available to the nation," that is, seized by the state. The bulk of the lands belonging to monasteries and the parish churches will be subdivided and sold publicly, by means of which the state debt will supposedly be paid off.

While waiting for the money to end up in the coffers of the state treasury, a new kind of paper money is put into circulation almost immediately, the value of which is theoretically backed by the confiscated ecclesiastical riches, henceforth known as *biens nationaux*, "national assets." This paper money is called assignats. (The name reflects the fact that the value of these banknotes "is assigned to the property of the clergy.") Out of fear for a successful counter-revolution that would likely permit the Church to recover its former property, the buyers of ecclesiastical real estate and other assets—mostly bourgeois and also a rich minority of the peasantry—will become grateful, zealous, and of course anticlerical sup-

---

15 Michalik, pp. 32-35, emphasizes women's anti-clericalism. The *calotte* is the traditional priest's cap. This term referred to the clergy, the Catholic Church and clericalism at that time. The little black cap had the same effect on the anticlerical revolutionaries as a red cape to a bull. On anti-clericalism in Paris before the Revolution, see Garrioch, pp. 197-98, 306-308.

16 *Chansonnier révolutionnaire*, p. 35.

porters of the revolutionary cause.

The majority of the peasants, however, are sharecroppers or landless day laborers, so they do not have enough money to buy nationalized ecclesiastical land. (We remember that they do not have enough money to buy the feudal land rights of their lords, either.) Anyway, formal *possession* of land is of far less interest to the peasants than the right to *cultivate* land. They would prefer to see the land become the property of the village community, or of the *nation*, or of any other type of collectivity, as long as they can work it in exchange for the most modest rent possible. Instead, the church lands are purchased by wealthy denizens from the nearest cities, or by those few peasants who have some capital, the so-called "cocks of the village" (*coqs du village*). To make things worse, the sale of the *biens nationaux* is complemented by the sale of an ancient social asset, namely communal lands, that is, "the meadows, woods, and marshes of the countryside, which cannot be cultivated but provide the poorest with an essential additional income," for example by allowing them to collect firewood or have their goats graze there.[17] The small peasants are thus left empty-handed, morphing into a landless "rural proletariat" that will in due course end up migrating to the big cities and new industrial centers to find work in factories or mines.[18] (However, a major exception to this general rule is the case of certain wine regions, especially Burgundy, where it appeared possible for many small vintners to purchase a minuscule lot, tiny but just big enough to permit a family to subsist.)[19] In any event, the peasants are disappointed by the revolution and, as a result, will prove to be extremely susceptible to counter-revolutionary propaganda. The well-to-do peasants, on the other hand, are happy with this development and join the bourgeoisie in the ranks of the fervent supporters of the Revolution.

On December 24, 1789, the Catholic Church receives yet another blow from the Revolution. The Constituent Assembly grants French Protestants not only complete freedom of worship, but also identical civil rights to those of Catholics. In September 1791, Jews will likewise be "emancipated." Protestants and Jews thus become supporters of the

---

17 Coquard, p. 94.
18 This issue is dealt with in detail by Lefebvre, in Hartig, pp. 136-70.
19 See Pauwels (2020a), p. 252-257.

Revolution, but the Church and its faithful, who were not exactly impartial from the start, thus find themselves even more firmly in the counter-revolutionary camp. Arno Mayer has masterfully revealed the implications of all of this and pointed out the strong similarities to the Russian Revolution, which will similarly liquidate the traditional privileges of the Orthodox Church. In any event, Catholicism has ceased to be the State religion in France; the country has taken steps that will ultimately lead to what is now called the "separation of Church and State."

The Constituent Assembly continues on its anticlerical momentum. On February 13, 1790, it decides on the suppression of (most, but not all) monastic orders and the closure of their monasteries. Tens of thousands of monks and nuns are dismissed and allowed to retire with a small state pension.[20] Sarcastically, the revolutionary anti-clericals sing:

Plus de moines langoureux,	No more languid monks,
De plaintives nonnes.	Complaining nuns.
Au lieu d'adresses aux cieux,	Instead of addresses to heaven,
Matines and nones,	Matins and nones,
On verra ces malheureux	We will see these unfortunates
Danser, abjurant leurs voeux![21]	Dance, recanting their vows!

On March 29, 1790, the first official reaction of Pope Pius VI to the events in France arrives: a condemnation of the Declaration of Human Rights. A bitter conflict arises between the French Revolution and the Catholic Church. On July 12, 1790, the Constituent Assembly promulgates the "Civil Constitution of the Clergy." This decree, an integral part of the constitution that is being prepared, defines the status of the Church in the new France. The number of dioceses, for example, is reduced from 139 to 83, that is, to one per *département*. (The *départements* are the new administrative areas established by the Constituent Assembly on December 22, 1789; they replace the old provinces, transforming the tangled administrative mosaic of the Ancien Régime into a centralized and hierarchical system of government. As Oliver Coquard notes, "the French realm is thus made more homogeneous, more unified.") In addition, there will henceforth only be one parish for every 6,000 inhabitants. Furthermore: from now on, priests will be elected (!) by the parishioners and, as "ecclesiastical officials of the State," they will receive a

---

20 See the articles by Marechaux and Marsden.
21 *Chansonnier révolutionnaire*, p. 42.

state salary.[22] The arrangements introduced by the Civil Constitution of the Clergy are truly revolutionary and obviously constitute a blow to the prerogatives of the Papacy. They offend the very pious Louis XVI, but on August 24, 1790, he finds himself obliged to give his approval. The inevitable papal condemnation of the Civil Constitution of the Clergy—and the principles of the French Revolution in general—will only come in spring 1791. In the meantime, the feud between Church and State in France, and between Paris and Rome, intensifies.

The city of Avignon and its surroundings, the Comtat Venaissin, have been a papal possession since the Middle Ages and therefore constitute an enclave of the Papal States in France at the time of the Revolution. On September 12, 1790, this territory is annexed by the revolutionary government, to the great joy of the majority of the population, but to the great displeasure of the Pope. Worse is yet to come. As of November 27, 1790, all priests are required to swear an oath of allegiance to the new Constitution, including the Civil Constitution of the Clergy. Almost all the bishops refuse to do so, and their example is followed by half of all the parish priests. (It has to be kept in mind that the bishops are overwhelmingly, if not exclusively, of noble background and therefore counter-revolutionary, while the parish priests are mostly of humble origin and therefore in favor of the Revolution.) The French clergy is henceforth divided between "constitutional" priests or "jurors" on the one hand, and "non-constitutional" or "refractory" priests, "non-jurors," on the other. The former receive authorization from the State to continue to exercise their ecclesiastical function but find themselves exposed to papal wrath; the latter retain the favors of the Vatican but risk prison terms or deportation and must therefore emigrate or go into hiding in order to escape such martyrdom.[23]

A full-fledged war now rages between the French State and the Church, which places the Church firmly on the side of the counter-revolution. In the pope's own words, the French Revolution is "fighting against the Catholic faith and the obedience that the people owe to their king." The revolution as a whole is condemned as a "heresy" against which a war—a holy war, a crusade—must be organized. Conversely, the revo-

---

22 Mayer, p. 421; Coquard, p. 89.
23 Mayer., pp. 422-24.

lution becomes more and more anticlerical, even anti-Christian and anti-religious. On October 5, 1793, for example, the Christian calendar is replaced by a republican calendar. Churches and monasteries are closed, sold publicly, and often demolished and quarried, with their stones and timber recycled as building materials. Relics like those collected by Saint Louis and kept in the Sainte-Chapelle, are burned or discarded. Bells are removed from the bell towers and melted down to make cannons. Christian names of streets and squares are changed. Children are no longer given Christian names, but *bona fide* "republican" names such as Brutus. The constitutional priests are encouraged to get married or simply to resign, and many of them do so.[24]

This "de-Christianization process" accelerates during the summer of 1792, with measures such as the suppression of the remaining monastic orders, the prohibition of religious processions, and the legalization of divorce; in short, a rigorous secularisation of the state and of society. de-Christianization reaches its highest point (or lowest point, depending on one's view) when, on November 10, 1793, in Notre-Dame, renamed the "Temple of Reason," a cult is organized in honor of the "goddess of Reason." The attendees gather around an "altar of philosophy," decorated with busts of Voltaire and Rousseau, and sing hymns to freedom. The goddess of Reason even appears on stage in the person of a famous opera singer! A few days later, on November 23, 1793, all the churches in Paris are closed.[25]

The intention is to replace Christianity with a new revolutionary kind of religion, but this endeavour meets with precious little success, especially outside of Paris. de-Christianization is an initiative of the ultra-radical revolutionary Parisians, namely the "Hébertists," followers of one of the most racial leaders of the Cordeliers, Hébert. The greater part of the revolutionary bourgeoisie, however, and even some radicals, doubt that it is a good idea to attempt to suppress religious feeling in the French people, be it Christian or any other. Robespierre, for example, will react in his own way against de-Christianization. At the end of 1793, he will restore freedom of worship and encourage faith in God, though not necessarily the God of Catholicism. On 20 Prairial of the year II (June

---

24   *Ibid.*, pp. 430-33, 437 ff. No less than 20,000 priests resigned, see Vovelle, p. 40.

25   Tulard, pp. 257-60; Kennedy, pp. 338-44

8, 1794), he organizes a grand ceremony at the Champ-de-Mars, with the help of the artist David, in honor of an undefined Supreme Being in whom all good French people are supposed to believe.[26] However, there is not even a shadow of hope that revolutionary France, with such gestures, can appease the hostility of the Vatican.

Let us return for a moment to the theme of the confiscation of ecclesiastical property. Before the French Revolution, the Church owned vast holdings in land and other forms of wealth, not only in France but in all the Catholic countries. This was especially the case in areas ruled by the Habsburgs, now Austria, the Czech Republic, Slovakia, Hungary, Croatia, and much of Poland. That situation remained unchanged until the end of the Second World War, when the new communist governments did not sell off to private interests but socialize the landed properties of the Church. With the fall of communism in Eastern Europe, however, the Church managed to repossess the lion's share of its former property. This factor undoubtedly explains why Pope John Paul II was so eager to see (liberal) democracy restored in Poland and elsewhere in Eastern Europe, while opposing democratization in Latin America where, since the time of the Spanish conquest, and thanks to that bloody conquest, the Catholic Church has owned plenty of land, something which could change with the dawn of democracy.

It is no coincidence that the Revolution was not only anticlerical but tended to be anti-religious. It is also a question of philosophy, of different world views. Like any religion, Catholicism essentially consists of a belief in immutable metaphysical truths, and it is in this sense intrinsically *conservative*. This is why the Catholic religion had been so well suited to the framework of the Ancien Régime: it taught that the world was the way it was because it was God's creation and God wanted it to be that way. In terms of the existing order, the key word was "amen," that is, "so be it." Conversely, wanting to change the established order was considered a sin. Christianity in general is in that sense *fatalistic*, a characteristic that is generally attributed to Islam. The philosophical temperament of the revolutionaries, on the other hand, was *voluntarist*, unwilling to resign itself to the existing order of things. The French revolutionaries believed that the existing order was bad, had to change, and could be changed.

---

26   Hazan (2014), pp. 318-23; Mayer, pp. 441-44; Vovelle, p. 41; Guillemin, pp. 107-10.

The Catholic religion calls on its believers to devote little or no attention to their own fate in this "valley of tears" that is the earth, but to focus instead on the Hereafter, where either bliss or damnation awaits them. In other words, like many other religions, Christianity preaches *passivity* on a social and political level, which, of course, does not mean that every Christian will bravely follow this path. The revolution, on the other hand, called for action, the revolutionaries clearly had an *activist* outlook on life, on the world. While the "religions of salvation," such as Christianity, asked each *individual* believer to focus on the *beyond*, the revolution was a *collective* effort to improve the lives of people *here and now*.

The Revolution was, in this way, a Prometheus, who, because of his "hubris," was doomed to arouse the wrath of the "Christian" Jupiter. It therefore does not surprise us that the French revolutionaries—followed by others—would turn away from Catholicism, Christianity, and religion in general. They would gravitate towards deism, a vague faith in a higher being (as with Robespierre), and seek alternatives such as worship of the goddess of Reason (like Hébert), or move even further towards agnosticism and, finally—like Marx—atheism. Conversely, religiosity, and particularly Christian religiosity, has always flourished in a counter-revolutionary context. Religiousness regressed where and when the revolution triumphed, as in France, and it similarly flourished together with the counter-revolution, for example France, Spain, and Chile under, respectively, Pétain, Franco, and Pinochet, without exception personalities who enjoyed the favors and blessings of the Vatican.

The sale of ecclesiastical possessions is confidently expected to restore the state's financial health. The Constituent Assembly therefore considers that the state can afford to offer a tax break to—and thus to appease—the common people and, above all, the restless Parisian populace. It is decided to do away with the import duties levied on goods brought into the capital. One of the most important of these goods is wine, almost as essential to ordinary Parisians as bread. The importance of bread and wine in pre- and even proto-industrial European societies such as France at the end of the 18th century has already been emphasized. In Paris, the shortages and costliness of bread spurred resentment against the monarchy, fueled popular discontent, and thus contributed to the outbreak of the Revolution. But the high price of wine—typical, as in the case of bread, of the "*soudure*," the lean period between June and October when the produce of the previous harvest begins to run out—also plays a role, especially in the cities encircled by a tax wall—Paris, of course, but also Lyon. In fact, Parisian women and men of the lower classes, for whom the high cost of wine in the city is much more painful than for well-to-do burghers, attacked and sacked some of the tollgates where the hated duty on wine was collected even before they stormed the Bastille, namely as early as the evening of July 10.

Hoping to appease the Parisian demos, the Constituent Assembly in February 1791 approves the abolition of the import duties on goods imported into the capital. A few months later, on May 1, 1791, that decision is implemented. On that day, exactly at midnight, hundreds of wagons loaded with barrels of wine and brandy, accompanied by an exuberant crowd, enter unhindered at the tollgates. The demolition of the customs wall around the capital begins.[27] The Revolution had been made by the wine-loving Parisians, and by providing them with inexpensive wine, the Revolution turned the Parisians into even more enthusiastic revolutionaries.[28]

The "little people" had always preferred the cheap white wine that was traditionally served in the *guinguettes*, the popular taverns located just outside the Parisian tax wall, but that was to change during, and because of, the Revolution. "Red wine," writes a French historian,

[a]ssociated with the revolutionary red, one of the three colors of the national flag, now supplants white wine, whose color has been connected since time immemorial with the monarchy. Red wine will flow freely during republican feasts, when the urban authorities will crack open barrels full of *vin rouge* for the enjoyment of the citizens. The red wine of the ordinary people is promoted to the rank of an egalitarian, republican, and patriotic drink.[29]

The frequent enjoyment of a *coup de rouge*, a glass of ordinary and inexpensive red wine, often as early as mid-morning will become a privilege enjoyed by the French working class for many years to come.

In 1792, France will adopt a national anthem known as the *Marseillaise*, about which more will be said later. It would inspire wine-loving

---

27 Garrier, pp. 140-46; Plack (2012), pp. 5, 11-12.
28 Nicolas, pp. 166-67; Plack (2012), p. 14.
29 Garrier, p. 140-46.

revolutionaries to create a version of their own, entitled *La Marseillaise du buveur*, "The Marseillaise of the Drinker"[30]:

Allons, enfants de la Courtille,	Come, children of the Courtille,
Le jour de boire est arrivé.	The day to drink has come.
C'est pour nous que le boudin grille,	The sausage sizzles for us,
C'est pour nous qu'on l'a préparé.	For us, it's been prepared.
Ne sent-on pas dans la cuisine	Can you smell it from the kitchen
Rôtir and dindons and gigots;	Roasts, and turkeys and legs of lamb;
Ma foi, nous serions bien nigauds,	My word, we'd be foolish,
Si nous leur faisions triste mine.	If we pulled long, sad faces.
À table, citoyens, videz tous les flacons;	Come to table, citizens, empty the flasks;
Buvez, buvez, qu'un vin bien pur abreuve	Drink, drink, let a pure wine refresh
vos poumons	your lungs

An Excursion to Varennes

Since the time of the French Revolution, most crowned heads of Europe have learned to adapt to the role of constitutional monarch. After all, it is hardly unpleasant to be destined from birth to play the role of head of state, live in a palace, cut ribbons, etc.; most people can only dream of such an existence. But Louis XVI will have none of it. He is still convinced that divine providence has predestined him, like all his ancestors, to reign over his subjects as an absolute monarch—or at least as absolute as possible. He is also quite annoyed that many of his noble peers have lost their titles, their chateaux and landed property, and have fled the country, hoping of course to be able to return once the French people have gotten over their fit of revolutionary delusion. Finally, the devout king is especially distraught about the revolutionaries' treatment of the Catholic Church, an institution of which the king of France is supposed to act as lord protector. It is therefore no surprise that, as the revolutionaries will later discover, he corresponds in secret with emigrated noblemen and with other European monarchs about the possibility of waging a kind of holy war against revolutionary France. By means of such a crusade, called for by the pope, the God-given social order is to be restored, an order in which everyone knows, and accepts, her or his predestined place. Under these circumstances, the royal family, assisted by a handful of loyal

---

30 Quoted in Garrier, p. 145. La Courtille, mentioned in this song, was a district just outside the Parisian tax wall which featured many wine taverns known as *guinguettes*.

and trusted court dignitaries, hatches a plan to escape the revolutionary cauldron of Paris and "emigrate" from France like countless aristocrats have already done. Thus begins to unfold the dramatic scenario of "That Night in Varennes," to borrow the title of a brilliant 1980s film based on these events.[31]

It is already late in the evening of June 20, 1791, and we find ourselves in the labyrinth of houses and streets filling the space that will some day become the interior courtyard of the Louvre, between IM Pei's pyramid, erected in 1989, and the small Arc de Triomphe du Carrousel, surrounded by a kind of "dusty steppe."[32] In the dark and narrow Rue de l'Échelle, an impressive carriage, known as a *berline* (sedan), waits for the royal family and those few trusted persons who will take part in the secret mission. To avoid attracting attention, they leave the Tuileries palace in disguise one at a time. Queen Marie-Antoinette is the last, she arrives fifteen minutes late. With everyone settled into the carriage, they set off into the darkness of night.

The destination is the fortress town of Montmédy, held by troops known to be loyal to the king, and located at a stone's throw of the border with the country that will eventually become Belgium. But in the 18th century this land is known as the Austrian Netherlands since it belongs to the Habsburg Empire, the homeland of Queen Marie-Antoinette. Austrian troops have already been concentrated in or near Montmédy for the protection of the king, if and when he arrives, and possibly to be used to march on Paris and restore the Ancien Régime. A shorter and more direct northerly route is avoided, since the border agents there are likely to be more vigilant. Just beyond the town of Châlons, in the village of Sainte Ménehould, the king is recognized by the postmaster, and in the next village, Varennes, 50 km from the safety of Montmédy, the trips comes to an end, While changing horses at an inn, the royals are arrested by zealous local revolutionaries.

It takes some time to organize the royal family's return to Paris, and the journey itself, a humiliating experience, starts on June 23 and will

---

31 *That Night in Varennes* (1982) was a French-Italian production directed by Ettore Scola, and starring Marcello Mastroianni, Harvey Keitel, Hanna Schygulla, Jean-Claude Brialy, and Jean-Louis Trintignant.

32 Hazan (2002), p. 43.

take a few days. The carriage is escorted by a military contingent and orders are given to allow neither displays of sympathy or contempt. The overnights involve very simple accommodations and meals. Arriving on the outskirts at the capital on June 26, it is decided to make a long detour around the city in order to avoid the eastern districts, mostly inhabited by sans-culottes who may be expected to be in a nasty mood. Bypassing the city center via the "new boulevards"—later to become boulevards de La Chapelle, Rochechouart, Clichy, etc.—located to the north, allows for the capital to be entered from the West. This happens at the Roule tollgate, located at what is to become the Place des Ternes. close to the site where the Arc de Triomphe will rise. Via the Champs-Élysées and Place Louis XV, the royal family heads for the Tuileries Palace. Countless Parisians have come out to watch. An eyewitness will leave the following description:

> The rooftops of the houses were bristling with men, women, and children, and so were the roofs of the tollgates; the trees were also full of people. And none of the spectators took their hat off [at the king's passage]. A majestic silence prevailed.[33]

Upon arrival at the Tuileries, however, the royal party is almost lynched by an angry mob as they get out of their carriage to enter the building that will not be their home much longer.[34]

With this inglorious attempt to flee the country, Louis has clearly shown that he will not settle for the compromise of a constitutional monarchy, which the Constituent Assembly has spent much time hammering out. He thus forfeits whatever goodwill he still enjoyed among the sans-culottes and the radical revolutionary bourgeoisie. The Jacobins and the Cordeliers now loudly demand his abdication, the abolition of the monarchy, and the establishment of a republic. In the Constituent Assembly, however, a majority continues to oppose such radical change, which would sound the death knell for any hopes to establish a constitutional monarchy.

This need to calm the revolutionary zeal must be viewed in a broader context. The bourgeoisie wants to replace the Ancien-Régime state, a regime that favors the nobility and clergy, with a state that is at the service

---

33   Quotation from Tulard, p. 172.
34   Miquel, pp. 300-04; Tulard, pp. 165-72.

of the bourgeoisie; this objective has in fact been achieved thanks to the elimination of the nobility, the plundering of the assets of the Church, and the subordination of the executive power, still in the hands of the king, to the legislative branch of the government, that is, the Assembly, dominated by the bourgeoisie. More far-reaching revolutionary changes are no longer necessary and are considered risky. As far as the bourgeoisie is concerned, it is now essential to consolidate its newly achieved position of power by crafting a constitution and promulgating laws that favor its cause.

Many members of the bourgeoisie within and without the assembly are henceforth far less fearful of their upper-class political opponents, the king, the nobility, and the clergy, than of those folks whose revolutionary deeds enabled the bourgeoisie to vanquish the champions of the Ancien Régime, namely the lower-class Parisians, especially the sans-culottes. Seen from the perspective of the well-to-do burghers, the sans-culottes are the capital's "populace," a dangerous lot on account of their expectations and demands, unpredictable behavior, energy, and newfound self-confidence. This is why, immediately after the storming of the Bastille, a censitary suffrage had been introduced, which means that only wealthy citizens can vote in elections for the Parisian Commune. On August 27, 1791, the Constituent Assembly decides to apply this system for all elections throughout France.

In addition, the bourgeois deputies who form the majority of the Constituent Assembly are in favor of laissez-faire ideas. This ideology, known as liberalism, reflects and suits their outlook. Implementing these ideas would benefit the entire nation, or so they firmly believe, but in reality it is primarily to the advantage of the bourgeoisie that the theory and practice of liberal notions happens to function, notions such as political freedom, economic freedom, free markets, free competition, and also the "freedom" of work, that is, the freedom for anyone to work, and conversely, the freedom to hire anyone to work.

From a liberal point of view, a limitation of this freedom is embodied by the guilds, the associations of craftsmen dating back to the Middle Ages, and by what will later be called "unions," that is, workers' associations. This is the rationale used to categorically prohibit such associations, which is done by means of a law promulgated on June 14, 1791 and named after the Breton lawyer who sponsored it, Le Chapelier. This piece of legislation also prohibits strikes, the primary weapon of workers' associations during conflicts with employers. This law will only be rescinded much later, and little by little, namely in 1864, 1884, and 1901.

It is obvious that in the Constituent Assembly, a majority is firmly determined to neutralize the mass of workers and other plebeians politically, not only in Paris, but in all of France, to subjugate it economically, and to repress its revolutionary energy now that this energy is no longer needed by a bourgeoisie whose revolutionary goals have essentially been achieved. For these moderate revolutionaries, the monarch remains useful as a counterweight to the growing threat perceived to be emanating from "those below," from the "dangerous classes." This is the reason why they stubbornly cling to the compromise of a constitutional monarchy, even though the king himself has displayed his aversion to such an arrangement with his flight to Varennes. Conversely, the sans-culottes, as well as the bourgeoisie's radical faction in the Assembly, who take the side of the little people, realize that the king presents a major obstacle to the progress of the revolution.

Thus we can understand why the Constituent Assembly decides, on July 16, 1791, to officially forgive Louis for the *"faux pas"* he committed with his escapade. This absolution is rationalized by means of the fiction, presumably concocted by Lafayette, that the king and his family were "kidnapped" and taken to Varennes. The revolutionary Parisians do not buy this story, however, and already the next day, on July 17, no less than 50,000 sans-culottes gather at the Champ de Mars to demonstrate against the decision of the Constituent Assembly, and at the same time, to express their discontent about unemployment, high prices and low wages. The authorities have no intention of making concessions: they declare a state of emergency and, under the leadership of Lafayette, the National Guard—made up exclusively of "active citizens," that is, members of the well-to-do bourgeoisie—sets out to restore order. The Guard raises a red flag as a warning that it is ready to use violence. But the demonstrators refuse to be intimidated; shots are fired, and around fifty are killed. According to the terse report of an eyewitness, "they shot workers like chickens."[35]

---

35 Quoted in Rudé, p. 89.

From this moment, the common people consider the red flag not only as the "flag of the carnage," as the "bloody symbol of bourgeois repression," to quote Jean Jaurès, but also as the symbol of the class struggle between the bourgeoisie and the demos, the two classes that had previously fought as allies—as one "Third Estate"—against a common class enemy, the tandem of nobility and clergy. Red will thus become the color of *le peuple laborieux*, the "working people," and the red flag will serve as the banner used by the working class to demonstrate its strength against the bourgeoisie, just as the bourgeoisie itself, embodied by the National Guard, had purported to show its power over the people at the Champ de Mars.

The Cordeliers take the lead in adopting the color red, and they do so by ostentatiously wearing red bonnets made of wool, of course, like all head coverings worn by the common people. Rightly or wrongly, these "Phrygian" caps are believed to have been worn by Ancient Greek and Roman slaves who had gained their freedom; they are therefore considered a symbol of liberty and opposition to any form of oppression.[36] With respect to flags, the sans-culottes remain faithful to the "blue-white-red," the tricolore which, already in the summer of 1789, symbolized their strength and the strength of the revolutionaries in general, including the bourgeoisie.[37]

Within the bourgeoisie, and especially within the petty bourgeoisie of the capital, there exists a minority of radical elements, namely the Jacobins and the Cordeliers, who continue to consider the combination of king, nobility, and clergy as the greatest threat. That does not mean that they identify with the sans-culottes and other common people, but in the conflict against the classes representing the Ancien Régime, an enemy not yet totally eliminated, they consider the sans-culottes as a useful, even indispensable partner. Following the example of the Third Estate in its struggle against the nobility and clergy, the Jacobins and the Cordeliers find a useful ally in the Parisian populace which, at this moment in time, is again becoming disgruntled and restless because of unemployment, shortages, and price increases, especially the price of bread.

In the Constituent Assembly, the petty-bourgeois radical revolu-

---

36   Soboul (1968), pp. 209-10.
37   Dommanget, pp. 23-29.

tionaries will harness the horse of the sans-culotterie to their cart in order to be able to impose their will against the revolutionary moderates, belonging to the well-to-do bourgeoisie and embodied by the Feuillants, who are in favor of maintaining the monarchy. The two radical clubs are starting not only to accept sans-culottes as members, but also to support the demands of the Parisian populace, and even to encourage them to demand higher wages and lower prices. The Champ de Mars demonstration, for example, was an initiative of the Cordeliers club.

For the time being, the (relatively) conservative burghers continue to command a majority in the Constituent Assembly and remain in control. They forge a new liberal constitution that officially transforms France into a constitutional monarchy. Maintaining the monarchy in this form reflects the hope of the bourgeoisie, writes Jean Suret-Canale "to be able to use royal power as a bulwark against pressure from the people."[38] The censitary suffrage, introduced in August 1791, plays a similar role. On September 14, 1791, Louis XVI meekly swears loyalty to this constitution, and on September 30, the Constituent Assembly officially declares that its task is accomplished. It is replaced by a Legislative Assembly, which meets for the first time the next day, on October 1. The conservative Feuillants are in the majority and therefore form the government. From their point of view, and for the bourgeoisie in general, the revolution is over. "They were optimistic," writes Annie Jourdan,

> ... they indulged in the illusionary thought that the revolution was indeed over. They felt that this was the optimal solution for France. The constitution had established great principles and henceforth, thanks to liberty, equality, and justice, everybody in the country would be happy. Continuing the revolution made no sense, as the abolition of the (constitutional) monarchy and the principle of private property would cause the country to descend into anarchy.[39]

Numerous historians, for example François Furet and Denis Richet, view things the same way. They believe that it would have been better if that 1791 constitution would have put an end to the revolutionary process set in motion in 1789. and that the revolutionary events that were to follow in the years 1792-1793 amounted to a tragic "mishap" (*dérapage*), one they blame on the Jacobins.[40] However, the Feuillants were deeply

---

38   Suret-Canale, p. 84.
39   Jourdan, p. 290.
40   Hartig, p. 10; Vovelle, pp. 25, 66-67. Furet and Richet formulated their the-

mistaken. The Revolution did not end in 1791, as Furet would have preferred it to do; it had barely started.

ory of the "derailment" of the French Revolution in a book published in 1965, *La Révolution française*.

5. 1792: From Monarchy to Republic

Red Wine and Blood in the Tuileries

After Varennes, great tension arises between the revolutionaries in Paris and the crowned heads of Europe. The latter worry greatly not only about the fate of Louis and his family—relations, via Marie-Antoinette, of the Habsburg emperor in Vienna—but even more about the anti-monarchical, anti-aristocratic, and anticlerical precedent being set in France, which, from their point of view, constitutes a nefarious example that may well be imitated in other countries. Furthermore, in Vienna, Berlin, and elsewhere, the émigrés, the aristocrats who have fled from France, are agitating in favor of an international crusade against revolutionary France, with as objective nothing less than the restoration of the Ancien Régime in their homeland.

In France itself, in mid-March 1792, the Girondins come to power. This is a group of politicians mainly composed of merchants and other businessmen and, as already mentioned, their hard core consists of gentlemen from Bordeaux, the seaport whose citizens are known as Girondins.[1] For a number of reasons, the Girondins yearn for a war, that is, a "continental" war, with as prime adversary the Habsburg Empire. But they oppose a war at sea, that is, a conflict against Britain, because that would constitute a threat to the trade, especially the very lucrative slave

---

1 The Gironde is the great estuary that is formed near Bordeaux by the confluence of the Garonne and Dordogne rivers and connects Bordeaux, in reality situated on the banks of the Garonne, to the sea.

trade, of Bordeaux, Nantes, and other seaports. Moreover, they firmly believe that revolutionary France has a universal mission, that it is predestined to reshape the rest of the world in its own image. Exasperated by the intrigues of the émigrés, they also hope to settle the account of these exiled counter-revolutionary diehards once and for all. A war is also expected to provide them an opportunity to deal harshly with the king and all those considered not to be unconditional supporters of the new revolutionary France. With a war, it will be possible to brand all the counter-revolutionaries as traitors to the fatherland and to treat them accordingly. In addition, it is hoped that a war of conquest will bring in money. Indeed, once again, the state coffers are empty and it is urgent to repay funds borrowed from the type of well-to-do burghers of whom the Girondins are the representatives.

Last but not least, the war strategy of the Girondins—representatives of the upper bourgeoisie throughout France—is also directed against the Parisian sans-culottes. The latter are once again restless and rebellious on account of high prices, particular for sugar and other foodstuffs. With a war, the energy of the Parisian populace can be directed into new channels, that is, diverted towards foreign foes, and the "plebeian youth, spearhead of a social revolution," can be physically removed from the capital, the revolutionary arena where the sans-culottes enjoy the "home-field" advantage.[2] Jacques Pierre Brissot, the leader of the bellicose Girondins, remarks in this context that a conflict against foreign enemies is necessary to restore peace in France itself, in other words, to neutralize the conflict between French people. "War," he proclaims, "is indispensable for the return of domestic peace in France."[3]

The radical elements, on the other hand, the Jacobins and the Cordeliers, are opposed to war. Why? They not only want to prioritize the pursuit of revolution in their own country, they also doubt that French soldiers will be welcomed abroad as liberators. Robespierre, for example, vainly warns that "no one likes armed missionaries." Even the king and the counter-revolutionaries in general yearn for a war, but for an entirely different reason. They wish for—and confidently expect—that the revolutionaries will be defeated, so that it will be possible to restore the An-

---

2   Guillemin, pp. 48, 83-84.
3   Jourdan, p. 47.

cien Régime.

The idea of a war against the crowned heads of Europe in defence of the revolution and against the counter-revolution, arouses great enthusiasm in Paris and in the rest of France. The bellicose enthusiasm of the French revolutionaries is stirred mightily by the lyrics of a song, the *Chant de guerre pour l'armée du Rhin*, "War Song for the Army of the Rhine." This ode to revolutionary war has been composed in Strasbourg by a certain Claude Joseph Rouget de Lisle in April 1792, within days after the Girondins' declaration of war against Austria. It conquers the hearts of the Parisians on July 30 of the same year, when a troop of volunteers from Marseille sings it loudly during a demonstration near the Tuileries Palace. Thus it becomes known as the "song [of the men] of Marseille," the *Marseillaise*.

Allons enfants de la Patrie,	Rise, children of the fatherland,
Le jour de gloire est arrivé!	The day of glory has arrived!
Contre nous de la tyrannie,	Against us tyranny's
L'étendard sanglant est levé,	Bloody standard is raised
Entendez-vous dans les campagnes	Listen to the sound in the fields
Mugir ces féroces soldats?	The howling of these fearsome soldiers
Ils viennent jusque dans vos bras	They are coming into our midst
Égorger vos fils, vos compagnes!	To cut the throats of your sons and consorts
Aux armes, citoyens,	To arms, citizens
Formez vos bataillons,	Form your battalions
Marchons, marchons!	March, march
Qu'un sang impur	Let impure blood
Abreuve nos sillons!	Water our furrows![4]

Other revolutionary songs also prove to be big hits. Some of these chants are less bloodthirsty, while others target the domestic, rather than the foreign enemy, for example *La Carmagnole*[5] and the very popular *Ah! Ça ira!* ("Ah! It will be fine!"), which aims squarely at the nobility:

'Ah! Ça ira, ça ira, ça ira,	Ah! It will be fine! It will be fine! It will be fine!
Les aristocrates à la lanterne!	The aristocrats to the lantern
Ah! Ça ira, ça ira, ça ira,	Ah! It will be fine! It will be fine! It will be fine,
Les aristocrates on les pendra!'	The aristocrats, we will hang them![6]

The *Marseillaise* will achieve national anthem status on July 14, 1795,

---

4   http://marseillaise.org/english/english.html
5   'Carmagnole.'
6   https://lyricstranslate.com/en/ca-ira-it-will-be-fine.html.

after the Revolution will have entered a far less radical phase; we will return to this theme later. It will have to surrender its crown twice, during the Restoration and during the Second Empire, but it will become the French national anthem again in 1870, shortly after the establishment of the Third Republic, to remain so until the present day. The *Marseillaise*'s title, lyrics, and melody will also serve as a model for numerous other national anthems, such as the Belgian *Brabançonne*. And it will be sung with enthusiasm by other revolutionaries, for example, by Russians in 1917. A lovely allegorical representation of the *Marseillaise*, sculpted by François Rude, can be admired in Paris on the front of the Arc de Triomphe.

Meanwhile, in Paris, the latent conflict within the former Third Estate, between the well-to-do bourgeoisie exemplified by the Girondins and their radical opponents, the mostly petit-bourgeois Jacobins, who cater to the sans-culottes, keeps festering. The former are happy with the state of affairs, anchored in the 1791 Constitution and the new political system, the constitutional monarchy. But the Parisian common people are not at all satisfied. What particularly bothers them is the fact that the king enjoys the right of veto and that "Mr. Veto" uses it to quash any decisions of the Assembly that he considers too radical. This royal obstructionism causes the anti-monarchist ire of the sans-culottes to flare up again and, on June 20, 1792, lead to a demonstration during which the crowd manages to penetrate into the Tuileries Palace through a side entrance. They burst into the king's apartment, stick a Cordeliers-style Phrygian bonnet on his head, and shove a glass of wine in his hand.

This occurrence might seem like nothing more than a picturesque vignette, but it has an important symbolic meaning: it demonstrates that everything has changed, that royal absolutism and the entire Ancien Régime are a thing of the past. The sans-culottes gleefully perform a parody of the royal audiences of old, during which attendees would respectfully parade one by one before the sovereign. But this time, instead of behaving with respect and according to protocol, the visitors physically touch the king and shout revolutionary slogans like "Tremble, tyrants!" in his ears. In the past, it was a custom to offer wine in honour of the monarch, and this *vin d'honneur* was drunk to his good health and prosperity. Now, everything is turned on its head, the roles have been reversed. The king is forced to drink to the health of the people, which henceforth considers itself the nation's sovereign, while he is the people's "subject"! It is also not a coincidence that the wine he is made to drink is red wine, as can be seen on a contemporary painting of the event. A few years earlier, during a visit to Paris City Hall following the storming of the Bastille, Louis had offered white wine for the people to drink to his health. The change can be explained by the fact that colors have great symbolic power. Red, already the color of revolutionary flags and caps, contrasts mightily with white, the traditional color of the monarchy and of the powdered faces, wigs, and silk stockings of the nobility, but also of the black clothes typically worn by well-to-do burghers.[7]

The aggression remains vocal, rather than physical, however, and everything ends fairly peacefully with the withdrawal of the unwanted plebeian visitors.[8] But among the common people, resentment against the king—formerly acclaimed as "our good king"—and against monarchs in general, will not stop growing. It is fueled by rumors about royalist conspiracies and by the seditious rhetoric of the Cordeliers and the Jacobins, who are increasingly agitating for the abdication of Louis, the abolition of the monarchy, and the establishment of a republican state.

In the meantime, the war is not going as planned. The enemy invades France and, on July 11 1972, the Assembly finds it necessary to officially proclaim what everybody already knows, namely, that "The fatherland is in danger!" Volunteers are asked to report to a recruitment office located at the Pont Neuf, in front of the statue of Henry IV. And countless sans-culottes, especially young people, thus leave Paris to join the army. On August 1, the capital receives the news that the commander of the enemy troops, the Duke of Brunswick, has threatened Paris with nothing less than total destruction if even a single hair from the royal wig is disturbed. This confirms the sans-culottes and all other dedicated revolutionaries in their belief that the king conspires with the enemies of the nation, so that the country can only be saved if Louis is eliminated.[9]

The Tuileries Palace will thus witness a second eruption of anti-royalist anger on August 10, and this time it will be a bloody affair, a massacre. Unsurprisingly, the trouble starts in the Faubourg Saint-Antoine, where the bells sound the alarm again, a crowd gathers and undertakes

---

7 Miquel, pp. 441-42.
8 Rudé, p. 100.
9 Coquard, p. 128.

the already traditional trek to the Hôtel de Ville, the hotbed of popular radicalism, embodied by the sans-culottes and the Jacobins. An armed band gathers, with no less than 20,000 men and women, mostly Parisian sans-culottes, but also what are called *fédérés* ("federates"), contingents of revolutionaries from cities like Brest and Marseille that are "federated," that is, allied, to the Parisians. They trek from city hall to the Tuileries, that is, from the architectonic symbol of popular power to that of its royal counterpart. Waving red flags show that the sovereign people is taking action against the "rebellious" executive power, the monarch. Upon arrival at the palace, the crowd loudly demands *déchéance*, "abdication"!

The "little people" thus give the royal Louis a sort of "red card," because they believe that the king's actions are disloyal so that he should no longer be allowed to perform his political task. On this day, the red flag becomes a symbol of the power of the common people, the Parisian sans-culottes, but the tricolor flag also remains important and popular. The troops of Marseilles, for example, carry a tricolor flag with a red bonnet on top. The tricolor—in the form of a flag or cockade—remains the emblem of choice of the Jacobins. When they will come to power in 1793, they will even make it compulsory to wear the tricolor cockade. The sans-culottes continue to favor the red color, but generally in the form of a bonnet rather than a flag. In fact, for the time being, the red flag will no longer be used by the revolutionaries, it will only reappear during the revolution of 1848 to become the revolutionary emblem par excellence in France and all over the world.[10]

The entrance to the Tuileries Palace is located on what will later be the Place du Carrousel. The name "Place du Carrousel" recalls the celebration of the birth of Louis XIV's first child in 1662, when a carousel happened to the main attraction. The palace is defended by the king's personal guard, some 900 men strong, and composed, like the Papal guards, of Swiss mercenaries. Fearing an encore of the humiliating events of June 20 or something even more unpleasant, the royal family flees from the rear entrance of the palace into the Tuileries Garden, passes the pond known as the "Grand Bassin," and ascends thirteen wide steps—steps which still exist today—connecting the gardens to the terrace of the Feuillants convent. The royals thus reach the Manège, where they find protection from

---

10   Dommanget, pp. 31-33.

the deputies. Numerous sans-culottes witness their escape and insult the king by shouting "*À bas le gros cochon!*" ("Down with the fat pig!"). The young Napoleon Bonaparte was reportedly present and made an unflattering, even quite vulgar remark about the king.[11]

IMAGE 14. Manège des Tuileries.[12]

In the meantime, the sans-culottes try in vain to fraternize with the Swiss guard, and suddenly the latter respond by opening fire. A veritable battle thus breaks, during which some four hundred attackers are killed. Approximately six hundred Swiss also lose their lives, either during the fighting or after their surrender, because most of the wounded are simply executed. In addition, a number of captured Swiss Guard officers will be found guilty and sentenced to death for giving the order to fire. They will

---

11   Poisson, pp. 13, 64-65.

12   Source: https://marais-louvre.fr/petite-histoire-de-la-salle-du-manege-des-tuileries

be guillotined on the Place du Carrousel, at the very scene of their alleged crime. In Lucerne, an impressive monument featuring a dying lion recalls these Swiss victims of revolutionary French violence.

Unfortunately for the numerous supporters of a constitutional monarchy, the experiment with such a revolutionary compromise had degenerated into a power struggle between the legislative and executive branches of government, between the National Assembly and the king. Because of the dramatic intervention of the sans-culottes, this conflict ends to the advantage of the former. Henceforth, the Assembly no longer has to take into account the executive power as represented by the king. Of the power of the monarch, who was once all-powerful in a state he viewed as his personal property—*L'État, c'est moi!*—nothing is left.

On the other hand, the deputies must now take the Paris Commune into consideration, where the Jacobins and the Cordeliers are very influential, and which had orchestrated the attack on the Tuileries. They must also consider the Parisian "mob" itself, that is, the armed sans-culottes who, on August 10, have demonstrated all too clearly what they are capable of. Furthermore, the sans-culottes will soon start to dominate the meetings of the Parisian sections as, one after the other, these remove the distinction between "active" and "passive" citizens, thus abandoning the censitary suffrage system. Hitherto monopolized by the wealthy citizens, the sections gradually fall into the hands of the ordinary people. Finally, increasing numbers of sans-culottes are now admitted into the ranks of the National Guard.[13]

The deputies of the Assembly, who are almost exclusively *gens de bien*, "people of property," must now take into account the political force of *gens de rien*, the "people who have nothing." For the time being, they have no other option but to make concessions, for example regarding the fate of the king. The latter is despised by sans-culottes, who publicly denigrate him as "Louis the traitor" or "Louis the Last." What is to become of him? For the time being, the Assembly keeps him under its protection, installing him for a few days in the Feuillants monastery. As was the case after his escapade to Varennes, he is treated with kid gloves: the plan is to "punish" him by placing him under house arrest at the Luxembourg palace. However, speaking on behalf of the sans-culottes, the Commune

---

13   Soboul (1968), pp. 160-61.

demands and obtains the incarceration of the entire royal family—as prisoners of the Parisian people—in an austere jail, an old fortress known as Le Temple, which will be described soon. On August 13, the royal family is transferred there.[14]

The Legislative Assembly must also make other, even more important concessions. On August 11, 1792, it abolishes the distinction between "active" and "passive" citizens. The date reveals that this is not done out of conviction, but out of fear: it is indeed the day after the attack against the Tuileries, the great show of force of what well-to-do burghers call the *canaille* ("rabble").[15] It is for the same reason that, on the same day, the republic is proclaimed, thus satisfying a demand voiced by the Jacobins, Cordeliers, and sans-culottes. This means the de facto end of the constitution, promulgated just one year earlier, that had transformed the French state into a constitutional monarchy. Another radical reform caters not to the big city, but to the countryside: "on August 25, seigneurial fees [are] abolished without compensation, thus satisfying a peasant demand that has remained unsatisfied since the Great Fear of 1789."[16]

The monarchy has not yet been abolished *de jure*, but *de facto* it is dead and buried. The Assembly draws the logical consequences, it dissolves itself and announces elections for a "National Convention" which must constitutionally formalize the new state of affairs. As there is no longer any class distinction between "active" and "passive" citizens, the elections are organized on the basis of universal suffrage, for men at least; women are excluded because of their supposedly "dependent" status.

As before, however, the candidates throughout France are almost exclusively members of the bourgeoisie and a majority of elected officials are either "notables" from the countryside, or wealthy citizens like the Girondins. Only two deputies are members of the working class. Paris, on the other hand, will mainly be represented at the Convention by the same radical elements that also dominate in the Commune, such as Robespierre, Danton, Marat, Desmoulins and the painter David. Robespierre has been described as being "close to the Parisians sans-culottes." So it turns out that radical Paris and the moderate countryside are taking very dif-

---

14 Guillemin, p. 71; de la Batut, vol. 1, pp. 121-22.
15 Soboul (1968), pp. 160-61.
16 De la Batut.

ferent paths.[17]

The champions of the constitutional monarchy, exemplified by the Feuillants, are most unhappy with the turn of events. One of their leaders, Lafayette, plans to march on Paris at the head of his troops to undo the changes, but the soldiers refuse to obey and he deems it prudent to flee the country.[18] We will see later that, like Lafayette himself, the constitutional monarchy will make an admittedly rather brief comeback in France, namely in 1830.

The Convention meets for the first time—still at the Manège—on September 20, 1792. The Girondins receive the support of a majority so they form the government. But the very first measure taken reflects the enormous influence exerted, right in the heart of Paris, by the Jacobins and the other revolutionary radicals who benefit from the support of the Commune and the sans-culottes. Most importantly, on September 21, the monarchy is now formally abolished and replaced by a revolutionary state, the Republic, a move certain to please—and appease—the sans-culottes. The following day will be considered the first day of year I of the Republic when, a year later, namely on October 5, 1793, a new revolutionary calendar is introduced. The months and the days will be given new names and Sunday will be replaced by a revolutionary day of rest, every ten days, the "*décadi.*" But this truly revolutionary way of marking time will never really catch on, and on January 1, 1806, Napoleon will reintroduce the Gregorian calendar.

At the end of the summer of 1792, foreign troops invade the French territory and march on Paris. It is on that occasion that Lafayette, one of the heroes of the first phase of the Revolution, but someone who has remained a monarchist at heart, flees abroad. In the gardens of the Palais-Royal, an effigy of his is burned by a thunderous crowd. More and more Parisians, above all sans-culottes, report voluntarily to join the army and depart for the front to defend the fatherland in its hour of danger. In the capital, a "great fear" suddenly breaks out, triggered by sinister rumours of a "conspiracy of the prisoners" (*complot des prisons*). Anonymous counter-revolutionaries are allegedly plotting to liberate and arm the aristocrats, priests, and other enemies of the Revolution who are

---

17   Tulard, pp. 221-22; Guillemin, pp. 94-96.
18   Hazan (2014), pp. 181-82.

being held in the Parisian prisons and can scarcely hide their joy when they learn that the Revolution is in trouble and is likely to come to an end. They are suspected of planning to massacre the wives and children of the patriots who have left for the front. "Thus is born a mass hysteria," writes the historian George Rudé, "that produces the massacres of [2 to 5] September, a kind of preventive but particularly violent cleansing of the prisons."[19]

During these September days, mobs of hundreds of bloodthirsty sans-culottes rush to the Parisian prisons, remove prisoners from the dungeons, and kill them like pigs at the slaughter, sometimes after a brief ceremony that is supposed to pass for a trial. In particular, they target priests who have been locked up because they refused to swear loyalty to the republican constitution. However, the vast majority of the victims are ordinary criminals. There is no certainty about the total number of victims. Some sources report 300 dead, others more than 1,000 or even 1,400, out of a total of 2,800 prisoners. Olivier Coquard points out that these massacres continued in the provinces, in cities like Meaux and Orléans, and that the victims numbered about 1,500 in total.[20]

On September 2, the abbey of Saint-Germain-des-Prés witnesses such a massacre. One of the buildings (long since disappeared), surrounded by thick walls with a small door as the only opening, serves as a prison. A crowd—in this case the term mob is appropriate—gathers at the entrance when, by chance, several carts appear, loaded with newly arrested priests. These unfortunates are massacred on the spot, followed by the other prisoners, who are taken one by one from their cells. The building where this massacre took place will disappear when, after the Revolution, the Boulevard Saint-Germain will be constructed; it stood behind the abbey's surviving church, in the middle of the Boulevard Saint-Germain, facing the numbers 135 and 137. Such horrible scenes—attended by numerous curious onlookers—are repeated at many other prisons, for example at the Conciergerie (which will be discussed later on), the Carmelite Convent (*les Carmes*) at rue Vaugirard, and the Salpêtrière women's prison, where the victims are mostly prostitutes.[21] The La Force Prison,

---

19   Rudé, p. 225 ; Guillemin, pp. 77-80. See also Vovelle, p. 90.

20   Coquard, p. 142.

21   Rudé, pp. 109-10; Poisson, pp. 99, 107-09, 116; Masson, p. 48.

where many noble acquaintances of the royal family are detained, also witnesses a massacre on September 2; the artist David calmly sketches the corpses as they are piling up.

During the Revolution, La Force will continue to function as a prison. Prisoners will be able to enjoy the services of a master chef who will cook delicious meals for them, possibly washed down with champagne, and even receive a visit from a wife or mistress to enjoy a few moments in private—if they can afford the high fees, that is. Before becoming a prison for women (the Petite-Force) as well as for men (the Grande-Force), only a few years before the start of the Revolution, around 1785, the building was the residence of the dukes of La Force, whose ancestor had been assassinated in another massacre, that of Saint Bartholomew's Day in 1572. All that will subsist of the prison in the 21st century will be a wall in the Rue Pavée, near the Hotel Lamoignon, where the historical library of the city of Paris will be located.[22]

In the Petite Force, out of 110 detainees, there is only one victim, the Princess of Lamballe, a lady-in-waiting of Marie-Antoinette. In the Grande Force, on the other hand, almost 170 of the approximately 400 detainees are killed. The entrance to the prison was the epicenter of the killing spree, it was located at No. 2 Rue du Roi-de-Sicile, where a plaque will recall the tragic event. The two prisons will be demolished in 1845.

The authorities of the Hôtel de Ville and in the Manège, such as Danton, who has just been appointed Minister of Justice, do not want or dare do anything to stop the slaughter. Marat and Robespierre lament it privately, but they refuse to publicly condemn the culprits. However, to avoid similar horrors in the future, people's tribunals are established to deal with the enemies of the revolution in an equally deadly but less anarchic fashion. A "cold," that is, systematic and disciplined terror, organized from above, will replace the "overboiling" (*bouillante*), anarchic and spontaneous terror from below.[23] We will return to this theme later.

The unexpected success of the French army of volunteers against the invading Austro-Prussian army on September 20 at Valmy, in Lorraine, proves to be a turning point in the war, even though it amounted to a mere skirmish, rather than a full-fledged battle. But the foreign invader

---

22 Poisson, pp. 33-35.
23 Mayer, pp. 119-20, 182-84.

has to withdraw ingloriously, the fatherland is no longer in danger, and the next morning, in Paris, the Convention proclaims the republic, thus thumping its nose at monarchical Europe, the great foreign nemesis of the Revolution. This assembly is now free to concentrate on the trial of "Louis Capet, former king [*ci-devant roi*] of France," thus called because the country's first king was called Hugues Capet. The suspended monarch stands accused of high treason.[24]

The Convention itself functions as the court, and the proceedings do not degenerate into a parody, a kind of show trial, far from it: the established legal rules are scrupulously observed.[25] The trial starts in the Manège on December 11, shortly after the discovery, in the Tuileries Palace, of an iron strongbox containing the king's very compromising secret correspondence with foreign monarchs. The proceedings will conclude on January 17, 1793, in the Tuileries Palace, henceforth to be known as the National Palace (*Palais National*), as the Convention has decided to move there from the Manège. He will be found guilty and condemned to death.[26]

Between August 1792 and January 1793, the royal family is detained in the tower of a medieval fortress, situated close to what will later become the Place de la République, looking very much like the Bastille and known as the Temple. Originally, that is, in the twelfth century, it served as the Parisian headquarters of the Knights Templar, an order of fighting monks that was liquidated by King Philippe IV le Bel, mainly in order to appropriate its vast assets. The Knights Templar owned chateaux and other fortifications known as "commanderies" just about everywhere in Europe. One stood in Berlin, namely on the spot an airport will later be built, appropriately to be called "Tempelhof," "court of the Templars," which would actually be a fine German translation for the French term "Temple." The Parisian Temple kept its name even after the dissolution of the Order of the Knights Templar, when it was taken over by another order of fighting, that is, crusading monks, the Knights of Malta. In the course of the centuries, the hull of the somber château became encrust-

---

24 Capet was the name of France's very first royal dynasty, the "Capetians," founded by Hugues Capet in 987.
25 Martin, p. 464.
26 See the comments in Mayer, pp. 184-89.

ed with barnacles in the shape of all sorts of dependencies, for example a 17th-century palace. Before the Revolution, the latter edifice was used to organize high-end receptions, dinners, and parties; the *wunderkind* Wolfgang Amadeus Mozart gave a concert there on one such occasion, hosted by Louis-François de Bourbon, a.k.a. the Prince de Conti.[27]

On the eve of the Revolution, the Temple complex was the property of the Duc d'Angoulême, a son of the Comte d'Artois, the latter a younger brother of Louis XVI who will be king himself, namely from 1824 to 1830, and rule as Charles X. But he has left the country and the edifice now belongs to the city of Paris, and the Commune decides to imprison the king there. The royal family is imprisoned not in one of the dependencies but in the keep (*donjon* in French) of the original, medieval fortress, called the "big tower" (*grosse tour*). This is a primitive and austere building, a particularly unpleasant abode, where Louis and his family will be mistreated and systematically subjected to all sorts of humiliations. This is how the situation is usually described in conventional historiography, but the reality was quite different. The royal family was provided with relatively comfortable accommodations, was treated respectfully, and received more than enough food of fine quality.[28] But it was definitely a prison, and the king was only allowed to leave it to attend his trial.

In any event, the sans-culottes are delighted with the supposedly harsh treatment meted out to the deposed monarch, "fat and brainless Louis" (*Louis sans cervelle*), and "his woman, the hypocritical and cruel Antoinette" (*sa femelle, Antoinette hypocrite et cruelle*). They gleefully express their satisfaction in this song, entitled "Punishment for Treason":

La famille sacrée	The holy family
Se sauve à, se sauve à l'assemblée.	Flees, flees to the Assembly.
Elle y fut condamnée,	There it is condemned,
De monter à la tour.	To move into the tower.
De monter à la tour,	To move into the tower,
Des fosses alentour,	Surrounded by a moat,
Madame à sa tour monte,	The lady likewise moves there,
Tout en rage et confuse de honte,	Befuddled with rage and shame,
Gros Louis se démonte.	Big Louis is embarrassed.
De se voir en prison.	To find himself in prison.
De se voir en prison,	To find himself in prison,

27 Gagneux and Prouvost, pp. 234-37.
28 Lenotre, pp. 109-10.

Et n'a-t-on pas raison?	We say it's just deserts!
De punir ce grand traître,	It is right to punish this big traitor,
Qui voulait toujours seul être maître	Who always wanted to be the sole master
Mais on lui fait connaître	But now we teach him
*Qu'il n'est plus rien du tout.*²⁹	That he is just a nobody.

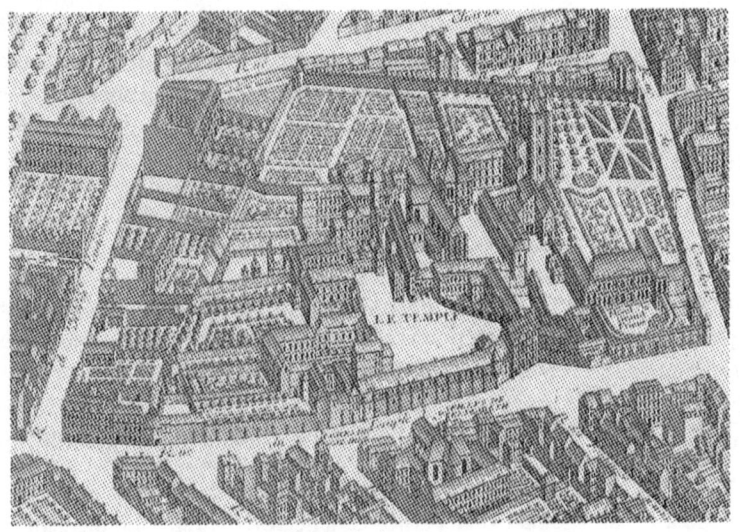

IMAGE 15. The Temple, with its high keep, on the Map of Turgot.

After the execution of Louis XV on January 21, 1793, the rest of the family will continue to languish in the Temple for quite some time. On August 1, 1793, Marie-Antoinette will be transferred to another prison, the Conciergerie. We will visit her there shortly. The little heir to the throne, the dauphin, who would have been called Louis XVII had he ever ruled, will remain alone in a dark cell. (On January 21, day of the "martyrdom" of Louis XVI, Marie-Antoinette had kneeled before her son who, as she saw it, was henceforth king.)³⁰ It is widely believed, though not certain, that the "child of the Temple" died of consumption (*phtisie*),

---

29   Lenotre, pp. 109-10.
30   Martin, p. 466.

as tuberculosis was called at the time, on June 8, 1795, and was buried two days later, without any religious or other ceremony, in a common grave in the cemetery of the parish to which the Temple belonged, that is, that of the Sainte Marguerite Church, situated at number 36 of the Rue Saint-Bernard, not far from Place de la Bastille. In 1894, a modest tombstone featuring a cross will be installed on a site where human remains are found, and a commemorative plaque will be affixed to the wall of the church. A physician who performed the autopsy kept the boy's heart, and it was discovered some years ago. DNA tests proved its authenticity, so the heart was placed in an urn and deposited in the former royal pantheon in the Basilica of Saint Denis.[31]

Republicanizing France, Deroyalizing Paris

The proclamation of the Republic in the late summer of 1792 triggers a process that may be described as a "deroyalization" of France that is simultaneously a "republicanization" and may also be described as a "revolutionization." It is a process that will take a lot of time and will experience progress as well as retrogression; and it is also a complex, multifaceted process.

First of all, the fact that France is henceforth a republic has iconographic implications. The royal fleur-de-lis disappear from public buildings, making way for republican symbols such as the initials R.F., "*République française*," and of course the famous motto "Liberty, Equality, Fraternity" (*Liberté, Égalité, Fraternité*). The white and/or blue flags of royal France are gone, replaced by the tricolore, which becomes the flag of the Republic even though it actually conjures up the constitutional monarchy, as we have seen earlier. The Republic had been able to opt for the red flag, but that was the color of revolutionary radicals, the revolution of the "little people," above all the restless Parisian demos. The Girondins and other bourgeois revolutionaries, who had been happy with a constitutional monarchy and were determined to slow down or even arrest the revolutionary momentum, have managed to prevent the use of the red flag.

In French, the name France is feminine, and it is therefore logical

---

31   Fraser, pp. 444, 446; Poisson, p. 18.

that the country is allegorically represented by a woman.[32] The France of the Ancien Régime was thus associated with a pious young woman, Joan of Arc, often represented with a cross and a lily-covered flag. The Republic, a term equally feminine *en français*, abandons the chaste Joan of Arc and opts to be symbolized by a beautiful and rather frivolous young woman who receives a nickname conjuring up not a lady but a woman of the people: Marianne. In all the town halls of France, a place of honor will be reserved for a bust of hers, typically with the face of a famous French actress or other celebrity such as Brigitte Bardot, Catherine Deneuve, Laetitia Casta, and Évelyne Thomas. Almost one hundred years after the founding of the Republic, on July 14, 1884, a huge and impressive statue of Marianne, created by the sculptor Léopold Morice, will be erected in Paris. It will arise in the middle of a vast square named after the form of government introduced by the Revolution, Place la République. The square and its statue are situated at only a few hundred meters from the site where the Temple once stood, the building that witnessed the demise of the monarchy.

Nowhere is the deroyalization-cum-republicanization more visible than in the capital, the formerly "royal city" of Paris, where this process may be said to have been launched by the demolition of the Bastille in July 1789. However, as in the rest of the country, that process gains momentum after Louis flees from his palace on August 10, 1792, thus triggering the birth of the Republic. In the capital, 1,400 streets with names directly or indirectly associated with the monarchy and the church are rebaptized, to use a non-revolutionary terminology the sans-culottes would certainly have repudiated.[33] However, arguably most symptomatic for the capital's metamorphosis is the fate of the proud royal squares that, more than any other urban features, have proclaimed Paris to be a royal city, a city belonging to the monarchy, the Ancien Régime in general, and its privileged classes, the aristocracy and the (high) clergy. These squares now receive new, radically different names and adopt an entirely new look.

Let us start by examining the fate of the most glorious of these magnificent open spaces, Place Louis XV. On August 11, 1792, the day af-

---

32   But Paris is masculine, hence the expression *le tout Paris*; see Higonnet, p. 21-22.

33   Lagorio, p. 86.

ter the storming of the Tuileries, that space's name becomes Place de la Révolution, and the statue of Louis XV is destroyed. (The square will be rebaptized Place de la Concorde in 1795, as we will see later.) Another fine *place royale* is Place Louis-le-Grand, later to become Place Vendôme, and it features an equestrian statue of that king, Louis XIV. That statue is taken down on August 16, 1792, shortly after the arrest of Louis XVI, and smashed into pieces, whereby a female sans-culotte is accidentally killed. The name of the square is changed to Place des Piques; this is a tip of the hat—or rather, Phrygian cap?—to the sans-culottes, whose traditional weapon is the pike. The new name simultaneously serves as a symbolic certification of the conquest of the proud "royal city" by revolutionaries coming mostly from the Faubourg Saint-Antoine and other eastern reaches of the city.[34]

An imposing former *hôtel particulier* at number 17 of this square, located next to the current Hotel Ritz, will become the Ministry of Justice. Under the window immediately to the left of the entrance, a large block of stone, bearing a horizontal line and the inscription "meter," will be embedded because the Academy of Sciences, by order of the Constituent Assembly, decided in May 1790 to develop a new uniform system of weights and measures, known today as the "metric system." Before that, there existed in France all kinds of non-metric systems of weights and measures, with their feet, inches, etc., which considerably hindered domestic as well as international trade. In this way, a new unit of length is born, the meter, "equal to the ten-millionth part of a quarter of a meridian." The metric system is officially adopted in April 1795 and is destined to conquer (almost) the whole world. In the 21st century, only three countries will still not use the metric system: Myanmar, Liberia, and the United States. To allow the French to see the exact length of a meter, "standard meters" (*mètres-étalon*), designed by Jean-François-Thérèse Chalgrin, later to be the architect of the Arc de Triomphe, are installed in 1796-1797 throughout the country, including no less than sixteen in the capital. The one on Place Vendôme is one of the last two subsisting into the 21st century, the other one can be seen at number 36 of the Rue Vaugirard.[35]

---

34   Sournia, p. 131.

35   Poisson, p. 111; Hillairet (1956), vol. 1, pp. 218-23 ; "Le mètre étalon de la Place Vendôme."

The Place des Victoires is also dedicated to the Sun King, and its name alludes to his military triumphs against foreign enemies. A minor addition causes it to be designated as Place des Victoires Nationales, thus celebrating victories not of the monarch but of the nation, that is, the French people, victories achieved not at the expense of foreign nations but of their own monarchs. The bronze figure of the fourteenth Louis is replaced with a pyramid honoring the attackers of the Tuileries on August 10, 1792, commoners from Paris and from elsewhere in France, including Marseille. As for the royal square dedicated to Louis XIII, it is renamed a number of times in honor of revolutionary actors such as the *fédérés* ("federates"), men from Marseille and other provincial cities, who had come to Paris to join the sans-culottes in actions such as the storming of the Tuileries Palace, and of revolutionary ideals, for example the indivisibility of the nation.

The Pont Neuf is not a royal square, of course, but very much a royal bridge, and it is viewed as the emblem par excellence of the royal city Paris had been. However, its decorative protectors, known as *mascarons*, prove unable to protect it against the evil revolutionary spirits. Henry IV may have been the most popular of France's royal rulers, but the revolutionaries have no use for any monarchs at all, so the statue of "Good King Henry" in the middle of the bridge is ripped off its pedestal on August 24, 1792, to be melted down except for some bronze sculptures that decorated the base; they will eventually find their way into the Carnavalet Museum of Parisian history.

The deroyalization of Paris is focused not only on all buildings, monuments, and symbols of the monarchy itself but also those associated with the monarchical state's two privileged classes, the nobility and the clergy. Countless noblemen have opposed the Revolution and have either been executed or fled abroad. Their prestigious urban residences, known as hôtels, are confiscated, auctioned off, and most of them thus become the property of well-to-do burghers. If they do not need an entire building, the new owners will tend to divide the edifice into a number of apartments or transform it into a place where travellers can temporarily stay in a room for payment. We have already seen that this will cause the term hôtel to refer to what used to be called *auberge* or *logis*, "inn."

Numerous particularly big or beautiful hotels, too expensive to be acquired by even the most prosperous members of the bourgeoisie, escape privatization but are acquired by the municipal or national government, thus morphing into offices for government administrations or museums. The Hôtel Salé in the Marais District, for example, built in the 1650s for a tax farmer who became rich collecting the *gabelle* or salt tax, which explains the name of the building—*salé* means "salted"—, and temporarily served as the Venetian embassy, is destined to become the Picasso Museum; and another fine hôtel of the same district, once owned by Madame de Sévigné, the Carnavalet, will eventually house the Paris Historical Museum.

The same fate, a change of ownership, befalls the extra grand, palace-like hôtels of the über-aristocrats in the "noble faubourg" of Saint-German, in some ways the *sanctum sanctorum* of upper-class Paris. Most if not all of its aristocratic denizens end up under the revolutionary blade or flee abroad, and their superb residences are taken over by the new republican government to become ministries or, if sold to foreign governments, embassies. After the flight of its owner, the Prince of Condé, the Palais Bourbon, the architectural prima donna of the Saint-Germain district, is thus confiscated by the state; it will become the meeting place of the lower house of the French Parliament, the *Assemblée nationale* or National Assembly. It is rather ironic that a central institution of the French Republic bears the name of the former royal family.[36] Another famous hôtel of the district, the Hôtel Matignon, will become the official residence of France's Prime Minister.

The Faubourg Saint-Honoré is another high-end and highly prestigious part of western Paris. It is bisected by the Rue du Faubourg Saint-Honoré, formerly a country road leading to the hill and village of Le Roule, located where the Arc de Triomphe will later arise. A superb hôtel there is the former residence of Madame de Pompadour, which became known as the Élysée Palace because its backyard abutted the Champs Élysées. That edifice is destined to become the residence of the President of the French Republic.

We finish this brief overview of the deroyalization-cum-republicanization of Paris at the site where this process had started, namely where the Bastille used to stand. In June 1792, the vast open space created by

---

36 Hillairet (1956), volume 2, p. 254.

the fortress's demolition, later to be known as Place de la Bastille, is given the name Place de la Liberté. One year later, a fountain is put up in the middle of the square, known as Fontaine de la Régénération, "Fountain of the Rebirth [of France]"; the water flows freely from the breasts of a plaster statue of the Egyptian goddess Isis, symbolizing Mother Nature. In the twilight of the Roman Empire, Isis was extremely popular, but her cult was outlawed when a rival, Christianity, became the state religion and used its power to eradicate all forms of paganism. In any event, at one time Isis reportedly had many aficionados in Gaul and it is even claimed that the name of the Parisii, the Gallic tribe that gave its name to the city, signified "followers of Isis." Interest in Isis revived with the Enlightenment and the emergence of Freemasonry, whereby the goddess was associated with the mysterious powers of nature. Because of the poor quality of its construction material, the monument will become dilapidated and therefore demolished after only a few years.[37]

Declericalization of the Capital

In the Ancien Régime, church and state had not been separated, the royal state and the Catholic Church had been inseparable twins. The Revolution is therefore not only antimonarchical but also anticlerical. Consequently, the deroyalization of Paris inevitably goes hand in hand with a host of measures that might collectively be described as a declericalization—or, if you prefer, desacralization, dechristianization, or just secularization—of the city.

Following the Revolution's introduction of anticlerical measures such as the nationalization of all church property on November 2, 1789 and the abolition of most monastic orders on February 13, 1790, many churches and monasteries are closed, become state property, and are sold to the highest bidder. The new owners are free to do as they please with the building and the land, and this often causes new streets, homes, and other buildings to appear on the site, so that not a trace will remain of the former ecclesiastical establishment. The old Dominican Monastery on Rue Saint-Jacques suffers this sad fate: nothing will remain of the complex, it will be replaced by residential and commercial properties.

---

37 "Fontaine de la Régénération."

In some cases, the new owners will find a new use for an ecclesiastical edifice, or at least part of it. This happens to another sanctuary dedicated to Saint James, the church of Saint-Jacques-de-la-Boucherie, so named because it is located in the central Parisian, right-bank neighborhood where the butcher shops (*boucheries*) used to be concentrated. The fact that one of its priests pronounced a funerary oration in honor of the revolutionaries killed during the storming of the Bastille, does not save that church. The building survives for some time because it proves useful as a meeting place for the revolutionaries of the parish but is eventually privatized and demolished, except for the imposing tower to be known as the Tour Saint-Jacques. After being used for some years as a foundry, the latter will be acquired by the city in 1824 and become an historical monument.

The greater the connection between a religious sanctuary and the monarchy, the greater the damage inflicted by the wrath of the revolutionaries. This is illustrated spectacularly by the fate of the Abbey of Saint-Denis, admittedly located outside of Paris but within easy reach of the anticlerical sans-culottes. The monastery is closed and its church, for centuries the burial place of French royalty, is temporarily used for the storage of supplies of flour; from the perspective of the common people, that is a useful purpose, because the availability of plentiful flour can help to maintain the price of bread at an affordable level. However, as the Revolution enters its most radical phase in 1792-1793, the royal tombs are vandalized, and the remains of 42 kings, 32 queens, and countless princes and other royal, noble and ecclesiastical seigneurs are tossed into common graves of the abbey's monks' cemetery. Fortunately, the church itself, a masterpiece of early Gothic architecture, survives. As for the site of the martyrdom of Saint Denis, the hill in northern Paris that had been named Montmartre, "mount martyr," it is renamed Mont Marat in honor of the revolutionary hero who was assassinated in his bathtub.

The Sainte Chapelle, the Gothic sanctuary of the former royal palace on Île de la Cité, where Saint Louis kept the relics he had acquired during his crusade in the Holy Land, also becomes the object of a thorough vandalization. Most of the relics are tossed into the Seine, while the gold and silver reliquaries are melted down. Much damage is done to the exterior as well as the interior of the building, including the stained glass windows. As in the case of Saint-Denis, it is a miracle that the Sainte

Chapelle will survive the revolutionary turmoil at all.

IMAGE 16. The Monastery of Montmartre in the 17th century.

Notre-Dame Cathedral also suffers from the twin antiroyal and anticlerical furor. Like all other church properties, the edifice becomes property of the state on November 2, 1789, and will remain so indefinitely. It will remain unavailable for use by the Catholic Church during many years, and instead of masses it witnesses ceremonies in honor of the goddess of reason or liberty. Much damage inside as well as outside is caused by pure vandalism, some of it as the result of the building's temporary use as a warehouse used for the storage of wine and food. This reflects the mentality of the all too often hungry (and thirsty) Parisian demos and poor folks in general, summed up as follows by Bertolt Brecht's already mentioned dictum, which could be summed up as, "food first, philosophy later." We will later learn more about what happened to Notre-Dame in the 19th century.

Many of the treasures Notre-Dame has accumulated over the centuries are destroyed or disappear. The statues of kings of biblical Israel are destroyed, and the same fate befalls other statues decorating the western façade. The heads of the statues, 21 of the 28, will be discovered during a 1977 excavation nearby and will be put on display in the Cluny Museum; as for the statues that will reappear in due course on the Cathedral's façade, they will be facsimiles.

Kings, aristocrats, saints, popes, cardinals, and so forth have become *personae non gratae* and are removed from monuments and names of streets and squares and evicted even from (former) churches. To be replaced, in one famous case, by heroes of the Revolution itself and of the great philosophers who are viewed as its intellectual godfathers. That exception is the former church dedicated to Sainte-Geneviève, patron saint of Paris, an imposing neo-classical building erected by the famous architect Soufflot during the time of Louis XV. It is perceived as an "in-your-face" architectural externalization of clerical power, the more since it sits on top of a left-bank hillock named after the same saint, the 33-meter high Montagne Sainte-Geneviève; featuring a big dome and a temple-like façade, it looks a lot like Saint Peter's in Rome. Unsurprisingly, it is thoroughly vandalized by the revolutionaries. However, the idea soon arises of transforming the gargantuan edifice into a Parisian version of the Pantheon in Rome. In that temple, Romans were able to worship all the gods; in Paris, Frenchmen will be able to worship earthly gods, namely gods of the French nation, deities of the revolution. Above the entrance, an inscription is affixed: "To the great men, the Grateful Fatherland." (At the time, the possibility of "great women" was not yet thought of.)[38]

The Parisian Pantheon also purports to be a republican counterpart to the former royal mausoleum of Saint-Denis. After the necessary modifications, most notably the removal of spires and windows, the metamorphosis from sacred to secular shrine is completed with the transfer into the building of the remains of Voltaire (July 12, 1791) and Rousseau (October 11, 1794). They are soon followed by those of Mirabeau and Marat. Marat, the famous martyr of the radical revolution, was originally buried under a weeping willow on the grounds of the Cordelier monastery that had been the home of the homonymous club; but he is reburied with pomp and circumstance in the Pantheon. As for Mirabeau, one of

---

38 See Caro, pp. 290-95, for a succinct but excellent description of the Pantheon.

the "fathers of the Revolution," his body will be removed from the Pantheon in 1794, after it is discovered that was involved with Louis XVI in a counter-revolutionary conspiracy orchestrated by the Austrian ambassador.

The declericalization of Paris by the revolutionaries involves not only buildings but also personnel associated with the Church. Monasteries are closed and the members of the religious orders are "set free." Many clergymen refuse to accept the anticlerical changes wrought by the Revolution but condemned by the Pope, and these "refractory" priests end up being imprisoned, guillotined, or forced into going underground or leaving the country. But even the many low-ranking members of the clergy who sympathized with the Revolution, accept the new arrangements and remain in their functions, adopting a low profile. The reason for that is the unpopularity of the Church, expressed by the slogan "*À bas la calotte!*" ("Down with the skullcap!"). This unpopularity is due to the fact that the clergy, like the nobility, was a privileged class; and it does not help, of course, that the Pope has condemned the Revolution as the work of the devil.[39] In this increasingly anticlerical revolutionary context, priests, monks, and nuns disappear from the capital's cityscape. The "new Jerusalem" Paris had been before 1789, is lost and gone forever.

By deroyalizing central Paris, then, the sans-culottes simultaneously continue their conquest of the capital and their revolutionary project. On their home ground, in the Faubourg Saint-Antoine, they similarly proceed to wipe out urbanistic, architectural, iconographic and other "fossils" of the Ancien Régime. The Faubourg receives a new name, reflecting the pride its denizens take in the fact that their neighborhood is the cradle and wellspring of the Revolution: Faubourg-de-Gloire, the "glorious suburb." And it is hardly a surprise that, on February 11, 1791, the Saint-Antoine Abbey is declared a national property. The abbey's church is demolished, and the rest of the complex becomes a hospital, something for which the suburb had a great need. In the 21st century, a few vestiges of the abbey remain, for example the door of the porter's house at 170 bis Rue du Faubourg-Saint-Antoine.

These changes—a mix of deroyalization and declericalization—

---

39   Michalik, pp. 32-35. The *calotte* is the traditional priest's cap, but the term referred to the clergy, the Catholic Church, and clericalism in general.

occur in Paris and elsewhere in France, but not in the country's major transatlantic colony, founded in the early 17th century and known as Nouvelle-France, "New France," the present-day Canadian province of Quebec. That territory was lost to the motherland during the Seven-Years' War of 1756-1763. When, a few decades later, the Revolution calls an entirely new France into being, nothing changes in Quebec. Change is unwanted there, especially since the British conquerors have turned over the colony's administration to the Catholic Church, which anathemizes the Revolution as the handiwork of Satan. In other words, when in Europe Old France becomes a New France, the overseas New France morphs into an Old France. To 21st-century Frenchmen, visiting Quebec will be like a voyage back in time, a *retour en arrière*, as they are greeted by blue-and-white flags proudly displaying no less than four *fleurs-de-lis*, separated by a large cross. *Parbleu*!

Louis the Last on the Scaffold

The king's trial starts in the Manège in December 1792. It ends on January 17, 1793 with a session in the Tuileries Palace, more in particular, in the Galerie des Machines, a large room situated to the south of the Marsan Pavillion, destined to survive into the 21st century, when it will be part of the Louvre Museum. "Louis Capet" is found guilty of having betrayed his country. But what will be his sentence? There are a number of options, but it comes down to a choice between exile or death. After numerous lengthy discussions, the Convention decides to vote on the issue and the partisans of the death penalty obtain a majority of a handful of votes, including that of the "former" Duc d'Orléans, who has changed his name to Philippe Égalité; he is one of the rare moderate candidates of the capital to be elected to the Convention. The sentence is carried out four days later.

As the place of execution, the Convention does not choose the Place de Grève where, during the Ancien Régime, the executions took place and where the guillotine officially entered service for the first time, on April 25, 1792; nor does it pick Place du Carrousel, opposite the entrance to the Tuileries, where, in September 1792, the commanders of the Swiss Guard were guillotined. Instead, the choice falls on the square which, until recently, used to be called Place Louis XV and which is located between the gardens of the Tuileries and the Champs-Élysées; later it will be known as Place de la Concorde. The largest and arguably most impressive of all "royal squares," dedicated to the glory of the monarchy, must witness the death of the man who is supposed to be the very last king. The death of the last king will also proclaim the demise of the "royal city" Paris used to be.

On the evening of January 20, Louis XVI "dines with appetite," then enjoys a "peaceful night's sleep."[40] The next morning, a father confessor of Irish origin by the name of Edgeworth de Firmont, celebrates mass in the king's room. And then, on a grey and rainy winter morning, the former sovereign embarks into a carriage and departs from the Temple. The vehicle travels along a string of wide streets that will later be called the "*grands boulevards*" to reach the waiting guillotine, and the trip will take 1 ½ hours. Since the plinth of the destroyed statue of Louis XV has remained in place, it proved impossible to mount the "machine of death" in the middle of the square. This is why it is installed about ten meters further west, that is, in the direction of the Champs-Élysées; a bronze plaque fixed in the pavement will later identify the site of the execution.

The king arrives at 10:20, and in a few minutes it will be all over. Dressed in a white shirt and grey breeches, that is, knickers, complemented below the knees with silk stockings, the 39-year-old monarch climbs the steps of the scaffold. He is allowed to undress himself and then his hands are tied behind his back. His confessor embraces him and addresses him with these words: "Son of Saint Louis, ascend to heaven!" Louis wants to address the crowd, but incessant drum rolls, specially ordered for this purpose, prevent his last words from being heard by anyone other than the executioner and his assistants. He allegedly shouted: "[my] people, I die as an innocent man." Then he speaks to the executioner, Sanson, who, before the Revolution, applied the death sentences in the service of the king himself: "Sir, I am innocent of everything with which I am accused. I hope that my blood may cement the happiness of the French"; to these words he presumably added "I surrender my soul to God." These were the last words of "Louis the Last."[41]

Without the slightest ceremony, the royal body is laid face down on

---

40 Coquard, p. 158.
41 Arasse, pp. 77, 86-87; *Les lieux de l'histoire de France*, pp. 298-99.

the plank of the guillotine, then the ax falls. In a flash, it's all over. Visually, as a spectacle, this kind of beheading has little to offer in comparison to the executions of the Ancien Régime, which sometimes lasted for hours and were accompanied by torture. To compensate for this deficiency, to treat the spectators to a minimum of spectacle, the executioner seizes the head by the hair and holds it up as a kind of trophy, to be seen by all those present.

Symbolically, however, the impact of this very brief moment is powerful. Separating the head of the king from his body inevitably brings to mind the ideology of the Ancien Régime, the idea that the king is the head in the figurative sense of the living body of the nation; with the fall of the ax, the nation is therefore rid of a head with which it can no longer live in harmony. There is also considerable symbolic value in *putting down* the man who once stood at the absolute top of the social pyramid, thus forcing the people to look up to him, while now everyone remains standing upright and are able to look down on him, albeit not literally so. Finally, considerable satisfaction is involved in witnessing the shortening (*raccourcissement*), by means of decapitation, of the individual who is at least symbolically the greatest, *le plus grand*, of all the aristocratic folks known as *les grands*, the "grandees," people who, on account of factors such as better food, also tended to be *plus grand* physically, in other words, taller, than the commoners, the "little people." With a height of approximately six feet, the king himself was in fact exceptionally tall.

The sans-culottes will describe the beheading of the king and aristocrats in general with great pleasure in terms such as "shorten, "As in this revolutionary song, sung at the time to the tune of the *Marseillaise*:

Ô toi, céleste guillotine,
Tu raccourcis reines et rois.
Par ton influence divine
Nous avons reconquis nos droits
(...)
Remplis, remplis ton divin sac
de têtes de tyrans! [42]

O heavenly guillotine,
You shorten queens and kings.
Thanks to your divine influence
We have regained our rights
(...)
Fill your divine bag
with the heads of tyrants!

The famous revolutionary song *La Carmagnole*, which became a kind of national anthem of the sans-culottes in 1792, similarly glorifies the "shortening" of the grandees:

---

42   Quoted in Arasse, pp. 96-97.

Il faut raccourcir les géants	We must shorten the giants
Et rendre les petits plus grands.	And make the little ones taller.
Tous à la même hauteur,	An equal height for all,
Voilà le vrai bonheur!	That means true happiness!

But how do the thousands of people gathered there react to the death of the king? At the very moment of the fall of the ax, a vibrant "Long live the republic!" springs from the throats of the spectators. What a contrast to what was always heard at the death of a monarch: "The king is dead, long live the king!" Otherwise, the crowd remains silent and calm. This calm is interpreted by the republicans as proof of the dignity of the people, which is no longer composed of *subjects*, and of its determination, via this daring act, to turn its back on the monarchical past and step boldly forward into a republican future. As far as the royalists are concerned, the overwhelming silence befits the tragic farewell—many of them see it as a martyrdom—of a loving father to his people; the royalists view this execution as a terrible crime, a regicide which is simultaneously a parricide. The ambivalence of the silence is matched by that of the scene that unfolds immediately after the beheading at the foot of the scaffold, where gallons of blood flow. Numerous spectators dip their handkerchiefs in the royal blood, while others crowd around the executioner and his helpers to claim pieces of clothing or strands of the king's hair. To preserve as holy relics, perhaps, as memories of the martyrdom of the father of the people? Or does this mean nothing more than the acquisition of an ordinary souvenir, a memento of an unprecedented historical event, the death of the tyrant? On this subject too, the witnesses have diametrically opposed opinions depending on whether they are republicans or monarchists.

The body is placed, head between the legs, in an open coffin, then taken very quickly by cart to the nearest cemetery, that of the parish of the Church of the Madeleine. Without the slightest decorum, the mortal remains of Louis XVI are thrown into a pit, to be joined there later by those of Marie-Antoinette. This cemetery will be closed and sold in 1794, but the owner maintained it and, after the fall of Napoleon, sold it to the new king, Louis XVIII, the former count of Provence. The latter will have the royal couple exhumed and reburied in the necropolis of the Basilica of Saint-Denis. In the old cemetery, in the year 1820, he will erect the so-called Expiatory Chapel, whose altar indicates the place where

Louis XVI was buried. The entrance to this complex is on Rue Pasquier, in the immediate vicinity of the Madeleine Church.[43]

IMAGE 17. Allegory of the Revolution, with an effigy of Jean-Jacques Rousseau, by Nicolas Henri Jeaurat de Bertry.[44]

---

43   Poisson, p. 84. For a detailed study of this chapel, see Darnis.

44   Source: https://www.worldhistory.org/image/16013/an-allegory-of-the-revolution

6. 1793-1794: The Radical Revolution

Rise of the Mountain Men

DURING CONVENTION MEETINGS AT THE MANÈGE, radicals like Marat, Danton, and a rising star, Robespierre, make it a habit to perch together in the upper rows of seats; they end up being called *Montagnards,* men from "the Mountain," *la Montagne.* A large number of them are members of the Jacobins or of that other radical club, that of the Cordeliers, and some are at the same time members of the very radical Commune at the City Hall. With regard to their social background, one can say that the members of the Mountain, like the Jacobins and Cordeliers in general, represent the petty bourgeoisie, that is, the Parisian petty bourgeoisie. Down below, in what is called "the Plain," is where the grand-bourgeois and moderate Girondins, are seated, a heterogeneous group to which the undecided belong, the unsure, the opportunists, but their most vocal representatives—and therefore the great antagonists of the Jacobins on the higher benches—are the Girondins. The latter are led by personalities such as Jacques-Pierre Brissot and are therefore also known as Brissotins. For the time being, the Girondins remain in power.

At the beginning of 1793, the newborn republic takes a hard hit. The war is not going well and and in France itself, after the execution of the king, royalist revolts erupt in the Vendée and in cities like Lyon and Toulon. In addition, food riots break out again in Paris. The sans-culottes, who are being asked to make more and more sacrifices for the revolution and, at the same time, to tighten their belts, are demanding the introduction of price controls. But the Girondins in government stubbornly oppose such a violation of liberal principles—in other words, "free market" principles—which are so dear to their hearts. And so their popularity plummets rapidly as, in the eyes of the sans-culottes, the Girondins are more and more associated with the hated "usurers and hoarders" (*usuriers et accapareurs*), that is, with these producers and merchants who are presumed to take advantage of the shortages to earn big money at the expense of the common people. More in general, it can be said that the sans-culottes, typically small producers and entrepreneurs, view as hereditary enemies the big producers and traders represented by the Girondins, as class enemies similar to the great landowners of the aristocracy. The ideal of the sans-culottes is a society without "the rich and fat" (*riches et gros*), an egalitarian society in which no one has more than what they themselves have, namely a minor asset in the form of a workshop, a retail store, or another small business.[1]

However, the Jacobins, the Cordeliers, and a group of extremists known as *les Enragés*, "the enraged" or "the furious," of which the best known is Jacques Roux, take side with the Parisian common people; they speak out in favor of the price controls demanded by the sans-culottes, in favor of what will be called a "Law of the Maximum."[2] At the Convention, the Montagnards therefore benefit increasingly from the support of the sans-culotterie, and this proves to be particularly useful in their power struggle against the Girondins. In the meantime, more and more sans-culottes join the National Guard and, starting in the fall of 1793, the sans-culottes dominate most Parisian sections. The revolution thus becomes not only more and more radical, it also increasingly involves the common people, it becomes a more real "popular movement."

The growing conflict between the Girondins and the Montagnards reflects a conflict of interests—and therefore of principles—within the bourgeoisie itself, namely between the interests of the patrician upper bourgeoisie and the plebeian petty bourgeoisie. In this conflict, the men of the Mountain seek the support of the sans-culottes, from whom, on the social level, they hardly differ, because the sans-culotterie, while far from homogeneous, is essentially also petty-bourgeois and not at all a

---

1 Soboul (1968), pp. 31-32, 71-74.
2 Hazan (2014), pp. 247-49.

kind of "vanguard of a future proletariat," as is sometimes suggested.[3] The Montagnards need the support of the Parisian "little people" against their grand-bourgeois and increasingly conservative rivals and, more in general, to save the Revolution—in other words, not out of conviction but because of tactical considerations. They are also prepared to allow the sans-culottes to play a limited active role in politics and even to indulge them with certain social-economic favors such as price controls and other interventionist measures; these amount to state interventions in economic life that are repugnant to the Girondins, champions of laissez-faire purity.[4]

The latent conflict between the Montagnards and the Girondins is at the same time a conflict between radicals and moderates; between supporters and opponents of the intervention of the lower classes in politics and of the intervention of the State in economic life; between those who want to radicalize the revolution and those who want to moderate and even end it; and ultimately it is also a conflict between Paris and the provinces, between the republican and radical capital and the rest of France, conservative or at least very moderate. (As Eric Hazan has written, between these two groups there was a "geographical difference," the Montagnard leaders being Parisian deputies, while the Girondins chiefs came from the south of France, the Midi, with the exception of one Parisian, namely Brissot.) The Girondins at the Convention thus suffer from a considerable disadvantage: the Convention meets in Paris, the den of the Jacobin lions, located at a stone's throw from the City hall, seat of the Commune, and from the faubourg Saint-Antoine teeming with restless sans-culottes. These sans-culottes also happen to be armed to the teeth, not only with pikes, but also with firearms and even cannon. Conversely, since the hot summer of 1789, the government no longer has the right to bring troops to Paris itself.[5]

Between May 31 and June 2, 1793, in Paris, unrest, once again provoked by the high prices, lead to demonstrations and end up triggering a direct attack by the sans-culottes against the Tuileries palace, now known as the Natonal Palace, into which the Convention moved only a few

---

3   Soboul (1968), passim; also Vovelle, p. 36.
4   Suret-Canale, pp. 85, 88; Vovelle, pp. 32-33.
5   Soboul (1968), p. 107; Hazan (2014), pp. 152, 200-02.

weeks earlier, on May 10.[6] This move from the modest Manège to the former royal palace symbolizes the twin fact that the legislative branch has triumphed over the executive branch of the government and that the monarchy has given way to the republic. The latter's principles are displayed in large letters on the walls: "Liberty—Equality—Fraternity." It is obvious that the attack on the Tuileries was orchestrated at the club of the Jacobins. In any event, faced with this new show of force emanating from "the street," recalling the famous 10th of August of the previous year, the Girondins, in the Assembly, are forced to transfer power to their radical opponents, the Montagnards. The Convention, which used to be a "Girondin Convention," is now a "Montagnard Convention." The Girondin deputies are relieved of their duties as deputies, presumably by the people, which claims the right to "dismiss" delegates who are not prepared to comply with its will. About twenty of their leaders are imprisoned; they are accused of treason and will end up on the scaffold, on Place de la Concorde, on October 31, 1793.

From these essentially Parisian Montagnards, who now rule the entire country, two things are expected immediately. First, on the international level, the rescue of the republican fatherland threatened by foreign enemies; and, second, with respect to economic policy, lower prices for the benefit of the ordinary Parisian people. Achieving this twin objective requires energetic measures and these will be taken by a new institution within the Convention that will function as a kind of revolutionary cabinet: the famous Committee of Public Safety. Robespierre turns out to be the figurehead of this committee and therefore the de facto head of government. The committee meets in what used to be the queen's room, located on the ground floor of the Pavillon de Flore, the south wing of the Tuileries palace. This pavilion will survive the destruction of the Tuileries Palace during the Paris Commune of 1871 and become part of the complex of the Louvre.

The draconian political, military, and economic measures taken by the "Jacobin-Montagnard regime"[7] which amount to a further radicalization of the revolution, will become known collectively as *la Terreur*, "the Terror," written with a capital letter to distinguish it from any other

---

6   Jacquin et al., p. 89.
7   This term is used by Larue-Langlois, p. 44.

form of terror. It will indeed be accompanied by coercion, violence, and bloodshed. Was this revolutionary Terror necessary or not, justified or not, was it the *sine qua non* of the survival of the young republic, or merely the whim of a fanatic and criminal clique of *buveurs de sang*, "blood suckers"? Was it the result of specific historical circumstances or the bitter fruit of the radical Jacobin ideology, is it comparable to other historical forms of terror or not, a historical banality or a singularity? This is a major issue that continues to divide historians today, not only in France but throughout the world.[8] It is an indubitable fact, however, that the Terror did deliver the desired results, in other words, that it saved the Revolution. Some reflections on the topic of the Terror will be offered in a later chapter.

IMAGE 18. Pavillon de Flore.[9]

8   This theme is dealt with in the brilliant study by Arno Mayer, *The Furies*.

9   Source: https://fr-academic.com/pictures/frwiki/80/Paris-PontRoyal-PavillonDeFlore-1814.jpg

With regard to the conduct of the war, at the end of August 1793, at a time when foreign armies again entered French soil, a draconian measure is taken, namely the forced mobilization of all available young men. This novel and indeed revolutionary initiative, called the *levée en masse,* the "mass levy" or "general conscription," is an unprecedented initiative, and many Frenchmen, especially peasants whose sons are called up for an indefinite period, are far from happy with it. Its architect is Lazare Carnot, a colleague of Robespierre within the Committee of Public Safety. The measure is obviously associated with coercion—and sometimes even violence—and is therefore part of the Terror system. However, the *levée en masse* will revolutionize warfare and prove to be an essential condition of the French military successes that will follow, thus saving the republic and later allowing spectacular conquests throughout Europe. Carnot's innovation is the embryo of the compulsory military service that will be introduced in virtually all European countries in the course of the 19th century. To be accepted, albeit without enthusiasm, by the population as a legitimate prerogative of the state.

On the economic front, too, radical measures—always accompanied by coercion and violence and therefore an integral part of the Terror system—will lead to the desired results, at least temporarily. In September 1793, a "revolutionary army" is created. Its mission is to requisition wheat and meat from the peasants, food required to feed the hungry and restless Parisian sans-culottes, and the mushrooming numbers of soldiers in the army. And in view of the bread shortages, the cultivation and consumption are promoted of a newfangled edible crop, the potato. The Paris Commune goes as far as to order "transforming the Tuileries Gardens into potato fields." Germain Chevet, the former florist of Marie-Antoinette, "is forced... to uproot the roses [in the Tuileries Gardens] and replace them with patriotic potatoes"[10] However, the sans-culottes dislike the "lack of flavor" (*non-gout*) of the "*cartoufles*" and continue to prefer bread.

A major handicap of the potato is indeed the fact that it is "*non-panifiable*," that is, cannot be used to make some form of bread, as it is possible to do with another staple from the New World, corn. It will only be much later, namely after "its meeting with deep-frying oil [*huile à friture*]," that

---

10 Toussaint-Samat, pp. 524-25.

the potato will experience "its democratic triumph." The denizens of Belgium are convinced that *pommes frites,* "fried potatoes," were invented in their country, most likely in the valley of the River Meuse, more specifically in and around the city of Liège, where it had long been a tradition to fry fish that way; the fact that this is the French-speaking part of the country presumably explains the now widely-used American terminology, "French fries," allegedly conjured up by Yankee soldiers stationed in Belgium at the end of the First World War. However, some claim that frites originated in Paris during the French Revolution, or perhaps a little earlier or later, and were at first called "Pont-Neuf potatoes," because they were originally sold at stands on the famous bridge; this may already have happened a few years after Antoine Parmentier started to promote the cultivation and consumption of potatoes in 1771. Maurice Edmond Sailland, a.k.a. Curnonsky (1872-1956), author, journalist, champion of regional cuisine, and 'prince of the gastronomes' declared in the 1920s that 'frites are one of the most spiritual creations of the Parisian genius.'[11]

During the elections for the Convention in August and September 1792, the provinces vote mostly for moderate representatives of the Girondin type, while Paris nearly exclusively opts for radical Jacobins and Cordeliers. Of course some Girondins and other moderates are also elected in Paris, but the presumably fanatic bourgeois revolutionaries, the Jacobins, form an overwhelming majority; in the capital, furthermore, the political space to the left of the Jacobins teems with ultra-radical, half-bourgeois, half-proletarian elements. Conversely, in the provinces, in towns as well as in the countryside, there are Jacobins, but they usually constitute a minority. The large and mid-size provincial cities are dominated by the Girondins and other moderates of bourgeois origin. In the provinces, moreover, numerous conservative and even openly counter-revolutionary elements are active that may be described as being to the right of the Girondins: aristocrats who have gone underground, for example, and "refractory" priests, who continue to enjoy much influence in the villages. In the countryside, the peasants are very attached to the traditions of their rural community and their province; for this reason, they are far from happy with the many aspects of the "modernization" of which the Revolution is a catalyst. Above all, the denizens of *la France profonde* resent the secularization, that is, the anticlerical and

---

11   Mongaillard; "Les secrets du Pont-Neuf"; Wheaton, pp. 82-84.

seemingly even anti-Christian measures taken by "Paris." Consequently, it is precisely those aspects of the Terror that are acclaimed in Paris by the sans-culottes that cause the inhabitants of the countryside to turn against the Revolution, namely, the requisitions by the revolutionary army, the price controls, and the compulsory military service. These measures make the revolution in general and the Montagnard regime in particular extremely unpopular in the countryside; they cause the already existing gap between the revolutionary city, Paris, and the countryside, essentially conservative and sometimes openly counter-revolutionary, to become deeper and wider.

Paris made the Revolution and, with the Terror, Jacobin Paris pushes the Revolution even further forward—or to the left, as one might also say.[12] Conversely, one can say that the provinces—that is, the provincial cities as well and the countryside—want to put the brakes on the Revolution, put an end to it, and, in some cases, turn resolutely against the Revolution and even take up arms in order to restore the Ancien Régime. It is in this context that we can understand what are called the "federalist" revolts of provincial cities like Marseille, Bordeaux, and Lyon during the summer of 1793. However, in the increasingly fierce conflict between the Revolution and its enemies, it will be especially the peasants of the countryside who tend to side with the counter-revolution, for example, in the guerrilla war in the Vendée and in the "war of the peasants," in the Austrian Netherlands, now Belgium, a land occupied, or liberated, depending on one's point of view, by the French revolutionary army.

While the Revolution—in many ways a modern and urban phenomenon—feels comfortably at home in Paris, we can say, conversely, that the counter-revolution takes root above all in the countryside. Which is logical, because, as we saw at the beginning of this story, it was in the countryside, in *la France profonde*, that the Ancien Régime had really been "at home." The uprisings in provincial cities like Lyons and Marseille, where the Girondins revealed themselves very active and influential, also reflected an "anti-Parisian resentment," due to the fact that "Paris controlled the Convention," as Eric Hazan has emphasized.[13]

We return to Paris and to the theme of the economic measures

---

12   Hazan (2014), p. 255-61.
13   Hazan (2014), pp. 255-61.

that are taken there within the framework of the Terror. The authorities are now dealing very harshly, at least for some time, with the real or alleged usurers, the infamous *accapareurs* or "hoarders," tormentors of the sans-culottes. And on September 29th, the famous "Law of the Maximum" is passed, which fixes the price of all kinds of commodities and other important products. This legislative achievement is greeted with enthusiasm by the common people. But the Montagnards do not introduce this measure out of conviction. They do it only for two reasons: first, because without support from the sans-culottes, it will be impossible to overcome the crisis; and second, because without such legislation, the sans-culottes are likely to turn against the Montagnards. The latter, including Robespierre, are and remain bourgeois by conviction as much as by origin. (Robespierre, for example, is the scion of "a petty bourgeois family involved in the practice of law and in business" in the town of Arras.)[14] As adherents of liberal principles, advocates of laissez-faire, they believe neither in the wisdom nor the desirability of price controls and other forms of regulation, in other words, in the kind of interventionist economic policy that will later be called a statist or dirigiste. It is therefore hardly surprising that Robespierre and his associates do not change one iota of the Le Chapelier Law, which prohibits workers' associations and strikes; neither is it surprising that Robespierre, like most of his Montagnard companions, "refuses to support the revolutionary republican citizens who demand equality between women and men."[15]

In any event, the Law of the Maximum, together with the requisitions from peasants and other, similar measures, achieve the primordial goal: inflation is brought under control, and the common people as well as the army receive sufficient food. The sans-culottes are also gratified by the fact that the revolutionary government lets them manufacture some war materiel or orders it from them, such as uniforms, even if most of the orders inevitably go to the big producers.[16] The alliance between the Montagne and the sans-culottes thus flourishes for some time. In stark contrast to their image in the provinces, Robespierre and his associates are extremely popular in Paris, where the Mountain is idolized and even

---

14   Vitu, referring to a book by Jean-Clément Martin, *Robespierre, la fabrication d'un monstre*.

15   Vitu.

16   Soboul (1968), pp. 77-81.

quasi-canonized as *sainte Montagne*, "holy Mountain"! However, the Law of the Maximum will gradually appear to be ineffectual. It is in fact systematically ignored by the producers and the traders, who prefer to offer their goods on a mushrooming black market; and these folks can count on the sympathy of many government leaders and officials who piously turn a blind eye to such practices.[17] All too soon, this will produce new shortages and price hikes, an alienation between Montagnards and sans-culottes and, finally, the fall of Robespierre and his associates. But we are not there yet. It deserves to be mentioned that Robespierre's government also undertakes something for the peasants of the countryside. In July 1793, a new law makes it unnecessary for peasants to *buy back* their lords' ancient feudal privileges but *abolishes* them.[18] It is a favor that will earn the Montagne precious little gratitude from the peasants.

Starting in the summer of 1793, particularly vigorous measures are also taken in the field of internal politics, in other words, against the domestic enemies of the revolution. It is especially in this context that the radical phase of the French Revolution will produce its (in)famous bloodbaths, associated with the guillotine, the instrument par excellence—and therefore the symbol—of the Terror. The assassination of Marat on July 13, 1793 is considered by his deeply shocked fellow revolutionaries as evidence that the revolution is threatened not only by dangerous foreign foes, but also by evil and treacherous domestic enemies. Ruthless action is therefore seen to be necessary. And, indeed, from the summer of 1793, the heads begin to roll.

The Terror culminates in a certain sense on September 17, 1793, with the approval by the Convention of what will be called "the Law of Suspects." This law permits the government—and the "revolutionary committees" of the Parisian sections[19]—to arrest anyone suspected of counter-revolutionary acts or even thoughts, of being "indifferent" or "lukewarm" (*insouciance, tiédeur*) vis-à-vis the revolutionary cause, or of any other form of "lack of civic responsibility" (*incivisme*).[20] The suspects are brought before revolutionary tribunals that must normally decide

---

17 See for example Rudé, p. 129.
18 Guillemin, p. 32.
19 Soboul (1968), pp. 180-83.
20 *Ibid.*, pp. 144-46.

within 24 hours about the guilt or innocence of the defendants. Those who are found to be innocent are released on the spot, but whoever is found guilty is condemned to mount within 24 hours the scaffold where the guillotine, the "revolutionary [or national] razor," will be waiting.

Topography of Terror:
Palace of Justice and Conciergerie

A first revolutionary tribunal was already established on August 17, 1792, to judge the "crimes committed against the people" one week earlier, on August 10, by the members of the Swiss Guard who had opened fire on the sans-culottes. The Swiss were condemned to death and guillotined on Place du Carrousel, site of the crime. The new revolutionary tribunals must likewise repress the enemies of the Revolution, but they also purport to prevent "that the people might be tempted to organize wild massacres" such as those of September 1792.[21] The revolutionary tribunals are supposed to be the instrument of a bloody but "cold" repression, that is, a form of terror orchestrated from above and subject to certain rules, a terror that aims to prevent new outbreaks of an even bloodier "hot," anarchic terror from below, as in September. "Let us be terrible so the people do not have to be so," is how Danton puts it.[22]

In the Middle Ages, the kings of France resided on the Île de la Cité, in a dark castle of which three towers will survive into the 21st century; one of them features a beautiful 15th-century clock adorned with royal lilies. But in the 16th century, the kings moved to the Right Bank, ensconcing themselves in a big, beautiful, and comfortable residence constructed in the trendy new Renaissance style: the Louvre Palace. The royal complex on the island became the city's palace of justice and was gradually reconstructed. Another part of the former royal edifice, located along the Seine and characterized by two massive round towers, morphed into the residence of an official, known as the *concierge* (housekeeper), who was responsible for the maintenance and operation of the former royal residence; hence the name "Conciergerie."

Since the king's move in the 16th century, the Conciergerie has been

---

21 Mayer, p. 190 ; Furet and Richet, p. 195.
22 *Ibid.*.

used as a prison, and this is still the case during the revolution. It is a particularly gloomy establishment, with large spaces as well as tiny dungeons and an interior courtyard divided by an iron gate into two sections, a courtyard for women and another one for men. During the Terror, there are as many as 1,200 prisoners at a time, but they keep coming and going. Every day, large numbers of new prisoners are brought in, but just as many depart for an appointment with the guillotine. In the evening, the names are announced of those who are due to appear the next day before the revolutionary tribunal, at the palace of justice. The tribunal holds its sessions in the "Grand Chamber" of the former royal castle, whence the fleurs-de-lis and other symbols of the monarchy have disappeared to give way to revolutionary icons such as the busts of Marat and Brutus.[23]

The revolutionary method of dispensing justice may be described as Manichean. It is a matter of white versus black, good versus evil; the accused is either guilty or innocent. Those who are acquitted can return home immediately, which is quite often the case. Even in the case of relatively minor misdeeds (or *avant-la-lettre* Orwellian "thought crimes"), there is only one penalty for those who are found guilty: death. In addition, everything must go very quickly. Normally, one single session is sufficient to decide whether it will be liberty or death.

The atmosphere at the Conciergerie is conjured up by this section of a song that was popular at the time, *La Trinité des républicains*, "The Trinity of the Republicans":

Non, rien ne peut se comparer	No, nothing can compare
À la sombre conciergerie.	To the gloomy conciergerie.
Le soleil craint de pénétrer	The sun does not dare to shine
La grille de barreaux garnie,	Behind its elaborate barred curtain,
Mais, demain, l'on me jugera,	But tomorrow I will be judged,
On fixera ma destinée	And my destiny will be sealed
Et le tribunal m'ouvrira	The tribunal will open for me
La porte... or la croisée.[24]	The gate to the prison... or to the afterlife.

Those condemned to death are executed the day after the trial, except if that happens to be "*décadi*," the day of rest of the Republican ten-day "week," which the executioner is also entitled to enjoy. On the morning

---

23   Hillairet (1969), pp. 204, 291-94; Sournia, pp. 103-06; *Les lieux de l'histoire de France*, pp. 302-03.

24   *Chansonnier révolutionnaire*, p. 158.

of the fatal day, in what is called *salle de toilette* ("washroom"), the prisoner has to hand over her or his personal belongings, the neck is freed and the hair is cut—so as not to impede the proper functioning of the cleaver. Then the condemned are conveyed, a dozen at the same time, on a cart which, accompanied by soldiers on foot and on horseback, begins the slow trek towards death.[25] We will soon follow one of these carts.

The most famous prisoner of the Conciergerie is Marie-Antoinette, who is transferred there from the Temple on August 1, 1793. The former queen is the object of particularly ardent hatred on the part of the revolutionaries. They contemptuously nickname her *l'Autrichienne*, a term which means "the Austrian woman" but also happens to contain the word *chienne*, "bitch." They are convinced that she instigated the king against the revolution from the start, which is basically correct. However, in pamphlets with pornographic illustrations, some radicals like Hébert also accuse her of all kinds of imaginary misdeeds, including adultery with Louis's brothers, lesbian relations with court ladies, incest with her little boy, and so forth. Such accusations are thrown in her face during her trial, but she puts up a spirited defense.[26] In other respects, too, she has to endure a lot of particularly nasty abuse. And it is of course inevitable that she is finally condemned to death.

The execution takes place on October 16, 1793. In the morning, in the *salle de toilette*, the "widow Capet" receives a very thorough haircut, but is given a bonnet to cover her head. She has asked to be driven by the guillotine in a closed carriage, like her husband, but this favor is refused. However, she is allowed to have a cart just for herself and she takes a seat in it around 11 a.m., dressed in white, hands tied behind her back, and her back turned towards the horses. This is how David sees her appear in the rue Saint-Honoré and draws a quick sketch that will be preserved for posterity.

The crowd at first remains totally silent, but suddenly begins to shout abuse at the former queen when her escorts provocatively exclaim: "Out of the way, make room for the Austrian woman!" However, Marie-Antoinette remains calm and dignified. And when, mounting the scaffold, she

---

25 Hillairet 1969, pp. 271-73.
26 Fraser, pp. 426, 431, more about Marie-Antoinette in the Conciergerie in Hillairet (1969), pp. 294-97.

steps onto the executioner's foot, she politely apologizes to him. Then the axe delivers her from her sufferings. In a farewell letter to her children, written in the Conciergerie prior to her departure for the scaffold, she wrote: "My God, have mercy on me! My eyes have no more tears to shed for you, my poor children, farewell, farewell. Marie Antoinette."

It is exactly a quarter past twelve when the blade comes down. And, of course, the executioner shows the head to the screaming crowd. Then the body is quickly transported to the cemetery of the Madeleine Church, but it proves necessary to wait some time before Marie-Antoinette can be buried next to Louis XVI, since the gravediggers just happen to be on their lunch break. Madame Tussaud, who will later open a museum in London that will become world-famous, takes advantage of the delay to fashion a wax effigy of the dead woman's face.[27]

After the fall of Napoleon, the monarchy will be re-established and the two brothers of Louis XVI will reign one after the other over the French. During this so-called Restoration of 1814/1815-1830, the cell where Marie-Antoinette was incarcerated will be transformed into a chapel, somewhat in the style of the Expiatory Chapel, and will subsist in that form into the 21st century. But the Conciergerie also preserves the memory of other famous prisoners, for example the twenty Girondins who, the day before their execution, organized a fine dinner there, abundantly washed down with great wines—from Bordeaux, we presume—and accompanied by many eloquent farewell speeches. The Conciergerie will continue to be used as a prison until 1934, at least partially, because from 1914 on, visits by tourists were allowed.[28]

For a little over a year, from May 1793 to June 1794, the guillotine stands on Place de la Révolution, formerly a royal square named after Louis XV. Without exception, the people sentenced to death at the Palace of Justice have an appointment with the guillotine and all have to make a one-way trip from the Conciergerie to the Place de la Révolution. It is a *via dolorosa* taken by the Widow Capet, Charlotte Corday, Philippe Égalité, Madame Roland, and all sorts of aristocrats and priests. But also by many devoted revolutionaries who, for some obvious or obscure reason, have incurred the wrath of the orchestrators of the Terror.

---

27   Fraser, p. 441.
28   "Conciergerie de Paris."

They include the Girondins, Danton, Desmoulins husband and wife, and Hébert. A total of 1,119 people will be guillotined on Place de la Concorde.

April 5, 1794. We follow a cart departing from the Conciergerie with, on board, ten people condemned to death. By his robust profile, one can recognize Danton and, next to him, Camille Desmoulins who, not that long ago, at the Palace-Royal, waving a pistol, incited the crowd to seize the Bastille. Today, it is obviously the Cordeliers who have a rendez-vous with the guillotine. But it is not because they were too radical that they are going to die, to the contrary: Robespierre and his consorts have accused them of being insufficiently ardent and overly tolerant towards certain enemies of the revolution. The Cordeliers in the death cart are folks who are considered too "indulgent," too eager to put an end to the Terror of which they are to fall victim.

We take the Pont au Change to the Right Bank and follow the Seine to the Pont Neuf. There, we swing a little to the right to reach the Rue Saint-Honoré, the main street that crosses Paris from east to west. We take a left turn, because we have to go west, towards the square at the beginning of the Champs-Élysées, the wide thoroughfare named after the Elysian Fields, the mythical land of the blessed, located in the confines of the setting sun. (It is for this reason that, during the Great War of 1914-1918, English soldiers will refer to being killed as "going west.")

The Rue Saint-Honoré is a long but relatively narrow street. It is crowded with Parisians eager to watch le *défilé de la mort*, the "pageant of death," from the narrow sidewalks and also from windows and balconies. Sometimes an icy silence prevails, but cries of joy and excitement are often heard and the passengers in the cart are frequently the object of cynical comments and insults and are even spat upon.

Of the condemned, quite a few happen to live on this street. Number 82, for example, is the residence of the Cordelier François Chabot, a former Capuchin monk, who coined the expression "sans-culotte"; he allegedly proclaimed Christ to have been the primordial sans-culotte! Accompanying him on his last journey is one of his neighbors, Claude Bazire, domiciled at number 77. The latter is known for having sponsored a law prohibiting the wearing of ecclesiastical clothes in public. He also introduced a bill obliging French citizens to address each other, as the sans-culottes are accustomed to do, with the familiar *tu* (thou) instead of the formal *vous*, in other words, to *tutoyer* instead of *vouvoyer* each other. The sans-culottes also make it a habit to call each other *citoyen* or *citoyenne*, "citizen," and they like to give each other a "fraternal kiss" (*baiser fraternel*). This egalitarian linguistic terminology contrasts starkly with the traditional terms of address favored by aristocratic and bourgeois "polite society": *monsieur*, an abbreviation of *mon seigneur*, "my lord," and *madame*, "my lady." The more radical revolutionaries detest these forms of address as linguistic fossils from the Ancien Régime.[29] However, the linguistic egalitarianism will not survive Robespierre's radical-revolutionary regime, and the polite forms of address, as well as the custom to use *vous* rather than *tu*, will make a comeback.

The cart passes in front of the Café de la Régence, located at the western corner of Place du Palais-Royal. Not so long ago, this establishment was frequented by characters such as Voltaire, Diderot, d'Alembert, Rousseau, and Benjamin Franklin; later, in 1844, Karl Marx will meet Friedrich Engels there. The painter Jacques-Louis David is a regular here. There he is, on the terrace of the cafe, sketching Danton on his way to the scaffold. It is from the same place that he had also drawn Marie-Antoinette on the way to the guillotine.[30] Standing upright in the cart, Danton recognizes the artist and insults him by loudly calling him a "lackey" (*valet*), meaning a spineless servant of Robespierre's regime.

Number 398 is the residence of the master carpenter Maurice Duplay, and it is in this building that Robespierre has rented an apartment looking out onto the courtyard since July 1791; he will continue to live there until his death. He has a relationship with Eléonore, the eldest of his landlord's three daughters. Their friends call her "Robespierre's fiancée" or "Madame Robespierre"; after the latter's downfall and execution, a few months later, she will be known as "Robespierre's widow." When the cart passes the house, Desmoulins exclaims loudly and prophetically: "Soon it will be your turn, Robespierre!" The Duplay house, including the bedroom of the architect of the Terror, will survive into the 21st century, and the courtyard will temporarily be home to a restaurant called

---

29 Soboul (1968), pp. 213-16 ; Miquel, p. 443.
30 Hillairet (1956), vol. 2, p. 201-02; "L'ancien Café de la Régence"; "Marie Antoinette."

"Le Robespierre."[31]

We arrive at Place de la Révolution, where the instrument of death is waiting patiently. From a distance, the guillotine looks like a door, a door through which many Frenchmen enter the beyond and through which France itself steps into its revolutionary future. The austere profile of "the great machine" also symbolizes the radical break between the past of the Ancien Régime and the Republican future.

Danton now ascends the scaffold. From him too, we may expect winged words for posterity, and we are not disappointed. The executioner, who prevents the great revolutionary from embracing and kissing one of his companions as a farewell, receives an insulting comment: "Fool, you cannot prevent our heads from making love [*baiser*] in the basket!"[32] Then, addressing the executioner again: "Show my head to the people, it is worth it." The blade drops, his head rolls, it is retrieved from the basket, and Danton's last wish is granted.

Since August 10, 1793, the first anniversary of the de facto end of the monarchy, a plaster statue of Lady Liberty has stood next to the base of the former equestrian statue of Louis XV, next to the guillotine. The proceedings here take place in her name. On November 8, 1793, Madame Roland, the "muse" of the Girondins, will address that statue from the scaffold with these winged words: "O Liberty, what crimes are committed in your name!"

The Constitution of 1793

On June 24, shortly after their advent to power, the Montagnards arrange for the Convention to vote for a new constitution, to be known as the "Constitution of the year I" or "Constitution of 1793."[33] This is a remarkable document which, unlike the "liberal" constitution of 1791, emphasizes equality, more so than liberty, even if it specifically recognizes typically liberal rights such as freedom of the press and freedom of wor-

---

31   Hillairet (1956), vol. 1, pp. 212-13; Poisson, pp. 78-80.

32   **Ed. Note:** 'baiser' in contemporary usage means 'kiss' but also had a prior meaning of 'making love.'

33   For a detailed analysis of the Constitution of 1793, see the study by Suret-Canale.

ship. The new constitution introduces universal suffrage for all French males, and even household staff receive the right to vote. However, "the recognition of women's citizenship is denied," as Olivier Coquard has written, despite the fact that "women [have] played a decisive role in the revolutionary action," the emergence of women's patriotic clubs and of "a feminist ideas and action" personified by some great female personalities, for example Olympe de Gouges, author of a Declaration of the Rights of Women (1791).[34] (She will be condemned to death and guillotined in November 1793, but it is not clear if this was done because of her feminism or, more likely, because of her support for the Girondins.) For women, the Revolution will not be a great liberating experience, even though some progress is being made. A new law thus makes divorce possible and another one provides for equal inheritance rights for daughters and sons.[35]

On the social level, the new constitution goes as far as to recognize certain socio-economic rights, such as the right to work, to education by the state and to public assistance for the needy. Such a program clearly postulates an active role of the state in the socio-economic life of the nation. It therefore violates the liberal principles so dear to the hearts of the Girondins, but it is clearly grist for the mill of the Parisian sans-culottes, whose support enabled the Montagnards to triumph over the Girondins at the Convention. The sans-culottes have been agitating for a long time for the recognition of the right to work, for public education, compulsory and free, for all French, female as well as male, and for recognition of the right of the poor to public assistance.[36] On the other hand, the new constitution also enshrines the right to hold property, that is, private ownership of the means of production, not to be confused with private personal possessions. This reflects the interests and the liberal principles which the typically petit-bourgeois Jacobins share with the overwhelmingly grand-bourgeois Girondins.

The threat posed by the enemies, both external and internal, to which Robespierre and his associates feel the only effective response is the combination of ruthless domestic repression, the Terror, and impla-

---

34   Coquard, pp. 188-89.
35   Garrioch, p. 322; Hazan (2014), p. 313.
36   Soboul (1968), pp. 90 ff.

cable warfare, means that the implementation of the new constitution must be postponed until after the war. At the start of the Year II of the revolutionary calendar, that is, in October-November 1793, the Convention begins to achieve successes in the life-and-death struggle against its enemies. The Republican troops, known as *les bleux*, "the men in blue," because of the color of their uniforms, gain the upper hand against the rebels in the Vendée, and Toulon is taken back from the royalists and their British allies; a young officer, Napoleon Bonaparte, an artillery specialist, shows himself to be particularly deserving there.

These successes make it possible for the Montagnards to implement even some very important parts of their radical constitutional program. On February 4, 1794, in the name of equality, the Convention abolishes slavery in all the French colonies, much to the chagrin of the surviving Girondins whose fortunes often happen to be generated by the slave trade and who regard slaves as a legitimate and untouchable form of property.[37] The same Montagnards, whom conventional historiography tends to condemn for their sponsorship of the Terror, undoubtedly a bloody affair that demanded thousands of victims, but undoubtedly not all innocent folks, thus abolished an institution which, during the thousands of years of its existence, victimized millions of human beings. But the general public is unaware of this, because most historians remain silent about this enormous contribution of Robespierre and his Jacobin associates to the advancement of democracy. (As the Franco-Colombian historian Rosa Amelia Plumelle-Uribe has rightly pointed out, there is a tendency in the West to devote a lot of attention to the crimes of which white people have been the victims, while entire genocides, committed by whites, but with non-whites as victims, such as that of the "Indians" of America and the genocidal system of slavery, are either glossed over or downplayed.)[38] In any event, thanks to the Convention, that is to say to the French Revolution in its most radical phase, France can be proud to have been the very first country to have abolished slavery. In 1802, however, Napoleon will annul this radical measure of the Convention in the name of respecting property rights. Slavery will be definitively abolished

---

37   See e.g. Munford, p. 524: "In Nantes, Rouen and Bordeaux ... were formed some of France's first large concentrations of capital—capital that later wended its way to large industrial establishments."

38   Plumelle-Uribe, *passim*.

in France in the context of another radical revolution, the one of 1848.

IMAGE 19. Abolition of slavery by the Convention on February 4, 1794.

Let us return for a moment to the theme of the abolition of slavery by the Montagnards, The abolition of slavery was celebrated in a revolutionary song entitled *La liberté des nègres*, "The Liberty of the Negroes." Here is the text of the final verse of that song:

> *Americains, l'égalité*
> *Vous proclame aujourd'hui nos frères.*
> *Vous avez à la liberté*
> *Les mêmes droits héréditaires.*
> *Vous êtes noirs, mais le bon sens*
> *Repousse un préjugé funeste...*
> *Seriez-vous moins interestings,*
> *Aux yeux des républicains blancs?*
> *La couleur tombe, and l'homme reste!*[39]

---

39   *Chansonnier révolutionnaire*, p. 163.

Americans [i.e. inhabitants of the New World, specifically, the French colonies], equality
Today proclaims you our brothers.
You have freedom
And the same hereditary rights.
You are black, but common sense
Rejects a fatal prejudice...
You are equally important,
In the eyes of white Republicans!
The skin color is not important, but the human being!

On the economic front, the Montagnards experience some difficulties. They appear to be unable, or more likely unwilling, to implement the Law of the Maximum. This results in price increases and a concomitant growing discontent among sans-culottes. The latter are the folks who put Robespierre and his companions in power, and it is on their support that the regime of the Montagne ultimately depends. Robespierre may be a radical but he is and remains a bourgeois and a believer in the free market. He therefore refuses to follow the radical economic policies touted by the Cordeliers, and especially their extremist wing led by Hébert, as the solution to the economic problems. In March 1794, Robespierre orders the main Hebertists to be arrested and guillotined, and this triggers an alienation between the Montagne and the sans-culottes. Almost simultaneously, the Montagnards are forfeiting the support of dedicated revolutionaries who have had enough of the Terror and advocate a more tolerant attitude towards the enemies on the right and the bourgeois opponents of the Law on the Maximum. These "indulgents," whose number includes Danton and Desmoulins, also end up under the revolutionary blade, namely, on April 5, 1793; we have already accompanied them on their transfer from the Conciergerie to the scaffold.

While Robespierre acquires more enemies on the political right, he also loses the little credit he still enjoys on the left, among the sans-culottes, because of some measures he takes either out of conviction or in a futile attempt to win friends on the right. First, he dissolves the "revolutionary army" tasked with requisitioning food from the peasants in the countryside to feed the inhabitants of Paris, and also institutions set up to track down the usurers and the monopolists, black beasts of the sans-culottes. Second, he promulgates a new Law of the Maximum, a very lax piece of legislation which allows prices to rise but inhibits wage increases.

This clearly spells the end of the *radicalizatio*n of the revolution, a radicalization which the common people had longed for and enthusiastically welcomed and supported as long as the Montagnards had pursued it. The revolution now takes a step backward, it starts to "de-radicalize." The Parisian demos is unhappy, and strikes break out, but the authorities intervene resolutely in the name of the Le Chapelier law. This terminates the alliance between the Montagne and the sans-culottes, whose admiration and love for Robespierre soon turn to contempt and hatred.[40]

With respect to the war, on the other hand, things continue to go well. In June, after a French victory at Fleurus, near Charleroi, in Belgium, the Austrian Netherlands are "liberated" and incorporated into France. The very first military use of an observation balloon contributed to this French victory. Paradoxically, however, this military success hardly benefits the Montagnard regime: the country is henceforth safer, and therefore the Terror seems less justifiable and the iron fist of Robespierre and others less essential for the survival of the Revolution.

DEATH MOVES TO PLACE DE LA NATION

Robespierre's fate is sealed because, without the support of the Parisian "little people," he is too weak in the face of the growing number of his opponents who are gradually acquiring a majority in the Convention. But the man glorified by many as "the incorruptible one" (*l'incorruptible*) can still rely on that other center of power, the Parisian Commune, a bastion of Jacobinism. For the time being, Robespierre and his associates thus continue to rule—and to apply the policy of Terror. The wheels of the death machine continue to turn unhindered, especially as this is the only way the Mountain, socially and politically isolated, can maintain itself in power. However, the Terror is becoming more discreet because its "theater" is no longer situated in the very heart of the capital.

On June 14, 1794, the guillotine moves from Place de la Concorde to Place de la Bastille, recently rebaptized to Place Antoine in honor of the inhabitants of the Faubourg Saint-Antoine. However, as in the case of Place de la Concorde, there too the local residents protest against the bloodshed in their neighborhood. After merely five days—and 75 exe-

---

40 Soboul (1977), p. 111-16, and Soboul (1988), p. 102-16. See also Guillemin, p. 113ff.

cutions—the guillotine moves again, this time to a square that used to be called Place du Trône, "Square of the Throne," in the Ancien Régime but is now known as Place de la Nation, "Square of the Nation." Death thus ensconces itself in the heart of a quiet, virtually rural district, situated to the east of the Faubourg Saint-Antoine, just outside the built-up center of Paris; on account of its quasi-rural character, this area may be described as a *rus in urbe*, "a bit of countryside in the city."

In the middle of the round open space, lined with trees, two square, 28-meter high columns, erected by the aforementioned architect Ledoux, form a monumental gate piercing the infamous wall of the tax collectors: they will still stand there in the 21st century. The original name of the square, Square of the Throne, referred to an enormous throne that was installed there for the young Louis XIV on the occasion of his return to Paris from Reims; he had made that trip to be anointed as king by the town's bishop in the Cathedral, as every king had done before him. After the fall of the monarchy, the revolutionaries sarcastically "rebaptised" the site to Place du Trône-Renversé, "Square of the Toppled Throne."

The towering throne of Louis XIV stood between the two tall pillars. The architect Ledoux, who incorporated them in the tollgate he erected there on the eve of the French Revolution, had planned to surmount them with statues symbolizing free trade and good fortune, but his plan remained unimplemented. The guillotine, the decapitation machine, is installed to the south of these two "headless" pillars. The duo also conjures up the Pillars of Hercules of Antiquity, marking the end of the familiar Mediterranean Sea and the beginning of the huge and mysterious Atlantic Ocean, the western "waters of death" that swallowed the sun, symbol of life, at the end of each and every day; the pillars were traditionally accompanied by the motto *nec plus ultra*, "there is nothing beyond": not a message that would have been appreciated by the women and men about to be dispatched by the guillotine to the Great Unknown.

The guillotine is set up to the south of these two pillars, will remain there for approximately six weeks, and will cause more than 1,300 heads to roll into its basket. During the Revolution, the "revolutionary razor" will dispatch about 2,500 people in Paris and 13,800 in all of France. That is a lot, but far fewer than many people imagine.[41] We will return

---

41   Statistics from Lévêque and Belot, pp. 14, 91.

later to the topic of the revolutionary terror and its victims, and compare it with the counter-revolutionary "white terror" and with the generally overlooked Napoleonic terror.

About half of the people who will be executed here, including *plus ou moins* 200 women, are ordinary citizens; the other half consists of high-ranking government officials, other prominent folks (*notables*), and members of the nobility and the clergy. The latter category includes sixteen Carmelite nuns from a convent in Compiègne, who mount the scaffold while singing *Veni Creator*. The tragic fate of these unfortunate women will inspire a book by a German author, Gertrud von le Fort, *Die Letzte am Schafott* (English title: "The Song at the Scaffold"). This book will be adapted by Georges Bernanos to serve as libretto for an opera put to music by Francis Poulenc, with as title *Dialogues des carmélites*, "Dialogues of the Carmelites"; written in 1956, this opera's world première will take place one year later in Milan's La Scala theatre, but performances in Paris will soon follow.

Another famous victim of the guillotine on Place de la Nation was the poet André Chénier. Awaiting his execution from Saint-Lazare Prison, he wrote a famous poem, *La jeune captive*, which started with these lines:

> *L'épi naissant mûrit de la faux respecté;*
> *Sans crainte du pressoir, le pampre, tout l'été*
> *Boit the doux présents de l'aurore;*
> *Et moi, comme lui belle, and jeune comme lui,*
> *Quoi que l'heure présente ait de trouble and d'ennui,*
> *Je ne veux pas mourir encore*[42]

> The scythe spares the wheat's young ear;
> Without fear of the press, the vine
> All summer drinks the dawn's sweet gifts;
> And I, likewise beautiful and young,
> Despite the sad and boring present hour,
> Do not yet want to die.

The road to death now leads to the east. Starting from the Conciergerie, the carts loaded with doomed passengers use the Pont au Change to cross to the Right Bank, then head for Place de la Bastille.

---

[42] The full text of the poem, the French original as well as an English translation, may be found here: https://allpoetry.com/La-Jeune-Captive.

At the Church of Saint Paul, in the Marais District, the crowd watching often includes priests who discreetly give the absolution to the Catholics in the carts, among them the sixteen Carmelite nuns. Past the site of the demolished Bastille, the cart follows the long street that used to be known as Rue du Faubourg-Saint-Antoine but has been renamed Rue du Faubourg-Antoine to the Place du Trône-Renversé.

As long as the "revolutionary razor" is installed on Place de la Nation, its victims are buried nearby, namely in the Rue de Picpus, on land belonging to a convent of Augustine nuns, or rather canonesses, founded in 1640 and closed in 1793. During the Middle Ages, this was the location of a hamlet called Picque-Pusse, and in the course of the years this name morphed into Picpus. (The name may originally have referred to the fleas, *puces* in French, that infested an inn of the district.)[43] A discreet burial place is needed, and the walled-in garden of this institution fits the bill perfectly. Two great pits are excavated—three, in fact, but the third one will never be used—to serve as common graves.

After a short, but frequently slow and arduous, trip from Place de la Nation in a cart painted in red, the corpses arrive at dusk. Their clothes are removed, they will be sold, and the revenue will be pocketed by the executioner. The lifeless bodies are subsequently stacked on top of one another in the sinister "Picpus hole" (*trou de Picpus*). The heads are stuffed into empty spaces between bodies. By planting herbs such as thyme and absinthe, it is vainly tried to chase away the stench that pervades the area; lime cannot be used in order to save space, it seems!

After the Revolution, the lot will be sold to a relative of one of the victims buried here. Thus it became possible to erect monuments for the numerous nobles who perished at Place de la Nation, seigneurs with prestigious names such as La Rochefoucauld, Montmorency, Polignac, and Choiseul. Their descendants also acquire the right to be buried here. In 1805, a convent will again be established on this site. It will even be the "mother house" (*maison mère*) of a new religious order, officially called the Sisters of the Sacred Hearts of Jesus and Mary, but soon to be known as the Picpus Sisters or simply as "the Picpus."[44]

The Cemetery of Picpus also features the tomb of the Marquis de

---

43   "Le faubourg Saint-Antoine."
44   Hillairet (1956), vol. 1, pp. 361-62; Poisson, pp. 120-21.

Lafayette, easily recognized by the small stars-and-stripes on top of it. His wife, Adrienne de Noailles, a blue-blooded aristocrat like her husband, was buried there in 1807; she wanted to be close to relatives who had been guillotined. Lafayette himself, known in France as the "hero of the two worlds" (*héros des deux worlds*), joined her later, in 1834. He was buried in earth he himself had brought back from America.[45]

As for the vast nearby square where the guillotine once loomed, after the fall of Napoleon and the restoration of the Bourbon monarchy, it was given back its old name, Place du Trône. In 1845, when the country was still ruled by a king, but this time by a scion of the House of Orléans, Louis-Philippe, the twin columns were crowned, so to speak, with statues of two famous medieval kings of France, Philip August and Saint Louis. By 1880, France was to be a republic again, and in that year the square was baptized Place de la Nation. A few years later, in 1889, on the occasion of the 100th anniversary of the storming of the Bastille, a sculpture entitled "The Triumph of the Republic" was placed in the center of the square. A huge number of socialists, communists, and other left-wing folks congregated on Place de la Nation in February 1934, and this huge demonstration marked the beginning of common anti-fascist action that yielded a Popular Front government led by Leon Blum, whose advent was to be welcomed by another major demonstration on the same square. May Day celebrations as well as strikes plus, during the German occupation, actions by the Resistance also contributed to turn Place de la Nation into a topographical icon of anti-fascism, republican patriotism, and left unity. Unsurprisingly, the German occupiers responded by vandalizing the "Triumph of the Republic" monument. After the war, the square continued to witness demonstrations, including some by Algerian *indépendentistes* that were bloodily repressed by the police on May 1, 1951 and on July 14, 1953.[46]

---

45 Jouve, pp. 22-23.
46 "Place de la Nation."

7. 1794-1799: From Thermidor to Brumaire

Thermidor: From City Hall to Place de la Concorde

IT WAS ONLY A QUESTION OF TIME before the *conservative* bourgeois opposition in the Convention ceased to be terrorized and attempted to bring down the *radical* bourgeois Robespierre and his friends. This attempt was successfully carried out on July 27 and 28, 1794, or 9 and 10 Thermidor of the year II of the Revolution, according to the republican calendar. That is why these events are described as the "Thermidorian reaction" or "Thermidor" *tout court*.

On 9 Thermidor, during a particularly stormy session of the Convention, Robespierre faces tough opposition for the very first time. He withdraws to City Hall, where he has been able to count on the support of the Commune and the Parisian sections. However, his adversaries have meanwhile obtained a majority in the Convention, and they send National Guard members from the wealthy districts of western Paris to City Hall. These men burst into the room where Robespierre has sought refuge, but run into resistance; pistol shots are exchanged, and Robespierre is shot in the face. It is not known who shot him, and it was perhaps a suicide attempt. Unconscious, his jawbone torn off, "the incorruptible" is dragged to the Conciergerie where, without the formality of a trial, he is ordered to be put to death.

The execution of Robespierre as well as some of his collaborators, including Saint-Just and Couthon, takes place the next day, the tenth day of Thermidor. For this special occasion, the guillotine is once again dressed on Place de la Concorde, in the heart of Paris, instead of on the distant Place du Trône-Renversé. "The incorruptible" is near death and unconscious and quite a few of his friends are also in bad shape; the blade brings them instant relief.

An anti-Montagnard song composed at the time, "Hymn of the Ninth of Thermidor" (*l'Hymne du neuf Thermidor*), offers this comment about the death of Robespierre:

C'en est fait... d'un tribun farouche,	The deed is done... the terrible tribune's
Le glaive a puni la fureur;	fury has been punished by the sword;
La liberté fut dans sa bouche,	His mouth was full of liberty,
Le despotisme dans son cœur.[1]	But despotism inhabited his heart.

Conventional historiography has similarly described Robespierre in the Thermidorian fashion as a bloodthirsty autocrat, while hardly ever mentioning his merits. And the same thing may even be said about the authorities of France and Paris where, even today, no name of a monument, street, or square conjures up the memory of the "incorruptible" lawyer from Arras. As is noted by Eric Hazan, "in 1946, when the newly liberated country may be said to have been in a revolutionary mood, the Place du Marché-Saint-Honoré, site of the original Jacobin Club, was named Place Robespierre, but this decision was cancelled in 1950 in the context of a political comeback of the French bourgeoisie; its hatred of Robespierre has burned brightly ever since Thermidor."[2] On the other hand, in the formerly very red suburb of Montreuil, a subway station bears the name of Robespierre. This has been so since 1936. This also happened to be a time when the left was in the ascendant in France, with socialists, communists, and other radicals forming a "Popular Front" government. Honoring Robespierre with the name of a subway station was an initiative of the communist leader Jacques Duclos.

It is remarkable that the sans-culottes did not lift a finger to save Robespierre. The hero of the ordinary people, so beloved by sans-culottes not so long ago, has indeed totally lost his popularity. The Parisian plebs feel betrayed by him and the other Montagnards and believe that his downfall will mean the end of the unpopular measures he has taken

---

1   *Chansonnier révolutionnaire*, p. 205.
2   Hazan (2002), p. 43. The communists, very popular at the time because of their active role in the Resistance, were partners in the governing coalition.

recently, especially his law setting limits on wages. But the sans-culottes will be terribly disappointed, their lot will not improve at all, *au contraire*. The new leaders of the country are representatives of the affluent bourgeoisie, and they intend to use political power for their own advantage, not to put themselves at the service of the demos; ideologically, moreover, they are committed to liberalism, so they are not prepared to introduce laws determining wages and prices or any sort of regulations of economic activities. They have confidence in the magic of the free market, they firmly believe it is good for themselves and therefore good for all Frenchmen. If, as a result of the interplay of supply and demand on the free market, prices rise and ordinary people die of hunger, well, too bad! All one can do is to wait for better days, because Adam Smith's "invisible hand" will ensure that everything is back to order sooner or later.

In any event, the economy is "liberated by the Thermidorian regime from the controls imposed earlier by the Jacobins, particularly the Robespierrists," to the advantage of the producers, merchants, landlords, speculators, and all sorts of war profiteers, but to the disadvantage of what are now called the consumers. In December 1794, all price controls are abolished. This is done even though the harvests have been poor and the country is at war, which causes the price of bread and other essential types of food to rise steeply. Conversely, there are fewer jobs and wages experience further downward pressure as a result of the measures such as the closure, in February 1795, of the state-run workshops that had been founded by the Montagnards to create jobs for the worst-off Parisian plebeians. In addition, the small producers of the Parisian sans-cullotterie no longer receive orders for the production of war material, henceforth the war will mean lucrative opportunities for the big producers. Soboul writes the following about this issue: There could no longer be any question of favoring small independent producers, now that complete economic freedom reigned and war production was viewed as the perfect working ground for the large-scale capitalist activities of the industrial bourgeoisie.[3]

The capital, in particular, is affected by the shortages, and the exceptionally high price of bread causes the sans-culottes to suffer from hunger. Unlike the Montagnards, the Thermidorians are unwilling to

---

3   Soboul (1968), p. 81. See also Guillemin, pp. 117-18.

undertake anything to try to lower prices of bread, wine, and other essentials. Worse, prices rise extra fast because new regressive indirect taxes are introduced; the customs wall around Paris, for example, which ceased to function in 1791, will be reactivated in October 1798, making wine again much more expensive within the city limits.[4] This causes unprecedented hardship for the little people of the capital, and police reports mention numerous cases of suicide. "Death and hunger went mostly after the poorest," writes historian Denis Woronoff, and adds:

> Seldom has the opposition of "the fat and the lean" been more obvious than at that time, and seldom have the social problems generated that much hatred on one side and fear on the other.[5]

In comparison with the policy of the Montagnard Convention, unquestionably *progressive* in many respects but too often overshadowed by Terror, the socio-economic course of the post-Thermidorian Convention may be described as *regressive,* and this is also the case politically. The new regime proceeds ruthlessly to undo the democratization introduced by the Montagnard Convention. The new masters of France are *grands bourgeois*, men of considerable property, and they intend to turn the French republic into a state at their service, to be described as a "republic of propertied men" (*république des propriétaires*), Conversely, these "people of means," (*gens de bien*), considering themselves to be "honorable men" (*honnêtes gens*), are determined to prevent the common people—the "rabble" (*canaille*), the "rebellious beggars" (*gueux*), the "have-nothings" (*gens de rien*)— from exerting the slightest pressure on the government via institutions such as the Commune.

The political organ of the overwhelmingly plebeian revolutionary Parisians, architecturally externalized by its home, the Hôtel de Ville, is shut down without any formalities. The Parisian municipal authorities cease to exist, the city loses its autonomy and finds itself, as Jean Tulard has written, "brutally placed under the tutelage of the French State."[6] When Napoleon comes to power, he will neutralize Paris as a center of revolutionary agitation by dividing the city into twelve arrondissements—to become twenty much later, in 1859—each with its own town

---

4 Pauwels (2020a), pp. 258-59.
5 Woronoff, pp. 18-23, quotation from p. 23.
6 Tulard, p. 365.

hall. How did Caesar put it again?: *Divide et impera*, "Divide and rule!" The Parisian city hall will be left standing, but until very late in the 20th century, the French capital will have no overall municipal authorities and therefore no mayor either. Along with the rest of the department of the Seine, of which it becomes a part, the capital will be run like any other department, namely, by a prefect, not elected locally but an outsider appointed by the French state, assisted by a police chief likewise appointed by the state. It will only be in 1977 that Paris will again have its own city council and mayor, but the city's police force will remain under state control indefinitely.

As for the Parisian sections, they have been stripped of all sans-culottes, Jacobins, and other radicals and are henceforth dominated by government officials, businessmen, doctors, lawyers and others "notables." Some sections thus even end up under the control of monarchists. Representatives of the lower classes are now also rigorously excluded from the National Guard; to achieve this, it suffices to decree that the members of the Guard must obtain their uniform and their weapons at their own expense. And it goes without saying that there is no longer any place for the simple man of the street—and even less for the simple woman of the street!—within the Convention itself. The distinction between "active" and "passive" citizens is reintroduced, and the right to vote is restricted to owners of a relatively large property. "That a country is to be ruled by those who own property is part of the order conferred by nature," is how Thermidorian Boissy d'Anglas proudly explains this arrangement. It is hardly surprising that, with such features, the new regime will soon be known as the "republic of the property owners."

Depantheonization of the Jacobins

The Thermidorians take aim not only at the lower classes, especially the Parisian sans-culottes, but also at the Jacobins, that is, the radical, progressive elements of the bourgeoisie who had shown themselves ready to collaborate with the sans-culottes and to defend and promote, at least to a certain extent, the interests of the common people, as Robespierre and the other Montagnards had done. The Jacobin club of Paris is closed during the night of November 11 to 12, 1794. The same fate will soon befall the Jacobin meeting places in the provinces. The club of the Cordeliers is eliminated a little later, in January 1795. The club will be dissolved in January 1795 under circumstances to be discussed in later pages. After that, the monastery buildings will be demolished, except for the Gothic refectory where the Cordeliers also met on occasion, as well as a few other architectural remnants; these remains will subsist into the 21st century at the numbers 11-15 of the rue de l'École-de-Médecine.[7]

Conversely, the Thermidorian regime reveals itself to be extremely indulgent towards the enemies of the republic, the main victims of the Terror under Robespierre. The policy of Terror comes to an end, but that is not all. The émigrés, aristocrats as well as the unconstitutional priests, are allowed to return to the country, their counter-revolutionary sins are forgiven, and they are hardly disturbed when they publicly resume their anti-republican activities, which is facilitated by the complete restoration of the freedom of worship, in February 1795.

Thermidor is associated with the end of the Terror and therefore receives glowing assessments from numerous historians. But the reality is much less rosy. The 48 hours following Robespierre's arrest witness a veritable orgy of executions by his supporters and 11 Thermidor breaks all the records for a single day, when 71 heads roll into the basket.[8] It is only then that Paris will be finished with the systematic terror, orchestrated by the national authorities, that is, the highly *visible* Terror, symbolized by the guillotine installed in the center of a square in the heart of the city in the middle of the country. But this terror gives way to another kind of terror, an improvised and even "savage" terror in the sense that death does not exist via the relatively humanitarian guillotine, but via lynchings and even torture. This kind of terror is much less visible, even in retrospect, that is, in the eyes of historians, because it rages mostly in the provinces; and it focuses on a very different kind of victims, for whom historians generally have little or no sympathy, namely folks who are held to be responsible for the Terror under the regime of Robespierre: the Jacobins. During this "counter-terror," the revolution thus eliminates the most enthusiastic revolutionaries, and it does so with the enthusiastic support of the counter-revolutionary elements whose return was made possible by Thermidor.

---

7   Poisson, pp. 104-05; Sournia, pp. 43-45.
8   "Französische Revolution," p. 156

In stark contrast to their very harsh intervention against the Jacobins and other radicals, the Thermidorians are indeed extremely indulgent toward all those who, politically, are positioned to their right, that is, the aristocratic and clerical émigrés. These partisans of a return to the Ancien Régime, irreconcilable enemies of the republic, even of a moderate republic like that which is the fruit of Thermidor, use this opportunity to take revenge on all that is Jacobin. In Paris, even moderate revolutionaries are shocked by the provocative public behavior of anti-Jacobin and sometimes even openly royalist young men of wealthy background; eccentrically dressed and armed with clubs they call their "constitutions," these *muscadins* ("dandies") or *jeunesse dorée* ("gilded youth"), a kind of anti-sans-culottes, rule the Palais-Royal, where the Café de Chartres is one of their favorite haunts.[9]

In any event, these are tough times for the Jacobins. Thousands of them are mistreated, arrested, prosecuted and in many cases executed. Thousands are simply lynched, especially in the south-east of the country and in other regions where the returning émigrés or the relatives of the victims of the previous terror are now free to take revenge on the Robespierrian *buveurs de sang* ("drinkers of blood"). This "white terror" will kill roughly as many as Robespierre's Terror, without the excuse of the threat represented by foreign enemies, because for France the war is now going very well. Especially in the Midi, the south of the country, thousands of Jacobins are executed or lynched in an orgy of violence. Cities like Lyon, Marseille and Toulon witness massacres in the prisons, massacres comparable to those of September 1792 in Paris. It is estimated that between 14,000 and 15,000 Jacobins are liquidated in southern France.[10] In only a few weeks, the "white terror" demands more victims in the single department of Bouches-du-Rhône than than the entire original Terror.[11] The French historian Edgar Quinet, who was certainly not an admirer of Robespierre, drew the conclusion that the anti-Montagnards "far surpassed" Robespierre "in the art of ridding themselves in cold-blooded fashion of their adversaries."[12]

---

9   Woronoff, p. 12 ff. More on this terminology in https://www.definitions.net/definition/MUSCADIN.

10   Mayer, pp. 209-20; Woronoff, pp. 34-35; Lévêque and Belot, p. 14.

11   Coquard, p. 217.

12   Quoted in Mayer, p. 217.

After Thermidor, General Bonaparte also finds himself temporarily in trouble, because he had sympathized with the Jacobins. He can save himself thanks to his friendship with Barras, one of Thermidor's "grey eminences." Barras is one of the most powerful men in France; as Minister of the Interior, he controls, for example, the police which, after Thermidor, developed into an increasingly important instrument of power (The Thermidorian state has been described, not incorrectly, as a "police state.") Barras resides in luxurious offices in the Luxembourg Palace and is known as the "king of the republic."[13] His friend Bonaparte, the opportunist Corsican, is quick to abjure Jacobinism.

Another facet of the anti-Jacobin reaction after Thermidor is the decanonization inflicted on the martyrs and other heroes on the side of the Jacobins, Cordeliers, and sans-culottes. The main victim is Marat. After his death, the latter was originally buried under a weeping willow on the grounds of the Cordelier monastery that had been the home of the homonymous club; but he was reburied with pomp and circumstance in the Pantheon, a mausoleum that the Constituent Assembly had erected in April 1791 for the heroes of the new revolutionary France. The Pantheon was intended to be a republican counterpart to the former royal mausoleum of Saint-Denis which had been vandalized by the revolutionaries.

Marat, martyr of the radical revolution, was the most famous of the Cordeliers and therefore incarnated radical republicanism, so the men who came to power with Thermidor are not grateful to him at all, to the contrary. His mortal remains are therefore unceremoniously "depantheonized," that is, removed from the Pantheon; Marat is reburied in the cemetery of the neighboring church of Saint-Étienne-du-Mont. Busts of the great Cordelier are broken into pieces and tossed into the Seine or onto garbage dumps. And David's famous painting—unquestionably his masterpiece, *The Death of Marat*, is removed from the interior of the Convention and "returned to sender," that is, given back to the artist. He will take it with him when, after the fall of Napoleon, he will emigrate to Belgium. Upon his death in Brussels, his family will offer the painting to the local Museum of Fine Arts, where it will join the Bruegels and Rubens as a major attraction. Marat would certainly spin in his grave if he found out that this museum is officially designated as a "royal" establish-

---

13 Jouve, p. 82.

ment.[14] On account of the obviously "ephemeral nature of heroic status," writes Ina Caro, it was decided to "institute a rule requiring that 'pantheonizations' could take place only after ten years had passed since 'the death of the great man' in question."[15]

The bourgeoisie or "middle class" is not a homogeneous class. In reality, the term describes two different and often antagonistic classes, the well-to-do, "patrician" grande (or haute) bourgeoisie or upper-middle class, and the low-income, sometimes even very poor, "plebeian" "petite bourgeoisie" or lower-middle class. Thermidor signifies a triumph for the former, the upper-middle calls, but a defeat for the latter, the lower-middle class. The grande bourgeoisie is now in control of Paris. And the sans-culottes, mostly petty bourgeois and champions of revolutionary radicalism, like their Jacobin allies, but also the dangerous revolutionary shock troops, are no longer needed or wanted there. They are forced to withdraw to the Faubourg Saint-Antoine whence, in the hot summer of 1789, they had stormed into the heart of the royal city to revolutionize the capital and the entire country. As it is, many sans-culottes have already left the revolutionary stage, having been recruited into the army and sent abroad to do battle against foreign, rather than domestic enemies. What is left of the radical revolutionary fighters now retires meekly to their faubourg and other plebeian neighborhoods.

Even so, the time of revolutionary eruptions is not yet over. The sans-culottes, and ordinary Parisians in general, have absolutely nothing more to say politically, and now they must manage without their former Jacobin allies and sympathizers within the bourgeoisie. It is therefore only "in the street" that they can express their growing discontent with the new regime. On the 12th of Germinal of the revolutionary year III, that is, on April 1, 1795, a first major demonstration starts spontaneously in the Faubourg Saint-Antoine. Consisting mainly of women, who had already gathered in front of bakeries early in the morning, a "mob" of denizens of the *faubour* treks to the Tuileries to express its grievances to the members of the Convention. They are dispersed without much difficulty by the troops concentrated there. But the fire of the discontent continues to smolder. The first day of Prairial—May 20—of the same year

---

14   Woronoff, p. 17.
15   Caro, pp. 294-95.

witnesses the last revolt of the sans-culottes. It is again a mostly female affair, initiated by women lining up at bakeries at sunrise. The alarm bells ring, and a large crowd of sans-culottes gathers and heads once again for the Tuileries. The Convention's meeting room is occupied and the crowd clamours loudly for "bread or death" and "bread and the constitution de 1793"! But one of the deputies, Jean-Bertrand Féraud, tries to block the crowd's access to the meeting hall and even provokes the demonstrators; a fight breaks out, a shot is fired, and Féraud is killed.[16] His head is stuck on a pike and thrust menacingly under the nose of the President of the Convention. But most of the Thermidorians are able to slip away. A handful of remaining Montagnards proclaim their sympathy for the demonstrators, but at the end of the day the latter withdraw without having achieved anything concrete.

The Thermidorian majority reestablishes control of the situation at the Convention. The army is called in and, on May 23, twenty thousand soldiers march to the Faubourg Saint-Antoine and enter the suburb via the Place de la Bastille. The creation of this vast square in 1789 had facilitated the sans-culottes' invasions of Paris in the wake of the fall of the Bastille; now the vast open space reveals itself to be useful for unfriendly traffic in both directions. Faced with such a show of force, the sans-culottes do not stand a chance. They surrender without even firing a shot, are immediately disarmed, and even have to give up their beloved pikes. Against the real or alleged leaders of these two revolts, known as "Germinal" and "Prairial," lawsuits are brought and a significant number of "terrorists" or "Jacobin conspirators" are executed or end up in jail.[17]

Various factors determined the failure of Germinal and Prairial. One was lack of leadership, organization, and political experience on the side of the sans-culottes, henceforth deprived of their Jacobin bourgeois allies. The Parisian demos lack capable leaders and has not yet been able to formulate a political program of their own. Moreover, large numbers of male sans-culottes have left Paris to serve in the army, hence the disproportionately large number of women in the revolutionary crowds involved in Germinal and Prairial. The remaining Jacobins will continue to remain active for some time, but after Prairial the defeated and deflated

---

16   Godineau, pp. 331-46; Alpaugh, p. 178.
17   Woronoff, pp. 25-29.

sans-culottes are down for the count.

Thermidor brings the radical phase of the Revolution to an end. There is no longer any prospect of a truly egalitarian republic, a project which, for a brief moment, namely, under Robespierre, seemed to be part of the possibilities. The modest but admittedly not insignificant progress that had been made during this radical phase towards some kind of "social democracy," is ruthlessly rolled back by the Thermidorians, who detest the ideas of social equality and interventionism in the economy. The Revolution returns to the bourgeois ideas of its initial phase, the ideas of the Feuillants and other "men of 1789." These were certainly progressive and even radical from the Ancien-Régime perspective, but conservative and even regressive in comparison with the ideas of the Jacobins, the "men of 1793," and certainly in comparison with the amorphous and unrealized egalitarian utopia of the sans-culottes. Soboul writes:

> Exhausted and disorganized, the common people had been defeated by the bourgeoisie with the support of the army ... The revolution was over. The Prairial revolt was the last, tragic episode in the class struggle that had raged between the factions of the Third Estate of 1789.[18]

The eclipse of the common people and its egalitarian ideal also find a linguistic reflection. The polite form of address, the *vouvoiement* or "use of *vous*," is making a comeback to the detriment of the familiar form, the *tutoiement* or "use of *tu*," introduced by the Montagnards, and the republican appellation "citizen" has to give way—not immediately, but gradually—to *madame*, "madam," and *monsieur*, "sir," terminology redolent of the Ancien Régime"[19]

However, the bourgeoisie which, after Thermidor, controls the Convention and thus holds power not only in Paris but throughout France, is and remains a revolutionary and republican bourgeoisie, and it does not want a return to the Ancien Régime and a restoration of the monarchy, not even a constitutional monarchy. A republic, a conservative republic, is the kind of state that serves the interests of the upper bourgeoisie. The monarchy, on the other hand, used to serve the interests of the nobility and the clergy and can be expected to do so again in the event of the restoration of the monarchy. In addition, countless Thermidorian bur-

---

18   Soboul (1977), pp. 119-20, 125-26.
19   Soboul (1968), pp. 215-16.

ghers have purchased lands formerly of the Church or castles formerly of the nobility at relatively low prices and quite a few of them are members of the Convention who voted for the death penalty for the king. A restoration of the Ancien Régime therefore constitutes a serious threat for their fortune and even their life; the white terror has demonstrated that royalists would exact a bloody revenge.

After Thermidor, the well-to-do bourgeoisie, statistically a tiny minority of the French people, finds itself high in the saddle of power, but far from comfortable and secure. The new regime feels threatened by the sans-culottes, whose revolutionary flame may not yet be fully extinguished, and by the remaining Jacobins, who still cannot be counted out. By putting an end to the Terror, that is, to the ruthless struggle of the republicans against all real or imaginary counter-revolutionaries, and by letting the émigrés of the nobility and the clergy return to France, Thermidor has also emboldened the counter-revolutionary, anti-republican forces, and these are now openly and aggressively striving to restore a constitutional monarchy or, even worse, a *retour en arrière* to the Old Regime. Even within the upper bourgeoisie's own ranks, some elements begin to view a return to the monarchy as a possible solution to the problems, including a possible comeback of the Jacobins.

SHOOTING RABBITS ON THE PLAIN OF GRENELLE

In the fall of 1795, the Thermidorians want to introduce a new constitution to stabilize their regime, in other words, to solidify and perpetuate the hegemony of the republican bourgeoisie. The elections required to do so are cynically and openly manipulated, for example, by a decision specifying that two-thirds of the delegates of the new legislative institutions must be made up of members of the existing Convention, in other words, by Thermidorians. This triggers a revolt by the royalists who believe, not without reason, that they would otherwise win the elections. Armed royalists, including members of the "gilded youth," assemble on Vendemiaire 13 (October 5) in the prosperous district of the stock exchange, known as "the money district." Shouting slogans such as "Long live the king!" and "Down with the Convention!," they head for the Tuileries, where the assembly, dominated by the Thermidorians, is in session. In this hour of danger, the "republic of the men of property" cannot count on the support of the Parisian demos and its fighting force, the sans-culottes. The latter had always been ready to defend the republican cause before, but Germinal and Prairial have proven that it is no longer "their" republic. That is why the army is called upon to come to the rescue.

IMAGE 20. Napoleon disperses a crowd of royalist demonstrators in front of the Church of Saint-Roch with "a whiff of grapeshot."

Barras, who has taken over the direction of operations, entrusts his protégé Bonaparte with the task of transforming the Tuileries into a kind of fortress. The Corsican orders his artillery to fire at virtual point blank range at a compact mass of royalists who have gathered in front of the Saint-Roch Church, located in the rue Saint-Honoré, planning to reach the Tuileries via a narrow side street. Between two and three hundred demonstrators are killed. Bonaparte laconically informs the Convention that he snuffed out the threat by spraying the royalist crowd with a "whiff of grapeshot." The Thermidorians are impressed and grateful. They will not only decide to forget his Jacobin antecedents but also reward him with a heap of promotions. A French historian writes: "From that day on, Bonaparte stood in the good graces of Lady Fortune; in three weeks, she brought him the marks of honor and promotions that constituted the basis of his rapid rise."[20]

Bonaparte's success has revealed that the survival of the regime, republican but antidemocratic and unpopular, henceforth depends on the army. Soon, the Thermidorians will again have to call on military leaders, including Bonaparte.

The first stone of the Church of Saint-Roch, patron saint of plague victims, was laid by Louis XIV in 1653, but work continued until approximately 1740. The very spacious interior of the church, almost as large as that of Notre-Dame, was to feature the tombs of some famous personalities, including Diderot, the philosopher, Le Nôtre, the architect who created the gardens of Versailles for Louis XIV, and of admiral de Grasse who, like Lafayette, was one of the French military personalities who helped the Americans win their War of Independence. In the imposing facade, with its Doric and Corinthian columns, the impacts of the artillery fire ordered by Napoleon will still be visible in the 21st century.

The Thermidorians are now free to pursue their plans for a new constitution and this "Constitution of the Year III" is promulgated on October 26, 1795. Two legislative institutions see the light of day: first, the Council of Five Hundred (*Conseil des Cinq-Cents*), consisting of members of at least thirty years of age, who will sit at the Palace-Bourbon; second, the Council of Elders (*Conseil des Anciens*), a sort of upper chamber of two hundred and fifty representatives, aged at least forty, who can approve or reject the laws passed by the Council of Five Hundred and who meet at the Tuileries Palace. The executive power is entrusted to a kind of cabinet of five men, known as *le Directoire*, the Directory, assisted by seven ministers; these five "directors" are elected by the Elders from a list proposed by the Five Hundred. The era of the Convention has come to an end, henceforth we find ourselves in the system—and in the revolutionary period—of the Directoire.

The Thermidorians have manipulated the electoral procedures to such an extent that barely one million Frenchmen bother to vote. And the candidates are almost exclusively "notables," that is, lawyers, businessmen, well-heeled farmers, journalists, civil servants and other solid burghers—precisely the kind of "honest people" who have supported the

---

20   Hillairet (1956), vol. 1, p. 205.

Thermidorian reaction and whose interests are defended by the regime. The Thermidorians thus constitute a majority in the two "People's Assemblies," just as they did at the Convention. And of course it turns out that the five members of the Directoire are high-profile Thermidorians, gentlemen like Barras, who were already pulling the strings at the time of the plot against Robespierre. However, numerous royalists and other counter-revolutionaries also manage to get elected to the two parliamentary institutions. The royalist danger has therefore not entirely vanished, despite the failure of the Vendémiaire revolt and the (relatively mild) repression that followed. To the contrary, during the new elections, in 1797, the royalists reap such success that, on Fructidor 17 (3 September) of that year, the Directoire annuls the results and has the army arrest the leading royalists. In doing so, the Thermidorians throw off the mask of legality they have hitherto worn so uncomfortably. "Fructidor" also causes the regime to take drastic measures against the counter-revolutionary émigrés and against the Church, considered not without reason as a bastion of royalism. This repression includes the banishment of numerous priests, to distant penal colonies.[21] As for the real or imaginary threat emanating from the left side of the political spectrum, the Directoire already repressed it in 1796.

During the harsh winter of 1795-1796, the Parisian little people are once again tormented by the cold and high prices, but the government does not care. Why not? Because for the businessmen, high-ranking civil servants, and other members of the upper bourgeoisie who constitute the Thermidorian elite, these are in fact good times. The manufacturers, for example, do very well because they supply the army with all sorts of equipment. The war drags on without an end in sight, as we will soon see, and permanent warfare means big business. The friends of the ruling clique can also enrich themselves through all manner of corrupt practices that will later be described as "a plunder of the republic." Under the auspices of the Directoire, we are thus witnessing, on the one hand, a small elite becoming very rich while the bulk of the population, especially in Paris, experiences an increasing pauperization.[22]

What remains of the Jacobins wants to come to the defense of the

---

21   Woronoff, pp. 75, 142.
22   *Ibid.*, pp. 135-37.

starving plebs. In November 1795, a new (crypto-) Jacobin club is founded, the Pantheon Club. Its meetings attract more and more people who listen approvingly to speakers calling for radical reforms and, preferably, a return to the constitution of 1793, which has become almost mythical. But the police are alerted and, in February 1796, General Bonaparte—him again!—arrives at the head of a troop of soldiers to shut down the club by order of the Directoire. Fortunately, this time there is no blood bath. Bonaparte is rewarded with another promotion: he receives the command of an army that is poised to wage war in Italy. There he will achieve spectacular victories, feats of arms that will make him famous and popular.

One of the members of the Pantheon Club is François-Noël Babeuf, a native of Picardy who, for some time, called himself Camille but finally opted for the first name of Gracchus, thus honoring two plebeian heroes of the republican eras of Rome's ancient history. After the closure of the Pantheon Club, he goes underground so that he can continue to agitate in favor of a new, truly egalitarian republic instead of the Directoir's "republic of the property-owners." Babeuf is sometimes described as an "extremist Jacobin" or a "left Robespierrist," but he wants to go further than Robespierre and la Montagne, "the men of 1793," for whom, however, he has nothing but praise. What the "people's tribune" proposes, is nothing less than the suppression of private property and the redistribution of the wealth of the country. Babeuf's objective is not merely a radical political revolution, but also a socio-economic revolution; he wants not only equality vis-à-vis the law, but also social equality. Hence the name he gives to his movement, les Égaux, "the Equals." And that is why Babouvism will be described—also by Marx and Engels—as a kind of embryonic communism, as communism *avant la lettre*.

Babeuf attracts a large number of collaborators and sympathizers, among them the Tuscan immigrant Philippe Buonarotti, a distant descendant of Michelangelo Buonarotti, the great Michelangelo. The man will survive his Babouvist adventure and in 1828 he will write a book about it. In early 1796, the hard core of Babeuf's partisans form what will be called a "Secret Directoire" or "Babouvist Committee" and this is how the "Conspiracy of Equals" (*conspiration des Égaux*) begins. The aim of this conspiracy is to unleash—not only in Paris, but also in the provinces and within the ranks of the army—a revolt of sans-culottes and soldiers, to overthrow the Directoire, and to establish a dictatorship. They distribute pamphlets, including the famous "Manifesto of the Equals" (*manifeste des Égaux*) of April 1796, written by one of Babeuf's collaborators, Sylvain Maréchal. On April 9, a poster appears on the walls of the Parisian suburbs, entitled "Analysis of the doctrine of Babeuf." It proclaims, for example, that "in a genuine community there can be neither rich nor poor" and that "the revolution is about ending inequality." Propaganda is also carried out by means of Babouvist songs such as "Le chant des Égaux" and the "Chanson nouvelle à l'usage des faubourgs." These are preferably belted out—for example, by singer Sophie Lapierre—in Babouvist rallying meeting places such as the Café des Bains Chinois, located on the site of 29 Boulevard des Italiens, of which the operator will turn out to be a police informer.

Les Bains Chinois (The Chinese Baths), constructed in 1787-1789, were an establishment in the style of the "tivolis"—mentioned during our promenade through pre-revolutionary Paris—that proved very trendy in the years before the revolution. But during the turbulent years starting in 1789, this complex of baths, shops, a restaurant, and a café, clustered around a central pagoda, lost much of its well-to-do clientele, including aristocrats who opted for emigration. Les Bains Chinois would subsist and even do well in the first third of the 19th century. However, in 1853 the building was to be demolished to make way for rental properties.

Babeuf's thought obviously purports to be an ideology for the sans-culottes, an ideology aiming to motivate the Parisian demos to undertake once again revolutionary actions like the attack on the Bastille or that on the Tuileries. It is however very doubtful that this can succeed. Not only does it turn out that after the failure of Germinal and Prairial, the revolutionary flame has been extinguished, but another problem has to do with the nature of Babouvist ideology. Babeuf errs when he talks about the "propertyless sans-culottes," that is, when he represents the sans-culottes as proletarians.[23] The sans-culottes are not proletarians, but mostly petty-bourgeois artisans and shopkeepers who are and remain attached to the principle of private property that Babeuf—like Jean-Jacques Rousseau—considers to be the main cause of all social evils. The conspirators can therefore not count on the support of the sans-cu-

---

23 Soboul (1968), p. 38.

lottes, despite their illusions in this respect. It is not without reason that "sans-culottisme" has been described as a mass movement without an ideology, and Babouvism, as an ideology without the support of the popular masses.

Yet another problem for the "people's tribune" and his supporters is the fact that, thanks to his spies like the manager of the Café des Bains Chinois and infiltrators like Grisel, one of the members of the Secret Directoire, the police are aware of their plans. Barras certainly knows what is going on, and Bonaparte perhaps too, but the latter will soon be leaving for the Italian front. It is no coincidence that, in April 1796, two draconian laws are passed, providing for the death penalty for all those who dare to make propaganda for the Constitution of 1793 and/or for the redistribution of private property. A little later, on 19 Floréal of the year IV (10 May 1796), the police strike. Babeuf is arrested, not at his home at number 29 of the rue du Faubourg-Saint-Honoré, but at number 21 of the rue de la Grande-Truanderie, where he and fellow conspirators like Buonarotti are plotting an uprising.

The Babouvists are temporarily locked up in the Temple, but on 10 Fructidor of the year IV (27 August 1796) they are transferred to be tried in the small, sleepy and conservative town of Vendôme, that is, far from possible sympathizers of the Babouvist cause in the Parisian suburbs. In Vendôme, the box of the accused also hosts a handful of Jacobins who have nothing to do with the conspiracy, for example Duplay, the owner of the house in the rue Saint-Honoré where Robespierre used to live and with whose daughter the "incorruptible" had a relationship. Duplay will be acquitted, but Babeuf and one of his friends, Darthé, will be condemned to death, not for their role in the conspiracy, but because they have agitated for the reintroduction of the constitution of 1793. Buonarotti and six other babouvists get away with deportation to a penal colony. On May 27, 1797, Babeuf and Darthé are guillotined and buried in a mass grave in the main cemetery of Vendôme. With this trial and its severe penalties, the Directoire makes it clear that the time of the uprisings in Paris is over and that the Revolution is definitely finished.[24]

Here are a few lines from a Babouvist "new song for the faubourg" (Chanson nouvelle à l'usage des faubourgs), reflecting the conspirators'

---

24   Larue-Langlois, pp. 59 ff.; Woronoff, pp. 55-65.

hope to see soldiers ally with the sans-culottes in an effort to overthrow the Directoire:

Le peuple et le soldat unis	United, the people and the soldier
Ont bien su réduire en débris	Managed to bring down
Le Trône et la Bastille;	The throne and the Bastille;
Tyrans nouveaux, hommes d'État,	You, politicians who are the new tyrants,
Craignez le peuple et le soldat	Fear the wrath of the people and the soldier
Réunis en famille[25]	Reunited in one family

The Babouvists were sorely mistaken. First, with their ideology, they found it impossible to galvanize the sans-culottes. Second, they did not have a shadow of a chance to break the alliance between the army—or, at least, the army leadership—and the Thermidorian regime of the Directoire. A "family reunion" of sans-culottes and soldiers under Babouvist auspices never took place. While the sans-culottes kept their distance from the "conspiracy of equals," the army proved to be downright hostile, as evidenced by an event in Paris in September.

During the Vendôme trial, the Babouvists who, in May 1796, managed to evade the wave of arrests, try to undertake something. They intend to take the five members of the Directoire who sit in the Luxembourg Palace as hostages and then convince the soldiers of the Grenelle barracks to support their coup d'état with arms. On September 9, they go to work, but once again the authorities are on the alert. It turns out that the Luxembourg palace is too strongly defended and so the rebels move on to Grenelle. At that time, Grenelle was a large plain on the southwestern outskirts of the capital, often flooded by the nearby Seine, only partly cultivated, some kind of countryside inside the city, where peasants and shepherds graze their cattle and sheep. (And Eric Hazan mentions that "Parmentier made his first attempts at cultivating potatoes there.") As mentioned before, the toponym Grenelle refers to a piece of land where rabbits were raised—and hunted.

Approximately 800 Babouvists meet in the courtyard of an inn called the Auberge du Soleil, a large house that will subsist into the 21st century at number 226 Rue Vaugirard, still displaying a large golden sun above the entrance.[26] Then they leave to try to convince the soldiers of the Grenelle camp to march on Paris to overthrow the Directoire. But the

---

25 *Chansonnier révolutionnaire*, p. 216.
26 Hazan (2002), pp. 229-30; Hillairet (1956), vol. 3, p. 45.

commander has been warned and, like Bonaparte, he orders to open fire. The rebels are shot like rabbits, more than one hundred of them are killed and the survivors flee in a panic. A number of "*Grenelliens*" drown in an attempt to swim to the safety of the opposite bank of the Seine.

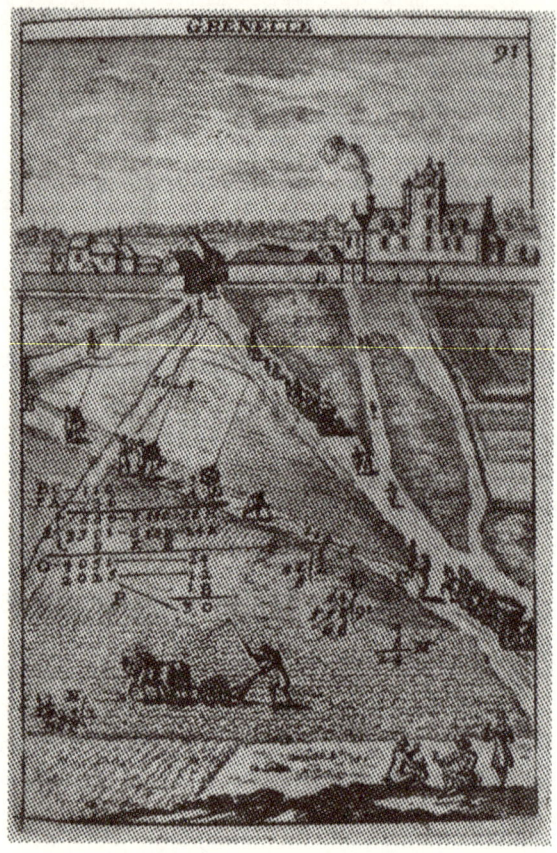

IMAGE 21. The Plain of Grenelle, with Paris in the distance on the left, in the 16th century.

In many ways, the Grenelle incident is the very last flicker of the revolutionary flame in Paris. As we know, the government is republican, of course, but it is no longer revolutionary and it eagerly takes advantage of the opportunity to organize a manhunt against all the Babouvists, Jacobins, and other ardent revolutionaries who are still at large. Some eight hundred people are arrested in Paris and surroundings, tried not by civil but military tribunals, and sentenced to prison terms, deportation, and even death. The executions are carried out in the military manner: the condemned are not guillotined, but shot, namely in the military camp of Grenelle, on the site where the Dupleix metro station will later arise. These details reflect the fact that the army has become the protector of the Thermidorian regime and even the guarantor of its survival. Can it last much longer before a military man is called upon to step forward and take charge of the Thermidorian state?

Coup d'état in Saint-Cloud

The Directoire will never be able to completely rid itself of royalist and (neo-) Jacobin threats. The central problem is that the undemocratic reality of the Thermidorian regime must be covered up by a thin layer of democratic varnish consisting of elections to the two legislative assemblies, elections that inevitably risk being won either by the royalists or by the Jacobins. Each time, the elections must either be manipulated to the advantage of the regime's official candidates or else one must resort to crude illegal measures such as the annulment of the elections and the arrest—on the basis of some pretext—of candidates of the opposition. But the bourgeois Thermidorian ship cannot forever navigate between a right-wing royalist Scylla and a left-wing Jacobino/sans-culottist Charybdis. The solution that Barras and his cronies will ultimately conjure up is to end the democratic charade and establish a military dictatorship. This will put an end to both the threat of a royalist counter-revolution and the danger of a Jacobin radicalization of the revolution, thus consolidating the republican system in its bourgeois and conservative Thermidorian manifestation.

To create the required military dictatorship, a general is needed who is not only reliable but also popular. A number of candidates meet the criteria but in the end, the choice falls on Bonaparte, "general Vendémiaire"; with his victories in Italy and despite the fiasco of his expedition to Egypt, transformed by his and his protectors' spin masters into a success, the Corsican has become very popular. What's more, like his wife, Josephine, he is "well connected with the business community," who have learned to profit from wars—and expect further victories and conquests from him.[27] After his return from the Middle East and on the occasion of a meeting of the Council of Five Hundred at the château of the Parisian suburb of Saint-Cloud, on the 18th Brumaire of the revolutionary year VII, that is, 9 November 1799, a coup d'état is orchestrated. Under the pretext of a "terrorist" or "anarchist" plot in which no one believes, and despite loud protests of the Jacobin representatives, all power is handed over to Bonaparte. He receives the title of First Consul, thus creating the illusion that the new regime is reviving the republican traditions of ancient Rome. Bonaparte will put an end to this farce on May 18, 1804 by crowning himself emperor at Notre-Dame, thus reviving another, far less democratic tradition of ancient Rome—and causing the republican era to come to an end. However, it was already with "Brumaire," that is, in 1799, that the inauguration of Napoleon's dictatorship had heralded the end of the Revolution or, to be more precise, of the first in a series of revolutionary convulsions in France, to become known as *la Grande Révolution*, the "Great Revolution."

The château of Saint-Cloud will be one of Bonaparte's numerous residences as consul and later as emperor. On March 31, 1810, it will serve as the venue of his second marriage, this time with Marie-Louise, daughter of the Habsburg emperor of Austria. During the Restoration, king Louis XVIII and his successor Charles X will spend much time there. In 1852, the château will witness the coronation of Napoleon III as emperor, and on July 15, 1870 it will be there that this nephew of Bonaparte will decide to declare war on Prussia. During this war, destined to be catastrophic for France, the Prussian and other German troops will besiege the French capital. The castle of Saint-Cloud will find itself to be on the front line and it will be bombarded by the German as well as French artillery and thus be transformed into a heap of ruins, to be completely cleared only in 1891. Afterwards, in Saint-Cloud, the château's park will remain, with a row of yews marking the site of the edifice and a museum recalling its history, including Bonaparte's coup d'état.[28]

---

27 Coquard, pp. 257, 261

28 *Guide bleu: Île-de-France*, pp. 413-15; *Les lieux de l'histoire de France*, pp. 325-26.

The advent to power of Napoleon is tantamount to the advent to power of the bourgeoisie, the haute bourgeoisie, of course, but definitely not the plebeian petty variety of that class. Napoleon will achieve a lot more for the cause of that class than eliminating the twin menace from the Left and the Right. He will consolidate the social-economic system that had been spawned by the Revolution in its early, moderate phase, a system whereby the French state—initially a constitutional monarchy, then a republic—was put in the service of the well-to-do burghers, above all the owners of means of production such as big manufacturing workshops and (increasingly) factories, bankers, merchants, and other businessmen. In 1804, this system will be legally "carved in stone" by means of the Civil Code, also known as the Napoleonic Code. This is a kind of legal Bible, an exhaustive collection of statutes with respect to persons and property, confirming principles that are dear to bourgeois hearts, above all the inviolable nature of private property. The Code Civil also reflects the 24-carat patriarchal mentality of the bourgeoisie, and of Napoleon himself, because it downgrades women to a form of property, or at least to "the status of a minor subject to the authority of the parents or the spouse" and "established a subjugation of women that is destined to last a long time."[29]

Arguably equally, or even more, important for the haute bourgeoisie will be the establishment, already in 1800, that is, immediately after the advent to power of the Corsican, of the Banque de France (BDF). That measure implies that Napoleon and the entire French state will henceforth be dependent on a private institution that happens to be the property of the country's financial elite, in other words, its richest citizens or, as one might say today, its "one percent." The bankers of the BDF will loan to the emperor—at high interest rates—the money he needs to rule and arm the country, to wage war, and to govern with much pomp and circumstance. This means that in Napoleon's empire, the emperor himself will not be the supreme authority, but instead the owners and major shareholders of the BDF. However, this truly shocking reality is obfuscated semantically by a name, Banque de France, that falsely creates the impression that it is a "national bank," in other words, an institution belonging to the state and thus to all French citizens and functions in their interest.

---

29 Marchioni, p. 31; Jones, p. 280-281.

The French historian Georges Dupeux once wrote that "in Napoleon, the bourgeoisie simultaneously discovered a protector and a master."[30] The former part of that dictum is correct, but the latter part is untrue: the bourgeoisie was Napoleon's mistress, even though he was made to look like the master in the eyes of the public. This fact is externalized by urbanistic and architectural changes. However, before we focus on these changes, something needs to be said about the nobility and the Church, actors who are not yet entirely counted out despite the triumph of the bourgeoisie.

Napoleon was allowed to govern France on behalf, and to the advantage, of the country's true masters, bankers and other *gens de bien*, people of property, predominantly members of the haute bourgeoisie, the upper-middle class, but, at least to some extent, also of the nobility. Under Bonaparte's auspices, aristocratic émigrés who had returned to France after Thermidor, were also allowed to enjoy the benefits the Corsican bestowed on the upper class or, to put it more accurately, the benefits the upper class bestowed on itself via the medium of Napoleon. Countless repatriated noblemen can recuperate their chateaux and are able once again, in collaboration with parish priests and other notables, to lord it over the denizens of their bailiwick in rural France. Thus they are neatly integrated into the Bonapartist system. A *modus vivendi* also emerges, embodied by the Concordat, between Bonaparte's regime and the counter-revolutionary institution par excellence, the Catholic Church. Catholicism admittedly does not regain its former status of the country's established religion but is officially recognized as "religion of the majority of Frenchmen," a status that comes with all sorts of financial and other privileges. Napoleon also abolishes the revolutionary calendar and reintroduces its Christian predecessor.[31]

NAPOLEON'S NEW PARIS

The fact that Napoleon's advent to power means the bourgeoisie's advent to power is reflected not only in legislation but also urbanistic and architectural changes, above all in Paris. The upper-middle class henceforth rules France, wants to make this crystal clear to Frenchmen and to the

30 Dupeux, p. 100.
31 Lyons, p. 138.

entire world, and therefore starts to thoroughly renovate the capital city as a wealthy new owner might do with a newly acquired home. Napoleon is the "architect" in charge of this task, and so the new Paris that he will create will simultaneously be *imperial*, that is, radiate the political, cultural and military grandeur of the *Imperium Romanum* as well as the Napoleonic empire, and *bourgeois*, and thus reflect the bourgeoisie's social and economic hegemony, interests, likes and dislikes.

Because of his foreign wars, the Corsican Augustus will often be absent from the capital for long periods of time. Even so, he will tackle a fair number of projects in the capital, though many will remain unfinished when he will depart from the scene in 1815. Napoleon's plans for the capital reflect his desire and determination to wipe out "Old Paris," not leaving "the slightest trace of it," as he was to formulate it at the end of his life, during his exile in Saint Helena.[32]

The "Old" Paris that he intends to get rid of, still consists mostly of quasi-medieval neighborhoods inhabited by poor folks, in other words, plebeian enclaves within a city that, before the Revolution, had been a royal city, dominated and indeed "owned" by the nobility and the Church. But, as Napoleon and most well-to-do burghers see things, Paris was invaded and temporarily colonized, as it were, by a mob of sans-culottes who, bursting forth from the Faubourg Saint-Antoine and other working-class suburbs, had stormed into the proud city like the Huns and other barbarians had once swarmed into the Roman Empire. With the consent and even cooperation of the petty-bourgeois Jacobins, this mob of *gens de rien* had taken over and desecrated the royal city, a process culminating in the execution of the monarch in the middle of the finest of all royal squares, renamed Place de la Révolution, or arguably even earlier, in the bloody conquest of the Parisian royal residence, the Tuileries Palace, in which Robespierre and his Montagnard cronies, the petty bourgeois fanatics who had emerged as leaders of the revolutionary populace, had the audacity to ensconce themselves while they terrorized the city and the entire country. Paris had been de-royalized and republicanized and appeared destined to look as plebeian as the Faubourg Saint-Antoine itself. However, thanks to Thermidor the tide had turned, and the Prairial uprising provided the bourgeois *gens de bien*, who now

---

32   For an excellent treatment of Napoleon as "master builder" of Paris, see Horne (2004), pp. 75-95.

held the reins of power, to castigate the demos, expel it from the city center, and drive it back into its suburban lair.

IMAGE 22. Napoleon's Elephant on Place de la Bastille.

To make it clear to the obnoxious *faubouriens* that the Revolution is now over and that the haute bourgeoisie is in power, Napoleon focuses his attention on the vast open space that had been created by the demolition of the Bastille. The name of that place, Place Antoine, is no longer acceptable, since it recalls and glorifies the role of the sans-culottes and their radical revolutionary ambitions; in 1802 it is therefore changed to an anemic Place de la Bastille. In the middle of the square, which had for some time been occupied by the Fountain of the Rebirth, the Corsican orders the construction of a new fountain in the shape of a gigantic, 24-meter high elephant. That beast is also made of plaster, but it is supposed to be replaced as soon as possible by one made of bronze; this will never happen and the plaster icon will remain in place for approximately thirty years. Why an elephant? Most likely because that animal symbolizes "a beginning as well as an end," an "alpha and omega."[33] On the place where the suburban plebs had started the Revolution on July 14, 1789, the jumbo thus proclaimed that the time for revolutionary action had come to an end, namely, with the advent to power of Napoleon. Since Napoleon represented the triumph of the bourgeoisie, positioning the beast on on the site of the Bastille—with its posterior turned ostentatiously to the adjoining Faubourg Saint-Antoine!—also amounted to a humiliating gesture by the haute bourgeoisie at the address of the petit-bourgeois and proletarian *faubouriens* who, in contrast to the bourgeoisie, had achieved so much for the Revolution but ultimately received so little from it.

As for Paris itself, the *royal* city has been ruined by the sans-culottes and the Jacobins, and an embryonic *plebeian* Paris, aborted by Thermidor, has to be cleared up and forgotten as soon as possible. The advent to power of Napoleon, champion of the cause of the bourgeoisie, makes it possible to transform the capital into a magnificent, outwardly imperial but intrinsically bourgeois metropole. This bourgeoisification of Paris requires, first of all, finishing the task inaugurated by the sans-culottes with the destruction of the Bastille, namely, the liquidation of the royal and clerical city Paris had been before the beginning of the Revolution.

The sinister complex of the Temple shares the fate of the Bastille, not so much because its high tower had likewise functioned as a kind of phallic symbol of royal power, but to prevent the building from becoming a center of pilgrimage for royalists. ("That prison must be demolished because it contains too many memories," is how Napoleon put it.)[34] On the other hand, Napoleon does not order the demolition of the great royal palaces. Not out of respect for the Bourbons, but because he likes the power, ceremonial, prestige, and sumptuous lifestyle associated with the monarchy. This preference of the Corsican is reflected in his decision to replace the Consulate with its pseudo-republican attributes by the Empire, a monarchical form of government. In Paris he often stays in the Tuileries, and he also likes another former royal palace, situated fairly close to the capital, Fontainebleau. But Napoleon stays away from Versailles, a palace that, to bourgeois Parisians, conjures up the absolutism of the

---

33 Chevalier and Gheerbrant, p. 399.
34 Quotation from Sournia, p. 95.

Ancien Régime and therefore the royalism that they consider as much of a threat as Jacobinism to the bourgeois regime of which the Corsican is the Lord Protector. But Napoleon undoubtedly also avoided Versailles because a sojourn in the shadow of the most prestigious of all French monarchs, the "Sun King," would have constituted a kind of humiliation for him.

Royal residences do not have to be demolished because they reveal themselves functional in the context of Napoleon's bourgeois empire. It suffices to remove the rare fleurs de lys that have survived the Revolution and to replace them with Napoleonic attributes, not only the imperial eagle but also the bee, symbol of the diligence considered by the bourgeoisie to be a hallmark of its class. One particular royal palace, the Louvre, appears to be useful as a home for the former royal art collections as well as for works of art looted by Napoleon in Italy, Belgium, and elsewhere in Europe.

As for the former royal squares, those were already the object of radical changes during the Revolution. The majestic square dedicated to Louis XV that had been renamed to Place de la Révolution and, having witnessed the execution of Louis XVI, received a new name from the Thermidorians in 1795. They came up with a neutral name, neither regal nor revolutionary, but reflecting their optimistic (and naïve) hope that the land—and its capital—would henceforth be blessed with political and social peace: Place de la Concorde.

The Place des Victoires was rebaptized even earlier, namely in 1792, to Place des Victoires Nationales, meaning victories of the people, the "nation," against its rulers. Even though these rulers referred to the former monarchs, the name reflected such a flagrant lack of respect for the authorities in general that it offended the bourgeoisie. Napoleon therefore dedicates the square to one of his generals, Louis Charles Antoine Desaix, whose statue arises in the center. Desaix had fought with Napoleon in Egypt and in Italy, where he had been killed in the Battle of Marengo. (That loss did not spoil the Corsican's appetite: after the battle, during dinner, he enjoyed "chicken Marengo," a dish improvised by his personal chef with local ingredients.)

The primordial royal square, dedicated to Louis XIII, was renamed to Place des Vosges in 1800. This was to honour the department of the same name, part of the old province of Lorraine, bordered to the east by the Vosges mountain range; the department's inhabitants had revealed themselves to be particularly enthusiastic fighters for France during critical early stages of the Revolution, when the Fatherland had found itself in great danger as it was invaded by foreign troops. The purpose of the re-naming was to stimulate patriotism and hostility to foreign enemies, sentiments that Napoleon and his bourgeois constituency found extremely useful and wanted to promote to the people of France and its capital.

The stately Place Vendôme was called Place des Piques during the Revolution, in honor, as we have seen, of the sans-culottes and their favorite weapon, but with Thermidor that name became taboo. In 1799 the square is renamed to Place Vendôme, a tip of the hat to César of Vendôme, an illegitimate son of King Henry IV and his mistress, Gabrielle d'Estrées. In the 17th century, this personality had been a military celebrity, and his family owned the land that was bought by Louis XIV and used for the construction of a royal square with his own statue in the center. On the square a new heroic warrior will henceforth be honoured, namely Napoleon himself. In 1806, a victory column in the Roman style, inspired by Trajan's column in Rome, will arise in the center of the square, to be crowned with a statue of the emperor, dressed in a toga, and looking like a triumphant Caesar. The column and its bas-relief sculptures commemorate his famous victory against the Austrians in the Battle of Austerlitz; the monument is made with the bronze of Austrian cannon captured during that battle.

The countless churches and monasteries that had earned pre-1789 Paris the nickname of "new Jerusalem" fare less well than their royal counterparts. Many of them had already been closed and often demolished or received a new, non-religious function long before Napoleon came to power, and that program of architectural and urbanistic anti-clericalism continues under his auspices. The monastery of Val-de-Grâce, for example, is transformed into a military hospital, and the famous abbey of Saint-Germain-des-Prés is demolished, except for the church, to make room, *entre autres*, for a broad new boulevard that will receive the same name.

A second aspect of Napoleon's "renovation" of Paris on behalf of the haute bourgeoisie is the obliteration of all traces of the radical phase of the Revolution. It is a paradox, but not a contradiction, that some ecclesiastical buildings will fall victim to this effort, for example the former dominican monastery that had been the home of the club of the Jacobins. After Thermidor, the opportunistic Corsican had quickly abjured the Jacobinism he had flirted with earlier. Hoisted into the saddle of power by Barras and other Thermidorian power brokers, he orders the demolition of the former Dominican church, which had become an architectural externalization of revolutionary radicalism à la Robespierre. The building is demolished in 1806 and a few years later a covered market arose on the site, first known as Marché des Jacobins and later as Marché Saint-Honoré. After World War II, when the Left will temporarily be very influential in France, the market square will for some time be called Place Robespierre. The market halls will be demolished in 1955 to make room for a parking garage, but in 1997 a modern new complex made of glass and steel will arise in its place, a combination of a market, shopping center, and offices, to be occupied mostly by a group of investment bankers, that is, the kind of folks from whom little sympathy can be expected for radicals such as Robespierre. However, admirers of the latter may find some solace in the fact that the main thoroughfare of the edifice is called Passage des Jacobins.

Napoleon proceeds to overhaul the entire neighborhood between the church of the Jacobins and the Tuileries. The Rue de Rivoli is created, that is, the street that is destined to become the major east-west thoroughfare of the city; and one of its side streets, the Rue de Castiglione, a name that, like Rivoli, commemorates one of his victories in Italy, connects the gardens of the Tuileries with Place Vendôme. This project involves the demolition of the monastery of the Feuillants, a building that used to be the home of moderate revolutionaries such as Lafayette. Those gentlemen had been champions of a constitutional monarchy, a formula that had temporarily been favored by the bourgeoisie but had been abandoned because Louis XVI and his entourage had failed to cooperate. The same urbanistic project also causes the disappearance of the Manège. That edifice had witnessed the proclamation of the Republic, a much too democratic system for the taste of the bourgeoisie, whose demand for a more authoritarian system fortunately (for the bourgeoisie) met supply in the form of Bonaparte's dictatorship.

Napoleon causes countless new buildings to appear in the capital, mostly in the neoclassicist style that had already become fashionable long before his advent to power. Many of these creations reflect the mentality and interests of the bourgeoisie. The Bourse or stock exchange, home and architectural icon of typically bourgeois capitalist activities, arises majestically, like a kind of Greco-Roman temple, on the site of a demolished nunnery: an architectural proclamation of the triumph of capitalism over clericalism. Napoleon also treats businessmen and bankers with infrastructure that greases the wheels of their industry and commerce. The construction of badly needed new bridges across the Seine, for example, creates new investment opportunities for private capital, with dividends in the form of tolls collected for the passage of persons as well as goods.

One of these bridges, the Pont de Iéna, named after a famous victory of Napoleon against the Prussians, connects the hillock of Chaillot with the Champ de Mars, the space where the Eiffel Tower will later arise. This project reflects Napoleon's interest in the development and embellishment, for the benefit of their inhabitants, of the western districts of the capital, formerly reserved for the aristocratic elite of high birth but henceforth virtually exclusively for an exclusively bourgeois elite of high income. Western Paris is blessed with the construction of wide new boulevards, similar to the already existing Champs Elysées, traffic arteries that converge on a star-shaped intersection, known as Place de l'Étoile. This creates golden opportunities for the maximization of capital, because investors can earn fortunes by constructing and selling or renting prestigious apartments. The new boulevards confirm the status of western Paris as the exclusive home of the capital's people of property, the *gens de bien*.

It is hardly surprising that many of these new thoroughfares, squares, and bridges receive the names of sites that witnessed Napoleonic victories, such as Iéna, Wagram, and Friedland. The Place de l'Étoile is supposed to develop into an even more impressive salute to Napoleon and the triumphs he achieved on behalf of the *grande nation,* an even more grandiose salute than the Austerlitz Column in the city center. It has to be another copy of an imperial monument in Rome, namely, an enormous triumphal arch. A monumental symbolic presence of the triumphant Napoleon, protector of the bourgeoisie, is certain to be welcome on Place de l'Étoile, epicenter of well-to-do western Paris, rather than on Place de la Bastille, where it was originally planned to be erected, but where a Napoleonic elephant ended up showing its derrière to the plebeians of the neighborhood. The project of the arch is launched as early as 1806 but will only be completed long after Napoleon's defeat in Waterloo, exile, and death. And enthusiasm for the project had already waned considerably after the catastrophic defeat in Russia.

The new Paris planned by Napoleon is not only simultaneously imperial and bourgeois, it is also militaristic, just like France's national anthem, the *Marseillaise*, its architecture breathes belligerence. The fact that bourgeois architecture can also glorify war will surprise all those who firmly believe that pacifism is one of the typical charms of the bourgeoisie. But it is a fact that Mars was not only the "patron saint" of Napoleon; via the medium of the military, in the form of a highly talented Corsican, the god of war showered great favors on France's bourgeoisie, and for these favors the supposedly peace loving burghers demonstrated their gratitude and respect also on the architectural level.

We have already seen that military means proved very useful to combat counter-revolutionary royalism as well as radical-revolutionary Jacobinism. Furthermore, under the auspices of the Corsican, warfare had revealed itself to be a cornucopia of profits for bankers and industrialists—something which, incidentally, it will remain in the 19th, 20th, and early 21st centuries. The years of Napoleon's rule, writes a German art historian, Arnold Hauser, were a golden age for suppliers of the army and all sorts of speculators.[35]

Last but not least: Napoleon's modifications of the Parisian cityscape are mostly financed not by means of taxation, an option that might have hurt bourgeois pocketbooks but with the loot of his long and impressive string of victories. With the help of Mars, Bonaparte ensures that the bourgeoisie is not saddled with the costs of transforming Paris into a bourgeois metropolis. It is not surprising at all that the new Paris will be bourgeois and simultaneously Napoleonic and martial: it is thanks to the duo of Napoleon and Mars that the bourgeoisie was able to come to power in the capital and in the entire country.

Before the Revolution, the Bourbon monarchs were the benefactors of the nobility and the high clergy, and so the aristocrats and prelates did not mind that the kings sprinkled their statues all over the capital, thus contributing mightily to turning Paris into a royal city. After the Revo-

---

35   Hauser, p. 675.

lution, Napoleon similarly reveals himself to be a generous benefactor of the bourgeoisie. Consequently, the well-to-do burghers do not mind that their golden boy transforms Paris into an imperial city radiating belligerence and glory, in other words, that the intrinsically bourgeois "new" Paris is covered with a relatively thick layer of Napoleonic gloss. They are even elated that the Napoleonic sparkle diverts attention from the fact that theirs is the new ruling class, whose interests are eagerly championed by a man who is not only their protector but also their servant.

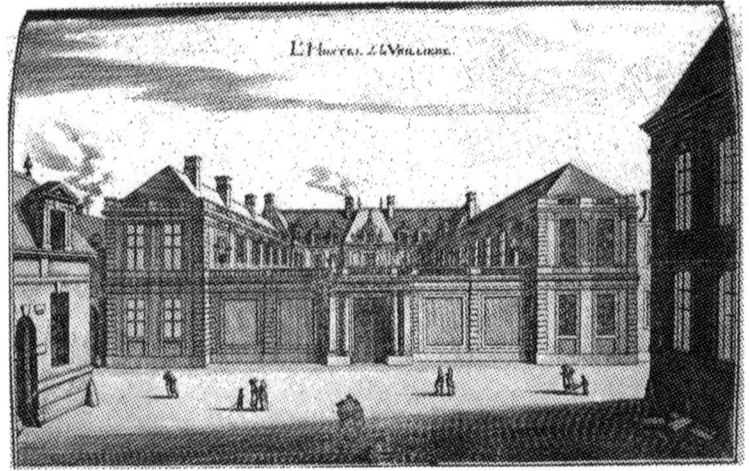

IMAGE 23. Hôtel de la Vrillière, later Hôtel de Toulouse, headquarters of the Banque de France in the Rue de la Vrillière.

The same cool calculation seems to have inspired a decision reached by the gentlemen—only much later to be joined by some ladies—of the Banque de France. The BDF initially found a home in a chic hôtel situated on one of the former royal squares, the Place des Victoires, associated with the "Sun King," who enjoyed showing off his great power. The address was most appropriate, because the establishment of the BDF in 1800 signified an enormous *victoire* for the haute bourgeoisie, it sealed the triumph of that class after ten long and turbulent years. However, the gentlemen of the Banque de France understood very soon that it was more prudent to obfuscate the absolute financial power they now enjoyed over the country, including power over the imperial government and the entire French state. In 1811 they therefore made a relatively short move of only a few hundred meters to a new headquarters in another imposing building, a hôtel erected by Mansart in 1635, but situated very discreetly in a quiet side street, the Rue de la Vrillière, and very close to the Tuileries Palace, where Napoleon often came to rule with much pomp and circumstance—but on their behalf.[36]

The *embourgeoisement* or bourgeoisification of Paris, the fact that the capital is becoming a bourgeois city, reflects the result of the complex class conflict the Revolution had been from the start in 1789 to the finish—or rather, as we shall see shortly, its suspension—in 1799. Looking back on those turbulent years, Napoleon will remark that "two kinds of people are involved in revolutions, those who make the revolutions and those who benefit from it."[37] This is true in the sense that France's *Grande Révolution* was made, not exclusively but certainly primarily, by the "little people," while the well-to-do burghers profited the most from it. The already mentioned German art historian Arnold Hauser shares this opinion and provides the following commentary:

> With the liquidation of the Revolution [in 1799] ..., the bourgeoisie emerges triumphantly from the struggle for social supremacy [*Vorherrschaft in der Gesellschaft*] ... The revolutionary struggle was fought with the help of the working class and would not have been successful without that contribution. But as soon as the [haute] bourgeoisie had achieved its objectives, it left its former allies in the lurch so that its class ended up being the only one to reap the fruits of the common struggle.[38]

Paris was one of the sumptuous fruits that were reaped by the bourgeoisie. The city had ceased to be royal, had momentarily threatened to become plebeian, but behind a Napoleonic-militaristic facade it was metamorphosing into an urban bastion of the bourgeoisie. However, a lot of water would have still have to flow under the Seine bridges before this metamorphosis was to be a *fait accompli*. Why? The revolutionary

---

36   *Les lieux de l'histoire de France*, p. 326 ; "Banque de France : Patrimoine Historique Architectural."

37   Bonaparte, p. 8.

38   Hauser, p. 675-76.

cataclysm was not really over, but merely suspended. New revolutions were on the way.

8. Reflections on France's Great Revolution

"1789," "1793," AND BONAPARTE

THE FRENCH REVOLUTION FROM 1789 TO 1799 was not a simple historical "event," but a long and complex development in which we can identify various stages. It started with the "revolt of the nobles" on the eve of 1789 and ended—but only in certain respects—in 1799, with "18 Brumaire," Napoleon Bonaparte's coup d'état. It is to be noted that some of these stages, including the important opening and closing stages, were more counter-revolutionary than revolutionary in nature. As far as the truly revolutionary developments are concerned, it is possible to identify two stages.

The first stage is "1789," the moderate revolution. This revolutionary phase puts an end to the Ancien Régime with its royal absolutism and feudalism, in other words, the monopoly of power of the monarch and the privileges of the nobility and the Church. Important achievements of "1789" are also the Declaration of the Rights of Man, the equality of all the French before the law, the separation of Church and State, a parliamentary system based on limited voting rights, and, last but not least, the creation of a "modern," centralized, and "indivisible" French state. Taken together, these achievements constitute an enormous step forward in the history of France, and they are anchored in a constitution that will be promulgated, not without some delay, in 1791.

The Ancien Régime, the France of before 1789, was associated with the *absolute* monarchy; the revolutionary system of "1789" is supposed to find a comfortable home in a *parliamentary* and *constitutional* monarchy. Due to Louis's recalcitrance, however, this experiment does not succeed, and so in 1792 a new form of state, the Republic, is born. "1789" has been made possible thanks to the intervention of the Parisian sans-culottes but it is essentially the handiwork of moderate folks, almost exclusively members of the well-to-do bourgeoisie. It is the latter who, on the ruins of an Ancien Régime that served the interests of nobility and the clergy, establish a state that must be at the service of the (upper) bourgeoisie. "It was the Terror and popular violence," writes Soboul, "that swept away the ruins of feudalism and absolutism for the benefit of the bourgeoisie."[1] On the political level, these solid burghers, originating from cities all over France, find a home in the club of the Feuillants first, then in that of the Girondins. But here in Paris, den of the revolutionary lions, the sans-culottes, and their Jacobin allies, they will never really feel at home..

The second revolutionary stage is "1793." This means the "popular," radical, egalitarian revolution, with social rights (such as the right to employment) and relatively far-reaching socio-economic reforms; it is enshrined in a constitution, that of the year 1793, but it will never be implemented. This revolution is radical, egalitarian, socially oriented and willing to regulate the economy of the country—and therefore to limit individual freedom to some extent—for the benefit of the community, "for the common happiness." Since the right to hold property is maintained, "1793" can be qualified as "social-democratic" rather than "socialist."

"1793" is the work of Robespierre and his fellow Montagnards, that is, essentially petit-bourgeois Parisian Jacobins whose principles are basically as "liberal" as those of the haute bourgeoisie, but whose measures also seek to satisfy the elementary needs of the Parisian sans-culottes; the latter are the indispensable allies of the Jacobins in their fight not only against the Girondins, but also, and above all, against the counter-revolutionaries. The radical revolution is essentially a Parisian phenomenon, a revolution made by and for Paris. And their opponents are essentially from outside Paris, they are mostly members of the haute bourgeoisie of the provincial cities, exemplified by the Girondins, merchants from Bor-

---

1   Soboul (1968), p. 158.

deaux, and of the peasantry of rural France. With "1793," the revolution becomes in many ways a conflict between Paris and the rest of France.

The counter-revolution—embodied by aristocratic émigrés, refractory priests, and the restless and even rebellious peasants of the Vendée and other provinces—is against "1789" as well as "1793" and it wants nothing less than a return to the Ancien Régime; in the Vendée, the insurgents are fighting for the king and the Church. The well-to-do bourgeoisie, entrenched in the great provincial cities of France, is hostile to "1793," but in favor of "1789." This class is against "1793" because, unlike the Parisian sans-culottes, it has nothing to gain and everything to lose from a radical revolutionary progress in the direction indicated by the constitution of 1793 with its egalitarianism and state intervention in the economy. The bourgeoisie is also opposed to a return to the Ancien Régime in which the state would again be at the service of the nobility and the clergy. "1789," on the other hand, signifies the creation of a French state at the service of the bourgeoisie, "1789" is the revolution of, and for, the bourgeoisie.

A return to the moderate bourgeois revolution of 1789, but with a republic instead of a constitutional monarchy, that is the objective and, in many respects, the result, of the "Thermidorian reaction" of 1794.[2] Thermidor produces the constitution of the year III which, as a French historian has written, "guarantees private property and liberal ideas [and] suppresses all that transgresses the boundaries of the bourgeois revolution and moves further, that is, in the direction of socialism."[3] The result of the Thermidorian recycling of "1789" is a state that has correctly been described as a "bourgeois republic" or as a "republic of property owners."

Threatened on the left by neo-Jacobinism and, on the right, by counter-revolutionary royalism, the system that the Thermidorians have cobbled together, that is, the Directoire, needs to be saved time and again by intervention from the army. To preserve its socio-economic hegemony, the bourgeoisie ends up entrusting its political power to a reliable general and this is how the revolution yields a military dictatorship. It is fair to say that, with "Brumaire," France's well-to-do bourgeoisie hands over to Bonaparte the political power it possesses so as not to lose it to the

---

2   Furet and Richet, p. 258 : "Thermidor renoue le lien avec 1789."
3   Morazé, pp. 165-66.

royalists or the Jacobins. In exchange for this favor, Bonaparte will in fact eliminate both threats and he will guarantee and solidify the socio-economic system of "1789," for example financially, namely, by founding the Banque de France in 1800, and legally, by the promulgation in 1804 of the Code Civil.

With respect to the Revolution, then, Bonaparte's dictatorship is ambivalent. On the one hand, the revolution is over, even liquidated, in the sense that it is the end not only of egalitarian experiments like those of "1793" but even of attempts to preserve the democratic republican facade of "1789." On the other hand, the essential accomplishments of "1789" are preserved and even consolidated.

To the question whether Napoleon was a revolutionary or not, one can answer as follows: he was for the revolution in the sense that he was against the royalist counter-revolution and, since two negatives cancel each other out, someone hostile to the counter-revolution automatically qualifies as a revolutionary. But we can also say that Napoleon was simultaneously for and against the revolution: he was for the moderate bourgeois revolution of 1789, that of the Feuillants-Girondins-Thermidorians, but he was opposed to the radical revolution of 1793, that of the Jacobins and the Parisian sans-culottes. Annie Jourdan quotes a contemporary commentator from Germany, a Prussian, who already understood that Bonaparte "had never been anything other than the personification of one of the various stages of the revolution," as he wrote in 1815.[4] That stage was the bourgeois revolution, that of 1789, which Napoleon noy only safeguarded within France but also exported to the rest of Europe.

By exporting the revolution, Napoleon had managed to arrest the revolutionary process, but he had no illusions. He confided to one of his advisers: "I am the bookmark that marks the page where the revolution came to a halt; but when I will be dead, it will turn the page and resume its march."[5]

To finish the Revolution—in the sense of preventing it from going beyond the achievements of "1789"—it had to be taken away from its cradle, Paris. In this regard, it made a lot of sense, at least symbolically, that Napoleon Bonaparte was handpicked to abduct the revolution from

4   Jourdan, p. 292.
5   Guérard, p. 277.

Paris, thus putting an end to the radical project of the petty-bourgeois Parisian Jacobins and sans-culottes and, conversely, to consolidate the bourgeois revolution. First, he was a native of Ajaccio, of Corsica, the farthest provincial capital from the administrative, economic, and political center of Paris.[6] Second, Napoleon was a "child of the Corsican gentry, in other words, the scion of a family that may equally well be described as grand-bourgeoisie but harboring aristocratic pretensions or as petty nobility with a grand-bourgeois lifestyle. In any event, in many ways, the Bonapartes belonged to the haute bourgeoisie or upper-middle class, the class which, throughout France, thanks to "1789," had achieved its objectives and sought to consolidate it via a military dictatorship in the face of threats emanating from the left as well as the right.

It is also worth noting that the decisive political step in the process of the liquidation of the Revolution, that is to say "Brumaire," was at the same time a geographical step away from Paris, the cradle of the revolution, the lion's den of Jacobinism and of the sans-culottes, far too revolutionary folks to France's well-to-do burghers. In addition, the move to the suburb of Saint-Cloud was also a leap, small, certainly, but nonetheless symbolic and not to be underestimated, in the direction of much less revolutionary and even more or less counter-revolutionary countryside. A very first symbolic step in this direction had already been taken when the Convention itself had transferred the guillotine from the Place de la Concorde to the Place de la Nation, that is to say from the heart of the revolutionary city—the square bearing the name of the Revolution, with in the middle the guillotine, revolutionary symbol par excellence!—towards the calm of the periphery which announces the conservative countryside. And is there not a similar symbolic dimension to the fact that the Parisian Jacobins suffered their last defeat in the quasi-rural district of Grenelle, far from the faubourg Saint-Antoine, the Hôtel de Ville, the Tuileries, and Place de la Concorde, the sites where, "playing at home," they had experienced their great revolutionary triumphs? The Grenelle "rabbit shoot" was a kind of prelude to Bonaparte's coup d'état, and it happened to take place in a location on the road from central Paris to Saint-Cloud.

Finally, with respect to Saint-Cloud, we can also point to a little

---

6   Furet and Richet, p. 405.

irony of history and topography, namely, the fact that this château was situated on the road from Paris to Versailles, the residence of the absolutist kings of the pre-revolutionary era. The fact that the coup d'état of 18 Brumaire took place in Saint-Cloud was a topographical reflection of the historical reality that, after the democratic experience of the revolution, France returned to the path of an absolutist political system similar to the one of which the Louis XIV, residing in Versailles, had been the "sun."[7] However, this time the destination was an absolutist system under a Bonaparte instead of a Bourbon and, more importantly, an absolutist system in the service of the bourgeoisie instead of the nobility.

Dialectic of Revolution and War

When we think of the dictatorship of Bonaparte, and also of the republic of the post-Thermidorian Convention and of the Directoire, we do not think so much of the revolutionary or counter-revolutionary events in the French capital, which come to mind when we think of the years from 1789 to 1794; what is conjured up instead, is an interminable series of wars, battles fought far from Paris and, in many cases, far outside the borders of France, battles which in Paris are recalled by the names of streets, squares, bridges, and railway stations like Jena, Rivoli, Wagram, and Austerlitz. This is no coincidence, because the wars were extremely functional for the primary goal of Thermidor and the Bonapartist dictatorship, namely, to preserve the achievements of "1789," but at the same time to prevent a return to the Ancien Régime as well a remake of "1793."

With their Terror, Robespierre and the Montagnards wanted not only to protect the Revolution, but also to deepen it, to radicalize it, to intensify it. This meant at the same time that they "internalized" the Revolution within France itself and, above all, in the heart of France, in the capital, Paris. It is not a coincidence that the guillotinings, closely associated with the radical Revolution, took place in the center of a square in the center of the city, itself located in the center of the country. To concentrate their own energy and that of the sans-culottes and of all the true

---

7   We remember that one of the first steps on the road to the Revolution had been the convocation of the Estates General in a building situated near the royal château of Versailles, of course, but on Avenue de Paris, that is, the road leading to the capital, which will reveal itself to be the hotbed of the revolution.

revolutionaries on this "internalization" of the Revolution, Robespierre and his Jacobin companions—unlike the Girondins—were in principle opposed to international wars, which they considered to be a waste of revolutionary energy and a threat to the Revolution. Conversely, the interminable series of wars which were subsequently waged, first under the auspices of the post-Thermidorian Convention, then under those of the Directoire, and finally under those of Bonaparte, amounted to an "externalization" of the Revolution, to an exportation of the Revolution—the bourgeois revolution of 1789—which at the same time served to prevent the further "internalization" of the Revolution, in other words, its "radicalization" in the style of 1793.

It was to arrest the revolutionary process in France itself, and especially in Paris, that Napoleon exported the Revolution—the moderate, bourgeois Revolution of 1789—to the rest of Europe. It was to prevent the mighty revolutionary current from excavating and deepening its own channel—Paris and the rest of France—that first the Thermidorians and later Napoleon caused its troubled waters to overflow the borders of France, inundate all of Europe, thus becoming vast, but shallow and calm.

The war abroad offered a solution to the burning social problems of Paris, problems that had triggered the great revolutionary events, such as the storming of the Bastille. The military service and the positive impact of the war on the national economy constituted a solution of sorts to socio-economic problems. The unemployed were largely absorbed by the army and military spending stimulated demand—in a "Keynesian" fashion—for products from factories such as those producing uniforms for the army. But, considered from the point of view of the partisans of the moderate Revolution, the foreign wars presented yet another advantage that should certainly not be underestimated. In Paris, countless young sans-culottes were stuffed into an army uniform and marched off to fight against an "external enemy" far away from their city instead of remaining in the nation's capital to confront the "internal enemy." For revolutionary collective actions such as the storming of the Tuileries, there were thus no longer sufficient numbers of men available. The revolutionary "mobs" henceforth contained mostly women and even children, and precious few men, too few to be able to repeat in Germinal and Prairial 1795 the success of the sans-culotterie of 1789. First the Directoire, then Bonaparte, will make this system permanent by introducing compulsory military service and embarking on an endless series of wars. "It was he [Napoleon]," writes historian Henri Guillemin, "who removed potentially dangerous young plebeians from Paris and even sent them as far away as Moscow—to the relief of the good burghers."[8]

Successful wars, followed by the occupation and pillage of foreign countries, also produced plenty of money for the treasury of the French state. (The Thermidorians had already realized that wars are good for business, that "wars generate profits," and in 1810 Napoleon was to declare publicly that "war is the source of the wealth of the country.")[9] With this money, it was possible to maintain an army, restore the country's financial health, and even throw some crumbs to France's little people, above all the notoriously restless Parisian populace, for example in the shape of subsidized and therefore low prices of bread and other essential foodstuffs; which served to still not only their physiological but also their revolutionary appetite. The social problems of Paris, and of France in general, were thus resolved by warfare and at the expense of foreigners.

Officially, the wars purported to share with the rest of Europe the benefits of the Revolution, that is, of the bourgeois Revolution of 1789; with that objective in mind, the sans-culottes went to war enthusiastically. (They would soon find out that Robespierre was right when he predicted that France's "armed missionaries" would not be welcomed with open arms by foreigners.) However, the news of great victories—made possible, at least to some extent, by the revolutionary enthusiasm of the troops—also aroused among the sans-culottes who remained in the country a patriotic pride. which was to compensate for the decline, after Germinal and Prairial, of revolutionary enthusiasm in Paris.[10]

With a little help from Mars, the god of the war, the revolutionary energy of the sans-culottes and the French people in general could be channeled along paths leading to destinations that were less radical from a revolutionary point of view. We are dealing here with a displacement

---

8   Guillemin, pp. 119-20. See also Vovelle, pp. 117-18. Compulsory military service was introduced by the Directoire on January 12, 1798, see Furet and Richet, p. 498.

9   Quoted in Guillemin, p. 58.

10   Woronoff, p. 78, observes in this context that the announcement of victories served to enhance "the depth of a patriotism in which Jacobin enthusiasm mixed with chauvinist exaltation."

process: the women and men of France people, including the Parisian sans-culottes, gradually lost their revolutionary *patriotism*, that is to say their enthusiasm for the revolution and the ideals of freedom, equality and, indeed, solidarity not only with the "nation" but also with neighboring peoples; instead, they increasingly worshiped the golden calf of *nationalism*, territorial expansion towards supposedly "natural" borders like the Rhine, and the international glory of the "great nation" and—after the 18 and 19 Brumaire—of its leader, Bonaparte.

Thus we can also understand the ambivalent reaction of the peoples of Europe to France's wars and conquests at this time. While some—the Ancien-Régime elites, for example, and the peasants—rejected the French Revolution *in toto* and others—above all local equivalents of Jacobins, known as, the Dutch "patriots"—rather unconditionally applauded it, many, and arguably most, zigzagged between the Charybdis of admiration for the ideas and achievements of the French Revolution and the Scylla of revulsion towards militarism, boundless chauvinism, and the ruthless imperialism of France—also in the field of the language.[11]

Numerous non-French people struggled with a simultaneous admiration and repulsion for the French Revolution. In others, the initial enthusiasm sooner or later gives way to disillusionment. We think of Beethoven for example. With his third symphony, Eroica, he initially lionized Napoleon enthusiastically as the embodiment of the Revolution; but eventually he would come to regard the Corsican as "an imperialist marauder who had betrayed the ideals of the Revolution" and compose music purporting to celebrate the victories of Wellington against this same Napoleon.[12] As for the British, many of them welcomed "1789" because they interpreted this moderate revolution not without reason as the importation into France of the type of constitutional and parliamentary monarchy they themselves had introduced a hundred years earlier,

---

11 French was considered to be the language of the Revolution and therefore destined to be "universalized"; conversely, other languages, certainly those spoken within France's own borders, were viewed as linguistic reflections of the counter-revolution that needed to be eradicated. "Let us eradicate the dialects," proclaimed a revolutionary in 1794, "the Republic is one and indivisible territorially and politically and must therefore be indivisible linguistically"; see the article by Jürgen Trabant.

12 Beethoven's attitude to the French Revolution and Napoleon is very well described in the book by Frida Knight; quotation from Knight, p. 66.

at the time of their so-called "Glorious Revolution." The poet William Wordsworth evoked this early enthusiasm with a famous verse:

> Europe at that time was thrilled with joy
> France standing at the top of golden hours,
> And human nature seeming born again...
> Bliss was it in that dawn to be alive,
> But to be young was very Heaven! [13]

However, with "1793" and the Terror, most, or at least many of the British—and, of these, especially the conservatives—viewed with disgust the events taking place on the other side of the English Channel. Their spokesperson was Edmund Burke, whose *Reflections on the Revolution in France*—already published in November 1790—was to become a veritable Bible for counter-revolutionaries not only in England but everywhere in the world. On the other hand, numerous Brits, including the majority of lower-class folks, were electrified by the revolution in France. Among their number was the poet Robert "Rabbie" Burns, who expressed the hope that in Britain and "the world o'er," the revolutionary example set by France might be imitated so that "tomorrow we shall don the Cap of Libertie."[14]

However, as Marx emphasized, the ideas of the dominant class tend to become the dominant ideas, and Britain proved to be no exception to this general rule. In the mid-twentieth century, George Orwell would be able to write that "for the average Englishman, the French Revolution means nothing other than a pyramid of chopped off heads."[15] He could have said the same thing about nearly all non-French, not only those of his era but even those of today. Here is an opinion, very similar to that cited by Orwell, but presented by an American tourist unsympathetic to the Revolution:

> From a tourist's point of view, my point of view, the Revolution is the missing heads of statues once lining the façades of Notre-Dame de Paris and Reims, burned reliquaries and broken shards of glass that once were stained-glass windows. It is the looted castles of the aristocracy and their missing furniture ... it is watching humanity step backward in time.[16]

---

13   Quoted in Bernal, p. 1059.
14   Quoted in the article by Alan Woods.
15   Quoted in Cohen and Major, p. 524.
16   Caro, p. 313.

IMAGE 24. "Glad Day," an engraving by William Blake from 1794-96. Similar to Rabbie Burns, Blake hoped the French Revolution could inspire a similar movement in Britain, depicted here as "The Dance of Albion."

A final, but important consideration is in order. First for the Thermidorians and then for the partisans of Bonaparte, the wars were wonderful in the sense that there were colossal amounts of money to be made by all kinds of businessmen. and especially for the good friends of the regime. The wars proved to be excellent for business. Especially thanks to deliveries to the army, exclusively entrusted to private companies after the fall of the Robespierre, fortunes could be made. Moreover, as long as the Napoleonic wars were victorious, they not only yielded high profit margins, but they also made sources of raw materials and market opportunities available to a French industry that was henceforth growing fast. French industrialists—and bankers—thus became able to play an increasingly important role within the bourgeoisie. It was under Napoleon that, in France, the industrial capitalism typical of the 19th century began to supplant the commercial capitalism typical of the previous few centuries. (This was also the case for Belgium, annexed at the time by France.)

It is worth noting that the accumulation of commercial capital in France had been made possible mainly thanks to the slave trade, while the accumulation of industrial capital had a lot to do with an almost uninterrupted series of murderous wars. In this sense too, Balzac hit the nail on the head when he wrote that "behind every great fortune there lurks a crime."

Until the time of Robespierre, and even under Robespierre, revolutionary France had also made war, but for the purpose of fighting the counter-revolution and defending the Revolution. It was after the fall of Robespierre, after Thermidor, that France revealed a militarist face and unleashed an endless series of wars, wars of conquest that were passed off as wars of liberation. "Under the Thermidorian regime," writes historian Annie Jourdan, "republican France became a warlike France."[17]

It is certainly not by chance that, among the numerous revolutionary songs of the time, it is precisely the very militarist *Marseillaise*, which focuses on foreign enemies, that was promoted to the rank of national anthem by the Thermidorians on July 14, 1795, and not, for example, the equally, if not more popular song *Ah, Ca ira!*[18] From a Thermidorian point of view, the latter chant was indeed extremely politically incorrect. It admittedly did not glorify "1793" but it did evoke the more radical facets of "1789" and attacked, in Jacobin fashion, the domestic enemy, that is, the class enemy, and he thus pleaded for an internalization instead of externalization of the Revolution, in other words, for a radicalization of the Revolution at home instead of the exportation abroad—via international warfare—of a watered-down version of the Revolution. (It should be taken into account that the term "aristocrats," used in *Ah, Ca ira!* to refer to the enemy, was used by the sans-culottes to designate not only the

---

17 Jourdan, p. 245.
18 **Ed. Note:** See lyrics for both songs on pp. [X].

traditional nobility but also the haute bourgeoisie and the rich, the *gens de bien*, in general.)¹⁹

The *Marseillaise* was the anthem of the French Revolution, more precisely of "1789"; at the same time it was also the quintessential battle song of the exportation of "1789" via international war. That ambiguity allowed the song, normally associated with the Republic, and defiantly belted out by the opponents of the coup d'état in Saint-Cloud, to continue to be used in the Napoleonic Empire. The emperor could hardly repudiate a song that had inspired the troops he had led to victory during the Italian campaign that had made him famous; but he clearly preferred a less revolutionary and republican, and even more warlike and patriotic song, *Le chant du départ,* and promoted it to national anthem in 1804. However, the *Marseillaise* was to make a comeback in 1814, when Napoleon's main enemy was a Bourbon monarch, Louis XVIII, restored to the throne by the Corsican's foreign enemies, and "its rousing tone was to accompany the last stand of the imperial guard at the Battle of Waterloo."²⁰

Bonaparte also retained the July 14 commemoration of the fall of the Bastille and kept the tricolor flag, a symbol not only of the Revolution of 1789, but also of French imperialism. But red, not only as color of a flag but also as color of a (Phrygian) bonnet, was to be *non grata* in his empire. Wearing the red bonnet, a symbol of Jacobin-style revolutionary radicalism, had in fact already been banned by the Thermidorians.

The wars waged by revolutionary and, even more so, Napoleonic France stimulated industrial development, in other words the development of an industrial system of mass production. Concomitantly, they sounded the death knell for the old "artisanal" system of small-scale production, in which artisans made products in a traditional, non-mechanized way, in their workshops. By means of war, the Thermidorian and Bonapartist bourgeoisie therefore not only made the sans-culottes—essentially a heterogeneous group of artisans, shopkeepers and other small producers—physically disappear from Paris, it also started to removed them from France's socio-economic landscape. During the Revolution in Paris, the sans-culottes could play a first-rate historical role; because of the revolutionary wars that liquidated the revolution, the sans-culottes

---

19   Soboul (1968), pp. 25-27; Hazan (2014), p. 175.
20   Lyons, pp. 138-39.

were to disappear from the historical stage. In this sense at least, the revolution did indeed devour its children.

Like a cannibal, the French bourgeoisie devoured its class enemy—and instead spawned another, even more dangerous one, namely the industrial "proletariat." In terms of economic production, the future henceforth belonged to machines, factories, industrialists and, as far as labor was concerned, wage-earning factory workers, and no longer to "independent" craftsmen. In this typically 19th century proletariat, the bourgeoisie will find a much more formidable opponent than in the sans-culottes, still a typical phenomenon of the end of the late 18th century and the pre-industrial era in general.

In many ways, the sans-culottes made the success of the Revolution possible, but the Revolution swept away the sans-culottes. This happened in the cities, and especially in Paris. In the countryside, a similar phenomenon occurred. The peasants made the revolution there but, due to the sale of ecclesiastical goods, mostly—though not exclusively—to the advantage of bourgeois urbanites and well-to-do peasants, the Revolution swept away the small peasants and turned them, first, into "cannon fodder" for the Napoleonic wars and, afterwards, into a rural proletariat. "The Revolution," wrote historian George Lefebvre, "by darkening the future of the poor peasantry, prepared its exodus; all that remained to be done was to build factories: the workers were already on their way."[21] (An admittedly important exception to this general rule was formed by the wine-producing regions, where even the acquisition of a tiny vineyard proved feasible and allowed the subsistence of small-scale viticultural operations.)[22]

In any event, not only in the north of France, then, where viticulture did not provide a safety-valve, a rural proletariat emerged and migrated not only to Paris but also to other urban centers such as Lille, Roubaix, Metz, Lyons, and Saint-Étienne to find work in the factories. Thus they morphed into factory workers, in other words, into urban proletarians who would take over the role of the sans-culottes, not only in the production process, but also in the social conflicts of the new era that began with the French Revolution.

---

21 See the remarks in Dupeux, pp. 109-11, with Lefebvre quoted on p. 111.
22 See Pauwels (2020a), pp. 253-57; Braudel, p. 95.

The Revolution, the triumph of the bourgeoisie over the nobility, eliminated the sans-culottes, without whose aid this triumph would not have been possible. But, at the same time, the Revolution also helped to produce a new class, the wage-earning workers who, during the next century and even longer, were to contest this bourgeois triumph. This will trigger new revolutions that will generate new wars—which will in turn generate other revolutions. We think for example of the Franco-Prussian war of 1870-1871, which was followed by the Paris Commune. The most spectacular example, however, will be the Great War of 1914-1918, which will be expected to put an end once and for all to the revolutions in Europe but which, to the contrary, will prove to be the mother of the great Russian Revolution.

With Bonaparte, the revolution ended, admittedly somewhat belatedly, where it was supposed to end, at least as far as the French bourgeoisie was concerned; with Bonaparte, the French bourgeoisie triumphed. It is therefore no coincidence that, in many French cities, the "notables," that is, the businessmen, bankers, lawyers and other representatives of the haute bourgeoisie like to socialize in cafés or restaurants bearing the name of Bonaparte, as the sociologist Pierre Bourdieu has remarked in one of his opuses. France's well-to-do burghers have always remained grateful to Napoleon for the great services he rendered to their class and, above all, for the fact that he knew how to consolidate the bourgeois socio-economic position in the face of threats from the right and the left. The cornerstone of this position was of course the right to hold property, a term which designates private ownership of the means of production and should therefore not be confused with personal possessions.

The most dramatic testimony to the fact that private property, the alpha and omega of any bourgeois system, was and remained inviolable under the dictatorship of Napoleon, was his restoration of slavery in the French colonies in 1802; indeed, at the time, slaves were still considered a legitimate form of property.[23] He sent an army to Santo Domingo[24] to put down an uprising of the island's slaves, who had been electrified by their earlier emancipation under the auspices of the Montagnards. The former slaves resisted bravely and ultimately effectively: the expedition

---

23   Munford, p. 540.

24   **Ed. Note**: A historic name for the island of Hispaniola, on which the modern-day countries of Haiti and Dominican Republic are located.

failed, and thus was born the world's very first state founded by former slaves who had liberated themselves: Haiti. (That development was not welcomed in the US, where slavery was to survive much longer. Following the success of the former slaves in Haiti, which was perceived to constitute a bad example, the island nation would pay a painful price for that 'original sin.')

The "bourgeois gentlemen" (*bourgeois gentilshommes*) who, before 1789, had aped the nobility which they hated and admired at the same time, also knew how to appreciate that, in the Napoleonic Empire, they too could acquire prestigious titles of nobility if they proved useful and loyal to the regime. Napoleon did in fact create a new kind of nobility, one in which membership was not based on birth, but rather on "merit." We must not underestimate the importance of such a socio-psychological factor: in this other republic born of a revolution, or at least an antimonarchist rebellion, the United States of America, the captains of industry and other bourgeois patricians also have a weakness for pseudo-aristocratic and presumably prestigious attributes. As in prerevolutionary France, when most kings of the Bourbon dynasty were called Louis, in "dynasties" of American industrialists and bankers the sons are given the same first name as the father, plus a Roman numeral; the great-grandson of oil tycoon John D. Rockefeller, the original Rockefeller, for example, is known today as John Rockefeller IV.

REVOLUTION AND TERROR

In France itself and in many other countries, many people, including politicians and historians, despise Robespierre, the Jacobins, and of course also the sans-culottes, blaming them for the bloodshed that accompanied their "popular" and radical revolution, "1793." These same people often profess great admiration for Napoleon, the savior of the bourgeois, moderate revolution, "1789." They condemn the "internalization" of the French Revolution, presumably because it went hand in hand with the Terror which, in France and especially in Paris, took a toll of thousands of victims, and they blame it on the Jacobin "ideology' and/or the supposed innate bloodthirstiness of ordinary 'people,' the "mob." They obviously do not understand—or do not want to understand—that the "externalization" of the revolution by the Thermidorians and by Napoleon, associated with international wars that dragged on for some twenty years, cost the lives of several million people, across all of Europe, including countless French people. In fact, one can say that these wars constituted a considerably larger and much bloodier form of terror than the terrorist regime of the Montagnards ever happened to be.

It is estimated that the Robespierrian Terror cost the lives of 50,000 people, which amounted to some 0.2% of the population of France. "Is that a lot, or little?," asks historian Michel Vovelle, who quotes these figures.[25] In comparison with the number of victims of the wars fought for the temporary territorial expansion of the "great nation" and for the glory of Bonaparte, it is very little. The battle of Waterloo alone, the last of Napoleon's presumably "glorious" career, killed or wounded between 45,000 and 50,000, "more or less": if we add the preliminary "skirmishes" of Ligny and Quatre-Bras, we arrive at a total of 80,000 or 90,000 casualties. And the battle of Leipzig, also lost by Napoleon, in 1813, but now almost entirely forgotten, claimed approximately 140,000 victims.[26] As for his catastrophic Russian campaign, the 1812 battle of Borodino, fought en route to Moscow, it ended with each square kilometer covered by no less than 3,000 Russian and French corpses. Finally, the track of the humiliating return journey out of Russia was littered with hundreds of thousands of dead and wounded. Napoleon had entered Russia with more than 500,000 French and allied soldiers, he exited with only 110,000.

However, no one ever speaks of a Bonapartist "terror," and Paris teems with monuments, streets, and squares glorifying the presumably "great" and "heroic" Emperor. Moreover, in a comparison of the terror of Robespierre with that of Bonaparte, should we not take into account the indisputable fact that death by the guillotine was quick and painless, compared to death on the battlefield? During a typical Napoleonic battle, only the lucky ones perished by a bullet in the chest. As for the wounded, Napoleon forbade their evacuation to the rear since using men for this task would have weakened the fighting battalions. Often terribly mutilated, the wounded were left to die a slow death and were sometimes

---

25 Vovelle, p. 141.
26 Rothenberg, pp. 81-82, 252-53.

devoured alive by wolves or stray dogs.[27]

Marx and Engels already noted that, by replacing permanent revolution in France, and especially in Paris, by a permanent war across all of Europe, the Thermidorians and their successors "perfected" the system of Terror, in other words, they shed infinitely more blood than the regime of Robespierre. In any event, it is undeniable that the exportation or "externalization," via warfare, of the moderate bourgeois revolution by the Thermidorians and Napoleon took a much heavier toll than the Jacobins' attempt to radicalize the revolution by means of Terror, in other words, to "internalize" the Revolution within France.

With respect to the spillage of blood that characterized "1793," the radical phase of the French Revolution, a few other remarks are in order. In Ancien Régime France, and in "old" feudal Europe in general, terror and violence had been used for centuries by the state as a means of achieving political goals and, more specifically, of keeping the lower layers of the social pyramid, "those below," under control. Particularly functional in this sense were not only the truly bestial public executions, supplemented by tortures that sometimes dragged on for hours, but also the burnings at the stake of witches, the atrocious repression of heresies like that of the Cathars (a.k.a. Albigensians) in the South of France. and, in Paris, the orchestrated massacre that has gone down in history as "Saint Bartholomew's night." For the "benefit of Parisians, this Ancien-Régime terror was permanently on display for hundreds of years in the macabre shape of the Gibbet of Montfaucon (*Gibet de Montfaucon*), looming on a hilltop just outside of the city, between what were to become the Square Amadou-Hampate Ba and the Place Robert-Desnos. The monumental arrangement displayed numerous corpses of executed folks, denied a decent burial and deliberately left hanging to rot; the idea was, as the French so delicately put it, "for the encouragement of others" (*pour encourager les autres*). The infamous gibbet was last used in 1629 and was dismantled in 1760.[28]

In comparison to the traditional "savage" or "hot" terror, the "disciplined" "cold" and "cold" terror of the French Revolution may actually be described as humanitarian. Torture, officially abolished by the Rev-

---

27 See the article by Arushev.
28 "Gibbet of Montfaucon."

olution, was not involved and, thanks to the guillotine, the condemned could "benefit" from a presumably immediate and painless death. The infamous massacres of September 1792, on the other hand, as well as the lynchings known as "lantern hangings" in the summer of 1789, evoked "hot" terror as the Ancien Régime had known it and reflected the brutalization of the populace which resulted from it. The remark made by Gracchus Babeuf after a hanging on the lantern in 1789 deserves to be quoted here:

> The plentiful corporal punishments, the practice of drawing and quartering, the tortures, the breaking on the wheel, burning alive at the stake, the whip, the gallows, the endless executions have taught us these atrocious customs! Our masters are now reaping what they themselves have sown.[29]

This factor too has to be taken into account when, as is so often the case during discussions about the French Revolution, the supposed "bloodthirstiness" of the people, or at least of its revolutionary elements, is discussed. In *A Connecticut Yankee in King Arthur's Court*, published in 1889, Mark Twain did so when, reflecting on the French Revolution, he made the following insightful remark about "France and the French before the ever memorable and blessed Revolution, which swept a thousand years of ... villainy away in one swift tidal wave of blood":

> There were two "reigns of Terror," if we would but remember and consider it: the one wrought murder in hot passion, the other in heartless cold blood; the one lasted mere months, the other had lasted a thousand years; the one inflicted death upon ten thousand persons, the other upon a hundred millions; but our shudders are all for the horrors of the minor Terror, the momentary Terror, so to speak, whereas what is the horror of swift death by the ax [sic, meaning the guillotine] compared with lifelong death from hunger, cold, insult, cruelty, and heart-break? A city cemetery could contain the coffins filled by that brief terror that we have all been so diligently taught to shiver at and mourn over; but all of France could hardly contain the coffins filled by that older and real Terror—that unspeakable bitter and awful Terror which none of us has been taught to see in its vastness or pity as it deserves.[30]

In addition, it is a fact, as Arno Mayer points out in *The Furies*, that revolutionary terror does not spring from a revolutionary ideology or from murderous plans hatched by revolutionaries, as far too many his-

---

29   Quoted in Munford, p. 538.

30   Quoted in Aptheker, pp. 112-13; "Mark Twain on the two Terrors," http://www.cultivatedlife.net/mark-twain-on-the-two-terrors.html.

torians claim, but from specific historical circumstances and, above all, from situations in which a revolution finds itself under great threat from internal and external enemies. The harassed revolutionaries thus come to the conclusion that compromise is no longer possible, that they are doomed, and with them the revolution, unless the enemies of the revolution and, with the latter, the counter-revolution, perish. In other words, the revolution ends up convinced that it must kill in order to survive. This certainly applies to the Terror of 1792-1793, when the Revolution was threatened by foreign as well as domestic counter-revolutionaries. Austrian troops invaded the country while royalist uprisings erupted in the Vendée region, triggering a kind of panic among the revolutionaries in the capital.

It must be recognized that there is some merit to the kind of thinking proposed by Mayer: revolutionary regimes that do not resort to terror or some other forms of violence and/or coercion, are virtually certain to be ruthlessly overthrown by the counter-revolution. This happened to be the tragic fate of Allende's democratic and peaceful revolution in Chile, smothered in blood during "the other September 11," the one of 1973, orchestrated by Pinochet. Had Allende's revolution used a modicum of violence against the leading political and military reactionaries, the major terror unleashed by Pinochet might not have come to pass—and the Chilean revolution might have been saved. In any event, in his masterful book, Mayer insists more than once on the fact that "the furies of the revolution are mainly nourished by the opposition of forces and ideas which are hostile to it."[31]

The majority of historians pay little attention to counter-revolutions or downplay their importance. There are many reasons for this, for example the fact that the counter-revolution normally does not formulate any theory. Another reason is the fact that counter-revolutions have tended to flourish in the countryside and not in the city; from a historiographical perspective, they, and their excesses, have therefore been far less visible and less shocking than the revolution's use of the high-profile guillotine for executions in the center of a square in the heart of the city in the middle of the country. In any event, the counter-revolution makes an equally—and probably even more eager—use of coercion, violence, and

---

31 Mayer, pp. 4, 23.

terror to achieve its objectives. Examples? The "white terror" during the Thermidorian reaction, a "savage" terror that raged primarily in distant provinces and, for that reason, easily escaped the attention of historians, And also the savage repression of the popular revolt in Paris in June 1848 as well as the mass executions of Parisian Communards in May 1871; the latter drama is described by Mayer as "the cruelest form of counter-revolutionary terror in Europe, between 1815 and 1917."[32] The panic-like fear of this kind of counter-revolutionary repression was undoubtedly one of the factors that help to explain the September massacres of 1792.

From the overwhelming majority of historians, politicians as well as contemporary journalists who condemn the Revolution because of the Terror, we may assume that they are not counter-revolutionaries. They are in favor of "1789," the moderate bourgeois revolution, but they are against "1793," the radical "popular," Jacobin revolution, the revolution that presumably "derailed," a project in which they see a forerunner of the even more radical—and anti-bourgeois—Russian Revolution. However, as we have seen, the exportation abroad and simultaneous consolidation at home of "1789," of the bourgeois revolution, provoked infinitely more terror, notably in the form of wars, than "1793." Furthermore, Robespierre and his companions organized their Terror not to implement some radical Jacobin ideological program, but to save the bourgeois revolution, i.e. "1789." They were convinced that this was not possible without bloodshed, and they were very likely right: "1793" saved "1789" from the clutches of the national as well as international counter-revolution. In addition, the Terror was not exclusively directed against the right-wing enemies of "1789," but also against its most radical leftist enemies, a fact illustrated by the execution of Hébert, the Cordelier leader who criticized the policy of the Montagnards as insufficiently radical. Of all the violence and bloodshed that characterized the French Revolution in the years following 1789—that is, of revolutionary terror in general and not only of the specifically Robespierrist Terror—it can therefore be said that much of it must be credited to the account of the counter-revolution and another considerable part to that of the moderate bourgeois revolution; in comparison, only a small portion of the total terror is attributable to the radical revolution of 1793, which, incidentally, may also be described as bourgeois, more specifically, petty-bourgeois.

---

32   Mayer, pp. 109, 119.

Tentative Evaluation of an Unfinished Revolution

Historians such as François Furet in France, Ernst Nolte in Germany, and Simon Schama in Britain like to bemoan the French Revolution on account of the violence and bloodshed associated with it. Schama, for example, has emphatically written that "from the very beginning—from the summer of 1789—violence was the motor of the Revolution."[33] This obviously ignores the historical fact, revealed in a thorough study, that more than 90 percent of all demonstrations and other collective actions of the revolutionaries in Paris between 1787 and 1795 did not involve any physical violence at all."[34] In any event, these historians compare the French revolutionary experience most unfavorably with the American Revolution, in their eyes a much more civilized historical phenomenon—sometimes eulogized as "a revolution without a revolution"!—and with the supposedly peaceful "evolution" towards modernity and democracy followed by Britain. Thanks to those historical developments, these two countries allegedly also succeeded in transforming the caterpillar of their "Ancien Régime" into the butterfly of a modern state, a democratic state which—like France—carries the banner of freedom, equality, and justice.

As the great Italian historian Domenico Losurdo has explained in a brilliant comparison of developments in France, the US, and Britain,[35] the developments in the US and in Britain may only be described as peaceful if one ignores some primordial historical facts. Britain's highly touted "evolution" towards democracy and other forms of "modernity" took centuries to come to fruition, because it started long before the French Revolution and obtained major successes, such as the introduction of universal suffrage, much later than France, namely only after the First World War—and, it deserves to be pointed out, after the Russian Revolution, without which universal suffrage would not have been introduced.[36] This evolution was an extremely protracted affair, and the main reason for this that was systematic and stubborn resistance, involving fre-

---

33   Schama, p. 859.

34   Alpaugh, p. 3.

35   Losurdo (2006), pp. 43-96.

36   See Pauwels (2016), chapter 28. At the end of WWI, quasi-revolutionary situations prevailed in France, Britain, Belgium, etc., and it was to avoid all-out revolution, as in Russia and in Germany, that the ruling elites quickly introduced reforms, including universal suffrage.

quent use of violence unleashed from "above," that is, from the British counterparts of the French counter-revolutionaries who, it must be added, have not yet been entirely vanquished.[37]

What comes to mind in this context are the civil wars of Cromwell's time, massacres, similar to those in the Vendée, of Catholic "rebels" in the Irish and Scottish periphery, and of course the decapitation of a king, Charles I, in the center of a square in the center of the capital, not Paris, but London—and in the old-fashioned and inhumane way, with an axe.

As for the American Revolution, it was not a real revolution, a movement of the demos, of *ceux d'en bas* [those below], but essentially a rebellion, a revolt against the authorities in London by *ceux d'en haut* [those above], namely, the colonial elite, an "English" patriciate of owners of plantations and plenty of slaves, as well as wealthy merchants, including slave traders, in other words, the US counterparts of France's landowning aristocracy and haute bourgeoisie.[38] And this revolt received indispensable armed support from the plebeian colonists, a kind of American version of the French sans-culottes.[39] Together, they pushed back against the authority of a government based in distant London.

This pseudo-revolution not only involved a full-fledged war against the British—in other words, the type of bloodshed for which historians generally do not show "red cards"—but also major massacres and mass deportations, whose victims were not only the numerous American colonists known as "Loyalists" because they remained loyal to the British Crown, but also the native population, the "Indians." Traditionally, massacres whose victims were Indigenous people have also also been whitewashed by American historians, who usually prefer to euphemize them as "Indian Wars." As mentioned, historians generally find wars to be legiti-

---

37   As mentioned earlier, Britain's Prince of Wales is still one of the biggest landowners; and nobles, as well as important prelates of the Anglican Church always automatically receive a seat - with a cushion on it! - in the Upper House of the British Parliament; furthermore, it can hardly be said that Church and State are separated in a country where the sovereign automatically also holds the office of head of the "national" Church.

38   See e.g. Amin, p. 44.

39   The important revolutionary role of the transatlantic demos—including sailors, indentured servants, slaves, etc.—before and during the American Revolution is the theme of the book by Peter Linebaugh and Marcus Rediker.

mate and justifiable, and most of that profession tend to overlook crimes committed against people of color.[40]

In addition, by maintaining slavery—one of world history's most spectacular forms of coercion and violence, in other words: terror—the American so-called revolution remained an unfinished symphony. A second revolutionary convulsion was required to finally bring about the formal abolition of slavery in the so-called "land of the free," but a system of crude and systematic discriminations victimizing Afro-Americans, known as "Jim Crow," would continue to exist for a very long time. This second phase, known as the War of Secession or the American Civil War, lasted from 1861 to 1865. It amounted to a gigantic bloodbath, a Moloch more deadly for the country than the Second World War was to be.[41] Yet in their zeal to present US history as peaceful in comparison to the French experience, historiographical illusionists such as Furet and Nolte ignore this terrible conflict and they pay little or no attention to the fate of "Indians" and Blacks. It is only in this questionable fashion that the myth of the dichotomy between a peaceful and sensible British and American evolution and a bloody, senseless French revolution can be kept alive.

While we are comparing the French Revolution to the American Revolution and the British "evolution," it should also be noted that the French revolutionaries pursued equality for all Frenchmen and that they realized this objective, though admittedly only in the sense of formal equality before the law. Of the American and British cases, the same can only be said if one ignores entire historical chapters. In its original phase, the American Revolution achieved absolutely nothing positive for the Afro-Americans, who remained slaves, arguably under worse conditions than before. And the American Revolution was also a catastrophe for the Indigenous population, the "Indians"; in the new state, they enjoyed no rights whatsoever but became the victims of a veritable genocide. According to a slogan that was to become popular in the new republic, "the only good Indian is a dead Indian"; and truly genocidal action followed these cynical words. This genocide provoked the admiration of Hitler and inspired his murderous plans with respect to Jews and other sup-

40   Losurdo (2006), pp. 59-63.

41   About 200,000 soldiers lost their lives during battles, but the total number of dead was to exceed 600,000.

posed "sub-humans" (*Untermenschen*).⁴²

To make it possible to favorably compare the historical developments in the US with the French Revolution, a supposedly gratuitously bloody affair, historians such as Furet have to avert their gaze from the millions—indeed: millions!—of Indians who, in the course of the 18th and 19th centuries, were massacred by the Americans. As an excuse for such negationism, one might perhaps cite the fact that, from a historiographic point of view, these bloodbaths were far less visible than the executions that took place in the public squares of major cities. Indeed, like the Thermidorian "white terror," the massacres of Indians took place far from the urban centers, in isolated "rural" settings, namely the American version of the French countryside, the Far West. Did it come to the attention of a single denizen of New York or Boston, in December 1890, that a few thousand "Injuns," including women and children and old folks, were massacred at Wounded Knee, a lost corner of faraway Dakota? Of this "Wild West," as the Far West was also known, it may indeed be said that it was "wild," not because it was inhabited by "savages," because the Indians were not savages at all, but because it was the scene where the supposedly civilized American settlers unleashed against the indigenous population a truly "wild" terror, a terror that made the revolutionary as well as counter-revolutionary terror in France look like the work of clumsy amateurs.

The result of the French Revolution was an inclusive society, a homogeneous "nation" in which even denizens previously treated as outsiders, Protestants and Jews, were henceforth members—*citoyens*, "citizens"—and enjoyed the same rights as Catholics. On the other hand, the result of the American Revolution was a "*Herrenvolk* democracy,"⁴³ that is, a society in which the advantages of liberty and equality were reserved for only a part of the population, the white citizens, while the two other

---

42 See for example Losurdo (2007), p. 99, about Nazi policy in Eastern Europe: "Germany is destined to penetrate Eastern Europe as a kind of Far West and to treat the 'natives' there like the Indians, never losing sight of the American model, whose 'fabulous inner force' was praised by the Führer." See also the studies by Stannard, Kakel, and Westermann.

43 Terminology introduced by Domenico Losurdo and inspired by the German term *Herrenvolk*, that is, "master race," the binary opposite, in the Nazi view, of *Untermenschen*, 'undermen,' such as Jews, Slavs, Roma, etc.

parts, the Afro-Americans and the Native Americans, were denied the rights associated with citizenship. [44]

The French Revolution *in*tegrated the minority that had been marginalized in the Ancien Régime; the American Revolution *ex*tegrated Blacks and Indians who, together, formed the majority of the population on the territory of the so-called "land of the free." A similar phenomenon occurred in Britain, where the passage from the absolute monarchy to democracy and modernity was generally achieved to the benefit of the English population and to the detriment, not of all, but of a majority of the predominantly Catholic Irishmen and Scots, who were either massacred by the thousands in battles—or rather, butcheries—such as those of Drogheda and Culloden, or driven off their land to make room for English landlords and their sheep. [45]

Executions, massacres, deportations, plus civil and international wars were thus not only a hallmark of the French Revolution, but also of more or less contemporary historical developments in the US and Britain. According to Arno Mayer, violence and bloodshed are inevitable whenever human history experiences a "new beginning," revolutionary or not. The reason: the privileged of the old system always react with violence and bloodshed to any attempt to dislodge them from their towers of power and privilege.

In revolutionary circumstances, violence and terror also flare up because of numerous other factors that Mayer also mentions, for example the desire to take revenge for earlier injustices and—indeed!—vulgar sadistic impulses on the side of the revolutionaries as well as counter-revolutionaries, because on both sides, the occasion makes not only the thief but also the sadist, the rapist, etc. In any event, when one wants to evaluate a "rapid historical acceleration" of a turbulent, revolutionary nature, one will not get very far if one focuses mostly on the bloodshed that it involved—which is not to say that it is unimportant—but one must above all examine the results of these revolutions. (And it must be taken into account that not all movements that are called revolutionary are genuine revolutions.)

Of the French Revolution, it can be said that it constituted a major

---

44 Losurdo (2007), p. 269; see also Losurdo's article in Klundt.
45 Losurdo (2006), pp. 55-59.

step forward for France, for Europe, and indeed for humanity, a liberating step away from the obscurity of the Ancien Régime and feudalism in general, and towards a bright, albeit distant, destination: democracy. After the Revolution, and because of the Revolution, France was a very different country in comparison to the France of the Ancien Régime. It was henceforth not merely a "state" looming high and in many ways threateningly above the heads of ordinary folks, but a "nation," a homogeneous state, highly centralized, and in many ways "modern"; and its inhabitants were no longer subjects of some monarch, but proud citizens with—at least in principle—the same rights and duties. The Church had lost its privileges and was henceforth separated from the state, something which most of us today deem to be a good thing. The nobility, which had previously dominated the social scene, had received a blow from which it was never to fully recover. The feudal "seignorial system," exploitative and abusive, was dead and buried. And every French person was henceforth entitled to be addressed as *madame*, "lady," or *monsieur*, "sir." Bread, even white bread, previously an unattainable luxury, and even croissants and similar deluxe baked delicacies were now available to all thanks to prices that were kept low, if necessary by state subsidies, with a tip of the hat to revolutionary radicalism and regrets to laissez faire.

After the Revolution, the French would also very much enjoy eating the meat of horses, animals traditionally used by the nobility and therefore considered to be "noble" animals, and *boucheries chevalines*, "horse butcher shops," would spring up in all French towns and even villages. Horse meat is wholesome and nutritious, but ordinary Frenchmen undoubtedly found its consumption extra satisfying because it amounted to a symbolic "cannibalisation" of the aristocratic class enemy, *ceux d'en haut*, the gentlemen who, seated on their "high horses," had always looked down on folks of the lower classes. The horse was indeed the "emblematic animal" of the nobility, and the latter's class ally in pre-revolutionary feudal times, the Catholic Church, had instituted a taboo on hippophagy in the early Middle Ages. In contrast to France and other countries thoroughly affected by the French Revolution, such as Belgium and Italy, lands that never experienced a real revolution and where the nobility was therefore able to solidly remain in the saddle, so to speak, horses continued to be "noble" animals, to be respected almost as much as the people riding them, and therefore not to be made available for consumption by the common people.[46]

The class that emerged as the great victor of the revolution and was henceforth to set the tone, not only economically but also politically, was the bourgeoisie, that is, the haute bourgeoisie or upper-middle class. (The chateaux in the countryside and the stately homes in Paris and other big cities were henceforth mostly inhabited by wealthy burghers, and only rarely by noble families.) But the petty bourgeoisie and even the lower classes in general would henceforth increasingly have to be taken into account, especially so after the introduction of universal suffrage in 1848. In other words, while the French Revolution certainly did not give birth to a democratic utopia, it had opened the Pandora's Box of the *democratization process*. The well-to-do peasants had been able to lay their hands on land and buildings formerly belonging to the Church and the nobility, so they too were among the "winners" of the Revolution. The small peasants, on the other hand, were victimized by revolutionary changes in the countryside, including the abolition of traditional communal practices in the villages, and they had no choice but to migrate to the urban centers of industry and mining and morph into wage-earning, propertyless proletarian workers. (As already mentioned, a notable exception to this general rule was the not inconsiderable number of peasants who managed to acquire a small vineyard, just big enough to continue to make a living, and continue residing, in the countryside.) In any event, it was thanks to the Revolution, which cherished liberal principles like freedom of enterprise, that industrial capitalism was able to unfold in France—albeit less majestically, because of viticulture, than in England or Belgium—with its controversial advantages for some and disadvantages for others, and with the virulent social conflicts that have been associated with it even since.

In France, the Revolution not only played into the hands of industrialization but also that of the urbanization which went hand in hand with it; and this urbanization concerned first and foremost Paris, the city that had been the main stage of the Revolution and, in many ways, had made the Revolution. Before the Revolution, France had been a predominantly rural society with Paris as the big exception, a kind of urban anomaly. After the Revolution, and because of the Revolution, France morphed into a predominantly urban society, but with Paris as the city of cities,

---

46 Von Paczensky and Dünnebier, pp. 268-71; see also the article by Bourcier.

the country's "megalopolis," and the French countryside—viewed from the Parisian perspective as a quaint but backward "province"—as a rural anomaly. After the Revolution, and because of it, writes Patrice Higonnet, "Paris was everything, the provinces were nothing."[47]

"1789," the moderate, bourgeois revolution, did not create heaven on earth for the French, but it greatly improved the lot of the vast majority of the population, in most cases not immediately, but certainly in the long run. "1793," the radical, petty-bourgeois and therefore plebeian revolution, provided a foretaste of what revolution can and—according to some—*must* lead to. "1793" showed the way beyond mere legal equality, towards social equality, towards a different, less "liberal" approach to the economy, towards social justice, social democracy, and even further, towards socialism. As for the question whether, in the long run, we should limit our aspirations to "1789" or if, alternatively, we should return to the path taken, ever so tentatively, by "1793," that is a question that still confronts us today. What Heinrich Heine said about the French Revolution still holds true today, not only for the French, but for all of us: "The Revolution has started, but it is far from terminated."

---

47   Higonnet, pp. 312-13.

Part III.
The Revolutions of 1830, 1848, and 1871

in Collaboration with Frans De Maegd

9. 1830: Three Glorious Days in July

For France, the fall of Napoleon, first in 1814, after the disastrous expedition to Russia, and then, definitively, with the Battle of Waterloo in June 1815, signified the triumph of the counter-revolution. The brother of the guillotined Louis XVI and uncle of his son who died in the Temple, Louis XVII, is placed on the throne as Louis XVIII by the statesmen meeting at the Congress of Vienna. The aristocratic émigrés return to the country, where many if not most of them are soon nicknamed the "Ultras" because, in their counter-revolutionary zeal, they aspire to go even "further"—*ultra*, in Latin—than the new king himself, who understands that the post-revolutionary situation requires tact and flexibility. The Ultras want to return to the days of the Ancien Régime but, after more than a quarter of a century of bourgeois rule, that is easier said than done. Taking revenge on the champions of the revolutionary cause and the supporters of Napoleon is possible, however, and this is what happens in a new outburst of "white terror." After the death of Louis XVIII, in 1824, his brother Charles X succeeds him. The new monarch sympathizes with the Ultras and pursues an even more reactionary policy than his predecessor. The general discontent generated by this, combined with an economic crisis reminiscent of the summer of 1789, will trigger a new revolution in July 1830.

Starting in 1826, France is plagued by a series of bad harvests, and the economy regresses sharply. The ordinary people are unhappy and the liberal opposition of the bourgeoisie and the intellectuals grows. Charles

X reacts by dissolving the parliament, which was powerless anyway, and proceeds to rule by decree, increasingly restricting the right to vote and suppressing press freedom. The bourgeois newspapers, for example the liberal *Le National* run by Adolphe Thiers, who will become one of the leaders of the coming revolution, protest loudly and call on the people to resist. In response to police raids into newspaper offices and printing facilities, many shops and factories close their doors and send their staff into the streets to demonstrate; some employers even pay their workers to do so. Members of the disbanded National Guard appear with guns they had concealed. On July 27, a full-fledged revolt erupts in the popular districts, including the Faubourg Saint-Antoine. Barricades are erected—more than 4,000, made with over 800,000 cobblestones, according to some sources[1]—and thousands of demonstrators wave the revolutionary tricolor and belt out the *Marseillaise* at the top of their lungs. The army attacks the barricades but is pushed back time and again. The capital's popular districts witness heavy fighting, especially in the area of Place de Grève and the Hôtel de Ville, which changes hands several times, but the architectural symbol of popular power ends up in the control of the insurgents. The revolutionaries will change the name of the square to Place de l'Hôtel de Ville and banish executions from it.

The troops are withdrawn after three days of fierce fighting, which leaves a thousand dead—800 from the people's side, 200 from the army ranks. Exasperated, Charles X abandons Paris and flees with his family from the château of Saint-Cloud via the port of Cherbourg to the safety of England.

The leaders of the revolutionary movement, again mostly well-to-do burghers, remember the lessons learned during the Great Revolution. They do not want a republic, for this form of government reminds them of "1793," the radical Revolution, but they have no objections to a constitutional monarchy, the formula opted for in "1789," the moderate phase of the Revolution.

Lafayette, a former Feuillant, and a handful of powerful bankers like Périer and Laffitte, come up with the seemingly ideal candidate for the throne: Louis-Philippe d'Orléans, son of "Philippe Égalité." He does not become "king of France," like his predecessors, because this title suggests

---

1 Higonnet, p. 60.

that the country is the property of the royal dynasty, but "king of the French," which implies that the sovereign has been chosen by, and is supposed to be at the service of, the people. The idea that a constitutional monarchy is a solution that is revolutionary and therefore democratic (or vice versa) and will therefore be welcomed by the 1830 avatars of the sans-culottes, is also intelligently conveyed by presenting Louis-Philippe to them as saviour of the nation, duly wrapped in the tricolore, on the balcony of the Hotel de Ville, architectural symbol of the common people's conquest of the capital. Likewise redolent with symbolism is the fact that this choreography involved having the new monarch trek respectfully for his anointing from his home, the Palais-Royal, associated with royalty, to the city hall, the downtown pied-à-terre of a mostly suburban demos; this hike conjured up the king's traditional trip to Reims for anointment by the archbishop—undertaken for the very last time, incidentally, by Charles X, in 1825.

France becomes a constitutional and parliamentary monarchy, known as the "July Monarchy." Louis-Philippe is expected to do what Louis XVI had not agreed to do, namely to play the role of a non-absolutist king, to settle for the sinecure's glory and other benefits but without commanding the power formerly associated with the throne. In short, "the king reigns, but does not govern," as Thiers put it.

In this arrangement, then, the sovereign has little to say, but the common people, who once again "made" the revolution, even less. More people are given the right to vote, but the censitary suffrage is maintained and continues to be very restrictive. Only very well-to-do burghers can vote, there are only 250,000 of them in all of France. And there are even more stringent criteria for being able to be elected, so that only 58,000 citizens qualify. (When questioned about this, the prime minister, François Guizot, famously replied that the solution was simple: "become rich!" (*enrichissez-vous.*)[2]

The rich bourgeoisie is thus able to monopolize power. Louis-Philippe's "July Monarchy," fruit of the revolution of 1830, is a (haut-) bourgeois regime, and Louis-Philippe has correctly been described as the "bourgeois king." A bourgeois regime implies a liberal ideology and liberal policies, reflected in the introduction of civil liberties and freedom

---

2   Noiriel, pp. 287-88.

of the press. The new monarchy, fruit of a revolution, also proves to be mildly anticlerical. The Catholic Church once again loses the role of state religion it had reclaimed in 1814-1815 at the Restoration. Finally, the revolutionary tricolor once again becomes the flag of France.

To commemorate the victims and the victory of the "Three glorious days"—26, 27, and 28 July, 1830—a 52-meter-high column will be erected in the center of the Place de la Bastille, the "July column." To make room for it, Napoleon's plaster elephant, which had been allowed to dilapidate during the Restoration, will be taken down in 1846, only a couple of years before popular risings in Paris (and elsewhere) would yet again demonstrate that the time of revolutions had not yet come to an end, as had been previously suggested by the "jumbo." The column is surmounted by an allegorical representation of freedom, holding in its hands the torch of liberty and the broken chain of tyranny; liberty is indeed the paramount object of desire of the bourgeois and *liberal*, rather than the plebeian revolutionaries. However, it was the latter who made the success of the revolution of 1830 possible and accounted for the majority of its martyrs, more than 400 of whom will be buried at the foot of the column, in underground vaults originally used for the storage or passage of water for the fountain.[3]

Perhaps the most famous memento of the 1830 Revolution is the painting originally entitled "Scenes on the barricades" (*Scènes de barricades*) but eventually to become known as "Liberty on the Barricades" or "Liberty Guiding the People" (*La Liberté guidant le peuple*); it was created in that same year by Eugène Delacroix, a scion of an aristocratic family but opponent of the restored Bourbon monarchy and a man with liberal sympathies. In this case too, the emphasis is on the role of the bourgeoisie in the Revolution and the liberal objective of that class. Liberty is symbolized by a young woman, wearing a Phrygian cap and holding the tricolor flag, thus conjuring up Marianne; she is inspiring and guiding the revolutionaries, she represents their objective, at least in the view of the artist. And their protagonist is a solid burgher, identifiable by his top hat. The plebeian characters, on the other hand, are relegated to the background—where Notre-Dame, emblem of Old France, is once again engulfed by the smoke of revolutionary events—except for

---

3   "Éléphant de la Bastille."

a boy swinging pistols and coming right at us. Perhaps he represents the next generation of lower-class proletarians who will be the main actors in the drama of the 1871 revolution, to be known as the Paris Commune? Incidentally, that street urchin is believed to have provided inspiration for the character of Gavroche in Victor Hugo's world-famous novel, *Les Misérables*, written in 1862, after yet another revolution, that of 1848. Delacroix's painting also inspired an equally famous work of art by the sculptor Frédéric Auguste Bartholdi's, entitled "Liberty Enlightening the World," but better known as the Statue of Liberty, donated by France to the United States in 1886.[4]

IMAGE 25. Inauguration of the Colonne de juillet in 1840.

The restoration of the monarchy in 1814/15 was not due to popular demand within France. Louis XVI was supposed to have been "Louis le dernier," the last king, and the French overwhelmingly favored either a bourgeois dictatorship under Napoleon or a republic. Louis XVIII could only return by riding the coattails of the victorious Russian, British, Austrian, and Prussian enemies of the Revolution and of Napoleon, without exception champions of Ancien-Régime style regimes.

---

4   Pool, p. 14.

This explains, first, why the Restoration was predestined to constitute only an ephemeral moment in the history of France; and, second, why Louis XVIII and Charles X were unable to undo the *embourgeoisement* of Paris inaugurated by Napoleon and to turn the capital once again into a royal city, even though they made a valiant effort to "reroyalize"—and "reclericalize"—the city.[5] That program included, first of all, building an "expiatory chapel" (*chapelle expiatoire*) on the site of the churchyard where Louis XVI and Marie-Antoinette had been buried after their execution on nearby Place de la Concorde. But the remains of the royal couple were transferred to the restored mausoleum of French royalty in the Abbey of Saint-Denis, which had been vandalized during the Revolution. The cell in the Conciergerie in which Marie-Antoinette had spent the last weeks of her life, was transformed into a kind of shrine commemorating the martyrdom of the queen despised by most of the ordinary Parisians. Statues of kings returned to born-again royal squares that also recovered their original names, and Henry IV on horseback reclaimed his old spot in the middle of the Pont Neuf.

The primordial royal square, dedicated to Louis XIII, renamed Place des Vosges in 1800, recovered its original name, Place Royale. As for Place de la Concorde, formerly the most magnificent of all royal squares, Louis XVIII intended to dedicate it to the memory of his brother, Louis XVI, the "king-martyr." His statue was to stand in the center, of course, framed by a chapel and a weeping willow. Work was started under Charles X, who laid the first stone in May 1826 and rebaptized the square Place Louis XVI. But the outbreak of a revolution in 1830 aborted the project, and the square became Place de la Concorde again. The neighboring bridge across the Seine, originally named after Louis XVI but briefly known as Pont de la Révolution, had predictably become Pont Louis XVI again in 1814; it was rebaptized Pont de la Concorde in 1830. As for the vast open space where the Bastille had once stood, the name it had received from Napoleon, Place de la Bastille, was not acceptable under the Restoration. With plans on hand to develop into yet another royal square, it was officially rebaptized Place Louis XVIII, but the Parisians preferred to refer to it as Place de l'Éléphant, referring to the elephant fountain in the middle of the square.

---

5   This "royalization" is described succinctly but effectively in Jones, pp. 303-20.

Of the many churches and monasteries that had fallen victim to the revolutionaries' anticlerical ardor, some were put back into service during the Restoration. The most famous example is the Pantheon, which became once again a sanctuary dedicated to Sainte Geneviève, patron saint of Paris. The famous inscription above the entrance was removed, but the tombs of Rousseau and even the famously anticlerical Voltaire were allowed to remain *in situ*; Louis XVIII displayed a regal sense of humor by stating that Voltaire would be sufficiently punished by having to hear mass daily![6]

A handful of entirely new churches were constructed; one of them was Notre-Dame-de-Lorette, inspired by Santa Maria Maggiore Basilica in Rome. However, the return of the old twin of throne and altar generated precious little enthusiasm among Parisians of the bourgeois variety and even less among the city's lower orders. As things turned out, the attempt to re-royalize Paris was as futile and doomed as the entire experiment of a *retour en arrière* towards a Bourbon monarchy in the style of the Ancien Régime. Paris did not want to become royal again. And all too soon it looked as if the city might revert to a plebeian urban persona, for dark revolutionary clouds gathered in the Parisian sky in the late 1820s.

---

6   Panthéon (Paris).

10. 1848: Red Flag on the Barricades

LOUIS-PHILIPPE'S REGIME is tailor-made to meet the needs of the haute bourgeoisie but is not to the taste of a not inconsiderable segment of that same class which, because of the restricted right to vote, is denied any input into the political process. The pressure mounting from this direction, for example via the relatively free press, results on the one hand in some concessions from the government, including a modest widening of the franchise; on the other hand, it also triggers repressive measures. And this stimulates republican sentiments within the opposition. The situation becomes critical when this latent political conflict is amplified and complemented during the years 1847-1848 by a serious economic crisis that rages not only in France but throughout Europe and brings unemployment and greater misery to the little people. It is yet another "subsistence crisis" like the one of 1789, during which shortages cause high prices, this time not only of bread but also of potatoes which have recently become an important staple in the diet of France's demos. As in 1789, the situation is ripe once again for a revolution in which discontented bourgeois, together with starving plebeians, will rise up together, overthrow the existing regime, and take over the reins of state.

The troubles erupt in January-February 1848, when the government seeks to close down political gatherings organized by the opposition and disguised as "banquets," events during which the extension of the right to vote is again called for. On February 22, demonstrating students are joined by workers as they prepare to march on the Chamber of Deputies, which meets at the Palais-Bourbon; under the July Monarchy, that building has come the symbolize the upper bourgeoisie's monopoly of power. The government feels strong because, in addition to an army of 30,000 men, it also plans to deploy the 40,000 strong National Guard. However, on February 23, a large part of the National Guard defects to the side of the discontented people.

Louis-Philippe creates the impression that he is prepared to introduce reforms by firing the widely detested prime minister, Guizot. And the situation seems to calm down. However, that same evening, a crowd of demonstrators wants to boo Guizot at his home, in the Capucines district, that is, between the site where the Opéra Garnier will be erected later, and the Madeleine Church. Approaching that sanctuary as they arrive from the Faubourg Saint-Antoine, they find their progress barred by an army unit that, allegedly following a provocation, opens fire and kills 52 demonstrators The bodies of these martyrs are transported in carts across Paris by torchlight, and this once again rekindles the revolutionary flame. In the popular districts, the alarm bells are ringing and the people—workers, students, and members of the petty bourgeoisie—start to erect no less than 1,500 barricades on which, in addition to the revolutionary tricolor, now also float numerous red flags.

The king refuses to resort to violence. To save his dynasty, he offers to abdicate in favor of his nine-year-old grandson, whose mother is to serve temporarily as regent. In the Chamber of Deputies, numerous representatives of the liberal bourgeoisie are in favor of such a compromise. However, in the name of the Parisian working class, François-Vincent Raspail, a scientist and publicist who has morphed into a revolutionary leader, declares that the workers will continue to occupy the barricades unless a republic is proclaimed. This means the end of the July Monarchy. On February 25, Louis-Philippe and his family escape from the Tuileries Palace and head for Le Havre, where the deposed monarch, disguised as a bourgeois gentleman and travelling as "Mr. Smith," will embark on a commercial liner and head for exile in England. As he departs from the Tuileries, a crowd of revolutionaries enters the palace and absconds with his throne, which they will deliver to the flames on Place de la Bastille, at the foot of the July Column. That is also where 200 of the revolution's 350 killed revolutionaries will be buried alongside the martyrs of 1830. The Second Republic is proclaimed—at the Hôtel de Ville, *naturelle-*

ment.

A painting by Henri Félix Philippoteaux entitled "Lamartine in front of the Town Hall of Paris rejects the red flag," recalls an important detail of the events that took place there on February 25. Its central figure is the poet Alphonse de Lamartine, one of the leaders of the revolution, a gentleman who typically champions liberal ideas and simultaneously abhors and fears the popular masses who have just pulled the chestnuts out of the revolutionary fire.[1] He is standing tall, literally as well as figuratively speaking, in front of the entrance to the Hôtel de Ville and is backed up by other bourgeois gentlemen. They are clearly determined to deny access to the building symbolizing popular power to a mob surging forward from the left, folks whose radical expectations are symbolized by the red flag carried by a Marianne wearing a Phrygian cap. Lamartine stands for the moderate, liberal revolutionary ideas, whose symbol par excellence has become the tricolore flag, prominent on the right side of the painting, conjuring up liberty, rather than equality and fraternity, a banner that also conjures up the kind of French nationalism that was first whipped up by the Girondins and later by Bonaparte in an effort to displace radical revolutionary fervor. Lamartine pleads successfully with the assembled revolutionaries not to abandon, in favor of the red flag of the social revolution, a tricolore that represented "the *glory* and *liberty* of the fatherland."[italics added][2] An ominous detail of the canvas is the fact that, likewise on the right, rallied behind the *blue-blanc-rouge* and grimly moving forward in good order is a mixed troop of armed men; it includes a few token common folks, among them a befuddled flag-bearer, but consists mostly of bourgeois *gens de bien* in top hats and above all of well-armed soldiers, while officers on horseback, devotees of "law and order," including one brandishing a sword, seem poised to order an attack against the disorderly motley crew of *gens de rien* on the left. A few months later, in June 1848, the military will indeed be mobilized by the bourgeois revolutionary leaders to crush another plebeian revolutionary outburst, as we will soon see. (Incidentally, the outstretched arms of the high-ranking officers loom rather ominously like a fascist greeting *avant la lettre*.)

---

1   Description of Lamartine in Duveau, pp. 84-86.

2   "Lamartine repoussant le drapeau rouge à l'hôtel de ville, le 25 février 1848" ; *Les lieux de l'histoire de France*, p. 345.

IMAGE 26. Lamartine, in front of the Hotel de ville, rejects the Red Flag.

Philippoteaux's painting illustrates clearly how the revolution of 1848, like its predecessor of 1830, was made by the ordinary people of Paris but hijacked, so to speak, by a bourgeoisie determined to prevent the populace from achieving its own revolutionary goals, focusing on social equality rather than political liberty. Much the same may be said about the revolution that had rocked the southern reaches of the United Kingdom of the Netherlands in 1830, leading to the creation of the state of Belgium; what originated there as a *social* revolution, made by the little people, was hijacked by the bourgeoisie and morphed into a *national* revolution.[3]

Within the provisional government, two antagonistic fronts emerge, conjuring up the two sides of Philippoteaux's painting. On the one hand, we perceive the bourgeois republicans, led by Lamartine, a poet and historian from the Burgundian city of Mâcon, where his statue still stands proudly along the banks of the Saône River. They wanted a political revolution, involving political changes that suit their needs; that objective has been achieved, they are satisfied, and now they want the revolution to end. They receive the support of the faction of the bourgeoisie that previously supported the Orleanist regime but, fearing a radicalization of the revolution, has converted to republicanism in order to be able to

---

3   See the book by Maurice Bologne.

continue to safeguard its interests in the political arena; these burghers are likewise keen to arrest the revolutionary process. The same attitude is displayed by the Catholic Church; formerly ardently monarchist, it now speaks out in favor of the republic form of state.[4]

On the other hand, the provisional government also features a left wing, that is, a number of folks representing the revolutionary little people, in other words, the working class, and these men push for radical reforms, not only of a political but even of a social nature. Albert, for example, whose real name is actually Alexandre Martin, is a simple worker, and Louis Blanc is a socialist theorist. Within the government, these personalities constitute a minority, but they can count on the support of the revolutionary Parisian workers who remain armed and who rule in the streets of the capital.

Under these circumstances, and against the wishes of many of its bourgeois members, the provisional government adopts an impressive series of political as well as social reforms, for example the introduction of universal suffrage for men, which will increase the number of voters from 250,000 to 9 million; the release of all political prisoners; complete freedom of the press; the abolition of the death penalty for political offenses; and, not least, the definitive abolition of slavery in the colonies. To combat the worrisome problem of unemployment, national workshops are established. But the left-wing members of the provisional government do not get their way when they propose to promote the red flag of revolution and socialism to the rank of national flag. Above all, it is the influential Lamartine who balks, and this is how the tricolor ends up being retained.

Louis Blanc is charged with the task of setting up the national workshops. He believes that this measure, combined with the introduction of universal suffrage, will solve social problems. He is convinced that the republic will thus become a "social republic" and ultimately cause socialism to triumph. Together with other workers' representatives, Blanc is installed in the Luxembourg Palace and there, in a magnificent setting redolent of the Ancien Régime, he and his associates may endlessly discuss things and make all sorts of plans. But he is not given any real power within a government whose other members are almost without exception opposed to his social policy project. Ironically, the latter meet at the City

---

4   Duveau, p. 62.

Hall, formerly the epicenter of popular power, and this is where all the important decisions are made—but not in the interest of the common people.

The grandiose plans of Louis Blanc yield no concrete results. The national workshops remain nothing other than but a kind of charitable institutions where, in exchange for alms, the unemployed are put to work in all kinds of generally useless tasks. However, the unemployment problem increases dramatically in importance as the number of workshop "members" rises steeply between March and early June, namely, from 20,000 to 110,000. To cover the mushrooming expenses, an additional tax is introduced, which makes the project of a "social republic" extremely unpopular among the middle class and the peasantry. This does not bode well for the upcoming general elections. A dichotomy emerges once again between a predominantly revolutionary capital and the overwhelmingly counter-revolutionary rest of France.

Louis Blanc realizes that the workshops do not meet his expectations and he dissociates himself from the project. And the Parisian workers are disappointed and unhappy with the state of affairs. They start to grumble and, influenced by radical leaders such as Auguste Blanqui, demand far-reaching reforms. The *Ceux d'en bas* are restless, and we seem to be on the verge of another explosion of popular anger. Pandemonium erupts when the election results turn out to be catastrophic for the radicals, who obtain only 100 of the 800 seats in the assembly of people's representatives. This means that conservative elements, consisting not only of bourgeois types who want to prevent a radicalization of the revolution but also outspoken counter-revolutionaries, come to power. On May 15, radical leaders including Blanqui, viewed from the conservative perspective as manipulators of the populace, as demagogues, organize a mass rally. Some 50,000 armed demonstrators burst into the Palais-Bourbon and proclaim the dissolution of the assembly that is meeting there. The crowd then treks to the Hôtel de Ville with the intention to form a revolutionary government. But the troops intervene, the revolutionaries are dispersed, and Blanqui finds himself once again in prison.

The counter-revolution now takes the initiative and, on June 21, the national workshops are closed down, a measure that plunges thousands of working-class families into misery. The government also prepares to draft all unemployed bachelors into the army, thus removing them from Paris, as the Thermidorians had done with young sans-culottes; "to rid Paris of its revolutionary forces," was the commentary of a contemporary.[5] The response to such provocations is not long in coming. On June 23, a revolt that starts, unsurprisingly, in the Faubourg Saint-Antoine, soon infects the other popular districts of Paris. Barricades are erected and defended by 30,000 armed workers. They are attacked by a force of approximately 100,000 soldiers under the command of General Louis-Eugène Cavaignac and, in some cases, swept away by cannon fire. (At the time, Victor Hugo resided in a home on Place des Vosges, a few hundred meters from the Faubourg Saint-Antoine, and he was an eyewitness to the revolutionary events; in one of his books, *Choses vues*,[6] he described in great detail an assault by the National Guard against a barricade near the Porte Saint-Denis.) The uprising ends up being smothered in blood. On June 26, it is all over. On the insurgent side, some 3,000 persons have been killed and no less than 15,000 prisoners will be deported to Algeria, colonized by France only shortly before.

The defeat of the revolutionary Parisian workers means that France is going to be governed by a heterogeneous group of conservative elements, lumped together in a "party of order," which has nothing but contempt for the republican state, in general, and abhors its system of universal suffrage, in particular. The situation resembles that which preceded Napoleon's orchestrated coup d'état of 18 Brumaire, when a solution was found in the form of a dictatorship. This time, power is again entrusted to a Bonaparte, namely, a nephew of Napoleon, Louis-Napoléon Bonaparte.[7] (In contrast to the original Napoleon, known as *Napoléon le grand*, "Napoleon the Great," his nephew will sarcastically be baptized *Napoléon le petit* by Victor Hugo.) His famous name allows the latter, first, to be elected as president of the republic and then, after an 1852 farcical coup d'état that Karl Marx will describe ironically as '*The Eighteenth Brumaire of Louis Bonaparte*,' to proclaim himself emperor. He adopts the name

---

5 François Pardigon, writer and revolutionary, who participated in the events of June 1848, as quoted in Hazan (2002), p. 342.

6 **Ed. Note:** Published in English as *Things Seen*.

7 Louis-Napoléon Bonaparte was the son of Louis, Napoleon's youngest brother, and Hortense de Beauharnais, daughter of Napoleon's first wife, Joséphine de Beauharnais.

Napoleon III as a tip of the hat to his cousin, Napoleon's son, whose full name was Napoléon François Joseph Charles Bonaparte; deceased in 1832, the latter survived his father, who had died in 1821, and was thus Napoleon II for about ten years, at least from a Bonapartist perspective.

IMAGE 27. Inauguration of the Saint Michael Fountain on August 15, 1860.

As a result, France's haute bourgeoisie no longer has any worries: a Bonapartist dictatorship once again guarantees the security of the existing social and economic order. It is not a coincidence that it is under

Napoleon III, that, in the Latin Quarter, a fountain is erected featuring a statue of Saint Michael, described by Eric Hazan as "the sword pointed at the back of a Satan ..., [representing] the triumph of good over the bad people of June 1848, ... the Second Empire crushing the demon of the revolution." The idea was that the Parisian common people would "recognize their image in the infernal beast thrown to the ground."[8]

Louis-Philippe departed ingloriously but left this mark on Paris. Not a royal mark, but a bourgeois mark, a grand-bourgeois mark that was simultaneously a Napoleonic one. Louis-Philippe was the "bourgeois king" and he was in many ways an avatar of Bonaparte who, as we have seen, was a kind of "bourgeois emperor." Both were brought to power, not by the petty bourgeoisie, of course, but by the *crème de la crème* of the bourgeoisie, industrialists, and bankers and such, to protect the interests of that class, and both did their best to meet this expectation. Military triumphs had made it possible as well as propagandistically useful to add a veneer of Napoleonic, militaristic, and chauvinist lustre to the intrinsically bourgeois renovation of Paris between 1799 and 1814/15. However, unlike Napoleon Bonaparte, Louis-Philippe could contribute no personal glory of any kind to a bourgeoisification program, launched by Napoleon but interrupted by the Restoration, that he restarted.

And so, while his reshaping of the capital[9] was predictably bourgeois, it turned out to be Napoleonic again, rather than Orleanist. And this project involved not only the completion of some of the emperor's pet projects but even the return to Paris, in 1840, of his mortal remains—his "boney parts" as the English joked—and their burial in a splendid edifice, the Invalides, located in the prestigious Saint-Germain district, part of the capital's bourgeois western reaches. That monument was to become one of the great architectural attractions of Paris. As for Napoleon's unfinished projects, it was under the auspices of Louis-Philippe that the Arc de Triomphe was finally finished and officially inaugurated on July 29, 1836.

The bourgeois-cum-Napoleonic renovation of Paris between 1830 and 1848 also included a *soupçon* of anti-clericalism, as it involved turning the great church of Saint Geneviève into a memorial to France's great-

---

8 Hazan (2002), p. 140.
9 The story of this reshaping is well summarized in Jones, pp. 310-43.

est children again, known as the "Temple of Glory" (*Temple de la Gloire*). That building, the Pantheon, could have been chosen as Napoleon's final resting place, but was not, presumably because the emperor preferred to rest among his veterans, for whom the Invalides complex had served as a retirement home since its foundation under Louis XIV, but more likely because he would have felt uncomfortable in the company of the likes of Voltaire and Rousseau, wrongly viewed by many as godfathers of the radical Revolution.

The bourgeoisie undoubtedly appreciated (even) more that the Orleanist regime's urbanistic and architectural initiatives in Paris included infrastructure projects that favored industrial development and/or greased the wheels of commerce. For example, the city was turned into the hub of a national railway network and witnessed the construction of big and beautiful railway stations, beginning with the Gare Saint-Lazare, opened for service in 1840. Railway lines and stations proved extremely helpful in bringing the industrial revolution to Paris. Indeed, factories were springing up along the periphery and triggered a rapidly increasing influx of workers immigrating from the provinces; a growing percentage of the city's *classes laborieuses* thus started to consist of wage-earning, genuinely proletarian industrial workers employed in factories rather than petty bourgeois artisans occupied in workshops. This turned eastern Paris into a bigger bulwark of the great unwashed than ever before.

This "red" Paris included not only the old cradle of restlessness and revolution, the Faubourg Saint Antoine, but also new working-class districts such as Belleville, formerly a village just outside the city walls, famous for its guinguettes; Bercy, located along the banks of the Seine, site of a cluster of wine warehouses; and the left-bank hillock known as Butte aux Cailles, one of the last Parisian heights to be covered with vineyards. Viewed from bourgeois western Paris, the city's expanding "East End" loomed increasingly like a major menace, a poor, dirty, and insalubrious hellhole inhabited by *canaille*, "rabble." (Not surprisingly, eastern Paris, a mosaic of polluted and unhealthy slums, insufficiently supplied with fresh water, was hit very hard by a major outbreak of cholera in 1832.) Astute observers like Alexis de Tocqueville predicted that a new revolution was likely to explode there.

The revolution feared but expected by Tocqueville and many others, visited Paris in 1848, and it involved both concessions to the "rabble," exemplified by the introduction of universal male suffrage, but also its bloody repression during the "June Days." And it ended with the establishment of another bourgeois regime, this time again under Napoleonic management. This meant that the reshaping of the capital, initiated under *Napoléon le grand*, could continue under *Napoléon le petit*. In fact, Paris was to be thoroughly revamped during the Second Empire, in the 1850s and 1860s. The mastermind of the renovation program was the prefect of the Seine Department, that is, Paris and surroundings, a personality called Georges-Eugène Haussmann but better known as "Baron Haussmann." He created new wide boulevards, vast squares, city parks, and major monuments that transformed the capital into a modern metropolis.

IMAGE 28. The Hausmannization of the l'île de la Cité (1862).

This process of "Haussmannization" (*Haussmannisation*) of the capital had a twin objective. First, the original idea, namely to continue and finish the transformation of Paris, a former royal city, into a city that, although featuring Napoleonic "bells and whistles," was intrinsically bourgeois, a city worthy of being the capital of a Europe and indeed an entire "Western world" dominated by a class whose name had originated in France, the bourgeoisie. Since the bourgeoisie's world view was liberal, Paris also turned into a world capital of liberalism, and the Haussmannization of the city has therefore been described with some justification as "a showcase [*vitrine*] of triumphant liberalism."[10]

Second, in view of the lessons learned in 1830 and 1848, Haussmannization purported to provide "protection against assault from within," in other words, against urban revolutionary action, action that could be expected to originate in the old slums located mostly in eastern but also in central Paris, *le vieux Paris* or "Old Paris."[11] Much of that Old Paris would fall victim to what Colin Jones had labelled "urban butchery" at the hands of the Baron, a man who sometimes referred to himself as a "demolition artist."[12]

Much destruction affected the ancient city center, where old houses were razed to make room for a network of wide streets and boulevards, slicing through the heart of the city like the *cardo* and *decumanus* of Roman towns almost two millennia earlier. Just as the Roman main streets used to intersect at a forum, Haussmann planned a north-south axis, a cardo, and an east-west thoroughfare, a decumanus, converging on a *grande croisée* or "great crossroads," a forum-like space, Place du Châtelet. That square had already been created by the first Napoleon, by demolishing a medieval "little castle" (*châtelet*) commanding access to the Île de la Cité via a bridge known as the Grand Pont and later as Pont au Change

Place du Châtelet was embellished with a monumental fountain and column commemorating the Corsican's early victories in Egypt and Italy, the Palm Tree Fountain. The square was made extra monumental by the construction of no less than two theatres, the Théâtre du Châtelet and the Théâtre de la Ville, as well as two fine brasseries, where the capital's well-to-do burghers would be able to enjoy entertainment and fine food and drink.

Haussmann caused a neo-cardo to stretch both north and south from the Place du Châtelet, slicing ruthlessly through lower-class neigh-

---

10 Noiriel, p. 359.

11 Mumford, pp. 369-70.

12 For details of Haussmann's program, see Jones, pp. 344-95. The quotation is from Jones, p. 352.

borhoods. The Île de la Cité was cleansed of its ancient slums and their proletarian inhabitants, of whom no less than 10,000 were expelled from their homes. This made room for an open space in front of Notre-Dame Cathedral, which, after the Revolution and the Napoleonic Wars, was in such a state of disrepair that Paris officials considered its demolition. Victor Hugo, who admired the great church and wanted it to be saved, wrote the novel *Notre-Dame de Paris* (published in English as *The Hunchback of Notre-Dame*) in 1831; the book proved to be an enormous success and contributed to the decision to restore the Cathedral, made official in 1844 by an order of King Louis Philippe. The restoration was planned and supervised by the architect Viollet-le-Duc and involved input by Victor Hugo; the project continued after the 1848 Revolution and the coming to power of Napoleon III. The latter sought to ingratiate himself with the Catholic Church because he relied on support for his regime from rural France, whose denizens were still overwhelmingly religious.

The urbanistic rearrangements on Île de la Cité also involved plunking down imposing government buildings such as an army barracks that would become the Prefecture in 1871 and, last not least, the city morgue, located just behind Notre-Dame and destined to remain there until 1910. And so, when Haussmann had finished implementing his "depressing projects," as Jacques Hillairet calls them, the island that constituted the historical cradle of the city had room for corpses but not for living little people. But it was henceforth crossed by a broad thoroughfare that linked the northern and southern stretches of the new cardo. To connect the two, a narrow street crossing the island, the Rue de la Barillerie, was widened to become the Boulevard du Palais, whose name refers to the Palace of Justice, a renovated former part of the medieval royal castle on the island; the new boulevard linked the exceptionally wide Pont au Change, which provided access to Place du Châtelet, with the Pont Saint-Michel and the Left Bank.[13]

On the Left Bank, a new thoroughfare, the Boulevard Saint-Michel, obliterated much of the old Latin Quarter, of which only a small section—crossed by narrow streets such as Rue de la Huchette—was to subsist, eventually to host countless Greek and other international eateries, catering not to the bourgeoisie but to university students and tourists

---

13   Hillairet (1969), pp. 67-68, 110-11; "The Morgue, favorite Paris attraction during the 19th century."

on a budget. To the north, another new thoroughfare similarly ripped through a district inhabited by *ceux d'en bas,* providing easy access to one of the new railway stations, the Gare de l'Est, inaugurated in 1849. It was called Boulevard de Sébastopol, a reference to one of the rare military successes of the new Napoleon, namely, the long and difficult but ultimately successful siege of the Russian city of Sevastopol in 1854-55, during the Crimean War.

A modern *decumanus,* linking western to eastern Paris, allowing for easy and rapid movement of persons and goods—and troops, of course, including cavalry and artillery—in both directions, via the Place du Châtelet, required far less Haussmannian intervention. That axis was already in place, it consisted of the Champs Elysées which predated the Revolution, the Rue de Rivoli, laid out under the first Napoleon, and the ancient but wide Rue Saint-Antoine, leading to Place de la Bastille and into the Faubourg Saint-Antoine. The "counter-insurgency" function of this artery was revealed by the establishment of a major army barracks in the Rue de Lobau behind the Hôtel de Ville. The garrison ensconced in this *caserne*, an institution unsurprisingly named after the original Napoleon, could not only easily deny access to city hall to any mob storming in from the Faubourg Saint-Antoine but also quickly rush eastward to quell uprisings anywhere in the city's restless eastern reaches; underground passages also enabled the military to quickly enter the building from the barracks to arrest popular leaders with real or perceived revolutionary intentions.

In addition, Haussmann arranged for the many narrow streets and "riotous slums" around Place de Grève to be razed, which likewise served to prevent the erection of barricades while facilitating bringing in artillery as well as infantry in the case of uprisings. The urban renewal known as Haussmannization proved to be a "key to undoing" what had been seen ever since 1789 as "the Place de Grève's role as epicenter of rebellion."[14]

The Baron added other east-west avenues and wide streets, namely, the Boulevard Saint-Germain on the Left Bank and, on the Right Bank, the streets Réaumur and Turbigo. Moreover, in the heart of eastern Paris, a relatively small square was enlarged to become a vast rectangular

---

14   Hillairet (1956), vol. 1, p. 59; Harison, pp. 408-09, 421.

space, eventually to be known as Place de la République, a kind of Place de l'Étoile, focal point of boulevards coming in from the west, such as the Boulevards Magenta and Saint-Martin. Not coincidentally, these thoroughfares were made wide enough to prevent the construction of barricades that might have blocked the progress of artillery and cavalry; and three of them, the Boulevards Beaumarchais and Voltaire plus the Avenue de la République—led straight towards the Faubourg Saint-Antoine and other eastern districts, looking very much like a threatening pitchfork, a weapon of mass destruction in comparison to the pikes of the sans-culottes. The cherry on the cake of this strategically important arrangement, so functional for "military and repressive purposes"[15] was the establishment, on Place de la République, of a massive cavalry barracks. It was originally named after Eugène de Beauharnais, son-in-law of Napoleon; another member of the Bonaparte clan was thus called upon—symbolically, that is—to make Paris safe for the bourgeoisie.

Like earlier rejuvenations of Paris, the city's Haussmannization was "self-financing" in the sense that land and houses of poor neighborhoods were forcibly sold at low prices to banks and wealthy individual investors who "replaced them with attractive prestige properties that could be sold or else rented out as homes and businesses." The new boulevards witnessed the construction of countless *immeubles de rapport*, buildings that could "bring in [money]" (*rapporter*) in the form rents of apartments, shops, and businesses. Haussmann's project thus stimulated "capital accumulation" by wealthy individuals and above all the big investment banks, the heavy guns of finance capitalism, that were emerging in France at the time, among them the Crédit Lyonnais, the Société Générale, and the Rothschild Bank.[16] The same banks also made money by loaning to the government the funds needed to help finance the operation; the loans were repaid with the revenue of indirect, regressive taxation, an additional burden on the Parisian underclass.[17]

No less than 350,000 "underprivileged" denizens of central Paris were thus evicted and forced to relocate to the eastern faubourgs. The poor moved out, and the rich moved in. The bourgeoisie henceforth en-

---

15 Jones, p. 366.
16 Noiriel, p. 359.
17 Jones, pp. 353, 365.

joyed more "living space" in a "Paris of luxury" that henceforth included not only western Paris but also most if not all of a "socially cleansed" central part of the city. The plebes, on the other hand, were squeezed together more tightly and uncomfortably than ever before in a "Paris of poverty," the more so since the capital's eastern reaches also happened to be the only part of Paris where working-class newcomers could afford to live. It was almost inevitable that a conflict was soon to erupt between those two very nonidentical halves of the city. In some ways, that conflict, the Paris Commune of 1871, was to be the "revenge of the expelled," an attempt to reclaim the city.

11. 1871: The Paris Commune

THE PARISIAN REVOLUTION OF 1871, which went down in history as the Paris Commune, was a complex, bloody, but also extremely important event. It was considered by Marx to be a veritable "proletarian" revolution and by Lenin as a precursor of the Russian revolution of 1917. We limit ourselves here to a succinct description.

As we have seen, Napoleon had in a sense put an end to the revolution by taking it out of Paris and exporting it to the rest of Europe *by means of war*. He had transformed the ardent revolutionaries of the Parisian little people, the sans-culottes, into chauvinist warriors on behalf of an imperial France. His nephew Louis-Napoléon, who, under the name of Napoleon III, could play the emperor of the French from 1852 to 1870, manages to achieve the opposite: via a war—a catastrophic, rather than a triumphant war—he brings the revolution back to Paris. Moreover, in a besieged and humiliated Paris, its disillusioned soldiers prove to be more passionate and radical revolutionaries than the sans-culottes had ever been. Eighty years earlier, the revolution had led to war; in 1870-1871, war leads to revolution. It is a scenario that will unfold again in Russia in 1905 after a war against Japan and again in 1917-1918 in Russia again as well as in Hungary and Germany, just before and after the conclusion of the Great War.

During the summer of 1870, Napoleon III frivolously unleashes a war against Bismarck's Prussia. The war is officially declared at the château of Saint-Cloud on July 15. Overconfident, the emperor leads his army towards the German border, but on September 1 and 2, his forces are routed near Sedan and he himself is taken prisoner. A few days later, on September 4, a bloodless revolution breaks out in Paris—during which the statue of Saint Michael is vandalized—and it ends with the "Second Empire" making way for a new republic, to be known as the Third Republic. This republic is of course proclaimed in the City Hall and a provisional government is formed there, composed almost exclusively of Parisians, many if not most of them lawyers. And so this revolution too is a Parisian phenomenon. However, the war continues, the Germans push deeper into France and, starting on September 19, the capital is entirely encircled. Thus begins a terrible siege that will last many months.

Although exposed to bombardment, undernourishment, cold, and disease, the populace of besieged Paris stubbornly opposes any attempt by the government to conclude an armistice with the Germans and end the war. On the other hand, because of the shortages and high prices, the working class and even the petite bourgeoisie, the lower-middle class—but not the haute bourgeoisie, which is far less affected by the situation—develop a growing desire for social justice and for a truly democratic and social state, possibly and even preferably, under the auspices of a Parisian Commune like the one ensconced in the Hôtel de Ville during the revolutionary years 1789-1794.

On January 28, 1871, a humiliating armistice is signed, but it is immediately repudiated by the Parisians. And, during the general elections established a week later, Paris votes overwhelmingly for the republican candidates, while the rest of the country votes for conservative candidates, especially monarchists. "The chasm between the city and the countryside had never been so deep," writes Gérard Noiriel, the author of a popular history of France.[1] The National Assembly displays its contempt for Paris by making a home first in the über-bourgeois and conservative city of Bordeaux, then in Versailles, former residence of the absolute monarchs, a town located closer to the capital, but symbolically lightyears away, and a government is formed under the leadership of Adolphe Thiers. The latter makes himself particularly unpopular in Paris by suspending payment of the meager remuneration granted to the Parisian members of the National Guard, a salary that was often the sole source of income for a Pari-

---

1 Noiriel, p. 369.

sian family. In addition, he announces the disarmament of all the capital's troops as well as the end of the moratorium, decreed during the siege of Paris, on the payment of rents and debts within the city.

On February 26, Thiers signs a provisional peace agreement with Germany, by which France loses not only Alsace but also a large part of Lorraine, and which also allows German troops to symbolically enter the capital and organize a parade on the Champs-Élysées.[2] The Parisians have had enough when, in Montmartre on March 18 at dawn, units of the army want to confiscate the guns of the capital's National Guard that are parked on top of the hill, approximately on the site where the Sacré Coeur Basilica will later arise. Someone sounds the alarm, the people rush in and protest loudly, shots are fired, and the clash causes numerous fatal and non-fatal casualties. But the scheme fails, mainly because many soldiers defect to the side of the Parisians. Two captured generals become the victims of popular vengeance: they are shot without formalities in the interior courtyard of a house in Rue des Rosiers, today located at number 36 rue du Chevalier-de-la-Barre, just behind the Sacré-Coeur Basilica.

With its tail between its legs, the regular army withdraws to Versailles, seat of the government of Thiers. In Paris, however, power is now in the hands of an improvised "central committee" of the National Guard, representing the sovereign people. After Parisian elections, held on March 26, this committee transfers power to a "Commune," a democratic administration of the city, composed of 90 members, inspired by the homonymous Parisian institution of the revolutionary years 1789-1794. This happens on March 28 during a ceremony at the City Hall which, this time, is not adorned with the traditional tricolor flags, but rather with red flags. To the cheers of the crowd, the National Guard marches by with bayonets on their rifles, cannons thunder, and the people loudly manifest their joy with shouts such as "Long live the Commune, long live the Republic!"

Still on that same day, the first meeting of the Commune takes place, during which the hope is expressed that similar institutions will be established in other cities of the land. There will indeed be attempts to emulate the Parisian example in Marseille, Lyon, Toulouse and elsewhere, but

---

[2] This agreement will lead to a formal peace treaty, signed in Frankfurt on May 10.

they will be nipped in the bud during the last days of March. A chasm of antipathy thus opens up between the revolutionary, "red," and "atheist" Paris of the Communards and the overwhelmingly bourgeois and conservative rest of France, personified by Thiers and the other civilians and military *Versaillais*, the "men of Versailles."

A crucial question about the Paris Commune has been debated endlessly by historians; namely, whether it was socialist, or communist, and/or Marxist. However, the Paris of the Communards was definitely a new and revolutionary kind of state by and for ordinary people, the demos, whether wage-earning workers or self-employed petty-bourgeois artisans, shopkeepers, etc. On the socioeconomic level alone, an entire series of measures are taken in a very short time, which can be described as socialist or at least social-democratic, and they recall "1793," the radical phase of the Great Revolution. As examples we can cite a guaranteed minimum weekly wage; the socialization of enterprises whose owners had fled from the city; compulsory and free education in state-run schools; pensions for the widows of members of the National Guard; legal equality between legitimate children and natural children; the cancellation of all rental debts; the separation of church and state; the abolition of the standing army and the proclamation of the National Guard as the nation's sole armed force; and even something that had not even been discussed in 1793: the right to vote for women.

Furthermore, although the Commune was established "on a nationalist basis," namely to organize the defense of Paris against the siege of the Prussian army, the Communards saw themselves as the representatives—and the combatants—not of a city or even of a nation, but of a class, of all "those from below" in Paris, France, Europe and even in the world, and they regarded their "state" not as a bourgeois and national republic but as a proletarian and internationalist project, as a "universal republic" or "workers' republic"; and they considered their struggle to be a class conflict, a conflict between the proletariat of all countries and the international bourgeoisie. Thus we can understand that the Commune attracted, hosted, and awarded citizenship to thousands of foreigners, including Germans, and that outlanders—women as well as men—were among their political and military leaders. As examples we can cite Léo Frankel, a Hungarian Jew, who was minister of labor, the Polish Jaroslaw Dombrowski, a general who died on the barricades, and Élisabeth Dimitrieff, a young Russian woman who helped organize the defense of Paris. The Communards believed in the international workers' solidarity, they were "internationalists" in the Marxist sense of the term.[3]

Within the Commune, "social interests, class interests are eclipsing the nationalist vision, the dominant ideology,"[4] and the Communards expressly repudiate French chauvinism, militarism, and imperialism associated with Napoleon Bonaparte. Of the latter, we know that his objective had been the suppression of revolutionary radicalism, of "1793," which may be considered to be a forerunner of "1871." Napoleon is symbolically repudiated by the Commune when it orders the destruction of the victory column he had erected in the middle of the Place Vendôme to immortalise his victory at Austerlitz against the Austrians; as far as the Communards are concerned, it is "a monument to barbarism, a symbol of brutal violence and fake glory, a tribute to militarism, ... a permanent attack against the great principles of the French Republic, fraternity."[5] On May 16, the Vendôme Column is toppled, which proves to be an arduous task, and plans are made to replace it with a monument commemorating the events of the previous March 18 in Montmartre. For the duration of the Commune, the square is called Place Internationale. After the fall of the Commune, a new column will be erected, complete with a statue of Napoleon. Incidentally, the painter Courbet was prosecuted, found guilty, and fined as well as imprisoned for his alleged involvement in this demolition.

We have seen that Napoleon was a great champion of the cause of the bourgeoisie, and also that the bourgeoisification of Paris had been obfuscated, so to speak, by plenty of Napoleonic glitter. The Communards understood this only too well, and their demolition of the column with the statue of the Corsican may be understood as a first step towards a *de*bourgeoisification of Paris, similar to the deroyalization of Paris at the time of the Great Revolution. Because of the intimate link between royalty and Church, the deroyalization of the capital had gone hand in hand with declericalization. The Communards' incipient debourgeoisification of Paris similarly involved declericalization.

---

3   Boulangé; Ross; Hazan (2002), pp. 286-87.

4   Boulangé, pp. 2-3.

5   Quotation from "*La Chute de la colonne Vendôme*."

Because he needed the support of the peasantry, Napoleon III's regime had closely associated itself with the Church, which remained very influential in rural France. This political strategy included an order, given when he was not yet emperor but still president and needed electoral support, for the retransformation of the Pantheon into a church in 1851, with, as cherry on the cake, the planting of a big cross on top of the dome. Even before they turned their attention onto Place Vendôme, the Communards removed that cross and raised the red flag, the flag of their Republic, on a newly secularized Pantheon. (After the Commune, France will be governed for some time by monarchists inclined to turn the Pantheon into a church yet again, but in the 1880s a republican majority will prevent this from happening, and Victor Hugo's 1885 death and solemn burial in the building will ensure that the Pantheon will remain a mausoleum for heroes of the nation.)[6]

In the meantime, in Versailles, Thiers, and company have not remained inactive. They were able to secure from Bismarck the release of numerous French prisoners of war, so that they now have an army of over 100,000 men available to undertake the reconquest of Paris, defended by approximately 30,000 or 40,000 men. Already in April, numerous skirmishes take place along the frontline to the west and south-west of Paris, as a result of which the Communards fall back on a line of defense that surrounds the capital. (They now undoubtedly regret that, after their success at Montmartre, they did not immediately march on Versailles, which was poorly defended; however, the Germans, whose troops had not yet withdrawn from the area, would almost certainly not have allowed this.)

It is during these fights that the "Versaillais" begin to shoot the Communard prisoners, as a result of which the Communards take hostages, including the archbishop of Paris. Later, these hostages will also be executed, notably after Thiers rejects a proposal to exchange them for imprisoned Communards, especially Louis Auguste Blanqui, who had played a leading role in the revolution of 1848, was elected president of the Commune, but had been taken prisoner by the Versaillais; Thiers presumably feared that a freed Blanqui might provide the Commune with effective leadership.

On May 21, the Versaillais troops enter Paris through the Porte de

---

6   "Panthéon (Paris)."

Saint-Cloud and thus begins the reconquest of the capital, a real civil war which will reach its climax during the "Bloody Week" (*semaine sanglante*) of May 21 to 28. In the wealthy western districts of the city, the Versaillais forces meet little resistance and they are even welcomed as liberators. The ease of this advance is also due to the wide boulevards that were laid out under Napoleon III by Baron Haussmann and make it virtually impossible to erect solid barricades. However, as the attackers approach the center of the city along an axis leading from the Champs-Élysées to the Place de la Concorde, the Rue de Rivoli and into the popular districts of eastern Paris, the resistance becomes fierce. The Communards defend themselves behind more than 500 barricades and they cover their retreat by setting fire to public buildings as part of what appears to be a kind of scorched-earth tactic. However, the government's troops themselves shell the city with incendiary bombs. In any event, the most famous among the many buildings that go up in flames are the Tuileries Palace and the Hôtel de Ville.

At the time of the Great Revolution, the Tuileries Palace was the "tabernacle of the monarchy" for the royalists but the "den of the counter-revolution" for the sans-culottes. It briefly became a "citadel of the Republic," namely, when the Convention moved into it. However, it morphed into an architectural icon of monarchical and/or bourgeois power again as Napoleon moved in, to be followed by the restored Bourbons, the bourgeois-king Louis-Philippe, and another Bonaparte. Thus we can understand that the Communards cause the palace to go up in flames of wrath as they are forced to evacuate central Paris. However, by this time a Communard "government" no longer exists, decisions are taken by "small, more or less isolated groups, and do not reflect the will of the Commune as a structured organization."[7]

The edifice is burnt down by around thirty Communards led by a butcher named Victor Bénot, on the night of May 22 to 23. Pointing to the burning palace, he is alleged to have told his companions that "the bird will not want to come back to his nest.[8] The building will burn for three days, and the ruins will only be cleared by 1883. In the early 21st century, only some flotsam and jetsam of the palace will subsist in lost

---

7 Guichard, p. 81.
8 Lagrange.

corners of the capital, for example on Square Georges Cain, in the third arrondissement, where the pediment of the central pavillion and its clock are still on view; and the Louvre conserves some statues that used to decorate the palace.[9] There has been talk of a restoration of the building.

Another symbolically important building that went up in flames, was the Hôtel de Ville, the architectural externalization of popular power in the heart of the city, the people's Tuileries, so to speak. In his memoirs of the fighting, a former Communard was to write that this ancient edifice, so closely associated with the power of the people, "was not allowed to survive its real master."[10]

A myth will later arise, claiming that these fires were started by women Communards determined to burn down all of Paris, the infamous *pétroleuses*, "petrol women." The myth undoubtedly reflects the fact that great numbers of women were actively involved in the Commune, as leaders as well as supporters, but also the patriarchal and misogynous sentiment of many if not most of the Commune's enemies.

The Left Bank also witnesses heavy fighting, for example in the district around the Pantheon, strategically important because it was used by the Communards as a kind of fortress and military headquarters. The action then moves to the heights known as Butte-aux-Cailles, in the area of the Porte d'Italie. The Communards repel no less than four assaults by Versaillais troops on their positions there. However, subjected to intense artillery fire, the defenders have to retreat to the districts of Belleville and Ménilmontant, on the Right Bank, and to the city's extreme eastern reaches, the very last bastions of the Communards.

The small hill of Butte-aux-Cailles used to be covered with vineyards and windmills. The name does not refer to *cailles*, as quails are called in French, but to a certain Caille family that owned a lot of land there. Today it is a peaceful district, and its Rue des Cinq-Diamants features the headquarters of the association Les Amis de la Commune, "Friends of the Commune."[11] At the end of the last century, a tiny square at the corner of Rue Buot and Rue de l'Espérance received from the municipality of Paris the name "Place de la Commune-de-Paris-1871." One can also see

9   "Les vestiges des Tuileries."
10 Lissagaray, p. 83.
11 Internet site of "Les Amis de la Commune": http://www.commune1871.org.

one of the famous Wallace fountains, of which there are no less than 108 in Paris. They were erected after the fall of the Commune at the initiative and expense of the British philanthropist Richard Wallace. The intention was to teach poor Parisians to quench their thirst with cool water instead of wine and strong drinks, presumably the cause of all social ills.[12]

The last fighting takes place in the Belleville District and a little further south, at the Père-Lachaise Cemetery. On Saturday, May 27, the troops of Versailles surround the necropolis, defended by 200 Communards. Among the graves, such as that of Balzac, who died in 1850, fierce fighting goes on all night, continuing with knives and other bladed weapons when the ammunition runs out. The butchery ends at a wall in the eastern corner of the cemetery, against which 147 prisoners are shot and buried in a mass grave. During the next few hours, they will be joined by some 2,000 corpses of other Communards—or "confederates" (*fédérés*), as these are also called—who were executed in the surrounding area.

It is in the district of Belleville, apparently in the Rue Ramponeau, named after the owner of the previously mentioned guinguette La Grande Pinte, that, on Sunday, May 28, the very last barricade is defended by a single Communard who, when his ammunition is exhausted, still manages to slip away.[13] However, according to some sources the very last barricade was that of the rue de la Fontaine-au-Roi, on which floated a huge red flag. Eric Hazan tells the story as follows:

> At the moment when the defenders are firing their final shots, a young woman arrives from the barricade in Rue Saint-Maur and offers to help them. They want to send her away from this place of death, but she refuses and stays. To the ambiguous story of the last barricade and the [Commune's] final hour, [the Montmartre singer, journalist and Communard] Jean.-Baptiste Clément was later to dedicate a famous song, *Le temps des cerises*.[14]

The defeat of the Commune is accompanied by a bloody repression, known as the "tricolor terror." A British historian who cannot be accused of sympathy for the Communards has described this episode as "an orgy of death."[15] Hastily formed war tribunals order the execution of captured Communards without due process. The victims are quickly disposed of in

---

12   Bracke, pp. 21-24.
13   Hazan (2002), pp. 301-02.
14   Hazan (2002), p. 302.
15   Horne (1971), p. 166.

mass graves in numerous cemeteries and along the Parisian fortifications and sometimes cremated in funeral pyres. Officially, there were 17,000 such executions, but historians estimate that the real figure was between 20,000 and 25,000, significantly higher than the total number of victims of the much more (in)famous Terror of 1793-1794. With 1,500 to 2,000 dead, the foreigners who participated in the Commune paid a heavy price for this repression. The Commune itself only had between 80 and 90 people executed in an explosion of popular anger, and that was an initiative of a few individuals, because no execution was directly ordered by the Commune authorities. When the uprising was over, some 40,000 people, men, women, and even children, were forced to walk to Versailles and locked up there in appalling conditions before being tried. And that resulted in many more executions as well as countless sentences to longer or shorter terms of imprisonment or hard labor and—in some 7,000 cases—deportation to penal colonies like New Caledonia.

The Père-Lachaise Cemetery bears the name of the father confessor of Louis XIV, François d'Aix de La Chaise, a Jesuit who lived in a country residence, just outside of Paris, that belonged to his order and was called Mont-Louis in honor of the Sun-King. In 1804, when Napoleon ruled the country, the city of Paris had a non-religious cemetery established on its grounds, officially called Eastern Cemetery (*cimetière de l'Est*) but soon popularly known as the cemetery of Father Lachaise.[16] Other than the Wall of the Federates (*mur des Fédérés*), now a memorial of the Commune, numerous other monuments recall this bloody page of the annals of the capital. One of them is the imposing mausoleum of Adolphe Thiers, black beast of the Communards. The latter are represented by the great revolutionary Blanqui who, for his role in the Commune, was "only" condemned to a prison term because of his poor health; set free in 1879, he died on the very first day of 1881.

Also to be found on Père Lachaise is the tomb of the Communard Eugène Pottier, author of the poem *The International* (*L'Internationale*), written while he lived in hiding to avoid the repression. In 1888, a worker of Belgian origin, Pierre Degeyter (or De Geyter), put the text to music and the *Internationale* thus became the anthem of the socialist and (later) communist internationals. Also worth mentioning is the tomb

---

16   Hillairet (1956), vol. 3, pp. 213-16.

of Jean-Baptiste Clément, who fought for the Commune, managed to escape, and was able to return to France later, after an amnesty. He authored the text of the song *Le temps des cerises*, which was to become the musical emblem of the Commune. This uprising did not take place in the time when cherries are picked, but the red berries obviously evoke the color of the red flag of the Commune and the blood of the fallen Communards.[17]

The Butte-aux-Cailles and the Wall of the Federates on Père-Lachaise are the main "places of memory" of the Municipality. But, in Paris today, there are other monuments that recall this revolution and, even more, the repression that followed it, even if many Parisians and most visitors to the French capital are unaware of their connection to the dramatic events of 1871.

The first monument of this nature is the shiny gilded statue of Joan of Arc, high in the saddle on top of a huge horse and triumphantly waving the banner of the kingdom. It was erected in February 1874 on Place des Pyramides, overlooking the site where the Tuileries Palace used to stand. This tip of the hat to the great heroine of monarchist and Christian France, an icon of the Ancien Régime and of French nationalism, may have purported to compensate for the Communards' destruction of the Vendôme Column, symbol of Bonaparte-style bourgeois France. Not surprisingly, in due course this statue became the focal point of rallies of France's rightwing forces, provocatively held on May 1, the day when the French Left meets on Place de la Bastille.

The second monumental expression of anti-Commune resentment is the gigantic pseudo-Byzantine edifice known as the Sacré Coeur, the Basilica of the Sacred Heart. Draped in the white color that used to be associated with the kings of France and located on top of the hill of Montmartre, this sanctuary dominates all of Paris. The Sacré Coeur was erected by order of the National Assembly, victorious in 1871 and dominated for many years by monarchists, in collaboration with the Vatican. It purported to function as an architectural token of repentance and penance, and was rather brutally plunked down on the very site where the

---

17 The song can be found on Youtube, e.g https://www.youtube.com/watch?v=OidIzOPERp8. For more on *Le temps des cerises* and its lyrics, see http://www.musimem.com/temps_des_cerises.htm. The lyrics of the *Internationale* may be found on: https://www.youtube.com/watch?v=PPExpmtdMEw.

"insurrection" of the Commune began on March 18 of 1871, when the Parisians prevented the Versaillais from seizing their guns. The name of "Sacred Heart" did not fall from the sky, it was the fruit not of divine but of earthly, social and political inspiration. The cult of the profusely bleeding "Sacred Heart" of Christ was launched in 1856 by Pope Pius IX as a means of fighting against freethinking within the bourgeoisie and, even more so, against supposedly godless socialism among the working class. It was hoped that the workers would realize that their sins were the cause of their misery and that they could therefore not expect salvation from "materialistic errors" but rather—through prayer and penance—from Jesus, whose heart was caused to bleed profusely because of all the sins of mankind.

IMAGE 29. Construction of the Sacré-Coeur, 1882.

The first stone of the Sacred Heart was laid in 1875, but construction made extremely slow progress due to problems with the expropriations and obstructionism from leftist politicians who denigrated the project as a "permanent provocation to civil war." The basilica, supposed to symbolically expiate the sins of the Commune, a Parisian revolution which, in many respects was the fruit of an international war, would not be completed until 1914. That happened to be the year when the great war began, the one we call the First World War. This "Great War" was to be the "mother" of a great revolution in Russia, whose protagonist, Lenin, viewed it as a new edition of the Paris Commune.

IMAGE 30. Repentant France offers the Basilica of the Sacred Heart, mosaic in the Sacré Coeur Basilica.

IMAGE 31. The Eiffel Tower illuminated during the World's Fair of 1889, by Georges Garen.

Conclusion
Paris, from France's Royal City to Bourgeois Babylon

THE "SHORT AND (BITTER)SWEET" revolution known as the Commune had permitted the capital's little people, its demos, to briefly take control of Paris. Suppressing that revolution allowed the bourgeoisie to reconquer the city—and to put the finishing touches on its bourgeoisification. The lower orders had been taught a lesson and found themselves once again compounded in the city's eastern reaches, including the Faubourg Saint-Antoine. It was from there that, in 1789, the sans-culottes had burst forth to enjoy an ephemeral conquest of the capital, establishing a headquarters in the Hôtel de Ville, executing the king in the most regal of all squares, and inaugurating the deroyalization—and accompanying declericalization—of the *ville royale*. Their popular, radical revolution failed, but it had triggered major changes in the nature and the outlook of the capital.

Before the start of the Revolution, Paris had been very much a royal city, littered with the kings' palaces, squares, and statues as well as the hôtels, churches, and monasteries of nobility and clergy. Those two classes, intimately associated with the monarchy, had dominated the city, politically as well as socially, in the absence of a ruler who preferred to live "far from the madding crowd," in Versailles, in a magnificent residence symbolically located in rural France, home ground of the Ancien Régime, rather than in its oversized urban anomaly, the megalopolis straddling the Seine like a colossus of Rhodes.

In the revolutions of 1789-1799, 1830, and 1848, the working class did all the heavy lifting and brought virtually all the sacrifices, but the bourgeoisie reaped most, though not all, of the political and social fruits of these convulsions. Similarly, the working class demolished royal Paris, or at least started that demolition. Of that achievement too, the bourgeoisie ended up being the major beneficiary. Each one of these three revolutions made it possible for the upper-middle class, whether Thermidorian, Bonapartist, or Orleanist, to "bourgeoisify" Paris a little more and simultaneously to make the city more Napoleonic. Without much glory to call its own, France's burghers were happy to borrow some glory, so to speak, from the man who had revealed himself to be their saviour and servant, the Corsican mafioso who was in many ways the godfather of bourgeois France.

Viewed in this context, the 1871 Commune was a valiant but unsuccessful attempt to reclaim Paris for its demos and thus to revolutionize and democratize the capital. During the Paris Commune, the capital briefly seemed poised to become plebeian again, to be ruled from the Hôtel de Ville, a kind of *maison du peuple,* rather than from a palace like the Tuileries, let alone Versailles. However, the outcome of that revolution determined that Paris was to be bourgeois, and to remain so for a long time, until the present day, in fact.

The bourgeoisification of Paris, the French capital, reflected the bourgeoisification of France in its entirety. Before 1789, when the country featured a feudal socio-economic system with a monarchical political superstructure, the country's bourgeoisie had no power; and the capital was a "royal city," radiating the might of the absolute monarchy and the wealth and privileges of nobility and aristocracy. And we remember that the Pont Neuf had been this royal city's emblem. But the series of revolutions that started in 1789, though mostly the work of the common people, the demos, allowed the haute bourgeoisie to come to power; in the process, Paris was transformed into a bourgeois city, redolent with, and radiating, the power and increasing wealth of the "rising" upper-middle class. That is not to say that the bourgeoisie would become all-powerful: even after 1871, the nobility and the Church remained very influential,[1] the petty bourgeoisie had to be taken into account, and the aspirations and restlessness of the working class would continue to haunt the well-to-

---

1   As I have argued in Pauwels (2016), echoing the view articulated by Arno Mayer in *The Persistence of the Old Regime.*

do burghers until the Great War and beyond.

However, in no other major Western—i.e. industrialized and capitalist—country, was the bourgeoisie's effort to achieve power as successful as in France, and no other capital was as thoroughly bourgeoisified as Paris. Russia, Germany, and the Habsburg Empire were monarchies whose capitals were to remain not just royal but imperial cities boasting mostly magnificent imperial and aristocratic palaces as well as exuberant churches. In Britain, the liberal upper-middle class became a partner, but only a junior partner, of a conservative landowning nobility that continued to set the tone politically, socially, and also architecturally and urbanistically. London thus continued to be an urban world with two feudal architectural poles, on one end the Tower, a medieval, Bastille-like fortress, a fossil of medieval absolutism, and on the other end the tandem of Buckingham Palace, a British Tuileries Palace, and Westminster Abbey, London's Notre-Dame; and it is not a coincidence that the style of most grand architectural creations of the time became known as "Victorian," reflecting, even emphasizing, its monarchical connections.

Paris would admittedly never become a 24-carat bourgeois nugget of urban gold, but in comparison with these other capitals, it was to look über-bourgeois. Not surprisingly, the city would be admired, visited, enjoyed, and praised by burghers female and male, old and young, conservative and avant-garde, from all over the world, or at least the "Western" world that was becoming increasingly industrialized, capitalist, and, indeed, bourgeois.

Arlette Farge, an expert on Paris in the 18th century, has described the city at that time as still "half-urban, half rural" (*mi-urbain, mi-rural*).[2] That is certainly an exaggeration, but she seems to have had the western half of the city in mind, where quasi-rural spaces such as the Grenelle Plain were to subsist well into the next century. In any event, the pre-1789 "royal city" was definitely still partly rural, featuring numerous little countrysides within the city limits. However, as the Hausmannian and other renovations of the 19th century involved a bourgeoisification of Paris, meaning that the city belonged more and more to the bourgeoisie and looked increasingly bourgeois, that is, grand-bourgeois with an unsubtle Napoleonic touch, Paris was divested of virtually all of its

---

2   Farge, p. 71.

miniature countrysides. The capital would admittedly retain quite a few green spaces, but only in the form of private gardens and manicured public parks, mostly belonging to, and enjoyed by, the well-to-do burghers; the vegetable gardens, orchards, vineyards, and such, on the other hand, genuinely evocative of the countryside and made by and for the working class, would almost all be gone by the end of the century. Only a few quaint fossils of country life would remain, such as the tiny vineyard on top of the hill of Montmartre.

In the Middle Ages, the bourgeoisie had originated as the class of denizens of the city, the *bourg*, in contrast to the residents of the countryside, peasants as well as noblemen. One could say that the bourgeoisie's triumph after the revolutions of 1789, 1830, 1848, and 1871 allowed it to turn all of Paris into a fully urban and therefore congenial environment by eradicating—even literally!—the last patches of countryside from the cityscape. The "city dwellers" conquered a Paris that was not yet fully urban; when their conquest was complete, Paris was completely urban, it was a city of cities, a perfectly comfortable and prestigious residence for a class that had always felt at home in an urban environment.

After the tragedy of the 1871 Paris Commune, France's "age of revolutions" was clearly over. This set the stage for the *embourgeoisement* of Paris to be certified symbolically, which was done in 1889. In that year, the centenary of the outbreak of the Great Revolution, the urbanistic triumph of the bourgeoisie was proclaimed architecturally by the erection of the Eiffel Tower. an oversized kind of totem pole, conjuring up modernity, science and technology, and progress, values associated with the bourgeois "tribe" in France and elsewhere, in general, and with France's bourgeois Third Republic, born in 1870, in particular. The "republican" pylon also functioned as a phallic symbol of the young, dynamic, and potent class the bourgeoisie perceived itself to be.

Rising high above the Grenelle Plain and therefore visible far and wide and conjuring up a lighthouse, radiating the bright light of modernity to the four corners of the land and, indeed, the world,[3] the tower also had the merit—from a bourgeois point of view—of overshadowing, and

---

3   See Chevalier and Gheerbrant, p. 959-960, for comments about the symbolic functions of towers. In this respect the Eiffel Tower resembled the contemporary Statue of Liberty with its torch, a work of art created by the French sculptor Frederic-Auguste Bartholdi, inaugurated in New York in 1886.

indeed humbling, the very horizontal Pont Neuf, emblem of the former royal Paris, suspended just above above the waters of the Seine, conjuring up the biblical "waters of darkness," the chaos before creation. As Eiffel's steel pillar similarly dwarfed and demoted also the venerable architectural icon of the ecclesiastical face of the royal city of old, Notre-Dame, it proclaimed the superiority of the new, republican, capitalist France of the bourgeoisie, to the old, monarchical, feudal France dominated by the nobility and the Church. Last but not least, the tower also usurped the Pont Neuf's reputation as hallmark of the French capital and effectively shifted the city's center of gravity from the Île de la Cité, heart of central Paris, to the city's bourgeois western parts, antipodes of the plebeian eastern districts such as the Faubourg Saint-Antoine.

IMAGE 32. Vegetable gardens in Grenelle, with the Eiffel Tower in the background, on a 1902 painting by Henri Rivière in the Musée d'Orsay (http://www.zone47.com/crotos/?q=18822925).

It was probably also not a coincidence that the bourgeois Tower-of-Babel-on-the-Seine was erected on a site with martial and Napoleonic overtones, namely, the Champ de Mars or "field of Mars," the god of war. This vast open space was formerly the training ground of the École Militaire, where the young Napoleon had studied to become an officer, a building whose main façade looks out on the tower. The presence of Eiffel's pillar also conveniently obliterated the memories, many of them far from dear to bourgeois hearts, of popular demonstrations and riots that took place here at the time of the radical phase of the Great Revolutions, especially the 1796 Grenelle massacre of the Babouvists. Arguably even more important about the tower's position was its vicinity to yet another Napoleonic *lieu de mémoire*, the Hôtel des Invalides, final resting place of the man who had been the godfather of bourgeois France while alive and the mascot of bourgeois Paris after his death.

Mircea Eliade, the great Romanian specialist in ancient myths and religions, has argued that archaic people tended to be overwhelmed by the vast, seemingly chaotic and in many ways mysterious and frightening world they inhabited, a world (or universe) of which they were only an infinitesimal, insignificant, and powerless part. They experienced the need to bring order and survey-ability to this world, that is, transform its *chaos* into a *cosmos*, a world that remained mysterious but was at least to some extent familiar, understandable, and less fearsome. This task was typically accomplished by finding and marking a *center*, that is, a place with great meaning in *space* as well as *time*, a *sacred* space: it was a geographic center of the world, in other words, a "navel" of the body of the earth, perceived as a human being, a mother; and it was also the place where the world had been created by the gods.

A very old and big tree and real or imaginary mountains, exemplified by the Mount Meru of Buddhism and Hinduism and by the pyramids of Egypt, might function as such a sacred spot, Alternatively, a pillar or tower could be constructed and proclaimed to be the center (or navel, axis) of the world and/or the locus of creation. Arguably the most famous example of such an *axis mundi* was the ziggurat or step-pyramid in the city of Babylon, the famous Tower of Babel. Towers symbolically functioned as a connection between earth and heaven, they enabled humans to ascend or at least approach heaven and, conversely, permitted the gods to descend on earth. Towers like the one in Babylon, known as Etemenanki, "temple of the foundation of heaven and earth," thus also marked a place sacred in time, because they were considered the site where the gods had come down for the purpose of creating human beings and their world. Towers of this kind were thus also viewed as ladders and featured steps, representing rungs, as in the case of the terraces of Etemenanki, the "hanging gardens" of Babylon.[4]

The Eiffel Tower's construction, location, most striking features, and history until the present time, may be interpreted with the help of these Eliadian insights. The revolutions that rocked France and indeed the entire world, from 1789 to 1871, brought about the demise of old feudal and monarchical France, dominated by the duo of the nobility and the Church. During nearly a century of *chaos*, a new *cosmos* was constructed in France, a capitalist rather than feudal order with a republic as a political exoskeleton and dominated economically and socially by the (haute) bourgeoisie. Other countries would follow suit, but France was first to achieve a virtually perfect bourgeois status, it was the primordial bourgeois state. The French capital, where most of the crucial revolutionary events had taken place, thus revealed itself to be the epicenter of an emerging international capitalist and bourgeois universe. Consequently, it was only fitting that the bourgeois metropolis erected a monument to confirm and celebrate its lofty status, sacred with respect to space as well as time: first, as epicenter of the new, bourgeois and capitalist world; and second, as locus of the uneasy birth, via revolution(s), of this new world. The Eiffel Tower, then the highest building in the world, was that monument, that "cosmic tree," but with its perpendicularity interrupted by three floors, it also conjured up a ladder, much as the terraces or "hanging gardens" had done in the case of the Tower of Babel, a step-pyramid. The Eiffel Tower indeed proclaimed Paris to be the Babylon of the new bourgeois cosmos.

In other European countries too, the bourgeoisie came to power over the course of the nineteenth or early twentieth century, via revolutions or not, but no capital was ever "bourgeoisified" as early and as thoroughly as Paris. Russia, Germany, and the Habsburg Empire were monarchies, linked with "established" Churches, whose capitals were to remain not just royal but imperial cities boasting mostly magnificent palaces as well

---

4   Eliade, pp. 25-43 ff.

as exuberant churches. In Britain, the liberal upper–middle class became a partner, but only a junior partner, of a conservative landowning nobility that continued to set the tone politically, socially, and also architecturally and urbanistically. London thus continued to be an urban world with two feudal architectural poles, on one end the Tower, a medieval, Bastille-like fortress, a fossil of royal absolutism. On the other end, the tandem of Buckingham Palace, a British Tuileries Palace, and Westminster Abbey, London's Notre Dame; and it is not a coincidence that the style of most grand architectural creations of the time became known as "Victorian," reflecting, even emphasizing, its monarchical connections.

In comparison with other capitals, Paris looked über-bourgeois after 1871. It is hardly surprising that the city was admired, visited, and praised by bourgeois women and men, young and old, conservative as well as avant-garde, from all over the world—that is, the "Western" world that was becoming increasingly industrial, capitalist and, indeed, bourgeois. From the four corners of the earth, well-to-do burghers converged on Paris like Catholic pilgrims converge on Rome or Muslim pilgrims on Mecca. Conversely, the forms and styles of a bourgeoisified Paris, most effectively symbolized by "Haussmannian" town planning and architecture, migrated to cities all over the world where the bourgeoisie likewise triumphed politically, socially, and economically. Featuring imposing residences and expensive "money-generating buildings" overlooking wide avenues or vast squares, as well as imposing government edifices, banks, stock exchanges, theatres, palace hotels, and deluxe restaurants, Bucharest, Brussels, and Buenos Aires, for example, tried very hard to resemble the French capital.

In 1871, the curtain came down on France's dramatic "Era of Revolutions." However, below, and occasionally above, the surface lower-intensity class conflict persisted, and with it, the symbolic "Battle for Paris" fought between rich and poor. The bourgeoisie believed itself to have won that battle, but its victory was never truly complete. Eastern Paris remained plebeian and as equally plebeian, even proletarian, revealed themselves in the mushrooming new suburbs to the east and north of the capital, such as Saint-Denis; that is where the immigrants settled who came from all over France as well as abroad, looking for work in the capital but unable to afford the high prices of accommodation in the city's center and western neighborhoods.

During the many years that have passed since the erection of the Eiffel Tower, Paris managed to remain bourgeois, but not as securely as one might think. This bourgeois supremacy was in fact threatened on a number of occasions. However, the German occupation of 1940-1944 did not constitute a problem in this respect. Under the auspices of the Nazi occupation and the collaborator regime of Vichy, both eager practitioners of policies of low-wages and high-profits, the bourgeoisie prospered in France and especially in Paris. Hitler, himself a *petit bourgeois* who had been coopted by Germany's *haute bourgeoisie* and ruled the Reich on its behalf, was an admirer of Paris; he did not wish to destroy the city but, in cooperation with architect Albert Speer, made plans to transform Berlin so that the German capital could replace Paris as bourgeois Babylon. The *Führer* also opined that many Frenchmen were not unhappy with the German presence in the "city of light" because it eliminated "the menace of revolutionary movements."

And, indeed, a potentially revolutionary situation threatening bourgeois supremacy in Paris, arose there in August 1944, when the Germans were pulling out of the city and Allied troops, coming in from Normandy, had not yet arrived. An opportunity thus opened up for the leftist, communist-led Resistance to come to power in the capital, and potentially in the entire country, and in this case radical anticapitalist reforms would almost certainly have been introduced. But that scenario was foiled by the decision-makers in Washington.

General de Gaulle, whom the Americans had previously ignored—a disgrace for which he would never forgive them—was hastily transferred by them to Paris, to be presented there as the uncontested supremo of the Resistance, which he really was not, and installed as head of the government of liberated France. As stage for his grand entry, the American "liberators," later more correctly described by de Gaulle himself as Germany's successors as "occupants" of France, wisely chose not Place de la Bastille, or another site in eastern Paris, but the same bourgeois western part of the city that had applauded the arrival of the Versaillais troops in 1871, where he was more likely to be safe and welcome. An American military escort made it possible for him to strut down the Champs Elysees, starting from the Arc de Triomphe, erected more than a century earlier in honor of another military hero morphed into the protector of France's upper-middle class. De Gaulle, a conservative representative of the French bourgeoisie, was to ensure that France's established bourgeois order would remain intact—with, as icing on the cake, a Paris as solidly bourgeois as ever.

That the bourgeoisification of Paris was never completely secured also became evident in May 1968, when workers and students went on strike and demonstrated in the Latin Quarter and elsewhere in the city centre and the situation threatened to degenerate into civil war or revolution. On the other hand, the City of Light also experienced attempts to perfect its *embourgeoisement*. Interpretable this way are the great projects that were undertaken in eastern Paris, first by de Gaulle's successor as President, Georges Pompidou, who arranged *à la* Haussmann for the clearance of the last slums of central Paris to make room for an art centre that was to receive his name. A little later, under the auspices of President François Mitterand, in theory a socialist but in reality a "bourgeois gentleman" (*bourgeois gentilhomme*), initiatives were put in place such as the construction of a new opera on Place de la Bastille and a new ministry of finance as well as a sports stadium in the working-class neighorhood of Bercy, officially purported to rejuvenate the city's east end for the benefit of its plebeian residents; in reality, Mitterand's urbanistic schemes came down to a gentrification for the benefit of the bourgeoisie and especially its *jeunesse dorée* or "gilded youth", for whom western Paris probably looms a tad too bourgeois in the sense of "dull."

In 2018, a new menace emerged for bourgeois Paris in the shape of a movement whose numerous and rowdy participants became known as the "yellow vests." The protestors were "the usual suspects," that is, plebeians from the capital's eastern districts and suburbs, but they were joined in their weekly invasions of the city by counterparts from all over France and even from abroad. They demonstrated not only on Place de la Bastille and elsewhere on their "home turf" in eastern Paris, but also, provocatively so, in the heart of the western "Paris of luxury," including the Champs Elysées. The *gilets jaunes* were gunning for the person and politics of President Macron, a former banker and as much as bourgeois-president as Louis-Philippe had been a bourgeois-king. Bourgeois Paris trembled as the movement dragged on until, in 2020, the COVID-19 pandemic provided a perfect rationale for outlawing large gatherings.

The organization of the Olympic Games in the French capital in

2024 may be viewed, and understood, from the same perspective. The modern Olympics have effectively been described as a form of "celebration capitalism,"[5] that is, a feast for the bourgeois "capitalist class" whose *crème de la crème* consists today of the hyper-rich owners, large shareholders, and managers of multinational enterprises, media moguls, their allied financiers, jurists, billionaire celebrities such as Lady Gaga and Céline Dion, and so forth. The primordial objective of this class is the maximization of profits. And the function of the Olympic Games is to enable the accumulation of riches with the collaboration of the host-city and the host-country, who are supposed to facilitate this *privatization* of the profits not exclusively, but primarily, by the *socialization* of the costs.[6] This elite of multinational capitalism sponsors the Games, and its members include mostly corporations whose home turf is the USA, now the centre of gravity of the capitalist world system, such as Coca-Cola; but they also include French companies like Louis Vuitton (LV), purveyor of all sorts of luxury products, a firm that flourished during the German occupation, (as mentioned not a bad time at all for France's bourgeois elite, typical consumers of the expensive goods made available by LV.)

This international elite was willing to hold its Olympic celebration in Paris, but in a congenial Paris, in a Paris in which they could feel at home, and that meant the western, bourgeois part of the city, the "Paris of luxury." Conversely, for the bourgeoisie, the "capitalist class" of Paris and all of France, the Olympic Games constituted a golden opportunity in two ways. First, to register unseen profits, for example by charging skyhigh prices for rooms in the fine hotels of western Paris that are pricey even at normal times, and also for balconies on the higher floors of favorably located "money-generating" buildings, whence well-heeled tourists could acclaim the passing athletes. Second, and more importantly at least for our purposes, for the bourgeoisie the Olympics also offered the possibility to reconfirm and even advance the *embourgeoisement* of the city—and to allow Paris to shine again, if only for a few weeks, as the Babylon of the international bourgeoisie. It was in this context that a "social cleansing"

---

5   See Boykoff, Celebration Capitalism and the Olympic Games, London: Routledge, 2014.

6   Boykoff, who developed the concept of "celebration capitalism," considers the Olympic Games as a reverse form of trickle-down economics, whereby the wealth actually trickles upward, from the poor to the rich.

(*nettoyage social*) of the city was carried out, namely the expulsion of the homeless and the concomitant "obfuscation of poverty" (*invisibilisation de la pauvreté*).[7]

Thus we can also understand why, on opening day, the boats loaded with thousands of athletes departed from the Austerlitz Bridge, situated on the cusp of the city's historic center and its eastern neighborhoods, the "Paris of poverty." By starting there, the Olympic show turned its back to plebeian Paris. Place de la Bastille, the primordial revolutionary *locus delicti*, and, behind it, the Faubourg Saint-Antoine, once the den of the revolutionary lion, much of it literally barricaded, could thus be left unseen and unmentioned—it sufficed that the Olympic torch had briefly passed through that district earlier, namely on July 14, Bastille Day. Unperturbed by unpleasant associations with the Revolution and with revolutions in general, the flotilla could thus happily descend the Seine to western Paris, the Paris where a sporty "celebration of capitalism" was as welcome as the troops coming from Versailles and General de Gaulle had been in 1871 and 1944, respectively.

Inevitably, the Games also had to make use of some of the sports infrastructure that happened to be located elsewhere, such as the national football and rugby stadium in the plebeian suburb of Saint-Denis, an impressive venue known as Stade de France. However, as many events as possible, including some of the most spectacular ones, took place in western neighborhoods. The marathons finished on the vast Esplanade des Invalides, and the cyclists arrived at the photogenic spot that could be viewed as the topographic focal point of the Parisian Olympics, virtually at the base of the Eiffel Tower, where temporary facilities had also been erected for events such as tennis and beach volleyball. That also happened to be the place where the athletes had disembarked from the boats to attend the opening ceremony. On that occasion, Eiffel's pillar, sparkling with thousands of lights, proclaimed to the Parisians, the athletes, and the entire world not only that the Olympic celebration of capitalism was welcome in Paris but also that Paris continued to belong to the bourgeoisie—at least until imperiled again by a second coming of the "yellow vests" or the appearance of yet another plebeian horde.

In the past, revolutions involved the attempted conquest, by *ceux d'en*

---

7   See Martinache, 2024.

bas, of a Paris dominated by *ceux d'en haut*, but each time the bourgeoisie managed to take control of the revolutionary movement and prevent the common people from taking over Paris—and the entire country. Might a second coming of the "yellow vests" or a new insurrection by other plebeians sooner or later trigger a new revolutionary explosion? If so, will the former "royal city" that became a "bourgeois Babylon" fall into the hands of the 21st-century avatars of the sans-culottes and Communards and experience a plebeian metamorphosis?

Bibliography

"À lire un extrait de 'Juin 1848. Le spleen contre l'oubli,' de D. Oehler," https://www.contretemps.eu/juin-1848-marx-baudelaire-spleen.

Alpaugh, Micah. *Non-Violence and the French Revolution: Political Demonstrations in Paris, 1787-1795*, New York, 2014.

Amin, Samir. *Le centenaire de la Révolution d'octobre 1917*, Paris, 2017.

Anderson, Perry. *Lineages of the Absolutist State*, London and New York, 1979; first edition: 1974.

Aptheker, Herbert. *The Nature of Democracy Freedom and Revolution*, New York, 1981.

Arasse, Daniel. *La guillotine et l'imaginaire de la Terreur*, Paris, 1987.

Arendt, Hannah. *On Revolution*, London, 2016; first edition: 1963.

Arushev, Mikhail. "Napoleon's Grand Army Medical Service: On the Battlefield," *Top War*, February 25, 2021, https://en.top-war.ru/180176-medicinskaja-sluzhba-velikoj-armii-napoleona-na-pole-boja.html.

"Banque de France: Patrimoine Historique & Architectural," https://www.banque-france.fr/patrimoine-historique-architectural.

Batut, Guy de la. *Les pavés de Paris: Guide illustré de Paris revolutionnaire*, 2 volumes, Paris, 1937.

Beaumont, Franck. "Insolite: Napoléon Bonaparte a habité le 9e arrondissement!," *Evous*, March 8, 2012, https://www.evous.fr/Insolite-Napoleon-Bonaparte-a-habite-le-9e-arrondissement,1174799.html#zUqRFO5Yd1vzI5U4.99.

Bernal, J. D. *Science in History. Volume 4 The Social Sciences: Conclusion*, third edition, Harmondsworth, 1965; first edition: 1954.

Best, Geoffrey (ed.). *The Permanent Revolution: The French Revolution and its Legacy 1789-1989*, London, 1988.

Bologne, Maurice. *L'insurrection prolétarienne de 1830 en Belgique*, Brussels, 2005.

Bonal, François. *Le livre d'or du Champagne*, Lausanne, 1984.

Boulangé, Antoine. "La Commune première révolution internationaliste," *NPA*, June 30, 2014, https://npa2009.org/idees/la-commune-premiere-revolution-internationaliste.

Bourcier, Jeanne. "La boucherie chevaline," *Chroniques d'un siècle*, October 9, 2016, http://jeannebourcier.unblog.fr/2016/10/09/la-boucherie-chevaline.

Bourdieu, Pierre. *Distinction: A Social Critique of the Judgement of Taste*, Cambridge/MA, 1984.

Boykoff, Jules. *Celebration capitalism and the Olympic games*, London, 2014.

Bracke, Krista. *Het andere Parijs*, Berchem, 2006.

Braudel, Fernand. *L'identité de la France: Les hommes et les choses*, Paris, 1986.

Canfora, Luciano. *Eine kurze Geschichte der Demokratie: Von Athen bis zur Europäischen Union*, Cologne, 2006.

Caro, Ina. *Paris to the Past: Traveling Through French History By Train*, New York, 2011.

Castelot, André. *L'histoire à table. Si la cuisine m'était contée...*, Paris, 1972.

Cetekk, Claude. *Nous avons bâti Paris*, Paris, 1987.

Chansonnier revolutionaire, Paris, 1989.

Cohen, M. J. and John Major. *History in Quotations*, London, 2004.

Cooper, Charlie. "Give us your Duchy: demand for Charles' £728m Cornish estate," *Independent*, September 28, 2012, http://www.independent.co.uk/news/uk/home-news/give-us-your-duchy-demand-for-charles-728m-cornish-estate-8190493.html.

Coquard, Olivier. *Quand le monde a basculé: Nouvelle Histoire de la Révolution française 1789-1799*, Paris, 2015.

Darnis, Jean-Marie. *Les monuments expiatoires du supplice de Louis XVI et de Marie-Antoinette sous l'Empire et la Restauration 1812-1830*, Paris, 1981.

Del Tufo, Vittorio. *Parigi magica*, Vicenza, 2022.

Deroy, Louis, and Maryanne Mulon, *Dictionnaire de noms de lieux*, Paris, 1992.

Dion, Roger. *Histoire de la vigne et du vin en France des origines au XIXe siècle*, Paris, 1977.

Dommanget, Maurice. *Histoire du drapeau rouge*, Marseille, 2006.

Dupeux, Georges. *La société française 1789-1970*, Paris, 1974.

Duveau, Georges. *1848 : The Making of a Revolution*, New York, 1967.

"Église des Feuillants," November 30, 2016, http://paris-bise-art.blogspot.ca/2016/11/eglise-des-feuillants.html.

Eliade, Mircea. *Le sacré et le profane*, Paris, 1965.

Farge, Arlette. *Le peuple et les choses. Paris au 18e siècle*, Montrouge, 2015.

Fierro, Alfred, and Jean-Yves Sarazin. *Le Paris des Lumières d'après le plan de Turgot (1734-1739)*, Paris, 2005.

Fournier, Edouard, and Jules Cousin. *Histoire des enseignes de Paris*, Paris, 1884.

"Französische Revolution," *GEO Epoche: Das Magazin für Geschichte*, No. 22, June 2006.

Fraser, Antonia. *Marie Antoinette: The Journey*, Toronto, 2006.

Furet, François, and Denis Richet. *La Révolution française*, new edition, Paris, 1973; first edition: 1965.

Garrier, Gilbert. *Histoire sociale & culturelle du vin*, Paris, 1995.

Garrioch, David. *La fabrique du Paris révolutionnaire*, Paris, 2015.

"Gibbet of Montfaucon," *Alchetron*, February 11, 2018, https://alchetron.com/Gibbet-of-Montfaucon.

Godineau, Dominique. *The Women of Paris and Their French Revolution*, Berkeley, CA, 1998.

Goubert, Pierre. *L'Ancien Régime*, 2 volumes, Paris, 1969-1973.

Guérard, Edmond. *Encyclopédie d'anecdotes modernes, anciennes, françaises et étrangères*, Paris, 1872.

Guichard, Sophie. *Paris 1871, la Commune*, Paris, 2006.

Guide Bleu: Île de France, revised edition, Paris, 1988; first edition: 1988.

Guillemin, Henri. *Silence aux pauvres!*, Paris, 1989.

Habakkuk, H. J. *Population Growth and Economic Development since 1750*, Leicester, 1971.

Hadjinicolaou, Nicos. *Histoire de l'art et lutte des classes*, Paris, 1974.

Haig, Diana Reid. *Walks through Napoleon & Josephine's Paris*, New York, 2004.

Harison, Casey. "The Rise and Decline of a Revolutionary Space: Paris' Place de Grève and the Stonemasons of Creuse, 1750-1900," *Journal of Social History*, Vol. 34, No. 2, Winter 2000, pp. 403-36.

Hartig, Irmgard (ed.). *Geburt der bürgerlichen Gesellschaft: 1789. Beiträge von Ernest Labrousse, Georges Lefebvre, Albert Soboul, Maurice Dommanget, Michel Vovelle*, Frankfurt am Main, 1979.

Hauser, Arnold. *Sozialgeschichte der Kunst und Literatur*, Munich, 1990.

Hazan, Eric. *L'invention de Paris. Il n'y a pas de pas perdus*, Paris, 2002.

Hazan, Eric. *A People's History of the French Revolution*, London and New York, 2014.

Heppner, Harald (ed.). *Reisen und Geschichte verstehen: Leitfaden für eine neue Weltsicht*, Vienna, 2007.

Higonnet, Patrice. *Paris: Capital of the World*, Cambridge/MA and London, 2002.

Hillairet, Jacques. *Connaissance du vieux Paris*, Paris, 1956; first edition: 1951

Hillairet, Jacques. *L'Île de la Cité*, Paris, 1969.

Hitler, Adolf. *Libres propos sur la guerre et la paix*, Paris, 1952.

Horne, Alistair. *The Terrible Year: The Paris Commune, 1871*, New York, 1971.

Horne, Alistair. *The Age of Napoleon*, New York, 2004.

Hussey, Andrew. *Paris: The Secret History*, New York, 2006.

Jacquin, Emmanuel, et al. *Les Tuileries au 18e siècle*, Paris, 1990.

Jaurès, Jean. *Histoire socialiste de la Révolution*, 7 volumes, Paris, 1901-1908.

Jones, Colin. *Paris: Biography of a City*, London, 2006 ; first edition: 2004.

Jourdan, Annie. *La Révolution, une exception française?*, new edition, Paris, 2006; first edition: 2004.

Jouve, Alice. *Paris: Birthplace of the U.S.A. A Walking Guide for The American Patriot*, Paris, 1997.

Kakel, Carroll P. , III. *The American West and the Nazi East: A comparative and Interpretive Perspective*, Basingstoke, Hampshire, and New York, 2013; first edition: 2011.

Kennedy, Emmet. *A Cultural History of the French Revolution*, New Haven and London, 1989.

Klundt, Michael (ed.). *Kapitalismus versus Barbarei?: Die Geschichtsschreibung der Neuen Weltordnung*, Cologne, 2007.

Knight, Frida. *Beethoven & The Age of Revolution*, New York, 1974.

Kossok, Manfred, and Editha Kross (eds.). *1789—Weltwirkung einer grossen Revolution*, two volumes, Berlin (East), 1989.

"La Chute de la colonne Vendôme," https://fr.wikipedia.org/wiki/La_Chute_de_la_colonne_Vend%C3%B4me#GirardinPirker2008.

"La circulation parisienne au XVIIIe siècle," *Histoires de Paris*, July 4, 2017, https://www.histoires-de-paris.fr/circulation-parisienne-xviiie-siecle.

Lachiver, Marcel. *Vins, vignes et vignerons: Histoire du vignoble français*, Paris, 1988.

Lacroix-Riz, Annie. *Les élites françaises entre 1940 et 1944. De la collaboration avec l'Allemagne à l'alliance américaine*, Paris, 2016.

Lacroix-Riz, Annie. *La NON-Épuration en France de 1943 aux années 1950*, Malakoff, 2019.

Lagorio, Carlos. *Pensar la modernidad : Una historia cultural de las revoluciones*, Buenos Aires, 2012.

Lagrange, Christophe. "Victor Bénot boucher, colonel, incendiaire, deux fois condamné à mort," *Les Amies et Amis de la Commune de Paris 1871*, December 15, 2023, https://www.commune1871.org/la-commune-de-paris/histoire-de-la-commune/illustres-communards/1310-victor-benot-boucher-colonel-incendiaire-deux-fois-condamne-a-mort..

"Lamartine repoussant le drapeau rouge à l'hôtel de ville, le 25 février 1848," *Paris Musées*, https://www.parismuseescollections.paris.fr/fr/musee-carnavalet/oeuvres/lamartine-repoussant-le-drapeau-rouge-a-l-hotel-de-ville-le-25-fevrier-1848#infos-principales.

"La prison de la Force," http://www.sjdc.fr/?page_id=1231.

"L'ancien Café de la Régence," https://www.paristoric.com/index.php/paris-d-hier/paris-disparu/2428-l-ancien-cafe-de-la-regence.

Larue-Langlois, Françoys. *Gracchus Babeuf tribun du people*, Paris, 2003.

"La pompe de la Samaritaine," http://paris1900.lartnouveau.com/paris01/lieux/la_pompe_de_la_samaritaine.htm.

'Le faubourg Saint-Antoine,' *Atlas historique de Paris*, https://paris-atlas-historique.fr/42.html.

Lefebvre, Georges. *La Grande Peur de 1789*, Paris, 1932.

"Le mètre étalon de la Place Vendôme," *Gavroche Père & fils*, December 6, 2011, http://www.gavroche-pere-et-fils.fr/le-metre-etalon-de-la-place-vendome.

"Le pont Notre-Dame," *Histoires de Paris*, https://www.histoires-de-paris.fr/pont-Notre-Damelutecia.

Leclerc, Mickaël. "Cholet. Histoire locale: 1709 ou l'hiver qui ravagea l'Anjou," *Le Courrier de l'Ouest,* January 5, 2020, https://www.ouest-france.fr/pays-de-la-loire/cholet-49300/cholet-histoire-locale-1709-ou-l-hiver-qui-ravagea-l-anjou-1b6b1866-2f03-11ea-b594-9b63193534d0.

"Les fondations religieuses au XVIIe siècle," *Atlas historique de Paris*, https://paris-atlas-historique.fr/24.html.

Les lieux de l'histoire de France, Paris, 2011.

"Les maisons sur les ponts," *Histoires de Paris*, https://www.histoires-de-paris.fr/maisons-ponts.

"Les morts violentes de l'histoire: Robespierre," https://www.rts.ch/play/radio/cqfd/audio/les-morts-violentes-de-lhistoire-robespierre?id=8946000&fbclid=IwAR2s5illoMFJ0HIwd5ndXo-5RBkuvqrxxMKX3pGkYCacCbm2bqML6AlKyq8.

"Les secrets du Pont-Neuf," https://www.pariszigzag.fr/secret/histoire-insolite-paris/les-secrets-du-pont-neuf#:~:text=Des%20hommages%20dans%20la%20culture%20fran%C3%A7aise&text=Enfin%2C%20selon%20la%20l%C3%A9gende%20parisienne,d'1%20cm%20carr%C3%A9).

"Les vestiges des Tuileries," *Paris Unplugged*, http://www.paris-unplugged.fr/vestiges-des-tuileries.

Lévêque, Jean-Jacques, and Victor R. Belot. *Guide de la Révolution française: Les lieux—les monuments—les musées—les hommes*, Paris, 1986.

"L'île Louviers, une île parisienne disparue," *Les yeux d'Argus*, August 29, 2017, https://lesyeuxdargus.wordpress.com/2017/08/29/lile-louviers-une-ile-parisienne-disparue.

Linebaugh, Peter, and Marcus Rediker. *The Many-Headed Hydra: Sailors, Slaves, Commoners, and the Hidden History of the Revolutionary Atlantic*, Boston, 2000.

Lissagaray, Prosper-Olivier. *Les Huit Journées de mai derrière les barri-

cades, Paris, 2017.

Losurdo, Domenico. *Democrazia o bonapartismo: Trionfo e decadenza del suffragio universale*, Turin, 1993.

Losurdo, Domenico. *Le révisionnisme en histoire: Problèmes et mythes*, Paris, 2006.

Losurdo, Domenico. *Il linguaggio dell'Impero: Lessico dell'ideologia americana*, Rome and Bari, 2007.

Losurdo, Domenico. *Liberalism: A Counter-history*, London, 2011.

Lyons, Martyn. *Napoleon Bonaparte and the Legacy of the French Revolution*, New York, 1994.

Mager, Wolfgang. "Soziale Ungleichkeit und Klassenstruktur in Frankreich 1630-1830," in: Hans-Ulrich Weber, *Klassen in der europäischen Sozialgeschichte*, Göttingen, 1979, pp. 66-93.

Marchioni, Jean. *Les mots de l'Empire*, Paris, 2004.

Marechaux, Xavier. "Married Priests in France, 1789-1815," *Age of Revolutions*, July 31, 2017, https://ageofrevolutions.com/2017/07/31/married-priests-in-france-1789-1815.

"Marie Antoinette," Le Café de la Régence, le 20 mai 2012, http://lecafedelaregence.blogspot.ca/2012/05/Marie-Antoinette.html.

"Mark Twain on the two Terrors," http://www.cultivatedlife.net/mark-twain-on-the-two-terrors.html.

Marsden, Kate. "Making Modern Gender Roles: The Case of Married Nuns in the French Revolution," *Age of Revolutions*, April 19, 2017, https://ageofrevolutions.com/2017/04/19/making-modern-gender-roles-the-case-of-married-nuns-in-the-french-revolution.

Martinache, Igor. "L'olympisme, stade suprême du capitalisme (de la fête)?," *Revue Française de Socio-Économie*, 1:32, 2024, https://shs.cairn.info.

Mayer, Arno J. *The Furies: Violence and Terror in the French and Russian Revolutions*, Princeton and Oxford, 2002; first edition: 2000.

McManners, J. "France," in: Albert Goodwin (ed.), *The European Nobility in the Eighteenth Century: Studies of the Nobilities of the Major*

European States in the Pre-Reform Era, New York and Evanston/IL, 1967, pp. 22-42.

Mennell, Stephen. *Smaken verschillen: Eetcultuur in Engeland en Frankrijk vanaf de middeleeuwen tot nu*, Amsterdam, 1989. (Original title: *All Manners of Food*)

Michalik, Kerstin. *Der Marsch der Pariser Frauen nach Versailles am 5. und 6. Oktober 1789 : Eine Studie zu weiblichen Partizipationsformen in der Frühphase der Französischen Revolution*, Pfaffenweiler, 1990.

Miquel, Pierre. *La Grande Révolution*, Paris, 1988.

Mongaillard, Vincent. "L'incroyable saga de la frite: on a tranché, le bâtonnet de patate est parisien!," *LeParisien*, July 17, 2021, https://www.leparisien.fr/societe/lincroyable-saga-de-la-frite-on-a-tranche-le-batonnet-de-patate-est-parisien-17-07-2021-IJJJGM2ZGRDOHDFC7GP5QU7NSQ.php.

Morange, Jean. *La Déclaration des droits de l'homme et du citoyen (26 août 1789)*, fourth edition, Paris, 1988; first edition: 1988.

Morazé, Charles. *The Triumph of the Middle Classes: A Political and Social History of Europe in the Nineteenth Century*, Garden City/NY, 1968.

Mousnier, Jehan. *Paris 18ᵉ arrondissement: Historique et pittoresque*, Paris, 1985.

Mumford, Lewis. *The City in History: Its Origins, Its Transformations, and Its Prospects*, San Diego, 1961.

Munford, Clarence J. "Les Libertés de 1789 in the Caribbean [sic]—Slave Revolution in St. Domingue," in: Kossok, Manfred, and Editha Kross (eds), *1789—Weltwirkung einer grossen Revolution*, Berlin, 1989, vol. 2, pp. 520-41.

Noiriel, Gérard. *Une histoire populaire de la France. De la guerre de Cent Ans à nos jours*, Marseille, 2018.

Obeyesekere, Gananath. *Cannibal Talk: The Man-Eating Myth and Human Sacrifice in the South Seas*, Berkeley/CA, 2005.

Parenti, Michael. *Democracy for the Few*, sixth edition, New York, 1995.

Paumgartner, Bernhard. *Mozart: Leben und Werk*, Munich, 1991.

Pauwels, Jacques R. *Beneath the Dust of Time: A History of the Names of Peoples and Places*, London and Colombo, 2009.

Pauwels, Jacques R. *The Great Class War 1914-1918,* Toronto, 2016.

Pauwels, Jacques R. *Bacchus in Gallië: Een geschiedenis van de Franse wijn*, Berchem, 2020. (2020a)

Pauwels, Jacques R. "France 1939-1945: From Strange Defeat to Pseudo-liberation," *Journal of Labor and Society*, August 23, 2020. (2020b)

Pricard-Méa, Denise. *Compostelle et cultes de saint Jacques au Moyen Âge*, Paris, 2000.

"Place de la Nation," *Left in Paris*, https://leftinparis.org/places/place-de-la-nation.

Plack, Noelle. "Intoxication and the French Revolution," *Age of Revolutions*, December 5, 2016, https://ageofrevolutions.com/2016/12/05/intoxication-and-the-french-revolution.

Plumelle-Uribe, Rosa Amelia. *La Férocité Blanche. Des non-Blancs aux non-Aryens: génocides occultés de 1492 à nos jours*, Paris, 2001.

Poisson, Georges. *Paris in the time of the Revolution 1789-1989*, Florence, 1989.

Pool, Phoebe. *Delacroix*, London, 1969.

Popkin, Jeremy D. (ed.). *Panorama of Paris: Selections from* Le Tableau de Paris *[by] Louis-Sébastien Mercier*, University Park/PA, 1999.

Quétel, Claude. *La Bastille. Histoire vraie d'une prison légendaire*, Paris, 1989.

Revel, Jean-François. *Un festin en paroles. Histoire littéraire de la sensibilité gastronomique de l'Antiquité à nos jours*, new edition, Paris, 1995; first edition: 1979.

Rockhill, Gabriel. *Contre-histoire du temps présent : Interrogations intempestives sur la mondialisation, la technologie, la démocratie*, Paris, 2017.

Rothenberg, Gunther E. *The Art of Warfare in the Age of Napoleon*,

Bloomington/IN, 1980.

Rudé, George. *The Crowd in the French Revolution*. London, 1967; first edition: 1959.

Sand, George et al. *Le diable à Paris: Paris et les Parisiens. Mœurs et Coutumes, Caractères et Portraits des Habitants de Paris ... etc., etc.*, Volume 2, Paris, 1846.

Schama, Simon. *Citizens: A Chronicle of the French Revolution*, New York, 1989.

Schivelbusch, Wolfgang. *Das Paradies, der Geschmack und die Vernunft: Eine Geschichte der Genußmittel*, Frankfurt am Main, 1983.

Sée, Henri. "The Economic and Social Origins of the French Revolution," in: Warren C. Scoville and J. Clayburn La Force, *The Economic Development of Western Europe: The Eighteenth and Early Nineteenth Centuries*, Lexington/MA, 1969, pp. 209-23.

Soboul, Albert. *A Short History of the French Revolution 1889-1799*, Berkeley/CA, 1977; original edition: *La Révolution française*, 1965.

———. *Les sans-culottes parisiens en l'an II: Mouvement populaire et gouvernement révolutionnaire (1793-1794)*, Paris, 1968.

———. *Understanding the French Revolution*, New York, 1988.

Stannard, David E. *American holocaust: The Conquest of the New World*, New York, 1993.

Suret-Canale, Jean. "La signification historique de la Constitution de 1793," in: Kossok, Manfred, and Editha Kross (eds), *1789—Weltwirkung einer grossen Revolution*, Berlin, 1989, volume 1, pp. 81-96.

Tableau de Paris: Bilder einer Grossstadt in Radierungen von Balthasar Anton Dunker nebst Erläuterungen, die auf die nämlichen Kapitel im Werk von Louis-Sébastien Mercier verweisen, Berlin, 1989.

"The Morgue, favorite Paris attraction during the 19th century," https://www.unjourdeplusaparis.com/en/paris-insolite/morgue-visite-favorite-paris-au-19e-siecle#:~:text=At%20the%20edge%20of%20the,slanted%20marble%20tables%20behind%20glass.

Thibault. "Les bourreaux dans la France moderne (XVe-XVIIIe siècles)," http://www.philisto.fr/article-62-les-bourreaux-dans-la-france-moderne-xve-18th-siecles.html.

Tilly, Charles. *Le rivoluzioni europee 1492-1192*, Rome and Bari, 1993.

Tisserand, Lazare-Maurice. *Topographie du vieux Paris*, Paris, 1897.

Toussaint-Samat, Maguelonne. *Histoire naturelle & morale de la nourriture*, Paris, 1987.

Trabant, Jürgen. "Langue et Révolution," https://www.bartleby-com/71/0530.html.

Varejka, Pascal. *Paris, une histoire en images: Architecture, economie, culture, société... 2000 ans de vie urbaine*, Paris, 2007.

Vitu, Marie-Line. "Robespierre, le grand mensonge," *Le Journal*, July 26, 2017, http://communication-ccas.fr/journal/robespierre-le-grand-mensonge.

Von Paczensky, Gert, and Anna Dünnebier. *Kulturgeschichte des Essens und Trinkems*, Munich, 1999.

Vovelle, Michel. *Die Französische Revolution: Soziale Bewegung und Umbruch der Mentalitäten*, Frankfurt am Main, 1985.

Westermann, Edward B. *Hitler's Ostkrieg and the Indian Wars: Comparing Genocide and Conquest*, Norman/OK, 2016.

Wheaton, Barbara Ketcham. *Savoring the Past: The French Kitchen and Table from 1300 to 1789*, Philadelphia/PA, 1983.

Williams, Eric. *Capitalism & Slavery*. Chapel Hill/NC and London, 1994; first edition: 1944.

Woods, Alan "Robert Burns—Man, poet and revolutionary," *In Defence of Marxism*, https://www.marxist.com/british-poets-french-revolution-5.htm.

Woronoff, Denis. *La République bourgeoise de Thermidor à Brumaire 1794-1799*, Paris, 1972.

www.ingramcontent.com/pod-product-compliance
Lightning Source LLC
LaVergne TN
LVHW042247070526
838201LV00089B/54